An Introduction to the Social Geography of India

This book discusses the significance of social geography, a multidimensional sub-discipline of geography encompassing social health, social security and social ethos. It presents the socio-spatial dynamics of the population in India through an understanding of the various issues related to migration, urbanisation, unemployment, poverty and public health. With a thorough analysis of various social indicators relating to health, education, income and employment, the volume presents a detailed picture of the social geography of India.

It discusses in detail,

- The origin, nature and scope of social geography, its relations with other social sciences and applications
- The nature and importance of social well-being along with welfare geography and the role of welfare state in ensuring social well-being
- The population of India and its attributes
- The status and spatial patterns of various social indicators relating to health, education and income and employment
- The composite indices which aggregate several social indicators such as the Human Development Index, Multidimensional Poverty Index and Sustainable Developmental Goals Index in the context of India.

This comprehensive book will be useful for students, researchers and teachers of social geography, human geography, population geography, demography and sociology. The book can also be used by students preparing for exams like civil services, UPSC, PSC and other competitive exams.

Dr Asif is an Assistant Professor in the Department of Geography, Faculty of Natural Sciences, Jamia Millia Islamia, New Delhi, India. He is an alumnus of the Aligarh Muslim University (AMU), Uttar Pradesh, India. He has worked as a research fellow with the Indian Council of Social Science Research (ICSSR) and as a research assistant with the University Grants Commission (UGC). He teaches undergraduate and postgraduate courses in social geography, economic geography and cultural geography, geographical thought, digital cartography and regional development. He has teaching experience of more than ten years at the university level. He has authored three books and has more than 20 research publications to his credit.

His research interests are in social and cultural geography, environmental issues, geopolitical issues, remote sensing and Geographic Information System applications in geographical studies.

Hemant is a PhD research scholar in the Department of Geography, Faculty of Natural Sciences in Jamia Millia Islamia, New Delhi, India. He has obtained his graduate degree in geography with distinction from Jamia Millia Islamia. He is an alumnus of the Jawaharlal Nehru University (JNU), New Delhi, India. He is a University Grants Commission – Junior Research Fellowship (UGC-JRF) awardee. He has specialisation in social geography, social identities, regional development, population geography, health geography and disaster management.

An Introduction to the Social Geography of India

Concepts, Problems and Prospects

Dr Asif and Hemant

LONDON AND NEW YORK

Designed cover image: ©Getty images

First published 2023
by Routledge
4 Park Square, Milton Park, Abingdon, Oxon OX14 4RN

and by Routledge
605 Third Avenue, New York, NY 10158

Routledge is an imprint of the Taylor & Francis Group, an informa business

© 2023 Asif and Hemant

The right of Asif and Hemant to be identified as authors of this work has been asserted in accordance with sections 77 and 78 of the Copyright, Designs and Patents Act 1988.

All rights reserved. No part of this book may be reprinted or reproduced or utilised in any form or by any electronic, mechanical, or other means, now known or hereafter invented, including photocopying and recording, or in any information storage or retrieval system, without permission in writing from the publishers.

Disclaimer: Maps used in this book are for representational purposes only. The international boundaries, coastlines, denominations, and other information shown in the maps in this work do not necessarily imply any judgement concerning the legal status of any territory or the endorsement or acceptance of such information. For current boundaries please refer to Survey of India maps.

Trademark notice: Product or corporate names may be trademarks or registered trademarks, and are used only for identification and explanation without intent to infringe.

British Library Cataloguing-in-Publication Data
A catalogue record for this book is available from the British Library

ISBN: 978-1-032-34961-9 (hbk)
ISBN: 978-1-032-45641-6 (pbk)
ISBN: 978-1-003-37800-6 (ebk)

DOI: 10.4324/9781003378006

Typeset in Sabon
by Deanta Global Publishing Services, Chennai, India

Contents

List of Figures	vi
List of Tables	x
Abbreviations	xi
Preface	xv
Acknowledgements	xvii
1 Introduction to Social Geography	1
2 Welfare and Social Well-Being	26
3 Population	49
4 Education	90
5 Health	131
6 Income and Employment	166
7 Measuring Social Well-Being	198
Index	239

Figures

2.1	Hierarchy of Needs by Abraham Maslow (1954)	29
3.1	(a) Population of India (2011), (b) Share of State/UT in Population of India (2011)	53
3.2	Population Density of India (1901–2011)	54
3.3	(a) Population Growth Rate of India (2001–2011) and (b) Population Density of India (2011)	55
3.4	(a) Birth Rate in India (2019) and (b) Death Rate in India (2019)	59
3.5	Population Growth Rate of India (1901–2011)	61
3.6	Sex Ratio of India (1901–2011)	63
3.7	(a) Sex Ratio of India (2011) and (b) Child Sex Ratio of India (2011)	63
3.8	Overall Male and Female Literacy Rate of India (1901–2011)	65
3.9	(a) Literacy Rate of India (2011) and (b) Literacy Gap Between Males and Females (2011)	66
3.10	(a) Male Literacy Rate of India (2011) and (b) Female Literacy Rate of India (2011)	66
3.11	(a) Scheduled Castes Population in India (2011) and (b) Scheduled Tribes Population in India (2011)	68
3.12	Age–Sex Structure of India	71
3.13	Overall Male and Female Age Structure of India	71
3.14	Demographic Transition in India (1901–2018)	73
3.15	Total Fertility Rate (TFR) in India (1951–2021)	74
3.16	(a) Total Fertility Rate (TFR) in India (2019–2021), (b) Rural Total Fertility Rate (TFR) in India (2019–2021) and (c) Urban Total Fertility Rate (TFR) in India (2019–2021)	75
3.17	Migrants by Reason for Migration in India (2011)	80
3.18	Overall Male and Female Migrants by Duration of Residence in India (2011)	81
3.19	Share of Migrants in Population of State/UT in India (2011)	82
3.20	Rural–Urban Composition of Population in India (2011)	84
3.21	(a) Most Spoken Language by State/UT in India and (b) Second Most Spoken Language by State/UT in India	87
3.22	Speakers of Scheduled and Non-Scheduled Languages in India	88
3.23	Projection of Population in India (2020–2100)	89

4.1	(a) Schools in India (2019–2020) and (b) Schools Per Lakh Population in India (2019–2020)	101
4.2	(a) Mean Enrolment Per School (2019–2020) and (b) Average Number of Teachers Per School (2019–2020)	103
4.3	(a) Pupil–Teacher Ratio (PTR) in Primary and Upper Primary Level of Education (Class I–VIII) (2019–2020) and (b) Pupil–Teacher Ratio (PTR) in Secondary and Higher Secondary Level of Education (Class IX–XII) (2019–2020)	104
4.4	(a) Per cent of Schools with WASH Facilities (2019–2020) and (b) Schools for CWSN (Children with Special Needs) (2019–2020)	105
4.5	(a) Gross Enrolment Ratio at Elementary Level (Class I–VIII) (2019–2020), (b) Gross Enrolment Ratio at Secondary Level (Class IX–X) (2019–2020) and (c) Gross Enrolment Ratio at Higher Secondary Level (Class XI–XII) (2019–2020)	107
4.6	(a) Dropout Rate at the Primary Level (Class I–V) (2019–2020), (b) Dropout Rate at the Upper Primary Level (Class VI–VIII) (2019–2020) and (c) Dropout Rate at the Secondary Level (Class IX–X) (2019–2020)	110
4.7	(a) Gender Parity Index at Elementary Level (Class I–VIII) (2019–2020), (b) Gender Parity Index at Secondary Level (Class IX–X) (2019–2020) and (c) Gender Parity Index at Higher Secondary Level (Class XI–XII) (2019–2020)	111
4.8	Enrolment by Social Category in School Education in India (2019–2020)	112
4.9	(a) Universities in India (2019–2020) and (b) Colleges in India (2019–2020)	115
4.10	(a) Pupil–Teacher Ratio in Higher Education (2019–2020) and (b) Mean Enrolment Per College (2019–2020)	118
4.11	(a) Gross Enrolment Ratio in Higher Education (2019–2020), (b) Gender Parity Index in Higher Education (2019–2020)	120
4.12	Male, Female and Total Enrolment by Social Category in Higher Education in India (2019–2020)	120
4.13	Expenditure on Education in India	127
4.14	Public Expenditure on Research and Development (R&D) in India as Per Cent of the GDP (2010–2019)	127
4.15	Employability of Graduates by Domain of Education in India	129
5.1	(a) Life Expectancy at Birth (2016–2020), (b) Male Life Expectancy at Birth (2016–2020), (c) Female Life Expectancy at Birth (2016–2020)	139
5.2	(a) Infant Mortality Rate (2019), (b) Under Five Mortality Rate (2020) and (c) Maternal Mortality Rate (2020)	141
5.3	(a) Prevalence of Anaemia in Women (2019–2021) and (b) Per Cent of Institutional Deliveries	143
5.4	(a) Out-of-Pocket-Expenditure on Health (2020) and (b) Per Cent of Households with at least One Member under Health Insurance Cover	144

5.5	(a) Fully Vaccinated Children of Age 12–24 months (2019–2021), (b) Vaccination Coverage in Children under Mission Indradhanush 2.0 (2019–2020) and (c) Vaccination Coverage in Women under Mission Indradhanush 2.0 (2019–2020)	146
5.6	(a) Distribution of Sub-Health Centres (SHC) (2019–2020), (b) Distribution of Primary Health Centres (PHC) (2019–2020) and (c) Distribution of Community Health Centres (CHC) (2019–2020)	148
5.7	(a) Hospital Beds per Lakh Population (2019–2020) and (b) Medical Colleges in India (2019–2020)	150
5.8	(a) Doctors in India (2019–2020) and (b) Physicians, Nurses and Midwives in India (2019–2020)	151
5.9	Distribution of Diseases by Categories and Age-Groups in India	154
5.10	Public Expenditure on Health in India (2016–2021)	156
5.11	(a) Distribution of Covid-19 Cases (2020–2022), (b) Distribution of Covid-19 deaths (2020–2022)	163
5.12	Covid-19 Vaccination in India (2022)	164
6.1	GVA (Gross Value Added) of Economic Activities	178
6.2	GVA (Gross Value Added) of Economic Sector	178
6.3	GVA (Gross Value Added) by Individual Economic Activity	179
6.4	Gross Domestic Product of India (2011–2021)	181
6.5	Per Capita Gross Domestic Product of India (2011–2021)	182
6.6	Employment by Economic Sector in India (2019–2020)	184
6.7	(a) Gross State Domestic Product (GSDP) at Current Prices (2019–2020) and (b) Gross State Domestic Product (GSDP) at Constant Prices (2019–2020)	185
6.8	(a) Per Capita Gross State Domestic Product (GSDP) at Current Prices (2019–2020) and (b) Per Capita Gross State Domestic Product (GSDP) at Constant Prices (2019–2020)	186
6.9	(a) Gross State Domestic Product (GSDP) Growth at Current Prices (2019–2020), (b) Gross State Domestic Product (GSDP) Growth at Constant Prices (2019–2020)	187
6.10	(a) Labour Force Participation Rate (LFPR) in India (2019–2020), (b) Female Labour Force Participation Rate (LFPR) in India (2019–2020), (c) Male Labour Force Participation Rate (LFPR) in India (2019–2020)	188
6.11	(a) Distribution of Main Workers in India (2011), (b) Distribution of Marginal Workers in India (2011)	189
6.12	Distribution of Working and Non-working Population in India (2011)	191
6.13	Distribution of Formal and Informal Workers in India (2019–2020)	192
6.14	(a) Poverty Rate in India (2011–2012), (b) Rural Poverty Rate in India (2011–2012) and (c) Urban Poverty Rate in India (2011–2012)	194
6.15	(a) Unemployment Rate in India (2019–2020), (B) Female Unemployment Rate in India (2019–2020), (c) Male Unemployment Rate in India (2019–2020)	196

7.1	Human Development Index (HDI) of India 2018–2019	205
7.2	Headcount Ratio of Multidimensional Poor in India (2021) Based on Data from NFHS Round 4 (2015–2016)	213
7.3	Sustainable Development Goals (SDGs) India Index 2020–2021	216
7.4	Gender Development Index (GDI) of India (2017–2018)	233
7.5	Gender Inequality Index (GII) of India (2017–2018)	236

Tables

3.1	India: Population Growth Rate (1901–2011)	60
3.2	India: Population Attributes by Religion (2011)	69
3.3	India: Migrants by Reason for Migration (2011)	69
4.1	Levels of Education in India	93
4.2	Number of Colleges in Districts	116
4.3	Enrolment in Colleges	117
4.4	India: Expenditure on Education	126
5.1	Population Norms for Public Healthcare Facilities	155
5.2	Causes of Morbidity-Related Deaths	155
6.1	Economic Indicators of Measuring Income	174
6.2	Economic Activities used in Calculating GDP by Gross Value Added (GVA) Method	176
6.3	GVA at Current Price 2020–2021 (in Crore Rupees)	176
6.4	GVA at Constant Price (2011–2012) 2020–2021 (in Crore Rupees)	177
6.5	Components of GDP by Expenditure Method	180
6.6	Components of GDP by Expenditure Method (in Per cent)	180
6.7	Gross Domestic Product (in Crore Rupees) of India 2011–2021	181
6.8	Gross Domestic Product (GDP) Year-on-Year Growth (in Per Cent)	182
6.9	Per Capita Gross Domestic Product and Growth (in Rupees)	183
7.1	Dimensions and Indicators of the Human Development Index	201
7.2	Categories of the Human Development Index (HDI)	203
7.3	Dimensions and Indicators of the Multidimensional Poverty Index (MPI)	208
7.4	Calculation of the MPI	209
7.5	India: Multidimensional Poverty Index 2021	212
7.6	Dimensions and Indicators of Gender Development Index (GDI)	229
7.7	Categories of the Gender Development Index (GDI)	232
7.8	Gender Inequality Index	234
7.9	Categories of the Gender Inequality Index (GII)	235

Abbreviations

AAG:	Association of American Geographers
ABR:	Adolescent Birth Rate
AICTE:	All India Council for Technical Education
AIDS:	Acquired Immuno-deficiency Syndrome
AIIMS:	All-India Institute of Medical Sciences
AISHE:	All-India Survey of Higher Education
ASFR:	Age-Specific Fertility Rates
AYUSH:	Ayurveda, Yoga and Naturopathy, Unani, Siddha and Homeopathy
B.ED:	Bachelors of Education
BCE:	Before Common Era
BMI:	Body Mass Index
BMN:	Basic Minimum Needs
BPL:	Below Poverty Line
CBD:	Central Business District
CBSE:	Central Board of Secondary Education
CCE:	Continuous Comprehensive Evaluation
CD:	Community Development
CE:	Common Era
CHC:	Community Health Centre
CISCE:	Council for the Indian School Certificate Examinations
CMNND:	Communicable, Maternal, Neonatal, and Nutritional Diseases
CWSN:	Children with Special Needs
DC:	District Collector
DHS:	Demographic and Health Surveys
DIET:	District Institute of Education and Training
DM:	District Magistrate
DPSP:	Directive Principles of State Policy
DTM:	Demographic Transition Model
EWS:	Economically Weaker Sections
FLN:	Foundational Literacy and Numeracy
GDI:	Gender Development Index
GDP:	Gross Domestic Product
GER:	Gross Enrolment Ratio
GFCF:	Gross Fixed Capital Formation
GHE:	Gross Health Expenditure

GII:	Gender Inequality Index
GIS:	Geographic Information Systems
GNP:	Gross National Product
GPI:	Gender Parity Index
GSDP:	Gross State Domestic Product
GVA:	Gross Value Added
HCR:	Headcount Ratio
HDI:	Human Development Index
HDR:	Human Development Report
HECI:	Higher Education Commission of India
HEI:	Higher Education Institutions
IB:	International Baccalaureate
ICDS:	Integrated Child Development Services
ICESCR:	International Covenant on Economic, Social and Cultural Rights
ICSE:	Indian Certificate of Secondary Education
ICT:	Information and Communication Technology
IEC:	Information Education and Communication
IGNOU:	Indira Gandhi National Open University
IIM:	Indian Institute of Management
IISER:	Indian Institutes of Science Education and Research
IIT:	Indian Institute of Technology
ILO:	International Labour Organisation
IMR:	Infant Mortality Rate
INC:	Indian Nursing Council
ISM:	Indian Systems of Medicine
JEE:	Joint Entrance Examination
KG:	Kindergarten
LFPR:	Labour Force Participation Rate
LGTBQ:	Lesbian, Gay, Transgender, Bisexual, Queer
MBA:	Masters of Business Administration
MBBS:	Bachelor of Medicine and Bachelor of Surgery
MDG:	Millennium Development Goals
MIS:	Management Information System
MMR:	Maternal Mortality Rate
MNC:	Multi-National Company
MOOC:	Massive Online Open Courses
NAAC:	National Accreditation and Assessment Council
NCD:	Non-Communicable Diseases
NCERT:	National Council of Educational Research and Training
NCPCR:	National Commission for Protection of Child Rights
NCT:	National Capital Territory
NCTE:	National Council for Teacher Education
NEP:	National Education Policy
NFHS:	National Family Health Survey
NHM:	National Health Mission
NHP:	National Health Policy
NIF:	National Indicator Framework

NIOS:	National Institute of Open Schooling
NIT:	National Institutes of Technology
NITI:	National Institute for Transforming India
NMC:	National Medical Commission
NNI:	Net National Income
NNP:	Net National Product
NPC:	National Planning Committee
NPP:	National Population Policy
NPR:	National Population Register
NSO:	National Statistical Office
NTA:	National Testing Agency
OBC:	Other Backward Classes
OECD:	Organisation for Economic Cooperation and Development
OOPE:	Out-of-Pocket Expenditure on Health
OPD:	Out Patient Department
OPHI:	Oxford Poverty Human Initiative
PCA:	Principal Components Analysis
PCV:	Pneumococcal conjugate vaccine
PDI:	Personal Disposable Income
PFCE:	Private Final Consumption Expenditure
PFRDA:	Pensions Fund Regulatory and Development Authority
PHC:	Primary Health Centre
PHD:	Doctor of Philosophy
PLFS:	Periodic Labour Force Survey
PNMW:	Physicians, Nurses and Midwives
PPP:	Purchasing Power Parity
PTR:	Pupil–Teacher Ratio
QOL:	Quality of Life
RTE:	Right of Children to Free and Compulsory Education Act
SARS:	Severe Acute Respiratory Syndrome
SC:	Scheduled Castes
SCERT:	State Council of Educational Research and Training
SDG:	Sustainable Development Goals
SDSN:	Sustainable Development Solutions Network
SEBI:	Securities and Exchange Board of India
SECC:	Socio-Economic Caste Census
SEDG:	Socially and Economically Disadvantaged Group
SHC:	Sub Health Centre
SMC:	School Management Committee
SRS:	Sample Registration System
ST:	Scheduled Tribes
TFR:	Total Fertility Rate
TPDS:	Targeted Public Distribution System
U5MR:	Under-Five Mortality Rate
UDHR:	Universal Declaration of Human Rights
UGC:	University Grants Commission
UIDAI:	Unique Identification Authority of India

UIP:	Universal Immunisation Programme
UNDP:	United Nations Development Programme
UNESCO:	United Nations Educational, Scientific and Cultural Organisation
UNFCCC:	United Nations Framework Convention on Climate Change
UNO:	United Nations Organisation
UNSD:	United Nations Statistics Division
USA:	United States of America
WASH:	Water, Sanitation and Hygiene
WHO:	World Health Organisation

Preface

Dear Reader,

I feel elated to introduce to you this book on the social geography of India. It is a culmination of nearly ten years of my hitherto experience of teaching and mentoring undergraduate, postgraduate and doctorate students at the university as a faculty of geography. This book has taken several months of meticulous research and detailed deliberations with faculties and scholars to finally attain its present form.

Why social geography? – it is a pertinent question that any learner of geography may be keen to ask. Aristotle, the legendary Greek philosopher said, "(Hu)Man is by nature a social animal". Human beings live and express themselves in social groups as family, community, society, state, etc. As social scientists, geographers are concerned with the welfare and development of the society and world, at large. When we discuss development, especially in the context of India, most of us would agree that health, education, employment and overall human development are essential for it. We felt the need for introducing a textbook that could acquaint the students, scholars and academicians of geography with the rich tradition of social geography while addressing the pertinent social issues around us, relating to social welfare and development.

The great geographer Wilbur Zelinsky in 1970 stressed for geographers to become 'diagnosticians, prophets and architects' of the social reality. By writing this book, our objective is to study scientifically and systematically the social reality around us. In India, the academic tradition of social geography has developed hand in hand with other social science disciplines such as sociology, economics, demography, linguistics, etc. There have been numerous academicians dedicated to its cause, including professors, who taught us and have inspired us to create this book. This book presents a novel perspective on social geography. We have addressed social issues which are considered indispensable and quintessential for the welfare and development of society, which include education, health and employment. This textbook will serve as a ready reckoner for students and readers who intend to understand the reality of these social sectors. Books on social geography are expected to address the cultural aspects of society such as ethnicity, tribe, caste, community, language, dialect and religion. In this book, we have treated these components demographically rather than sociologically, as we believe the existing textbooks discuss these aspects in sufficient detail.

Chapter 1 discusses the origin, nature and scope and development of the discipline of social geography within geography, from the age of the renaissance to modern times along with methods and philosophical themes in the discipline. The development of social geography in India has also been outlined. In Chapter 2 on "Welfare and Social

Well-being", certain important concepts such as needs, social well-being and social indicators have been discussed along with the development of the discipline of welfare geography and the welfare state in India. Chapter 3 on population discusses the Census of India, population composition and demographic attributes of the Indian population including aspects such as population growth, distribution, sex ratio, literacy rate, age structure, religious composition, migration, linguistic demography and policy on population. Chapter 4 is on education in which the organisations, levels, constitutional provisions and policies related to both school and higher education have been discussed. Essential social indicators like Pupil–Teacher Ratio (PTR), Gross Enrolment Ratio (GER), Gender Parity Index (GPI) and Dropout Rate have also been discussed. A detailed discussion has also been presented on the education policy in India and the contemporary issues related to education. In Chapter 5 on health, the principles and aspects of health, organisations of healthcare in India, related constitutional provisions, essential social indicators like Life Expectancy, Infant Mortality Rate (IMR), Under-Five Mortality Rate (U5MR), Maternal Mortality Rate (MMR), immunisation and expenditure have been discussed. Health-related policy along with the Covid-19 pandemic in India has also been discussed. In Chapter 6 on income and employment, essential economic concepts related to economic activities, measurement of national income, GDP (Gross Domestic Price) have been discussed along with the social dimensions of employment, unemployment and poverty. In Chapters 4–6, social indicators related to health, education and employment have been discussed. Often, in public discussions, composite indicators are used to simplify and compare the state of welfare and development of societies. In Chapter 7, such composite indices have been discussed which are acclaimed globally, namely Human Development Index (HDI), Multidimensional Poverty Index (MPI), Sustainable Development Goals (SDG) Index, Gender Development Index (GDI) and Gender Inequality Index (GII).

This book attempts to present a research-based detailed discussion on social geography and certain social aspects, which concern us all, with particular reference to the Indian context. Learning is a process and in the pursuit of academic excellence, despite our best efforts, a few aspects of this book may fall short of your expectations. We will look forward to responses from our readers to improve this book in future.

Dr Asif

Acknowledgements

A book may have the words of a writer but it is the product of the direct and indirect contribution and support of various people who make it possible for a book to be written and published. First and foremost, we present our gratitude to the Almighty for the successful completion of this book. We would like to thank our editors Lubna Irfan and Angelin Joy and our publisher Routledge, Taylor & Francis Group for accepting this project and guiding us throughout. This book would not have materialised without their constant support over many months. We would thank our parents and families for their emotional guidance. We would like to thank:

- Prof. Najma Akhtar, Vice-Chancellor of Jamia Millia Islamia (JMI), New Delhi, India, for providing an environment propitious to the pursuit of academic excellence,
- Our professors and teachers who have dedicated their lives to geography and set precedents of excellence for us to follow. We extend special thanks to:
  - Prof. Hifzur Rahman, Professor of Geography (retired) at Aligarh Muslim University (AMU), Uttar Pradesh, India
  - Prof. MH Qureshi, retired Professor of Geography (retired) at the Centre for the Study of Regional Development (CSRD), Jawaharlal Nehru University (JNU), New Delhi, India
  - Prof. Atiqur Rahman, Professor of Geography at Jamia Millia Islamia (JMI), New Delhi, India
  - Prof. Haroon Sajjad, Professor and Head of the Department of Geography at Jamia Millia Islamia (JMI), New Delhi, India
  - Prof. Mary Tahir, Professor and former Head of the Department of Geography at Jamia Millia Islamia (JMI), New Delhi, India
- Dr Aijaz Hussain and Dr Sameena Qazi at the Department of Geography, Jamia Millia Islamia (JMI), New Delhi, India, for their insights in preparation of the manuscript
- Zainul Abedin, PhD research scholar at the Department of Geography, Jamia Millia Islamia (JMI), New Delhi, India, for helping us with the preparation of manuscript and maps
- SK Zafarul Haque Tanweer, an officer at the Indian Revenue Service (IRS) for his support

In addition, I, Dr Asif would thank my wife, Farah Fatima and children, Ahmad Faraz and Umaiza for their support and encouragement in my professional endeavours.

Finally, we remain eternally grateful to Jamia Millia Islamia (JMI), Jawaharlal Nehru University (JNU) and Aligarh Muslim University (AMU), three institutions of excellence that have been nurturing and enriching the great tradition of geography.

Dr Asif
*** Hemant***

Chapter 1

Introduction to Social Geography

Introduction

Geography, as a discipline, is concerned with the spatial organisation and analysis of features and phenomena occurring on and in the vicinity of the surface of earth. Conventionally, on the basis of subject matter, two divisions of geography are identified: (i) physical geography and (ii) human geography. Physical geography deals with the naturally occurring features and phenomena on the surface of earth, whereas human geography is concerned with the distribution and analysis of human activities within nature and society.

The exposition of human activities has always been a major pursuit in geography so that in antiquity, Herodotus (485–425 BCE) in Greece presented a descriptive account of the struggle of the Greeks against the 'barbarians'. Strabo (64 BCE–20 CE), during the Roman period, wrote *Geographica* as a geographical treatise of the known world for better comprehension and training of imperial officers. Such encyclopaedic tradition continued till the 'Age of Explorations' which existed till the 17th century, occurring in the accounts of Marco Polo (1254–1324), Bartolome de las Casas (1484–1566), Captain James Cook (1728–1779), Major James Renell (1742–1830), etc.

In the post-Renaissance period of the emergence of modern geography around the 17th century, the concern of geographers was mainly to explore and provide encyclopaedic description of the features and phenomena on the earth's surface, both natural and social. The description of human activities was in the social context. There was a tacit understanding that humans are social animals, and thus, human activities occur within the society or the social space they are placed within. Hence, in the early days, what is known as human geography was conceived as social geography. Thomas Walter Freeman (1908–1988), a geographer from Britain, in the book *A Hundred Years of Geography* (1961) has commented on the social aspect of geography that "undoubtedly the attraction of human geography was its social interest, its study of ways of life of people in many places, and at many stages of civilisation" (Freeman, 1961). The Irish geographer Anne Buttimer (1938–2017) noted the ontological essentiality of the social aspect in geography, "Since human activities characteristically are group activities, how can human geography be anything else but social?" (Buttimer, 1968).

DOI: 10.4324/9781003378006-1

Definition

Social geography is the sub-discipline of geography that is broadly concerned with the spatial organisation of society. It deals with social phenomena and their spatial components and, in the process, provides the essential linkage between society and space. It can be defined as the study of the spatial organisation of social phenomena as they occur within and across social groups, in the social space they occupy.

The Canadian geographer James Wreford Watson (1915–1990) described social geography in 1957 as, "the identification of different regions of the earth according to associations of social phenomena related to the total environment" and defined, "social geography is not a systematic treatment of society in relation to its environment, but a genetic description of social differences as they are related to other factors and to differences in areas of the earth surface" (Watson, 1957). British sociologist and pioneer of social geography Raymond Edward Pahl (1935–2011) in the essay 'Trends in Social Geography' (1965) defined social geography as the study of the pattern and processes in understanding socially defined populations in their spatial setting (Pahl, 1965). In simpler terms, social geography can be considered to be the study of the society from a spatial perspective. This is achieved by the examination of the social groups, social contexts, social processes, social relations and social differences that produce and reproduce space dynamically.

In *A Dictionary of Geography*, Francis John Monkhouse defined social geography as

> often used simply as the equivalent of human geography, or in the United States of America (USA) as Cultural Geography, but usually it implies studies of population, urban and rural settlements, and social activities as distinct from political and economic ones.

In the same dictionary, he defined human geography as "the part of Geography dealing with man and human activities" (Monkhouse, 1965). This presents the ambiguity faced in defining social geography as a consequence of the wide range of subject matter included in it. The subject matter of social geography has been so varied that Buttimer, writing in the *International Encyclopedia of Social Sciences* (1968), preferred to describe social geography as "a field created and cultivated by a number of individual scholars rather than an academic tradition built up within particular schools" (Buttimer, 1968).

Nature and Scope

Social geography is concerned with a wide range of social features and phenomena in the spatial dimension. Studies in social geography can range from the anthropological origin of humankind to the information societies (Castells, 1996) or *simulacra* shaping social relations in the present-day world (Boudrillard & Glaser, 1981). Naturally, the discipline of social geography is multi-faceted that has a myriad of concepts, some of which are discussed as follows:

1. **Society**: It is the functional unit of individuals occupying a particular spatial environment, interacting with each other and having values and beliefs expressed in the form of culture.

2. **Social Group or Social Community**: It is a set of individuals sharing common values, beliefs or identities and having a sense of unity. They may be occupying real space organised in the form of nation-states, cities, neighbourhoods etc. or they may exist in virtual space in the form of online social communities.
3. **Social Interaction**: It refers to the communication between two or more individuals, which may be religious, economic, political, academic, etc. in nature and is expressed in the form of exchange, competition, conflict, cooperation and accommodation within the society.
4. **Social Relationship**: It is the association or connection between an individual and society or a group of individuals based on their social interactions that are perceived to have personal meaning and provide a sense of community.
5. **Social Values**: Social values are collective standards or rules with which people are expected to follow or act in accordance (Kluckhohn, 1951; Tsirogianni & Gaskell, 2011).
6. **Social Institution**: It refers to the organised grouping of individuals with a common purpose and defined roles following similar norms and having similar beliefs and values.
7. **Social Process**: It refers to the ways and manners in which social interactions, relationships and ultimately social life are constructed and produced.
8. **Social Identity**: It refers to the self-concepts made by people as a member of a social group or functioning within a social structure (Tajfel, 1978). Social identity is strongly linked to space or the 'sense of belonging' to certain places.
9. **Social Structure**: It refers to the stable ordered arrangements of social groups and social institutions in society, which influence the functioning and status of individuals.
10. **Social System**: It is the functional interrelated organisation of individuals, groups, institutions and structure of the society.
11. **Social Change**: It is the transformation or alteration of the state of society. The pursuit of social change may arise due to inequality or oppression. It may occur in two ways, either radically through social revolution or liberally through social reforms.
12. **Social Justice**: It refers to the pursuit of the creation of a more just society by reducing inequalities and ensuring fair distribution of wealth, opportunities and privileges within it. It has been a central theme for social geographers and has found application in the claims of right to the city, right to health, right to education, right to a clean environment, right to fair treatment irrespective of sexuality, gender, disability, race, ethnicity or nationality. Social geographers are concerned with how rights are influenced by the state and corporate actors acting in space.
13. **Social Well-Being**: It is the well-being pertaining to social connections, relationships and personal expressions within one's social setting. It is used as a generic term for various overlapping and broad concepts that include quality of life, welfare and the standard of living etc.
14. **Social Welfare**: It is the social well-being of people ensured by the fulfilment of their basic needs; social goods and social services such as food, health, education, sanitation, etc. by the social institutions (Elizalde, 2014). This may be done entirely by the state or with the help of private institutions, corporations, etc. It

has been recognised as an essential obligation of the society, and particularly the state towards its citizens.
15. **Social Theory**: It refers to the set of statements used for the explanation of social life which may include the spatial distribution of social groups, the social construction of space and the various other facets of political–economic institutions and development.

Social geography as an academic discipline deals holistically with humankind in the context of total geographical milieu. This milieu comprises various categories as they correspond to various types of human activities, such as political, economic and cultural. The scale of these activities or phenomena ranges from the individual to the international level. The range of scale of studies in social geography is discussed as follows:

1. **Individual:** At the individual level, studies in social geography include exploring individual identities, perceptions, discrimination, sexualities, etc.
2. **Family:** At the family level, several issues as discrimination, ostracisation, exclusion, housing, consumption, well-being, intra-family relations, etc. are studied.
3. **Social Group:** Most of the studies in social geography relate to understanding the perceptions, attitudes, activities, distributions of social groups or communities. These social groups derive their identities on the basis of (a) the physical space they share such as urban community, forest tribes, gated community, (b) the values and beliefs they share such as religious communities, digital communities, (c) the social identities they share such as caste communities, queer communities or combination of these factors.

The spatial range of social geography studies can vary at the following levels: (1) **Neighbourhood Level**, e.g. the 'ghettos' or the neighbourhoods of the Afro-American community, gated communities, slums, etc.; (2) **City or Village Level**; (3) **Regional Level**, e.g. Himalayan region; (4) **National Level**; and (5) **International Level**, e.g. South Asia, Nordic region. Research in social geography may also pertain to unreal or virtual spaces, i.e. spaces which may not exist on the map but shape the social interactions of individuals such as digital spaces. Social space is the central theme in social geography. French geographer Paul Claval (1932–) highlighted the importance of social space "to understand the geography of a place means to understand the social organisation of those who inhabit it, their mentality, their beliefs, their representations" (Claval, 1964).

Comprehension of the socio-spatial organisation is the prime motivation in social geography. This process often begins with exploring the origins of society. In social geography, social groups become actors or the agency that construct and transform social interactions and social networks which find manifestations in the space they occupy. The society is organised in the form of a socio-spatial structure and functions as a social system. This organisation and functioning are influenced by the political distribution of power, economic distribution of resources and cultural expression of values, beliefs and attitudes. Very often, the interlinked political, economic and cultural factors, acting in cohesion, create an unequal social order in which resources, power and opportunity become concentrated in the hands of few, that is, inequality in socio-spatial distribution occurs. For instance, in the social structure defined by the presence of the caste system in India, few higher castes appropriated power, resources and knowledge, whereas the majority of the population of the lower castes were deprived of it. Similarly, the society in France prior to the French revolution of 1789 was marked by stark inequalities in possession of wealth, resources and political power. In Russian society, for instance, on the eve of the October Revolution of 1917, the society had clear divisions between the aristocracy that had all the power and wealth and the working class and peasants who were condemned to penury.

The unequal distribution of power, resources and knowledge is created through social processes making those social groups disadvantaged which are (i) placed at the lower levels of the social hierarchy or social structure or (ii) situated (relatively) away from the centres of political, economic or cultural power in society. This is elucidated with an example from India: as explained earlier, the social order marked by the caste system has historically led to the deprivation of the communities belonging to the lower castes, for instance, the Scheduled Castes (SC) who are placed at the bottom in the social hierarchy of caste. Similarly, the tribal people or Scheduled Tribes (ST) have been disadvantaged because they have occupied spaces at the fringe of political and economic power. In this way, inequality is perpetrated by social and spatial processes acting together. The general concern of social geography is with the issues related to equity, oppression, and justice and understanding how differences and inequalities are produced and reproduced in space and the ways in which they are experienced and challenged.

Spatial analysis in social geography is based on interrelated political, economic and cultural factors acting with material reality and producing social contradictions. Such analysis is motivated by the need for social change (Asheim, 1979; Johnston, 1981). Social geography considers social structure from an interactionist perspective and aims to study how social life is constituted spatially through the structure of social relations (Jackson & Smith, 1984). Social theories are powerful tools that are constructed and utilised to explain the organisation and functioning of society and the resulting consequences. Social geographers are placed in a perplexing position with regard to social theory because they are placed in the social space they observe, and hence, it is challenging to remain disinterested. So, the British geographer Derek Gregory (1951–) referred to social theory as 'an intervention in social life – it is an intervention because social theory does not take place in some isolated laboratory, not applied from outside, but worked with to make social life intelligible' (Gregory, 1994).

Evolution of Social Geography

During the early period of modern geography, social geography was synonymous with human geography. In fact, what is considered to be human geography in the present day was originally known as social geography because human activities occur within a socio-spatial context. This is evident in the work of German geographer Alexander von Humboldt (1769–1859), particularly in the essay 'The Island of Cuba' (1856) in which he described the social conditions and slavery prevailing under the imperial rule on the island (Humboldt, 1856). This was preceded by the inquisitive cynical essay of Thomas Robert Malthus (1766–1834), *An Essay on the Principle of Population* (1798) where he warned of the catastrophic consequences societies that would become liable to deal with if population growth occurred uncontrollably (Malthus, 1798). Earlier, in 1725, Italian philosopher Giovanni Battista Vico (1668–1744) postulated that the development of human societies everywhere followed an identical series of stages (Joyce & Burgess, 1966). German geographer historian Johann George Kohl (1808–1878) examined the significance and social function of various types of settlement in his works. Eduard Hahn (1856–1928), an ethnologist from Germany, in 1896 traced the evolution of livelihoods and presented an exposition of the religious and social origins of several economic activities. In the 18th and 19th centuries, thinkers in the Western World had begun to develop a distinction between nature and society as humans organised themselves into societies to fulfil their needs and thrive in the natural world.

The conceptualisation of democracy in France (1789), the rise of national consciousness due to the unification of the German Empire in Germany (1871) and the foundation of the first modern democratic republic state in the USA (1776) are accompanied by the dominance of liberal and rational thought that resulted in the development of the 'scientific' approach to knowledge. This scientific approach was concretised in the works of the French social philosopher Auguste Comte (1798–1857), notably *Cours de Philosophie Positive* (1829). He was a proponent of the application of scientific methods of the natural sciences, which were empiricism and positivism, to the study of social phenomena. This would result in (a) the formulation of rationally explicable laws and theories in social sciences based on sound scientific methods and (b) the application of such laws and theories to usher in the desired monitorable changes in society through social-economic planning (Dixit, 1997).

The consciousness of the 'social' was present in the minds of geographers whether, Carl Ritter (1779–1859), Ferdinand von Richthofen (1833–1905), Friedrich Ratzel (1844–1904), Paul Vidal de La Blache (1845–1918), Alfred Hettner (1859–1941) or Halford Mackinder (1861–1947). Social geography has a tradition that has a history dating beyond a century (Dunbar, 1977). The first person in the Anglo-American tradition to use the term 'social geography' was George Wilson Hoke, whose paper 'The Study of Social Geography' was published in 1907 (Hoke, 1907).

Social geography did not receive much attention till the beginning of the 20th century primarily due to two reasons: firstly, the realm of physical geography was still largely being explored and developed scientifically so the majority of geographers accorded only secondary importance to the study of society in geography, attending primarily to the description and explanation of 'diverse natural phenomena as they occurred in interrelation on the surface of the earth' (Richthofen, 1903) and secondly, to lend scientific calibre to geography as an academic discipline in the same manner as that of physics or chemistry, geographers addressed natural phenomena which could be dealt through empirical, mathematical and cartographic methods while largely eschewing the study of socio-spatial organisation and functioning of society which required qualitative research as well. What existed as social geography, with the passage of time, then became human geography, so as to analyse human activities from a disinterested 'value-free' position. Thus, the first reason corresponds to the lack of interest in subject matter, whereas the second reason indicates the methodological issues presented by social geography.

The term 'social geography' originated in France as *geographie sociale* in the works of anarchist geographer Elisee Reclus (1830–1905). The first known occurrence of the 'social geography' is in *Nouvelle Geographie Universelle* (Universal Geography) of

Reclus written in 1884. He used this expression in several of his letters and in his last work *L'Homme et la terre* (Man and Nature) written in 1905 (Reclus, 1905). Social geography found expression in the works of the sociologists of the Le Play school inspired by the French sociologist Frederic Le Play (1806–1882), who discarded the prevalent *a priori* explanations of society and used case study as a method for investigation of the actual social conditions of families of workers and peasants in France. His technique of writing monographs and producing a descriptive encyclopaedic inventory of social facts was used later by Vidal de La Blache and his students in France and Herbert John Fleure (1877–1969) in Britain. Le Play's conceptualisation of *lieu-travail-famille* was later reformulated by the British sociologist-geographer Patrick Geddes (1834–1932) into 'place–work–folk' and discussed in Chapter 2.

Germany: German geographer Friedrich Ratzel (1844–1904) in the monumental work *Anthropogeographie*, Volume I, published in 1882 described society from the classic ecological perspective within its natural environment and the role of human agency in transforming nature and dealing with physical barriers. In the second volume of *Anthropogeographie* (1891), based on his study of the tribes and the evolution of society in North America, he noted that every human migration was characterised by (a) an area of origin, (b) a specific cause and (c) a particular route to destination. The societies created by migrants at their destination were expressions of their memories, skills, traditions and culture. Such migrant societies in the newly inhabited spaces resulted from two spatial forces: (a) the local geographical environment of destination, and (b) the culture and technology that had been produced in the geographic environment of origin (Ratzel, 1891).

France: In European traditions, social geography developed as an approach to human geography rather than a sub-discipline, especially in the French school of geographical thought (Bartels & Peucker, 1969). The pioneer of geography in France, Paul Vidal de La Blache (1845–1918) and a leading thinker of possibilism, noted that geography was a science of places and not a science of men (Blache, 1913). His conceptualised *genre de vie* (way of life) as a product, sets of techniques, cemented through tradition, continuously being produced as a result of the interaction of society with nature, expressed spatially in the form of 'pays'. The *genre de vie* of different societies varied spatially and assumed the form of functional social order to fulfil material necessities of life (Blache, 1911; Sorre, 1948). Vidal de La Blache (1903) summarised this process as:

> It is man who reveals a country's individuality by moulding it to his own use. He establishes a connection between unrelated features, substituting for the random effects of local circumstances a systematic cooperation of forces. Only then does a country acquire a specific character, differentiating it from others, till at length it becomes, as it were, a medal struck in the likeness of a people.
> (Gregory et al., 1986)

Camille Vallaux (1870–1945), a student of Vidal de La Blache, wrote the book *Geographie Sociale*, published in 1908 and 1911 in two volumes. The leading disciple of Vidal de la Blache, Jean Brunhes (1869–1930), synthesised the Vidalian concept of *genre de vie* with the Schluterian tradition of *Kulturlandschaft* (cultural landscape) the 'visible landscape' (Brunhes, 1924). He considered the physical and cultural phenomena to be in a state of perpetual change to be studied on the temporal scale. He added the dimension of group psychology or social psychology to describe in the true Vidalian sense, how similar environments were utilised in different ways at different periods in history to give rise to different landscapes by different cultures. He placed social geography as the third level in a threefold structure of human geography that included (i) the primary groups of family, kith and kin, (ii) the secondary groups at workplace and (iii) the third groups of the social systems and institutions that make the society functional and determine access to land and property (Brunhes, 1910).

Albert Demangeon (1872–1940), the French professor of geography and a student of Vidal de La Blache, placed social groups at the centre of analysis in the human geography tradition and pioneered the use of field surveys to obtain information on social questions (Demangeon, 1942). He noted, "To explain the geographical phenomena of which (hu)man has been the witness or contriver, it is necessary to study their evolution in the past with the aid of documents". (Darby, 2002) French geographers Maximilien Sorre (1881–1962) and Pierre George (1909–2006) examined social geography from a system's perspective. Sorre investigated the process of transfer of populations and cultures through international migrations. For him, society represented a system of techniques: family and kinship systems, livelihoods (genres de vie) and religions, having specific influence on the spatial organisation of society (Sorre, 1948). George interlinked the social and economic aspects of human behaviour with the social aspect representing one facet of the economic (George, 1946). The French sociologist Henri Lefebvre (1901–1991) introduced the concept of the (social) production of space (Claval, 1984) developing on topics he had written since the 1930s, finally culminating into 'La Production de L'Espace' (Lefebvre, 1974). According to Lefebvre, the production of space could be absolute which is the natural space or in more subtle and complex ways resulting in the construction of social spaces or spaces to which certain meanings were attached by society. He conceptualised this production of space as a three-part dialectic between everyday practices and perceptions (*le percu*), representations or theories of space (*le concu*) and the spatial imaginary of the time (*le vecu*) but this production was certainly not value-free but served to advance the hegemony of the dominant classes. He noted,

> Social space is a (social) product ... the space thus produced also serves as a tool of thought and of action ... in addition to being a means of production it is also a means of control, and hence of domination, of power.
>
> (Shields, 1991)

In France, the subject matter of social geography coincided with human geography itself while in Germany it was perceived more narrowly with the landscape school.

French sociologist Emile Durkheim developed the concept of 'social morphology' based on the distribution and organisation of human populations across the world which encompassed the analysis of the size, density and attributes of the population to understand the ways in which these factors construct and shape the relationships between people and social groups (Durkheim, 1899). The concept of social morphology was later developed and applied by the geographers of the school of urban ecology and social relevance movement.

The Netherlands: The Dutch sociologist Sebald Rudolf Steinmetz (1862–1940), in Amsterdam, developed the school of 'Sociography' as a new unique subject matter by combining geography and ethnography. Its methods were mainly theoretical, based on writings on society, social sub-divisions and societal patterns. Sociography later morphed into a meta-discipline, by combining studies of literature, sociology, politics, culture and economics (Steinmetz, 1912–1913). The Utrecht School of Social geography in The Netherlands, which emerged in the 1930s, started with studies on the relationship between social groups and living spaces and developed special emphasis on urban society in the backdrop of globalised processes of urbanisation, climate change, globalisation and infrastructural changes. Dutch professor of social geography Christiaan van Paassen (1917–1996) conceptualised the world as comprised of socio-spatial entities of different scales. In the 1962 article titled, 'Geographical Structuring and Ecological Complex', he presented the concept of 'syn-ecological complex' as a structural whole of cohabiting households, their facilities and their activities (Passen, 1965). He identified two types of social consciousness, namely, historical and geographical consciousness. Geographical consciousness, according to him, was an ecumenical whole, the consciousness of society as a whole in which (hu)man is placed, and thus, people are bound to places and areas (Easters, 1962). In the Dutch school of geography, *sociale geografie* equalled the French *geographie sociale*.

Sweden: In Sweden, Torsten Hagerstrand (1916–2004) and Sven Godlund (1921–2006) applied quantitative and cartographical techniques to study social processes such as migration, rural–urban interaction, circulation, innovation diffusion, etc. focusing on *hembydsforskning* (home area studies), and chorographic ethnological studies of material culture to define cultural regions (Crang & Thrift, 2000).

USA: American geographer Ellsworth Huntington (1876–1947), who wrote *Civilization and Climate* (1915) linked civilisational development with climate. He went as far as to relate the social features such as race, religion, languages and institutions with geographical location, topography, soil, climate and other physical conditions on the other (Huntington, 1915). Geographers CC Huntington and Fred Carlson in *Environmental Basis of Social Geography* (1930) presented a discourse in opposition to environmental determinism, supplanting 'human' in the geography of man by 'social' and suggested that "it must not be supposed ... that environment alone can furnish all of this explanation of social causation" (Huntington & Carlson, 1929). Percy M Roxby (1880–1947), a US geographer and student of AJ Herbertson (1865–1915), in 1930 identified social geography as one of geography's four main branches along with historical geography, regional geography and physical geography (Roxby, 1930). Harlan H Barrows, a geographer at the University of Chicago in his address titled *Geography as Human Ecology*, to the Association of American Geographers (AAG) as its president identified social geography as one of the three major divisions of geography (Barrows, 1923).

In the 1920s, the geographic thought experienced 'paradigmatic shift' from descriptive and deductive physiographic programmes to a possibilist inductivist approach. During this period, American academic geography was dominated by the Berkeley School of Cultural Geography led by Carl Ortwin Sauer (1889–1975), whereas the socio-spatial distribution was taken up by the Chicago School. Sauer developed the concept of the 'cultural landscape' or the morphology of landscape constructed from a historical perspective (Sauer, 1925). As a matter of fact, he rejected environmental determinism and rigid positivism (Duncan, 1980) and introduced the 'superorganic' concept of culture in geography (Solot, 1986).

Chicago School: In the USA, the social organisation of space was taken up by the geographers of the 'Urban Ecology School' at the University of Chicago, notably in the works of Robert Ezra Park (1864–1944), Ernest Watson Burgess (1886–1966), Roderick Duncan McKenzie (1885–1940) and Louis Wirth (1897–1952). They employed urban ecological models to examine the socio-spatial organisation, such as the Central Place Model of Burgess in 1925, the Sectoral Model of Homer Hoyt (1895–1984) in 1939 and the Multi-Nuclei Model of Urban Growth by Chauncy Harris (1914–2003) and Edward Ulman (1912–1976) in 1945. Earlier, Mark Jefferson (1863–1949) formulating the 'Law of the Primate City' supported indeterminism as opposed to the prevailing thought of environmental determinism of his teacher William Morris Davis of 'environmental control and man's response'. He accorded great importance to the human creative ability expressed in socio-spatial organisation.

Louis Wirth in the essay 'Urbanism as a Way of Life' (1938) described rural and urban communities as the opposite ends of the spectrum and described the city as "substitution of secondary for primary contacts, the weakening of bonds of kinship, the declining social significance of the family, the disappearance of neighbourhood and the undermining of traditional basis of social solidarity ... leading to isolation and less interaction" (Wirth, 1938) but also as "centers of freedom and toleration, the home of progress, of invention, of science, of rationality" (Wirth, 1956). Burgess envisaged the spatial morphology of the urban society in the form of concentric rings expanding radially outwards from the centre, with the Central Business District (CBD) in the centre encircled by the slum area (or the zone of transition), which in turn is encircled by the zone of workingmen homes farther out; then the middle-class residential area and the bungalow section of the upper affluent class or the commuter zone on the periphery (Zorbaugh, 1929; Wirth, 1928).

Crime sociologists Clifford Robe Shaw (1895–1957) and Henry Donald McKay (1899–1980) projected urban crimes into three types of maps: (a) **Spot Maps**: These maps depicted social problem areas and spatial occurrences of crime with a focus on juvenile delinquency; (b) **Rate Maps**: These maps divided the city into blocks of one square mile and represented the population by attributes of age, gender, ethnicity, etc. and (c) **Zone Maps:** These maps demonstrated the major problems clustered in the city centre.

The magnum opus of this school was the book *The City* (1925) authored by Robert Park and Ernest Burgess that was built on the foundations of urban history, urban sociology and urban studies. It combined social and spatial theory with ethnographic observation, focusing on urban individuals within the social structures and institutions, seeking patterns of racial and ethnic segregation and criminal patterns, and the spatial transformation of the city over time. Thus, social geography in the USA developed with the union of sociology and geography (Park & Burgess, 1925). In the second school of urban sociology in Chicago, Otis Duncan (1921–2004) and Leo Schnore (1927–1988) in 1955 described ecology as the study of interaction between environment, technology, population and social organisation. Milla Aissa Alihan in 1938 presented a critical analysis of traditional materialism and emphasised the sociological implications in the context of ecological study (Alihan, 1938). Walter Irving Firey (1916–) in the work 'Land Use in Central Boston' (1947) postulated that ecological study should explain "the territorial arrangements that social activities assume" in human adaptation to space (Firey, 1947). Canadian geographer James Wreford Watson (1915–1990) applied the ideas of the Chicago school of urban ecology in his theory of urban geography that the urban landscape can be systematically explained in terms of social structure. Working in the city of Hamilton, he recognised different urban zones such as the zone of transition and cultural shatter belts associated with the different socio-economic groups (Watson & Watson, 1977).

In the 20th century, till the Second World War (1939–1945), what constitutes the subject matter of social geography was treated within the various sub-disciplines of geography such as human geography, economic geography, population geography, political geography, cultural geography and most importantly, regional geography. The academic focus in geography was on the regional geography perspective, on 'areal differentiation' rather than 'spatial interaction', as in the words of Richard Hartshorne (1899–1992), "Geography is concerned to provide an accurate, orderly, and rational description and interpretation of the variable character of the earth's surface" (Hartshorne, 1939). This was a period when geography was fast losing ground to disciplines such as geology, meteorology, oceanography, sociology, anthropology that resulted in an identity crisis. During this phase, the identification and explanation of the distributional patterns of various natural and social phenomena in the form of distinct spatial units or regions provided the unique subject matter to geography and appeared to dissipate the crisis.

Emergence as a Discipline

Social geography, as it is understood in the present-day context, emerged from the much-needed geographic turn in the 1960s to respond to the problems of the post-war era. The benefits of the post-war project of 'building of a better world' were distributed unfairly appropriated by the political, economic and social elite. This was evident both in the nations of the western world and the third world of former colonies, manifested in the civil rights movement of the Afro-American community in the USA, the Vietnam War and anti-war protests, political assassinations, the second wave of the feminist movement, the anti-apartheid movement in South Africa, the rise of environmentalism, the petrodollar crisis of the 1970s resulting in economic uncertainty, recession and widespread job losses. It should be noted that this was also the period when the success of the anthropogenic project of the conquest of nature had become ubiquitous. The problems faced by humankind then were not viewed as functions of disadvantaged geographies or lack of natural resource endowments. Social problems such as poverty, unemployment, oppression and discrimination increasingly came to be recognised as the products of the unjust social, economic and political order produced and sustained by humans. The emergence of social geography was a consequence of this consciousness, impregnated by the belief that social problems could be overcome with the mindful and just applications of the scientific method to the social problems of spatial distribution.

In the 1970s, the debate within American human geography shifted to political–economic processes with the felt need for social change (Ley, 1977; Jackson, 1981). When social geography emerged as a distinct tradition during the 1960s, it was used to identify and explain patterns in the distribution of social groups and social phenomena, thus being closely connected to urban geography and urban sociology (Johnston, 1987). However, in a much similar fashion to geomorphology, social geography transitioned from studying features to processes during this period. The paradigm shift was ushered in by the book *Social Justice and the City* (1973) authored by David Harvey. In this book, Harvey expounded the inequalities of social distribution and the hegemonic appropriation of city spaces by the dominant classes, using a structural Marxist approach in which the functioning of the capitalist system was identified as the root cause of socio-spatial inequalities. This was preceded by the work of the American geographer Richard Morrill (1939–) who mapped the spatial distribution of the ethnic minority concentrations in the urban space of Seattle and interpreted the expanding 'ghetto' as the geographic manifestation of a social phenomenon – the physical as well as social segregation of a disadvantaged group discriminated against by a more powerful one. He viewed the 'ghetto' as a product of social incompatibility, poverty and relative power. He explained the residential differentiation based on racial segregation so that the

> high income residents have been able to keep the most desirable corridor (usually far from the industrial areas) into the center, either as areas of old mansions, or as high-rise apartments. The much larger number of low-income residents who had to walk or rely on the streetcar were able to compete for access to this employment by accepting much less space and quality.
>
> (Morrill, 1971)

William Bunge in *Fitzgerald: Geography of a Revolution* (1971) studied the spatial organisation of social inequality on the scale of neighbourhood in Fitzgerald, Detroit, USA. He posed questions on how cities could be better organised to address inequalities. Bunge presented the insider perspective of living in ghetto and the structural constraints found in that space.

Geographers began taking up the real-world social problems developing crime geography (Morenoff et al., 2001; Newman, 1972; Herbert, 1997), health geography (Mayer, 1982; Monmonier, 1976; Gatrell, 2002), welfare geography (Smith, 1973), etc. Significant research included problems of poverty and deprivation, social discrimination exclusion, education and housing. British geographer Neil Smith (1954–2012) highlighted the structuring of social spaces to sustain and aggravate social differences and inequalities, producing 'uneven development', at both the local and global scales (Smith, 1984). Feminist Marxist scholars have expounded that the spatial organisation of society favours free market capitalism and advances the hegemony of the elites while at the same time disenfranchising women (Kodras et al., 2010). The inclusion of social elements into a systematised general framework for spatial analysis in geography gained traction during this period (Bobek, 1959). Various sub-disciplines evolved that included geographies of sexuality, leisure, tourism, consumption, etc. Contemporary scholars of the various sub-traditions within geography have identified a wide spectrum of different social geographies (Smith et al., 2010). In sum, the overwhelming emphasis of social geography in recent years has been to analyse how the spatial organisation of society creates inequalities in distribution resulting in differences between social groups.

Social Movements which are mobilisations of social groups with the objective of changing social, economic and political order by challenging the dominance of sociocultural and political–economic elites have been of major interest in social geography. These movements have spatial expressions and claim the right to participate in the construction of spaces. For instance, the Black Consciousness Movement in South Africa in the 1960s to challenge apartheid sought freedom and inclusion of the native communities; the *Chipko* Movement in the 1970s in Uttarakhand was a reaction of the Himalayan community to preserve their ecumene; the protests in the USA against the World Trade Organization in 1999 sought freedom to shape urban spaces without the penetrative influence of capital; the Arab Spring in the Middle East in the 2010s was an eruption of the people to claim spaces controlled by the dictatorial autocratic regimes; the Occupy Wall Street movement of 2011 demanded inclusion of the bottom 99 per cent of the population in urban, political and economic spaces and present the case for fair distribution of wealth. Social geographers are interested both in how social movements originate and operate spatially and their demands for the reorganisation of society.

Social Regions

The overarching objective of social geography is to understand, explain and analyse the spatial organisation of society, in terms of social features and social phenomena. The distribution of social features such as literacy rate or sex ratio can be delineated cartographically and identified as social regions through a formal approach. However, the identification of the distributive patterns of social phenomena is more complex as various indicators have to be taken into consideration coupled with functional interpretation of the phenomena in terms of their underlying social processes. These are discussed below:

1. **Formal Approach:** In this approach, social regions are identified based on social indicators. One or more than one indicator can be taken at a time. It follows from the traditional concept of areal differentiation and spatial distribution through deduction. This approach may not dwell on functional explanations of the underlying social process but remain limited to the identification of the distributional pattern of certain social regions. The objective is to search for social wholes in space and explanations for spatial patterns they express, for instance, the urban zones in the models of Burgess (1925), Hoyt (1939) and Harris-Ullman (1945).
2. **Functional Approach:** In this approach, social regions are considered to be dynamically produced by the operating social processes in the totality of their political, economic, historical and cultural contexts. In this approach, the spatial analysis tradition developed during the quantitative revolution of the 1950s is utilised. The social indicators are used to identify zones of influence, nodal organisation of space, spatial significance of social institutions, etc. For instance, the British geographer Emrys Jones (1920–2006) in his work *A Social Geography of Belfast* (1960) demarcated social regions and viewed them as products of historical and religious forces (Jones, 1960).

Thus, the analysis of the spatial dimension in social geography can be said to have two basic approaches. The first approach is concerned with the delineation and explanation of the formal distribution and patterns of social features through areal differentiation and considers social space as a mosaic of social areas defined by the social features of the occupant groups. In the second approach, the main concern is with the functional interpretation and spatial analysis of the spatially distributed social phenomena with due consideration to the underlying social processes along with the nodal organisation of social space as a network of spatial relations radiating around nodes (*points privilegies* of Sorre) and interacting via arteries of circulation. In recent years, social geographers have also been contributing to interdisciplinary research and regional planning.

Methods in Social Geography

As in other social sciences, the methodological approaches to studying social geography can broadly be classified into quantitative and qualitative. A large number of studies, however, also employ the mixed method incorporating both quantitative and qualitative aspects into their research.

1. **Quantitative Method**: This method is largely a legacy of the quantitative revolution of the 1950s. In this method, descriptive and inferential statistical techniques are used for the analysis of spatial and social indicators, which social geographers try to measure as objectively as possible. The typical linear research method used includes the steps of data collection, data processing, data analysis and, finally, data interpretation. Correlation and regression analysis, composite index and Z-score computation, principal components analysis (PCA) and principal axis factor analysis (PAFA), areal association and spatial autocorrelation are some of the techniques typically used in such studies. The quantitative method was applied by the Chicago school in social area analysis and factorial ecology. Eshref Shevky (1893–1969) and Wendell Bell (1924–2019) of the Chicago school of Urban Ecology developed the technique of 'social area analysis' for the identification of social areas. It related urban growth and morphology with social structure. They examined social rank, family, status and ethnicity in the case of Los Angeles and San Francisco using statistical census tract data. Shevky and Bell demarcated social areas on the basis of three indexes of social rank, degree of urbanisation and segregation. Following this, they conceptualised 'societal scale' or the number of people in relation and the intensity of these relations. They discovered that the process of urbanisation led to residential differentiation and social organisation occurred in the form of concentration of groups along cultural and ethnic lines (Shevky & Bell, 1955). However, this technique was largely quantitative and mechanistic and could not holistically portray the urban social reality. However, later it was used in multivariate statistical techniques, mainly principal components analysis and cluster analysis, and for various planning research exercises (Brindley & Raine, 1979). Social area analysis nevertheless played a defining role in the historical development of social geography by a systematic treatment of urban social space (Anderson & Bean, 1961; Timms, 1971). As a method, social area analysis was abandoned in favour of 'factorial ecology', which did not begin with any a priori identified parameters but used a host of variables under 'socio-economic status' (Johnston, 1978). These variables were then analysed using quantitative techniques such as correlation, and the results automatically identified which variables or factors shaped the socio-spatial organisation in a particular region. However, factorial ecology could not account for the impact of

non-quantifiable parameters such as social values, social structure, cultural practices on the socio-spatial setting (Lebowitz, 1977). British geographer Paul Cloke (1959–) developed the 'rurality index' in the 1970s which provided a composite measure of living conditions in England and Wales based on social indicators such as household amenities, occupations and commuting patterns (Cloke, 1983).
2. **Qualitative Method**: In social geography, the qualitative method is based on holistic comprehension of social groups and their interactions within social space by going beyond statistical techniques. The subjectivity of perceptions, beliefs, practices and values of the people involved is accorded primary importance. Social geographers try to incorporate this subjectivity and present it objectively to make their studies credible. Qualitative techniques include in-depth interviews, semi-structured interviews, biographical methods, focus groups, participatory observation, action research, case study design, etc. Early academicians of the Chicago school followed the ethnographic approach, whereby they observed the daily routines of migrants, ethnic communities, labouring classes, delinquents and thieves, the marginalised communities through the methods of participant observation, life history and field survey (Spates & Macionis, 1982). Humanist geographers such as Anne Buttimer and Edward Relph (1944–) in their studies have examined the geographies of everyday, mundane, life of individuals and social groups at personal and local levels. These works have established the qualitative method as a credible method and valid alternative to the 'quantitative revolution'.
3. **Spatial Method**: Social geography examines the social phenomena as they occur in space. It should be kept in mind that geography is a spatial science, and hence, spatial representation of phenomena is a method unique to geographers. The scope of geography extends to the phenomena that are mappable. The spatial method includes cartographic or Cartesian representation of phenomena. This is done by using maps, aerial photographs, satellite imagery or any Cartesian plane. In fact, the use of the spatial method is one of the major factors distinguishing social geography from sociology. The spatial method is derived from the combination of qualitative and quantitative techniques with geometry. In recent times, Geographic Information Systems (GIS) and remote sensing techniques have ushered in an era of digital cartography that has been used extensively in the field of social geography.

Philosophical Themes

Philosophical approaches provide the ontological and epistemological foundation to the studies, research and theories in social geography; ontological in the sense of explaining what is being studied and epistemological in the sense of how it is being studied and understood. These approaches are not the rule book of studies in social geography but enrich the knowledge and understanding of those studies. The philosophical approaches are discussed below briefly:

Naturalism: Naturalism is the belief in the organic unity of humans and nature. It is based upon the ideals of methodological unity in the natural and human sciences, and thus, seeks causal explanations for the operation of geographical and social phenomena. The founders of modern geography such as Alexander von Humboldt, Carl Ritter, Ferdinand von Richtofen, Freidrich Ratzel and Paul Vidal de La Blache were naturalists in the sense that they firmly believed that the laws that guided natural phenomena and social activities were essentially united (Entrikin, 1985).

Positivism: Positivist approach is based on obtaining knowledge through direct sensory observation or sense experience, known as the empirical method. The origin of the positivist approach lies in the works of the French philosopher August Comte (1798–1857) and the group of thinkers known as the Vienna Circle. According to this approach, scientific theories should be based on empirical observations or rational logic and must be testable and verifiable. Only those objects and phenomena should be studied or theorised which can be observed and measured. The positivist philosophy of Comte enumerated five principles for scientific knowledge:

1. *Le Real*: Scientific knowledge should be based on directly observable and empirically verifiable sensory experiences of reality.
2. *Le Certitude*: The scientific method across disciplines had to be uniform having certitude so as to make it highly verifiable and acceptable.
3. *Le Precis*: The description, presentation and explanation of scientific knowledge should be as precise, concise and clear as possible. Ethical value-based judgements should not affect the observation and judgements of the observer who should be disinterested in the phenomenon being observed.
4. *Le Utile*: Scientific knowledge should be developed to have some social utility.
5. *Le Relative*: Scientific knowledge is never complete and scientific truths are contingent truths.

Hence, metaphysical questions, personal perceptions and social values cannot be studied scientifically according to positivism. Hence, the spatial organisation of society is studied in terms of quantifiable variables such as population attributes, ethnicity and income levels. Emile Durkheim conceptualised the study of society by 'social facts' and 'social morphology' which was informed by the empirical positivist approach (Durkheim, 1982). Positivist approach was expressed in the quantitative method which influenced a significant number of studies in social geography in its early phase in the 1960s, although the development of critical theory resulted in greater use of mixed methods.

Behaviouralism: Behaviouralism emerged as a response to the quantitative revolution of the 1950s which treated social phenomena statistically and mathematically, with little importance to the human agency in shaping social phenomena. This led to the rise of behavioural geography which combined quantitative methods with psychological and sociological knowledge to analyse human behaviour in the social context. Its emphasis was on the cognitive perception of reality by individuals, decision-making which was not always optimum or rational and differed in varying contexts. Behavioural geographers criticised spatial science's study of *Homo economicus* (economic man). The behavioural tradition in geography was enriched by the works of Gilbert White on *Human Responses to Floods* (1945), Robert Kates on flood plain management (1962), WK Kirk on people's perception of the environment (1963), Julian Wolpert on *The Decision Process in a Spatial Context* (1964), Peter Gould on mental maps (1966) and Allan Pred on behavioural matrix (1967) culminating in the session of the Association of American Geographers (AAG) on Behavioural Geography (1969).

Humanism: The humanistic approach accords foremost importance to the subjectivity of human agency, creativity and awareness (Jackson & Smith, 1984). It consists of three approaches, namely idealism, phenomenology and existentialism. Yi-fu Tuan, Edward Relph, Anne Buttimer, David Ley, Marvyn Samuels and Nicholas Entrikin were the pioneers of humanistic geography. The idealistic approach to humanistic geography was advocated by Entrikin, Guelke and Harris and believed that real world cannot be known independently of the mind; hence, social phenomena can be comprehended only from an individual perspective. Phenomenology placed importance on the subjective meanings of place and space as they mean to people with equal emphasis on experience, identity and human agency in spatial construction (Buttimer & Seamon, 2015). Buttimer (1976) inspired by the phenomenology of Husserl discussed the concept of the 'lifeworld' to provide a subjective sense of intimacy between place and people. The existential approach viewed social landscapes as constructed historically by people. Humanistic approach reoriented the centre of geography to people situated in their social context based on subjective experience and qualitative methodologies (Relph, 1976). David Ley pushed social geography towards a humanist approach through ethnographic studies for examining the 'taken-for-granted realm of experience' and the social realm of 'shared meanings' (Ley, 1977). Ley mapped the 'environmental stress surface' as the mental topography of psychic stress with centres of gang turf, drug peddling and fears of people in a predominantly black area (Gould & White, 1974). Kay Anderson (1958–) and Susan J Smith (1956–) noted that emotions constitute an underrecognised set of social relations shaping the social world and constructing people's 'sense of place' (Anderson & Smith, 2001). Humanistic geographers represented spatial variations of social organisation through photographs, graffiti, quotations and mapping of various cultural activities.

Critical Approach: The critical approach to social geography focuses on the reflective assessment and critique of existing social, economic and political structures to make the discipline socially relevant to real-world problems. Critical geography is used as an umbrella term that includes Marxist, feminist, postmodern, post-structural and queer approaches. Critical geographies are characterised by a rejection of positivism, the possibility of progress, alteration of existing social structures, rejection of grand ideologies and faith in the agency of everyday change (Agger, 1988). Geographers such as David Smith (1936–) and David Harvey expressed wider social concerns in the 1970s and 1980s through their welfare and Marxist approaches. Apart from identifying spatial locations of social problems, they emphasised the 'why' questions or the underlying social processes that led to such problems. They exposed the unequal class relations in housing and labour markets in various urban, rural and regional settings.

Structuralism: Structuralism is "a theoretical approach to human geography which is characterised by a belief that in order to understand the surface patterns of human behaviour it is necessary to understand the structures underlying them which produce or shape human actions" (Aitken & Valentine, 2006). According to the structural approach, social and cultural structures within society shape individual behaviour. The social structure is based on material reality and interaction constructed by social interactions (Lippuner & Werlen, 2009). Structuralism seeks an explanation of the social phenomena in the operation of the overarching social, economic and political structures. The British sociologist Anthony Giddens (1938–) and the French sociologist Pierre Bourdieu (1930–2002) propounded the structuration theory, whereby they conceptualised social structure to be in a state of continuous change and dynamism. Derek Gregory in the book *Ideology, Science and Human Geography* (1978) attempted to align spatial explanations in geography with the concept of structure as formulated by the French ethnologist Claude Levi-Strauss (1908–2009). Later on, beginning the 1970s, geographers interpreted the social structure using the Marxist approach.

Marxism: Marxism is the school of thought based on the method of historical materialism seeking explanations for social phenomena through the dialectic approach or the operation of oppositely placed forces such as rich and poor, developed and undeveloped, bourgeoisie and proletariat. Marxist interpretation of spatial organisation of social phenomena is rooted in understanding how the surplus generated by the means of economic production is appropriated and distributed unequally by the social structure and political economy. Marxist geography is equated with radical thought in geography because of its criticism of the value-free positivist spatial analysis without considering how the capitalist production method influenced socio-spatial organisation (Peet, 1985). Marxist tradition in geography has overlapped with radical, critical and structural approaches. British geographers David Harvey (1935–), Richard Peet (1940–) and Nigel Thrift (1949–) are the pioneers of the Marxist approach in geography. Harvey criticised the positivist spatial science of the city, which failed to consider that "the city has to be regarded as a functioning totality within which everything is related to everything else" (Harvey, 1973). Lee (1976) pointed out the concentration of capital in the major urban centres of Europe. However, the Marxist approach was criticised by Ray E Pahl (1975) who argued that social problems and inequalities are bound to arise regardless of the mode of production. The failure of the regional planning of the Soviet city, and the Soviet Union at large, which sought to extricate the social inequalities proved the persistence of socio-economic inequalities under state socialism inspired by Marxist thought.

Feminism: The feminist approach tries to analyse and interpret the subjugation and marginalisation of women and individuals of non-binary sexualities through social practices and beliefs operating in the structures defined by patriarchal hegemony. Feminist expressions in the form of writings, art, theories and social movements present the claims of the marginalised sexes on social, political and economic spaces. Researchers such as Kim England, Larry Knopp and Ruth Fincher combined feminist and Marxist approaches to illustrate how hegemonic inequalities were sustained through privileged capitalist class relations, and patriarchal practices in urban spaces, housing stock and social services. American geographer Richard Symanski working on the geography of sexuality highlighted the economies of prostitution in England and the USA at different scales of state, metropolitan, street, etc. (Symanski, 1981). Queer theory developed as a tradition within feminist geography seeking rights, recognition and justice for people of heteronormative sexual identities, namely the Lesbian, Gay. Transgender, Bisexual, Queer (LGTBQ+) community. This theory challenged the presumption that all space is heterosexual. Feminist geographers have posed social queries regarding the spatial organisation of gendered lives and how social spaces reinforce gendered roles as well as offer opportunities to challenge systems of patriarchy and sexism.

Post-colonialism: This approach developed in the 1970s and 1980s focusing specifically on the socio-spatial problems of the Third World or the former colonies of imperial powers. Post-colonial approach shifted the debate on social realities away from the 'centres', i.e. former colonial powers towards the 'margins' or periphery, i.e. former colonies. Scholars such as Edward Said (1935–2003) and Frantz Fanon (1925–1961) highlighted the epistemological construction of former colonial spaces in the Western world through the binary logics of white and black, orient and occident, coloniser and colonised, north and south (Said, 1978). This construction reinforces differences and inequalities. The tradition of subaltern studies developed within this approach through the works of postcolonial feminist scholars, such as Gayatri Chakravorty Spivak (1942–) and Chandra Talpade Mohanty (1955–), who challenged the conception of the female in Western feminism through the construction of the 'third world women'. Post-colonialism also inspired studies of cultural construction and differences especially the creation of 'otherness' (Blunt & McEwan, 2002; Anderson et al., 2007).

Postmodernism: Postmodernism developed in the 1990s as an intellectual movement that rejected the structure of modernity, which included grand theories (of Newton, Marx, Einstein, Keynes, etc.), certainty of scientific truth, consideration of society as an amorphous whole, historical contextualisation of social life and social theory, and disavowal of objective construction of knowledge (Soja, 1989). Postmodernism replaced this meta-narrative with scepticism, heterogeneity in the geographical method and liberal social enquiry from different standpoints or perspectives including artistic experimentation with the overarching emphasis on understanding social reality (Dear & Flusty, 1998). Michael Dear classified postmodernism into three components of (i) postmodern style, (ii) postmodern method and (iii) a postmodern epoch (1986). The postmodern style expressed social reality in artistic forms of paintings, poetry, pop and subaltern culture; the postmodern method consisted of techniques such as deconstruction as popularised by the French philosopher Jacques Derrida (1930–2004), psychoanalysis, critical interpretation, ethnography, etc.; the postmodern epoch has been concomitant with a period when mainstream narratives have been replaced by a multiplicity of narratives, since the 1980s. In geography, the postmodern approach has been utilised to study how certain aspects of social life and previously taken-for-granted assumptions about work, space, identity and social interaction are constructed and perceived differently by different people.

Posthumanism: The humanistic approach studied the spatial organisation of society with human agency at its centre, in a binary perspective of the human and non-human. The posthumanist approach replaces this binary with an emphasis on the connections between 'human' and other forms and relations (Castree & Nash, 2006). Posthumanism considers human life and activities within the context of relations in space. This includes the material and immaterial relations of humans with plants, food, pets, technoscience, gadgets, artificial intelligence, illnesses, experience of death, etc. For instance, Heidi Nast discussed the evolution of human–pet relations in the framework of 'dominance–affection–love' and noted that

> post-industrial isolations and narcissisms have made pets into screens onto which all sorts of human needs, desires, and investments can be and are being projected,

such projections (are) part and parcel with larger socio-spatial uneven processes of wealth accumulation and investment.

(Nast, 2006)

The posthumanist perspective is associated with 'Hybrid Geography', which investigates the complex hybrid geographies through which humans and nonhumans interact (Whatmore, 2002).

Ethical Approach: This approach has been developed extensively by the British geographer David Marshall Smith (1936–) in the texts *Geography and Social Justice* (1994), *Geography and Ethics: Journeys in a Moral Terrain* (1999) and *Moral Geographies* (2000), going beyond the quantitative and theoretical engagements in social geography and reflecting on the need to realign geography with social responsibility according to moral and ethical compass. A similar stance has been expounded by David Harvey in *Rebel Cities: From the Right to the City to the Urban Revolution* (2012) in which he dwelt on social problems plaguing modern urban societies such as cultural tensions, anxieties and discrimination. This has been accompanied by a geography of care for marginalised social groups such as the specially abled that has attracted active scholarship on their spatial experience and reality (Castrodale & Crooks, 2010). As a consequence, a renaissance of the moral concerns articulated earlier through welfare geographies and social justice theory has occurred. These geographers have called for morally self-conscious research and action, as well as a more ethically reflective approach to the understanding of geography, imagining fairer, equal and inclusive societies in future. Smith has noted that "People who have lost their place, for one reason or another, must be provided with or find another. There is no question about it. People need it. They just do" (Smith 1994).

Social Geography in India

Social geography in India developed in close collaboration with other social science disciplines, namely sociology, history, social anthropology, economics, political science, education and social linguistics. The studies in the field of social geography have had a bi-directional temporal orientation, firstly, the historical construction of the spatial organisation of Indian society as in the past and secondly, in the present towards addressing the contemporary issues through an authentic interdisciplinary approach. Some of the pertinent social issues addressed include underdevelopment of tribal, rural and caste communities; poverty, educational backwardness, displacement of people, disparities arising from development, etc. The social geography course at the Centre for the Studies of Regional Development (CSRD) at the Jawaharlal Nehru University (JNU) beginning the 1970s adopted the interdisciplinary approach in the quest to make geography socially relevant. Several other institutions have also taken up studies related to the field of social geography, through the respective departments of geography, in Delhi University, Calcutta University, Madras University, Banaras Hindu University, Aligarh Muslim University, Jamia Millia Islamia, Bombay University, Poona University, etc. The Indian Council of Social Science Research (ICSSR) has served as a premier national institution in the field of social science research related to social geography. Pioneers of social geography in India include Prof. Moonis Raza (1925–1994) whose notable works in the field include *Atlas of the Child in India*

(1986) and *Atlas of Tribal India* (1990) among others; Prof. Aijazuddin Ahmad whose works include *Social Structure and Regional Development* (1993), *Mountain Population Pressure*, a multi-volume work on *Muslims in India* (1993–1996) and a book *Social Geography* of India (2002); VLS Prakasa Rao whose notable text is on *Urbanisation in India: Spatial Dimensions* (1983) and Prof. Sachidanand Sinha who has worked on multiple themes including education, spatial segregation, caste and tribal inequalities.

Conclusion

Social geography in the present times has reoriented its focus on social change while addressing the issues of inequalities of socio-spatial distribution perpetrated by the current social, economic and political order. Social geography studies have become critical of the social reality, especially as the myth of value-free research has exploded. Space is the essential stage on which social phenomena unfolds and social geographers examine differences and similarities across and between spatial units. Ed Soja (1980) redefined the spatial organisation of society through the conceptualisation of the 'socio-spatial dialectic', by which social relations construct certain spaces and these spaces shape social relations or processes. Derek Gregory explained the space–society relation through 'spatiality' by which "all organised space is seen as rooted in a social origin and filled with social meaning" (Soja, 1980). Social inequalities are an undeniable phenomenon in the spatial organisation of society and geographers have a role in addressing them, either through contributions in policy-making and knowledge enhancement or through direct engagement with the disadvantaged and marginalised social groups. These developments have also led to the evolution of nuanced critiques of dominant social narratives with research in spatial segregation, transnationalism, multiculturalism, heteronormative sexualities and social welfare (Peach, 2002). The role of social geographers has thus become to utilise the theoretical foundations and research methods for undertaking studies while understanding their social responsibilities as social scientists. Social geography thus remains concerned with how differences and inequalities are experienced by social groups organised in space.

References

Agger, B. (1988). *Critical Social Theories: An Introduction*. Herndon, VA: Avalon Publishing.
Aitken, S., & Valentine, G. (2006). *Approaches to Human Geography*. London: Sage.
Alihan, M. A. (1938). *Social Ecology: A Critical Analysis*. New York: Columbia University Press.
Anderson, J. M., Kirkham, S. R., Browne, A. J., & Lynam, M. J. (2007). Continuing the Dialogue: Postcolonial Feminist Scholarship and Bourdieu - Discourses of Culture and Points of Connection. *Nursing Inquiry*, 14(3), 178–188.
Anderson, K., & Smith, S. J. (2001). Emotional Geographies. *Transactions of the Institute of British Geographers*, 26(1), 7–10.
Anderson, T. R., & Bean, L. L. (1961). The Shevky-Bell Social Areas: Confirmation of Results and a Reinterpretation. *Social Forces*, 40(2), 119–124.
Asheim, B. T. (1979). Social Geography - Welfare State Ideology or Critical Social Science? *Geoforum*, 10(1), 5–18.

Barrows, H. H. (1923). Geography as Human Ecology. *Annals of the Association of American Geographers, 13*(1), 1–14.

Bartels, D., & Peucker, T. K. (1969). Annals Commentary: German Social Geography. *Annals of the Association of American Geographers, 59*(3), 596–598.

Blache, P. V. (1911). Les Genres De Vie Dans La Géographie Humaine. *Annales de géographie, 20*, 289–304.

Blache, P. V. (1913). Des caractères distinctifs de la géographie. *Annales de Géographie, 22*, 289–299.

Blunt, A., & McEwan, C. (2002). *Postcolonial Geographies*. New York: Continuum.

Bobek, H. (1959). Die Hauptstufen der Gesellschafts-und Wirtschaftsentfaltung in geographischer Sicht. *Journal of the Geographical Society of Berlin, 90*, 250–298.

Boudrillard, J., & Glaser, S. F. (1981). *Simulacra and Simulation*. Ann Arbor: University of Michigan Press.

Brindley, T. S., & Raine, J. W. (1979). Social Area Analysis and Planning Research. *Urban Studies, 16*(3), 273–289.

Brunhes, J. (2000). *Human Geography: An Attempt at a Positive Classification, Principles and Examples*. London: Forgotten Books.

Brunhes, J. (1924). *Human Geography*. London: G.G. Harrap & Co.

Buttimer, A. (1968). Social Geography. In D. Sills (Ed.), *International Encyclopedia of the Social Sciences* (Vol. 6, pp. 134–145). New York: Macmillan.

Buttimer, A., & Seamon, D. (2015). *The Human Experience of Space and Place*. London: Routledge.

Castells, M. (1996). The Rise of the Network Society. In M. Castells (Ed.), *The Information Age: Economy, Society and Culture* (Vol. 1). Oxford: Blackwell.

Castree, N., & Nash, C. (2006). Posthuman Geographies. *Social & Cultural Geography, 7*(4), 501–504. doi:10.1080/14649360600825620.

Castrodale, M., & Crooks, V. A. (2010). The Production of Disability Research in Human Geography: An Introspective Examination. *Disability & Society, 1*, 89–102.

Claval, P. (1964). *Essay on the Evolution of Human Geography*. Paris: Beautiful Letters.

Claval, P. (1984). The Concept of Social Space and the Nature of Social Geography. *New Zealand Geographer, 40*(2), 105–109.

Cloke, P. J. (1983). *An Introduction to Rural Settlement Planning*. London: Taylor & Francis Inc.

Crang, M., & Thrift, N. J. (2000). *Thinking Space*. London: Psychology Press.

Darby, H. C. (2002). *The Relations of History and Geography: Studies in England, France and the United States*. Exeter: University of Exeter Press.

Dear, M., & Flusty, S. (1998). Postmodern Urbanism. *Annals of the Association of American Geographers, 88*(1), 50–72.

Demangeon, A. (1942). *Problèmes de géographie humaine*. Paris: Armand Colin.

Dixit, R. D. (1997). *Geographical Thought: A Contextual History of Ideas*. PHI Learning Pvt. Ltd.

Dunbar, G. S. (1977). Some Early Occurrences of the Term "Social Geography." *Scottish Geographical Journal, 93*(1), 15–20.

Duncan, J. (1980). The Superorganic in American Cultural Geography. *Annals of the Association of American Geographers, 70*, 181–198.

Durkheim, E. (1982). *Rules of Sociological Method*. New York: Simon and Schuster.

Durkheim, E. (1899). Social Morphology. In S. Lukes, *The Rules of Sociological Method* (pp. 241–242). London: Palgrave.

Easters, V. (1962). *Geographical Structuring and Ecological Complex*. Amsterdam: Royal Dutch Geographical Society, p. 79.

Elizalde, A. (2014). Social Welfare. In A. C. Michalos (Ed.), *Encyclopedia of Quality of Life and Well-Being Research*. Dordrecht: Springer.

Entrikin, J. N. (1985). Humanism, Naturalism, and Geographical Thought. *Geographical Analysis*, 17(3), 243–247.
Firey, W. (1947). Land Use in Central Boston. *Social Forces*, 26(2), 230–232.
Freeman, T. W. (1961). *A Hundred Years of Geography*. London: Gerald Duckworth & Co.
Gatrell, A. C. (2002). *Geographies of Health: An Introduction*. Oxford: Blackwell Publishers Ltd.
George, P. (1946). *Les Regions Polaires*. Paris: Armand Colin.
Gould, P., & White, R. (1974). *Mental Maps*. Harmondsworth: Penguin Books.
Gregory, D. (1994). *Geographical Imaginations*. London: SAGE.
Gregory, D., Johnston, R., Pratt, G., Watts, M., & Whatmore, S. (1986). Cultural Geography. In D. Gregory, R. Johnston, G. Pratt, M. Watts, & S. Whatmore (Eds.), *The Dictionary of Human Geography* (p. 130). Oxford, UK: Blackwell Publishers Ltd.
Hartshorne, R. (1939). *The Nature of Geography*. Chicago: Franklin Classics Trade Press.
Harvey, D. (1973). *Social Justice and The City*. Athens: UGA Press.
Herbert, S. (1997). Territoriality and the Police. *The Professional Geographer*, 49(1), 86–94.
Hoke, G. W. (1907). The Study of Social Geography. *The Geographical Journal*, 29(1), 64–67.
Humboldt, A. V. (1856). *Political Essay on the Island of Cuba: A Critical Edition*. Chicago: The University of Chicago Press.
Huntington, C. C., & Carlson, F. A. (1929). *Environmental Basis of Social Geography*. New York: Prentice-Hall Inc.
Huntington, E. (1915). *Civilization and Climate*. Connecticut: Yale University Press.
Jackson, P. (1981). Phenomenology and Social Geography. *Area*, 4, 299–305.
Jackson, P., & Smith, S. (1984). *Exploring Social Geography*. Hemel Hempstead: George Allen and Unwin.
Jackson, P. A., & Smith, S. J. (1984). *Exploring Social Geography*. London: Routledge.
Johnston, R. (1987). Theory and Methodology in Social Geography. In M. Pacione (Ed.), *Social Geography: Progress and Prospect* (pp. 1–30). London: Croom Helm.
Johnston, R. J. (1978). Urban Geography: City Structures. *Progress in Human Geography*, 2(1), 148–152.
Johnston, R. J. (1981). *The Dictionary of Human Geography*. Oxford: Blackwell.
Jones, E. (1960). *A Social Geography of Belfast*. Oxford: Oxford University Press.
Joyce, J., & Burgess, A. (1966). *A Shorter "Finnegans Wake."* London: James Joyce; Anthony Burgess.
Kluckhohn, C. (1951). Values and Value Orientations in the Theory of Action. In T. Parsons, E. A. Shils, & E. C. Tolman (Eds.), *Towards a General Theory of Action* (pp. 388–433). Cambridge: Harvard University Press.
Kodras, J. E., Jones, J. P., & Falconer, K. F. (2010). Contextualizing Welfare's Work Disincentive: The Case of Female-Headed Family Poverty. *Geographical Analysis*, 26(4), 285–299.
Lebowitz, M. D. (1977). A Critical Examination of Factorial Ecology and Social Area Analysis for Epidemiological Research. *Journal of the Arizona Academy of Science*, 12(2), 86–90.
Lefebvre, H. (1974). *La Production de L'Espace*. Paris: Anthropos.
Ley, D. (1977). Geography and the Taken-for-Granted World. *Transactions of the Institute of British Geographers*, 2(4), 498–512.
Lippuner, R., & Werlen, B. (2009). *Structuration Theory*. Jena: University Jena.
Malthus, T. R. (1798). *An Essay on the Principle of Population*. London: McMaster University Archive for the History of Economic Thought.
Mayer, J. D. (1982). Relations Between Two Traditions of Medical Geography: Health Systems Planning and Geographical Epidemiology. *Progress in Geography*, 6(2), 216–230.
Monkhouse, F. J. (1965). *A Dictionary of Geography*. London: Aldine Publishing Company.
Monmonier, M. S. (1976). Jacques M. May. *The Professional Geographer*, 28(1), 93.

Morenoff, J., Sampson, R. J., & Raudenbush, S. (2001). Neighborhood Inequality, Collective Efficacy, and the Spatial Dynamics of Urban Violence. *Criminology, 39*, 517–560.

Morrill, R. L. (1971). The Persistence of the Black Ghetto as Spatial Separation. *Southeastern Geographer, 11*(2), 149–156.

Nast, H. J. (2006). Critical Pet Studies? *Antipode, 38*(5), 894–906.

Newman, O. (1972). *Defensible Space; Crime Prevention through Urban Design.* New York: Macmillan.

Paassen, C. V. (1965). *Over vormverandering in de sociale geografie.* Groningen: Wolters.

Pahl, R. E. (1965). Trends in Social Geography. In R. Chorley & P. Haggett (Eds.), *Frontiers in Geographical Teaching* (pp. 81–100). London: Arnold.

Park, R. E., & Burgess, E. W. (1925). *The City.* Chicago: University of Chicago Press.

Peach, C. (2002). Social Geography: New Religions and Ethnoburbs – Contrasts With Cultural Geography. *Progress in Human Geography, 26*(2), 252–260.

Peet, R. (1985). An Introduction to Marxist Geography. *Journal of Geography, 84*(1), 5–10.

Ratzel, F. (1891). *Anthropogeographie.* Leipzig: F. Grunow.

Reclus, E. (1905). *L'homme et la terre.* Paris: Librairie universelle.

Relph, E. (1976). *Place and Placelessness.* London: Pion.

Richthofen, F. F. (1903). *Driving Forces and Directions of Geography in the Nineteenth Century.* Berlin: University Book Printer G. Schade.

Roxby, P. M. (1930). The Scope and Aims of Human Geography. *Scottish Geographical Journal, 46*(5), 276–290.

Said, E. (1978). *Orientalism.* New York: Pantheon Books.

Sauer, C. O. (1925). The Morphology of Landscape. In C. O. Sauer (Ed.), *Land and Life: A Selection From the Writings of Carl Ortwin Sauer* (pp. 315–350). Berkeley: University of California Press.

Shevky, E., & Bell, W. (1955). *Social Area Analysis: Theory, Illustrative Application And Computational Procedures.* Stanford: Stanford University Press.

Shields, R. (1991). *Places on the Margin.* London: Routledge.

Smith, D. M. (1973). *The Geography of Social Well-Being In The United States: An Introduction To Territorial Social Indicators.* New York: McGraw-Hill.

Smith, D. M. (1994). *Geography and Social Justice.* Oxford: Wiley-Blackwell.

Smith, N. (1984). *Uneven Development: Nature, Capital and the Production of Space.* New York: Basil Blackwell.

Smith, S. J., Pain, R., Marston, S. R., & Jones, J. P. (2010). Introduction: Situating Social Geographies. In *The SAGE Handbook of Social Geographies.* London: SAGE.

Soja, E. (1980). The Socio-Spatial Dialectic. *Annals of the Association of American Geographers, 70*(2), 207–225.

Soja, E. (1989). *Postmodern Geographies: The Reassertion of Space in Critical Social Theory.* New York: Verso.

Solot, M. (1986). Carl Sauer and Cultural Evolution. *Annals of the Association of American Geographers, 76*(4), 508–520.

Sorre, M. (1948a). La notion de genre de vie et sa valeur actuelle. *Annales de géographie, 57*, 193–204.

Sorre, M. (1948b). *Les Fondements De La Géographie Humaine.* Paris: Colin.

Spates, J. L., & Macionis, J. J. (1982). *The Sociology of Cities.* New York: St. Martin's Press.

Steinmetz, S. R. (1912–13). Die Stellung der Soziographie in der Reihe der Geisteswissenschaften. *Archiv fur Rechts- und Wirtschaftsphilosophie, 6*(3), 492–501.

Symanski, R. (1981). *Immoral Landscape: Female Prostitution in Western Societies.* Toronto: Butterworth-Heinemann.

Tajfel, H. (1978). *Differentiation Between Social Groups: Studies in the Social Psychology of Intergroup Relations.* London: Academic Press.

Timms, D. (1971). *The Urban Mosaic*. Cambridge: Cambridge University Press.
Tsirogianni, S., & Gaskell, G. (2011). The Role of Plurality and Context In Social Values. *Journal for the Theory of Social Behaviour, 41*, 441–465.
Watson, J. W. (1957). The Sociological Aspects of Geography. In G. Taylor (Ed.), *Geography in the Twentieth Century* (pp. 463–499). London.
Watson, J. W., & Watson, J. (1977). *The Canadians: How They Live and Work*. Toronto: David & Charles.
Whatmore, S. (2002). *Hybrid Geographies: Natures Cultures Spaces*. London: SAGE.
Wirth, L. (1928). *The Ghetto*. Chicago: University of Chicago Press.
Wirth, L. (1938). Urbanism as a Way of Life. *American Journal of Sociology, 44*, 1–24.
Wirth, L. (1956). *Life in the City*. Chicago: University of Chicago Press.
Zorbaugh, H. W. (1929). *Gold Coast and Slum*. Chicago: University of Chicago Press.

Chapter 2

Welfare and Social Well-Being

Introduction

Social well-being is a major theme of research in social sciences. It is also considered to be the ultimate objective of the policies and programmes of development. The term 'social well-being' has two connotations: (i) the well-being of an individual in relation to society and (ii) the well-being of society as a whole. In scientific disciplines, where the importance is on the well-being and development of the individual such as pedagogy and clinical psychology, the first connotation takes precedence. These disciplines consider social well-being as one of the various aspects of the overall well-being of the individual that include physical, mental and emotional well-being. They consider social well-being as the perception of the individual on their integration, coherence and contribution to society. Disciplines that study social phenomena such as geography, economics and sociology put a greater emphasis on the second connotation. They use social well-being in the sense of the overall well-being of society.

Social Well-Being: Definition and Components

Well-being is a multidimensional and subjective concept. It can be defined simply as the 'state of feeling healthy and happy' or in more complex terms as 'the state of being or doing well in life; happy, healthy or prosperous condition; moral or physical welfare of a person or community'. There are eight widely recognised dimensions of well-being (Swarbrick, 2006; Mackey, 2000), which include (not necessarily in order but overlapping):

1) **Physical Well-Being**: It exists when the physical needs of the individual are fulfilled and the body remains healthy and disease free.
2) **Emotional Well-Being**: It refers to the ability to handle stressful conditions and adapt to change successfully.
3) **Social Well-Being**: It is the well-being pertaining to social connections, relationships and personal expressions within one's social setting.
4) **Spiritual Well-Being**: It refers to living with a sense of purpose and meaning in life and may or may not include alignment with religious beliefs.
5) **Intellectual Well-Being**: It is the recognition and expansion of creative abilities, knowledge and skills.

DOI: 10.4324/9781003378006-2

6) **Occupational Well-Being**: It is the personal satisfaction and enrichment derived from work.
7) **Financial Well-Being**: It is the satisfaction with one's financial situations to provide for present and future needs.
8) **Environmental Well-Being**: It is the occupation of a pleasant and healthy environment, comprising the living space and physical conditions, that enhances overall well-being.

Well-being is achieved by a harmonious balance of these dimensions, which are interdependent and vary from individual to individual (Stoewen, 2017). Consequently, every individual has a different understanding of what well-being means. Social well-being and the well-being of the individual are inseparable. Kenneth Wilkinson, in his book *Community in Rural America* (1991), noted that "the well-being of the individual is not possible without the well-being of the community". Social well-being is achieved when the needs of people are satisfied. Some of the basic components of social well-being include nutrition, shelter, education, health, leisure, social stability, surplus income, physical environment, security (Larson, 1996).

Social well-being is used as a generic term for various overlapping and broad concepts including quality of life (QOL), welfare and standard of living. However, defining these terms has always been a challenging task. Standard of living refers to the level of income, comforts and services available, generally applied to a society or location, rather than to an individual. Welfare refers to the provision of goods and services instituted by the community to enhance the quality of human existence. Quality of life (QOL) is the general well-being of individuals and societies considered to be a function of biophysical, environmental and social conditions (Papageorgiou, 1976). It consists of two aspects – (a) personal, which is operationalised as well-being and (b) spatial and also the quality of place (McCann, 2004). Social well-being is thus the sum total of circumstances in which people are able to fulfil their basic human needs such as food, water, shelter and health with equal access and they are capable of coexisting harmoniously in communities with opportunities for improvement (Roy, 2018). The concept of social well-being is normative in nature. Its conception is based on needs and wants. It is inherently associated with the fulfilment and satisfaction of individual and collective needs and wants. These needs and wants can be both objective and subjective. According to Paul Knox (1975) "well being is … the satisfaction of the needs and wants of the population". Needs and wants vary across different social, economic and political contexts across spatio-temporal dimensions and are measured via social indicators.

Understanding Needs

Maslow's Hierarchy of Needs: American psychologist Abraham Maslow (1908–1970) in 1954 presented a hierarchical arrangement of human needs. This hierarchy consisted of five tiers in a pyramidal structure (Maslow, 1943). He identified two types of needs, namely (a) deficiency needs (D-needs) and (b) growth needs (B-needs). The deficiency needs arise out of deprivation from the basic needs. On the other hand, growth needs arise from the desire to grow as a person. The hierarchy of needs presents a linear sequence, and the fulfilment of higher needs happens only after lower needs have been fulfilled, even if partially. The hierarchy begins with the physiological needs quintessential for survival which include food, water, shelter, sleep and culminates in the satisfaction of the need for self-actualisation. At any point in time, a person may want to fulfil multiple needs in the hierarchy and the basket of needs a person wants to be fulfilled is integrated with their socio-economic situation. Survival is the motivation for the satisfaction of physiological needs. While state welfare may be restricted to the bottom layers of the hierarchy but social well-being of the individual may require the fulfilment of several layers of needs within it (Maslow, 1954). The five-stage hierarchy of needs includes the following:

1. **Physiological Needs**: These include biological requirements for human survival and optimal functioning of the body, for example, air, food, drink, shelter, clothing, sex, sleep. These needs are the most important as all the other needs become secondary until these needs are fulfilled.
2. **Safety Needs**: The needs for security and safety include the need for order, predictability and control which are fulfilled by the family and society, for instance, employment, police, schools, business and medical care.
3. **Love and Belongingness Needs**: The third level of human needs consists of social needs, involving feelings of love, belongingness, friendship, intimacy, trust, acceptance and so on.
4. **Esteem Needs**: These needs include the needs to achieve and realise self-worth, accomplishment and respect. Maslow classified esteem needs into two categories: (a) esteem for oneself in the form of dignity, achievement, mastery, independence and (b) the desire for respect from others.
5. **Self-Actualisation Needs**: These are the highest needs in Maslow's hierarchy. They include the realisation of a person's potential, self-fulfilment, personal growth and individual development (Maslow, 1962). For example, the desire to become an ideal parent or manager or the desire for creative expressions through paintings, poetry or inventions.

The universal existence of human needs has been proven empirically across different cultures. However, the ordering of the needs within the hierarchy has been debatable (Figure 2.1).

Approaches to Addressing Needs

The hierarchy of needs by Maslow presents a wide spectrum of needs. However, the realisation of such a wide variety of needs for the social well-being of all individuals becomes complex from the perspective of development, planning and welfare. Hence, one approach can be to address a few essential needs such as housing, health, food, education. Another approach can be to create such socio-economic conditions that can provide people with the capability and freedom for the fulfilment of a wide variety of needs. Some of the approaches are discussed in the following:

1. **Basic Minimum Needs (BMN) Approach (1976)**: The Basic Minimum Needs (BMN) approach for social well-being and poverty eradication was introduced by the International Labour Organisation (ILO) at the World Employment

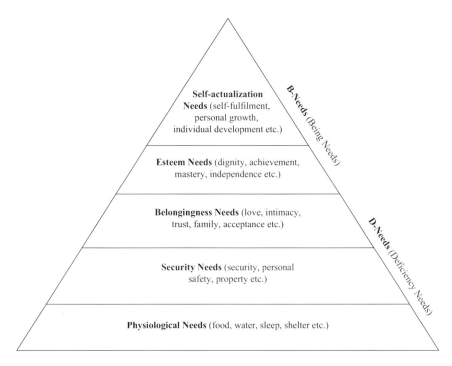

Figure 2.1 Hierarchy of Needs by Abraham Maslow (1954)

Conference in 1976 (Jolly, 1976). The ILO identified a bundle of needs in the form of goods, commodities and services required for a dignified human existence identified as the six Basic Minimum Needs (BMN). These are (1) health, (2) education, (3) food, (4) water supply, (5) sanitation and (6) housing. A welfare state is expected to fulfil at least these BMNs. Several governments globally have incorporated this approach in their poverty eradication programmes. However, this approach faced sharp criticism for reducing social well being to minimal human existence.

2. **Capabilities and Freedom Approach (1985):** According to renowned Indian economist Amartya Sen (1933–), social well-being is a complex phenomenon and can be understood as groups of 'doing' and 'being', which together can be called 'functioning'. Sen developed the 'capabilities approach' to social well-being, building on the foundations of the concept of basic needs. He argued for conceptualising social well-being by accounting for both objective and subjective needs; well-being is what people can be and can do, rather than simply on what they have (Sen, 1985). The capabilities of the individual are realised by their functioning within society. The realisation of this functioning is enabled by freedom or a set of interlinked freedoms: (a) political freedoms and transparency in social relations, (b) freedom of opportunity, including freedom to access credit and (c) economic freedom for protection from abject poverty through income supplements and

unemployment relief (Sen, 1999). The absence of one or more of these freedoms results into poverty or a lack of social well-being. The novelty in Sen's approach is that it goes beyond the narrow perspective of commodities or income in assessing social well-being. Building on the capability approach of Amartya Sen, the United Nations Development Programme (UNDP) in 1990 (and since continued) introduced the composite index called the Human Development Index (HDI).

3. **Having, Loving, Being Approach (1990)**: Finland sociologist Erik Anders Allardt (1925–2020) simplified Maslow's hierarchy of needs to understand social well-being or quality of life, substituting the vertical pyramid with a horizontal triad. While the Basic Minimum Needs approach to social well-being was resource-centric and the approach of Amartya Sen was individual-centric, Allardt merged these two approaches in the social context. He conceptualised social well-being as a system with the three dimensions of (a) having, (b) loving and (c) being. 'Having' refers to the fulfilment of physiological or material conditions, which people need to satisfy to survive; 'loving' refers to the fulfilment of social needs, such as social support, self-identity, etc. and 'being' refers to the ability of an individual to achieve personal growth. Allardt argued that social well-being in all three dimensions could be measured objectively as well as subjectively.

Social Indicators

Social indicators gained prominence as part of the 'Social Relevance' movement in the 1960s in countries of Western Europe and North America. American economist Mancur Olson (1932–1998) defined social indicator as

> a statistic of direct normative interest which facilitates concise, comprehensive and balanced judgments about the condition of major aspects of a society. It is, in all cases, a direct measure of welfare and is subject to the interpretation that if it changes in the "right" direction, while other things remain equal, things have gotten better, or people are better off. Thus, statistics on the numbers of doctors or policemen could not be social indicators, whereas figures on health or crime rates could be.
>
> (Micholas, 2014)

The Australian Bureau of Statistics defined social indicators as, "measures of social well-being which provide a contemporary view of social conditions and monitor trends in a range of areas of social concern over time" (McEwin, 1995). The United Nations Statistics Division (UNSD) definition of social indicators (1994) is

> social indicators can be defined as statistics that usefully reflect important social conditions and facilitate the process of assessing those conditions and their evolution. Social indicators are used to identify social problems that require action, to develop priorities and goals for action and spending, and to assess the effectiveness of programmes and policies.

The social indicators movement began in the USA in the 1960s, highlighted by the publication of a study titled 'Social Indicators and Sample Surveys' (1966) by Raymond

Augustine Bauer on behalf of the American Academy of Arts and Sciences and another report titled, 'Toward a Social Report' by the Lyndon B Johnson administration in 1969. This movement was a reaction against the reductionist conception of human development that reduced social well-being to physical and economic indicators (Rapley, 2003). According to Bauer, social indicators were "statistics, statistical series, and all other forms of evidence that enable us to assess where we stand and are going with respect to our values and goals" (Bauer, 1966). Earlier, American sociologist William F Ogburn at the University of Chicago in the 1930s and 1940s had presented his theory of the measurement of social change and published the two-volume book *Recent Social Trends* (1933), a landmark contribution to social reporting and assessment of social well-being. The objective of the social indicators movement was to monitor changes over time across a broad range of social phenomena going beyond the traditional economic indicators and giving considerable significance to indicators of social well-being (Andrews, 1986; Noll & Wolfgang, 1994). In 1974, the first volume of the international journal *Social Indicators Research* was published; and social indicators were soon widely adopted by national governments and international agencies, such as the United Nations Organisation (UNO) and the Organisation for Economic Cooperation and Development (OECD).

Classification: Social indicators can be broadly classified into: (a) subjective social indicators, which measure the quality of life from the point of view of the individual under examination, and (b) objective social indicators, which measure variables that have some significance for measuring the quality of life or social well-being from the point of view of any independent observer (Land, 1983). These two types of indicators can be further classified into:

1. **Descriptive Subjective Indicators** (for example, self-reported happiness, satisfaction with job)
2. **Evaluative Subjective Indicators** (for example, self-reported good health, victims of criminal offenses)
3. **Descriptive Objective Indicators** (for example, percentages of eligible voters casting ballots, university graduates)
4. **Evaluative Objective Indicators** (for example, crime rate, unemployment rate, poverty rates)

Subjective indicators record relatively intangible and individually experienced aspects of life, for instance, generic positive or negative feelings, specific feelings of fear, attitudes, beliefs, knowledge, motives, goals, needs, wants, happiness, satisfaction, etc. (Cummins, 1996). Ethnography, case studies, interviews, visual and art methods are used for assessing subjective social well-being (Forgeard et al., 2011). According to Paul Knox, well-being relates to the satisfaction of the needs and wants of the people associated with different elements of well-being which can be evaluated through objective or universalistic measures and can be called social indicators (Noll, 2004). Most of the contemporary studies on social well-being use mixed methods (Woolley, 2009). For instance, McCracken (1983) in the 'Dimensions of Social Well-being: Implications of Alternative Spatial Frames, Environment and Planning' identified seven social indicators of male and female income earners, employment rate, age-standardised mortality ratio, level of education, and households with telephone connections and television sets for the exposition of social well-being (McCracken, 1983). Ilbery (1984) in his book *Core Periphery Contrasts in European Social Well-being* presented 27 indicators, out of which seven major elements such as housing, health, education, economic growth, national well-being, leisure and recreation describe the effective inequality in European social well-being (Ilbery, 1984).

Social Well-Being in Geography

The study of social well-being has been one of the intrigues of geographers for a very long time. Alexander von Humboldt (1769–1859), the foremost geographer of the classical period of modern geography, wrote compelling descriptions of the inequality perpetrated by slavery and racism on the island of Cuba. In the book, *The Island of Cuba* (1856), he noted that

> To remedy the evil, to prevent public calamities, and to console the unfortunate beings who belong to an ill-treated race, and who are feared more than acknowledged, it is necessary to probe the sore; for there exists in social, as well as organic bodies, reparative forces, which, when well directed, may triumph over the most inveterate evils.
>
> (Vila, 2018)

Humboldt's account was a general representation of the spatial organisation of Cuban society and not a specialised study of social well-being. The British geographer Patrick Geddess (1854–1934) described the organisation of society in the framework of 'Place-Work-Folk' on the lines of French sociologist Frederic Le Play (1802–1886) (Mairet, 1957). According to this framework, families are the central social units from which all else develop, and from 'stable, healthy homes' providing the necessary conditions for mental and moral development come healthy children who are able to fully participate in life (Tyrwhitt, 2021). This framework of Geddess was based on the harmonious balance of the individual and family within their environment and, thus, the well-being of society.

Russian geographer Peter Kropotkin (1842–1921) was born into aristocracy but turned anarchist on observing the plights of the socially deprived classes in the feudal society of Russia. The structures of social inequalities present across different societies in Europe diverted his attention from physical to social geography so much so that he refused the offer to take charge as the Secretary of the Russian Geographical Society in 1871. Writing on inequality, he lamented,

> but what right I had to these highest joys when all around me was nothing but misery and struggle for mouldy bits of bread; … all those sonorous phrases about making mankind progress, while at the same time the progress-makers stay aloof from those whom they pretend to push onwards, are mere sophisms made up by minds anxious to shake off a fretting contradiction.
>
> (Kropotkin, 1899)

The idea of well-being was very central to the thinking of Kropotkin. In *The Conquest of Bread*, he noted,

> All is for all! If the man and the woman bear their fair share of work, they have a right to their fair share of all that is produced by all, and that share is enough to secure them well-being. No more of such vague formulas as 'The right to work', or 'To each the whole result of his labour'. What we proclaim is The Right to Well-Being: Well-Being for All!
>
> (Kropotkin & Weigl, 2008)

The study of social well-being gained prominence in geography with the rise of the 'Relevance Movement' of the 1970s based on social justice. This movement was a response to the various crises of the period. In the post-war period, the nations of the Global North had experienced unprecedented economic growth and recovery, but its benefits accrued more to the richer sections which resulted in a significant rich–poor divide. The 1960s also witnessed the Civil Rights Movement in the USA whereby the people of Afro-American origin demanded realisation of equal social and economic rights. The Vietnam War that began in the late 1960s was viewed largely as a battleground of the Cold War powers and the suffering of the Vietnamese people divided opinions globally and especially in the USA. The petrodollar crisis of 1973 precipitated a steep recession accompanied by rising inflation which resulted into a period of great economic uncertainty. These events shifted the emphasis of enquiry in geography from the study of marginal land to the study of marginal social space. The British geographer David Harvey (1935) in the book *Social Justice and the City* (1973) discussed how the capitalist mode of production impacted the spatial organisation of cities and argued that geography cannot remain disengaged, impartial and 'objective' at a time when urban poverty and associated ills were reigning high (Carey, 1975; Harvey, 1973).

The geographical perspective of social well-being studies is still being developed theoretically. Geography has mainly borrowed the theoretical framework for well-being studies from economics (Smith, 1977). Harvey elaborates, "There is an urgent need to combine social imagination with geographical space. In true sense the social imagination confirms that man realises the meaning of his existence only in the context of society he lives in". According to him,

> Geographical perspective enables the individual to recognise the role of space and place in his own biography to relate to the space he has around him and to recognise how transactions between individuals and between organisations are affected by the space that separates them. It allows him to recognise the relationship which exists between him and his neighbourhood.

In 1971, a 'Survey of Regional Variations in Britain' was conducted under which the 'Studies in Economic and Social Geography', by BE Coates and EM Rawstron, described and mapped variations in a range of key economic and social indicators. They were of the opinion that they were refining 'the regional idea' of geography by utilising statistical evidence relevant to planning and policy. Earlier, in two issues of 1969 and 1970 in the radical journal *Antipode*, the geographer Richard Morrill outlined the potential role of geography in 'the transformation of society'. He opined that geographers have a responsibility to ask questions about the 'rightness' of existing spatial patterns. Wilbur Zelinsky in a paper entitled 'The

Role of Geography in the Great Transition' (1970) identified the urgent agenda for the human geographer as 'the study of the implications of a continuing growth in human numbers in the advanced countries, acceleration in their production and consumption of commodities, the misapplication of old technologies, of the feasible responses to the resultant difficulties'. In 1974, geography and public policy were the central focus at the annual conference of the Institute of British Geographers where Coppock delivering his Presidential address highlighted the challenges, opportunities and implications of the involvement of geographers in public policy research. The text *Geography and Inequality* (1977) by BE Coates, Ron Johnson and Paul Knox used 'objective' social indicators to map spatial inequalities across the United Kingdom, the USA, France, India and other world regions in housing, education, nutrition and health care.

Socio-spatial justice is central to the realisation of social well-being. It implies full participation of all social groups and a geographical enquiry should aim at realising a social space in which both material well-being and social inclusion are guaranteed for all. David Marshall Smith (1935–) noted the importance of raising awareness towards reducing inequalities:

> Although the teaching of Marx or Christ is likely to be a more potent source of enlightenment than a geography text, we can at least play a part by creating an awareness of the extent to which American society is geographically unequal.
> (Smith, The Geography of Social Well-Being in the United States: An Introduction to Territorial Social Indicators, 1973)

Smith (1973, 1977), Knox (1974) and various other social scientists developed a social welfare approach as a central theme in geography. The beginning of social well-being studies in geography was embedded in real-world problems and its development has sought to address issues around structural social inequalities (Wilkinson & Pickett, 2010; Byrne, 1999).

Welfare Geography

The quantitative revolution of the 1950s in geography had led to the treatment of space as banal and the formulation of spatial laws and theories predicated on the quantitative methods of neoclassical economics. This tradition of 'locational analysis' ignored the socio-economic and political realities of space. In the 1970s, the quantitative methods were countered by a rise of 'radical geography' seeking radical changes in society. Welfare geography emerged as a liberal perspective in the tradition of critical geography, raising questions of spatial inequalities related to social welfare or social well-being. The British geographer David Marshal Smith was the founding father of this school of thought. He was influenced by the Annual Meeting of the Association of American Geographers (AAG) in 1971 in Boston. In a paper that followed, he wrote that there were

> sound logical reasons for studying many social phenomena that have traditionally tended to be ignored. These would include such matters as racial segregation, poverty, hunger, infant mortality, morbidity, drug addiction, mental illness, suicide,

illegitimacy, sexual deviance, welfare services, medical care, crime, justice, and the incidence of areas or regions of social deprivation, and so on.

(Smith, 1971)

Smith challenged the asocial views of subject matter and method in human geography while focusing on profoundly significant aspects of social life.

Welfare geography is concerned with spatial inequalities in living standards. Socio-spatial redistribution of resources has been the primary concern of welfare geography. Reduction of socio-spatial inequalities was fundamental to the development of the welfare state which seeks to mitigate it by providing free or subsidised services of healthcare and education, and transfer payments such as unemployment allowances and old-age pensions (Smith, 1994). In the welfare geography approach, the emphasis is on spatial inequality and territorial justice (Gregory et al., 2009).

The approach of DM Smith in welfare geography highlighted the complex intersections between social injustice and spatial inequality which results in haves and have-nots existing in all societies and the spatial differentiation into rich and poor places at a range of geographical scales from the city to the nation. Smith called welfare geography 'an alternative framework for human geography'; a 'moral' or ethically charged vision into the heart of human geographical enquiry. Two of his works *Human Geography: A Welfare Approach* (1977) and *Where the Grass is Greener: Living in an Unequal World* (1979) formed introductory texts in the development of welfare geography. These works were largely descriptive and were predicated on the abstract formulation used in welfare economics and gave it empirical soundness. It provided for evaluation of the existing welfare configurations, in terms of 'who gets what, where and how'. The central tenet of welfare geography is 'who gets what, where and how'. Here, 'who' refers to the people of any spatially disaggregated society, 'what' refers to the goods and bads (services, commodities, and environmental quality) enjoyed (or suffered) by the population, 'where' refers to the spaces of distribution and consumption and their scale and 'how' refers to the social, economic and political processes through which the observed spatial patterns arise.

Thus, welfare geography paves the way for a welfare state with the framework that guides its decisions with respect to welfare provision: (a) what are utilities (goods and services) to be provided, (b) where are the utilities to be provided (in terms of the scale and extent of provision), (c) how are the utilities to be distributed (institutional arrangements for provision) and (d) who gets these utilities (target groups – universal or selective).

Smith argued that the general level of welfare can be empirically derived as a function of the sum of levels of welfare or social well-being across the spatial units comprising that society. Social well-being can be measured through territorial social indicators, consumed or experienced as utilities or disutilities by people living in different territories. In a spatially disaggregated society, the general level of welfare can be written as:

$W = f(S_1, ... S_n)$, where S is the level of social well-being in a set of n territorial subdivisions. Welfare is thus the function of the distribution of goods and bads among groups of the population occupying spatial units. Social well-being is defined in terms of what people actually get:

$S = f(X_1, ..., X_m)$, where X is the quantity of the m goods and bads consumed or experienced. Social well-being can also be expressed in terms of the distribution within the spatial units:

$S = f(U_1, ..., U_k)$, where U is the level of well-being or satisfaction of each of the 'k' population subgroups. In these expressions, the terms can be assigned different weights and combined according to any suitable function, representing the combination of spatial levels of well-being. For identifying social well-being and spatial distribution, the development of social indicators is very important. Such indicators may be related to income, employment, housing, education, etc.

Smith argued for critical normative analysis of the distributions of societal goods and bads through the lens of moral and ethical geography with the objective of achieving a better state of affairs with respect to any or all of the criteria of what, how, for whom and where is the welfare improvement. He was also of the opinion of going beyond the economic goods to measure welfare. He stated that welfare can never be singular, geographically even or merely material.

Smith opened an arena for true interdisciplinary studies to address the issue of welfare. He noted,

> The welfare approach logically requires a holistic social science perspective, including economic, social and political factors, and also consideration of moral philosophy which underpins concept of social justice. In this rapidly changing world, where new political and economic institutional arrangements can benefit populations unequally, there is renewed interest in the issues raised by the welfare approach.
>
> (Smith, 1994)

The field of welfare geography is dynamic as the concept of welfare remains ever changing with socio-economic progress, and ensuring uniform spatio-social distribution will always be challenging. Hence, the scope of the welfare approach is relevant and dynamic. For instance, the quality of environment and resilience to hazards which was ignored earlier, is now being increasingly included in the measurement of welfare by researchers and governments. Welfare geography provides an empirically valid framework to assess the welfare programmes and regional development plans of the government, colloquially fit into 'who got what, where and how'.

However, Smith also admitted that welfare geography was rooted in welfare economics and required a Marxian refinement by attuning it to the context of political economy. David Harvey's statement in *Social Justice and the City* (1973) has been presented as a critique of the moderate approach of welfare geography as "masochistic assemblage of some huge dossier on the daily injustices to the population of the ghetto, over which we beat our breasts and commiserate with one another before retiring to our fireside comforts" (Harvey, 1973).

However, the geography of welfare opened up a new arena for enquiry and research in human geography with relevant social applications. The issue of welfare remains relevant irrespective of the economic organisation of the society, whether capitalist, socialist or communist. It also gave a moral and ethical compass to the geographer to be aware of the socio-economic reality of the space around them and contribute to the alleviation of the problem of spatial inequalities.

Welfare State

Welfare state describes a collective range of social policies that aim to provide basic services such as health, education, etc., free of cost or at subsidised rates. It is a concept of government in which the state or the well-established network of social institutions plays a key role in the protection and promotion of the economic and social well-being of citizens. It is based on the principles of equality of opportunity, equitable distribution of wealth and positive liberalism. Facilitation of distributive justice is viewed as one of the major objectives of the welfare state. A welfare state is a state that is committed to providing basic economic and social security for its citizens by protecting them from the risks associated with old age, unemployment and sickness. Protection is provided by a range of social services, including healthcare, education and old-age pensions (Weir et al., 1988).

The sociologist TH Marshall described the welfare state as a distinctive combination of democracy, welfare and capitalism (Marshall, 1950). According to Marshall, history was the progressive development of rights: civil rights in the 18th century, political rights in the 19th century, and social rights in the 20th century. The welfare state was an embodiment of the social rights of the people. Richard Titmuss (1907–1973), the pioneering thinker of social policy, viewed the welfare state as a response mainly to the fear of social revolution, the need for a law-abiding labour force, the portrayal of the social conscience of the rich, and the competition of political parties and pressure groups for power. In his opinion, the most important force was solidarity and mutual aid which formed the working-class ethic (Titmuss & Abel-Smith, 1987).

In the opinion of historian Asa Briggs (1921–2016),

> a welfare state is a state in which organised power is deliberately used (through politics and administration) in an effort to modify the play of market forces in at least three directions—(i) first, by guaranteeing individuals and families a minimum income irrespective of the market value of their work or their property; (ii) second, by narrowing the extent of insecurity by enabling individuals and families to meet certain 'contingencies' and (iii) third, by ensuring that all citizens without distinction of status or class are offered a certain agreed range of social services.
>
> (Briggs, 1961)

The functions of the welfare state can be divided into four types: (1) protective function: it implies providing protection from deprivation through pensions, unemployment allowance or basic income. (2) Preventive function: it implies preventing deprivation through insurance schemes, employment generation, etc.. (3) Promotive function: it implies enhancement of income as well as capabilities through education and scholarships. (4) Transformative function: it implies promotion of social equity and inclusion, for instance through labour laws and reservation.

The purpose of the welfare state is to reduce socio-economic inequalities by assuring equitable standards of living for all. This is sought to be achieved by (i) the recognition that every member of the community is entitled to a minimum standard of living; (ii) the commitment to a policy of economic stability and progress and (iii) prioritising optimum employment as one of the top priorities of public policy.

Evolution of the Welfare State: In the 3rd century BCE, emperor *Ashoka* in India put forward his idea of a welfare state. His *dhamma* (path) was adopted as the state policy in which he declared that his subjects were his children. The Major Rock Edict II records that the state provided for medical treatment of people and animals, construction of roads, wells and tree planting (Sastri, 1988). In the medieval period, Mughal emperor *Akbar* (1542–1605) introduced a liberal tax regime with provisions for the remission if the crops failed and also provided agricultural loans. He abolished the pilgrim tax on Hindus and *Jaziya* tax for non-Muslims in 1563 and 1564, respectively (Habib, 1992). In China, emperor Wen (203–157 BCE) of the Han Dynasty introduced welfare measures including pensions for the old in-kind as well as monetary support for the widows, orphans and the childless elderly (Hulsewe, 1987). The Roman Plebeian Council is known to have approved the programme known as *Cura Annonae*, later implemented by the Roman state to distribute free or subsidised grains to its population (Hanson et al., 2017). In Arabia, the ruler of the Rashidun Caliphate Umar (584–644) instituted welfare measures through the *Bayt al-mal* (treasury), which was used to stockpile food to cope with disasters and emergencies (Crone, 2005).

In the modern period, the term 'welfare state' originated in the 1940s in the United Kingdom by Archbishop William Temple in the book *Citizen and Churchman* (1941) where he contrasted the welfare state to the warfare state. The catastrophic destruction during the Second World War (1939–1945) provided the impetus for the development of the welfare state which assumed the 'paternal' responsibility of welfare and social well-being of its citizens. This was evident in nations of the Global North or what is commonly known as the Western world.

The classical liberal theory of the free market, proposed by Adam Smith, David Ricardo and others in the 18th to the 19th century, opposed government intervention in functioning of the economy as it was based on the belief that in the free market, everyone sought profits in their own interests. Ultimately, the free market would make everyone wealthy. This was the origin of the school of thought known as capitalism, which came under severe attack when, in England, the report of the Royal Commission appointed to investigate the coal mining industry exposed the brutal working conditions in the mines, the exploitation of women and children, barbarous long working hours and the absence of safety devices, thus creating both physical and moral hazards.

Thinkers such as Charles Dickens, Robert Owen, John Stuart Mill, Thomas Hobbes, Karl Marx and Friedrich Engels wrote in favour of restructuring the socio-economic order in favour of the common citizenry and the working class. During 19291933, the liberal capitalist state experienced an unprecedented crisis in the form of the Great Depression as a result of which it became imperative to examine the functioning and foundations of a capitalist economy. The socio-economic consequences of the modern industrial capitalist system made it inevitable for the state to become a 'welfare state'. The *laissez-faire* (minimum governmental interference in the economy) system had competition without responsibility and limited or no obligation of the entrepreneur towards the workers. As a consequence, there were wide disparities in income, ownership of resources, social power, high rates of unemployment and poverty and a glaring rich–poor divide, or in the Marxian parlance, the bourgeoisie–proletariat divide, which ultimately led the state to engender redistribution and welfare.

Otto von Bismarck, the first Chancellor of Germany, created the *sozialstaat* (social state or welfare state) in unified Germany in the 1880s by introducing a number of social security programmes such as old-age pensions, accident insurance and medical care based on dedicated taxes or 'contributions'. This later formed the basis of the modern European welfare state in Italy, France and the Nordic states. Even though the welfare programme was instituted by Bismarck to suppress social democracy, yet on the economic front, it resulted in rapid industrial growth by ensuring social well-being of the working class in Germany. However, the legacy of the Bismarckian welfare state has been debated by researchers.

Benjamin Disraeli, former Prime Minister of the United Kingdom, wrote in the novel *Sybil* (or the Two Nations) (1845) that "power has only one duty – to secure the social welfare of the people" (Disraeli, 1845). The United Kingdom introduced welfare reforms in the early 20th century by enacting a series of laws such as the Old-Age Pensions Act 1908, Labour Exchanges Act 1909, the Development Act 1909, which heralded greater state intervention in economic development, and the National Insurance Act 1911. These reforms, termed as Edwardian legislations (1905–1914), introduced free school meals, school medical service, old-age pensions for the poor financed by tax, national health and unemployment insurance, supported by a national network of labour exchanges. The minimum wage was introduced in the United Kingdom in 1909 for certain low-wage industries. Later, the welfare state of the United Kingdom developed as a symbol of the solidarity of the British people during the Second World War (1939–1945); a set of social services that would be available to all British citizens. These services were granted recognition by the Beveridge Report (1942).

In Australia, the economic depression in the 1890s coupled with the rise of the trade unions and labour parties led to welfare reforms that included old-age pension (1900), disability pension (1910) and maternity allowance (1912). During and after the Second World War (1939–1945), Australia under Labour Government created a welfare state by introducing national schemes for child endowment (1941), widow pension (1942), and unemployment, sickness and special benefits (1945).

American sociologist Frank Lester Ward (1841–1913) was the 'philosophical architect of the welfare state' in the USA. He argued for state welfare or state aid for the needy. He believed that a universal comprehensive system of education was essential for a democratic government to function successfully (Ward & Commager, 1950). His works laid the foundations for the welfare state in the USA, where welfare was introduced in the wake of the catastrophic socio-economic consequences of the Great Depression (1929–1933). In 1935, President Franklin D Roosevelt introduced the 'New Deal' which was centred on the colloquial 3Rs: relief for the unemployed and poor, recovery of the economy and reform of the financial system to prevent a repeat depression. This paved the way for active state intervention in the economy to promote distributive justice. Canada introduced wide-ranging social welfare programmes between the 1930s and the 1960s through services of medical care, public education up to graduate school, social housing, guaranteed income supplement, child tax benefit, old-age security, employment insurance, workers compensation, etc.

The Nordic countries, such as Iceland, Sweden, Norway, Denmark and Finland employ a system known as the Nordic model developed progressively since the 1930s beginning in Sweden. The welfare state involves a transfer of funds from the state to the citizens for a range of services such as healthcare, education and housing – at a flat rate, which means that all individuals receive equal benefits from the state irrespective of their economic or social status. The welfare state is funded through redistributionist taxation (Ferragina & Seeleib-Kaiser, 2011, p. 592).

In Latin America, three types of welfare states have developed, mainly after the 1980s. These include (a) state-productivist, (b) state-protectionist and (c) family welfare regime. The state-productivist regime endeavours for the expansion of human capital and market inclusion of the labour force, as in Argentina and Chile. On the other hand, the state-protectionist model protects citizens from market risks such as unemployment and poverty, found in countries such as Costa Rica, Uruguay, Cuba, Brazil and Mexico. Family-dependent welfare states exist in Guatemala and Nicaragua, where people largely depend on family and relatives for social security (Fleury, 2017).

In recent years, particularly after the rise of Neo-liberalism in which the general tendency of the state has been to roll back and let market forces influence the economy more liberally, a 'mixed welfare economy' model has emerged. In this model, which has been adopted by most countries, the state recognises its responsibility for welfare but the welfare programmes are typically implemented by corporations or trusts. These organisations function with profit motives, although with back-end support from the government (Katz & Sachsse, 1995). For instance, the largest market share of life insurance in India is of the Life Insurance Corporation (LIC), a public enterprise with a corporate functioning. The intervention of the Bretton Woods twins, namely the World Bank and the International Monetary Fund in the structural adjustment of several economies, has redirected public expenditure away from basic needs provisions to increasing conditions conducive to employment. Consequently, while education has generally been prioritised, healthcare, housing and basic human needs have been ignored (Corbridge, 1993; Lustig, 1995).

Typology of Welfare State: There are various classifications of the welfare state. Three such classifications by Esping-Anderson (1990), Richard Titmuss (1974) and Korpi and Palme (1998) are discussed below:

A. **Esping-Anderson's Classification (1990)**: Danish sociologist Gosta Esping-Andersen (1947–) in his work *The Three Worlds of Welfare Capitalism* (1990) identified three types of welfare state. It was based on the empirical observation of social welfare expenditure of 18 Organisation for Economic Cooperation and Development (OECD) countries in the 1980s (Bambra, 2007).

   This classification was based on several variables for the measurement of social well-being that included (a) de-commodification index or the extent to which individuals and families could maintain an acceptable standard of living, independently from market participation, (b) social stratification based on a wide range of indicators of how key institutions of the welfare state operate in structuring class and social order and (c) public–private nexus that examines the relative roles of the state, family and market in welfare provisions (Asatiani & Verulava, 2017). Consequently, Espring-Anderson identified three types of welfare states:
   1. **The Liberal Welfare State**: In the liberal welfare state, there is minimal interference of the state in the market. Welfare benefits are designed so as not to distort the market. The benefits for working-age adults tend to be minimal. Social rights are weak and the private social benefits provided by firms deepen the stratification within society. Benefits such as health insurance and

pensions are linked with employment. The weak, poor and marginalised eligible for welfare receive relatively modest cash and voucher benefits. The development of workforce capacity and enabling conditions as incentives and fair regulations propitious for employment generation is considered to be the primary role of the state. 'The shadow state', or institutions such as private insurance companies, and not-for-profit trusts which are not part of the state apparatus perform a significant role in welfare (Wolch, 1990). Countries that follow this model include the USA, India, Canada and Australia.

2. **The Conservative Welfare State**: In the conservative welfare state, generous social benefits are provided but the market-based status differentials are preserved. Welfare benefits are provided through state funds in which the size of benefits is linked to previous contributions. The conservative welfare states depend heavily on the traditional institutions of the Church and the family to promote social well-being. Nations that follow this model include Germany, Austria, France and Italy.

3. **The Social Democratic Welfare State**: It is based on principles of universalism and social equality in which welfare benefits are provided to all citizens as a matter of entitlement. Social democratic welfare states provide extensive welfare benefits to support the family, particularly women in their traditional responsibilities, for example, childcare and education. The government intervenes extensively in the markets to ensure social protection and equitable redistribution of wealth and income through taxes. The state thus becomes the guarantor of social rights. This is the welfare model of the Nordic nations of Finland, Denmark, Norway, Sweden, Iceland and so on. These nations also report the highest levels of human development and happiness year after year, measured by the Human Development Index (HDI) and the World Happiness Index, respectively.

On examining the East Asian nations, a new type of welfare state termed as the **Confucian welfare state** regime has also been identified. This type of state is characterised by a low level of government investment in social welfare and the central importance of the family in providing social safety net (Walker & Wong, 2005; Aspalter, 2006). In reality, most countries incorporate features of more than one model.

B. **Richard Titmuss' Classification (1974)**: The British thinker of social policy Richard Morris Titmuss (1907–1973) theorised the development of welfare state in relation to various socio-economic factors such as the fear of social revolution, the solidarity of the working class, the competition of political parties to attain power. He classified the welfare state into three types based on the relative responsibility and intervention of the state in providing welfare (Titmuss, 1974). The three types are as follows:

1. **Residual Welfare State**: In the residual state, the state intervenes to provide welfare as a last resort. It is based on the premise that the needs of the individual can be fulfilled only through (a) the market and (b) social organisations as family or parish. It is only when both these systems collapse and fail to satisfy basic individual needs, the state steps in to provide social welfare. This is made available on a temporary basis. For instance, when the poverty in the United Kingdom became widespread, the Poor Law (1834) was implemented

for the benefit of the impoverished. The residual conception of the welfare state is based on the capitalist thought of *laissez-faire* or minimum intervention of the government in the economic functioning of the society. It has subsequently been abandoned by most of the nations.
2. **Industrial Achievement-Performance Welfare State**: In this model, state makes the provision of social welfare as a catalyst for the growth of the economy and the formation of class loyalties. It is also known as the 'Handmaiden model'. The state links welfare benefits to the people in proportion to their economic contribution, for instance, the contribution of individuals to the pension funds is supplemented by interest on the sum contributed. Hence, the greater the contribution, the higher will be the pension afterwards.
3. **Institutional Redistributive Welfare State**: In this model, social welfare is treated as a good in itself which must be distributed to the people in the society. The emphasis is on providing universal services, such as free education or primary healthcare, sponsored by the state. It is based on the principle of social equality and is more prevalent in socialist economies.

C. **Korpi and Palme Classification (1998)**: The Swedish social scientists Walter Korpi (1934–) and Joakim Palme (1958–) classified welfare state based on multivariate criteria including benefit eligibility, principles for benefit levels and forms of welfare programmes. This classification presents a spectrum of welfare states, including states where welfare is organised voluntarily with little or no support from the state, and states where welfare provisions are need-based and targeted, to states where people receive universal welfare for the fulfilment of their basic needs (Korpi & Palme, 1998). Korpi and Palme identified five types of welfare states:
1. **The Voluntary Welfare State**: In this state, welfare is arranged through a number of voluntary funds, trusts and charities. The eligibility depends on membership contribution but benefits are relatively low.
2. **The Targeted Welfare State**: In this state, minimum benefits are provided to selected population groups after a test of need, for example, Australia.
3. **The Bismarckian-Corporatist Welfare State**: It is modelled as the first welfare state developed in Germany under the leadership of Otto von Bismarck. In this state, people receive benefits in proportion to their previous earnings and contributions made to the state fund. It follows a state corporatist which involves joint governance by representatives of both employers and employees, for example, Germany, Italy Austria, Belgium, France and Japan.
4. **The Beveridgean Basic Security Welfare State**: It is modelled on the welfare system of the United Kingdom devised in the post-Second World War period. It offers relatively low flat-rate benefits to all the people enrolled in a programme. For example, Canada, Denmark, Ireland, the Netherlands, New Zealand, Switzerland, the United Kingdom and the USA follow this model. In India, the PM-KISAN (Kisan Samman Nidhi) scheme which provides a flat benefit of Rs 6000 to all non-income tax-paying farmers represents such a welfare system.
5. **The Encompassing or Hybrid Welfare State**: It is a synthesis of the Beveridgean and Bismarckian systems. It provides certain universal benefits such as subsidised or free education, combined with earnings-related benefits, in terms

of say old-age pension to the economically active population. It is mostly followed in the Nordic nations of Norway, Denmark, Finland and Sweden.

Criticism of the Welfare State

Thomas Malthus (1766–1834), the renowned thinker, was a vocal opponent of social welfare. Being a clergyman and devout Christian, he believed that the poor need to realise their well-being the hard way by practising frugality, self-control and chastity (Edwards, 2007). In his address to the Central Committee of the Communist League, written after the failed revolution of 1848 in France, Karl Marx warned that welfare measures designed to increase wages, improve working conditions and provide social insurance were bribes for temporarily weakening the situation of working classes and the revolutionary consciousness essential to achieve a socialist economy (Marx, 1850).

French sociologist Michel Foucault was critical of the welfare state because the state uses the welfare systems to scrutinise, monitor and police the population by collecting vital information on social groups, which has been exacerbated by the digitisation of governance (Foucault, 1977; Rose, 1999).

Feminist studies of welfare states highlight the role of ideology about gender roles and families as a central factor in determining the type of welfare state. Feminist analyses have broadened the scope of inquiry to social services relevant to the family and policies related to women's rights, often neglected in the welfare state (Orloff, 1993).

The critics of the welfare state have expressed apprehension about the creation of a large bureaucracy required for administering it and the resultant tax burden on the wealthy meritorious citizens (Ryan, 2012). Serious apprehensions have been raised on the sustainability of social welfare programmes, especially pensions. This is due to the demographic transition, with ageing populations and smaller workforces, particularly in the countries of the Global North which has put severe pressure on the welfare state.

Since entitlements in the welfare state are based on citizenship, migrants tend to be excluded from social security systems (Goodhart, 2014). There are several administrative problems related to the welfare state including determination of the desirable level of services by the state; ensuring that the system of personal benefits and contributions meets the needs of individuals and families while at the same time offering sufficient incentives for productive work; ensuring efficiency in the operation of state monopolies and bureaucracies; and the equitable provision of resources to finance the services over and above the contributions of direct beneficiaries.

India: A Welfare State

In 1947, when India attained independence from colonial rule, there were innumerable social and economic problems and challenges. Socio-economic inequalities and disparities were very pervasive. Socially disadvantaged groups such as the *Dalits* (Scheduled Castes), *janjatis* (Scheduled Tribes), women, children and the economically backward classes such as the poor, industrial labourers, small peasants and farmers were in a distressed situation. The Gross Domestic Product (GDP) of India was a mere Rs 2.7 lakh crores accounting for a miniscule 3 per cent of the global GDP. The overall literacy level was pitifully low at around 12 per cent while the female literacy rate was just 8.86 per cent. According to various estimates, in 1947, the annual per capita income was only Rs 249.6 while the poverty rate in India was about 80 per cent or about 250 million people were below the poverty line. The level of industrialisation was very low and agriculture alone accounted for 54 per cent of the GDP and 60 per cent of the workforce was dependent on it for income (Rangarajan, 2014). Due to the weak condition of the economy and the glaring social differences, the founders of the Indian democratic republic envisioned development on socialist lines to achieve distributive justice and welfare.

The Directive Principles of State Policy (DPSP) were inscribed into the Constitution taking into account the limited resources at the disposal of the state while ensuring that it provides for the welfare and social well-being of the citizens. The DPSP, enshrined in Part IV (Articles 36–51) are the guidelines that aim to create social and economic conditions by which the welfare of citizens can be achieved. Thus, the objective of these principles is to establish social and economic democracy through a welfare state. Even though these principles are non-justifiable and non-enforceable in the court of law, the Constitution in Article 37 states that it shall be the duty of the State to apply these principles in making laws. However, the directives lend soul to the Constitution and have been termed as the 'Conscience of the Constitution' (Austen, 1966). Following is the list of DPSP that seek to promote welfare measures in India:

1. **Article 38**: To promote the welfare of the people by securing a social order permeated by justice – social, economic and political and to minimise inequalities in income, status, facilities and opportunities.
2. **Article 39**: To secure (a) the right to adequate means of livelihood for all citizens; (b) the equitable distribution of material resources of the community for the common good; (c) prevention of concentration of wealth and means of production; (d) equal pay for equal work for men and women; (e) preservation of the health and strength of workers and children against forcible abuse; and (f) opportunities for the healthy development of children
3. **Article 39-A**: To promote equal justice and to provide free legal aid to the poor.
4. **Article 41**: To secure the right to work, to education and to public assistance in cases of unemployment, old age, sickness and disablement.
5. **Article 42**: To make provision for just and humane conditions of work and maternity relief.
6. **Article 43**: To secure a living wage, a decent standard of life, and social and cultural opportunities for all workers.
7. **Article 43-A**: To take steps to secure the participation of workers in the management of industries.
8. **Article 45**: To provide early childhood care and education for all children until they complete the age of six years.
9. **Article 46**: To promote the educational and economic interests of SCs, STs and other weaker sections of society and to protect them from social injustice and exploitation.
10. **Article 47**: To raise the level of nutrition and the standard of living of people and to improve public health.

The term 'Socialist' added in the Preamble by 42nd Amendment, 1976 implied the achievement of socialist ends through democratic means. It is based on the reasoning that since wealth is generated socially, it should be shared equitably by society through distributive justice, and not concentrated in the hands of a few. The proclamation of the 'socialist' nature of the state has made it the moral responsibility of the government to regulate the ownership of property and resources, to reduce socio-economic inequalities and to ensure social well-being of the people.

Several other laws and legal provisions have been made for providing a legal mandate to social welfare. These include:

- The **86th constitutional amendment, 2002** made free and compulsory elementary education for children from the age of 6 to 14 years, a fundamental right under **Article 21A**. The Right to Education Act, 2009 was enacted for the effective implementation of this fundamental right.
- **National Food Security Act, 2013** made food security a statutory right. This law makes it obligatory for the government to provide food grains to approximately two-thirds of the country's 1.2 billion population at a subsidised rate. It includes the Mid-day Meal Scheme, Integrated Child Development Services (ICDS) scheme and the Targeted Public Distribution System (TPDS) and recognises the entitlements of children, pregnant and lactating women.
- **Mahatma Gandhi National Rural Employment Guarantee Act, 2005 (MGNREGA)** was enacted to guarantee the 'right to work'. Its objective is to enhance livelihood security in rural areas by providing at least 100 days of wage employment to at least one member of every rural household whose adult members volunteer to do unskilled manual work in a financial year. One-third of the employed have to compulsorily be women.
- The **Maternity Benefit Act, 1961** and the **Equal Remuneration Act, 1976** ensure the interests of women workers by making maternity leave legal and ensuring equal pay for equal work.
- *Pradhan Mantri Jan Arogya Yojana* (**PMJAY**) or the National Health Protection Scheme was introduced in 2018 as the largest health insurance scheme, aiming to provide a health cover of Rs 5 lakhs per family per year for secondary and tertiary-care hospitalisation to the 100 million poorest and most vulnerable families.
- **National Health Mission (NHM)** was launched in 2013 for universal access to equitable, affordable and quality healthcare services that are accountable and responsive to the needs of the people.
- **National Social Assistance Programme (NSAP)** of the Government of India provides financial assistance to the elderly, widows and persons with disabilities in the form of social pensions.

The expenditure on social services (education, health and other social sectors) by the Centre and States combined as a proportion of Gross Domestic Product (GDP) increased from 7.7 per cent in 2019–2020 to 8.8 per cent in 2020–2021. Of the 7.7 per cent in the previous year, 3.1 per cent went to education, 1.6 per cent to the health sector and rest to other social service segments including housing, urban development, the welfare of SCs, STs and Other Backward Classes (OBCs), labour welfare, social security, nutrition and relief on account of natural calamities. The public expenditure and the state of various sectors of social welfare will be discussed in detail in later chapters.

References

Andrews, F. M. (1986). *Research on the Quality of Life*. Ann Arbor: Institute for Social Research.
Asatiani, M., & Verulava, T. (2017). Georgian Welfare State: Preliminary Study Based on Esping-Andersen's Typology. *Economics and Sociology*, 10(4), 21–28.
Aspalter, C. (2006). The East Asian Welfare Model. *International Journal of Social Welfare*, 15, 290–301.
Austen, G. (1966). *The Indian Constitution - Cornerstone of a Nation*. Oxford: Oxford University Press.
Bambra, C. (2007). Going Beyond the Three Worlds of Welfare Capitalism: Regime Theory and Public Health Research. *Journal of Epidemiology and Community Health*, 61(12), 1098–1102. doi:10.1136/jech.2007.064295.
Bauer, R. A. (1966). Social Indicators and Sample Surveys. *The Public Opinion Quarterly*, 30(3), 339–352.
Briggs, A. (1961). The Welfare State in Historical Perspective. *Archives Europe´ennes de Sociologie*, 2, 221–258.
Byrne, D. (1999). *Social Exclusion*. Milton Keynes: Open University Press.
Carey, G. W. (1975). Social Justice and the City by David Harvey. *Geographical Review*, 65(3), 421–423.
Corbridge, S. (1993). *Debt and Development*. Oxford: Blackwell Publishers.
Crone, P. (2005). *Medieval Islamic Political Thought*. Edinburgh: Edinburgh University Press.
Cummins, R. A. (1996). The Domains of Life Satisfaction: An Attempt to Order Chaos. *Social Indicators Research*, 38, 303–328.
Desai, A. (1980). The Environmental Perception of an Urban Landscape: The Case of Ahmedabad. *Ekistics*, 47(283), 279–285.
Disraeli, B. (1845). *Sybil*. Salt Lake City: Project Gutenberg.
Edwards, J. R. (2007). The Costs of Public Income Redistribution and Private Charity. *Journal of Libertarian Studies*, 21(2), 3–20.
Esping-Andersen, G. (1990). *The Three Worlds Welfare Capitalism*. Cambridge: Polity Press.
Fleury, S. (2017). The Welfare State in Latin America: Reform, Innovation and Fatigue. Cadernos de Saúde Pública, 33, e00058116.
Forgeard, M. J., Jayawickreme, E., Kern, M. L., & Seligman, M. E. (2011). Doing the Right Thing: Measuring Wellbeing for Public Policy. *International Journal of Wellbeing*, 1(1), 79–106.
Foucault, M. (1977). *Discipline and Punish: The Birth of the Prison*. New York: Pantheon Books.
Goodhart, D. (2014). *The British Dream: Successes and Failures of Post-War Immigration*. London: Atlantic Books.
Gregory, D., Johnston, R., Pratt, G., Watts, M. J., & Whatmore, S. (2009). *A Dictionary of Human Geography*. Sussex: Wiley Blackwell.
Habib, I. (1992). Akbar and Social Inequities: A Study of the Evolution of His Ideas. In Proceedings of the Indian History Congress (pp. 300–310). Mumbai: Indian History Congress.
Hanson, J., Ortman, S., & Lobo, J. (2017). Urbanism and the Division of Labour in the Roman Empire. *Journal of the Royal Society Interface*, 14(136), 20170367. doi:10.1098/rsif.2017.0367.
Harvey, D. (1973). *Social Justice and the City*. Athens: University of Georgia Press.
Hulsewe, A. (1987). Han China: A Proto "Welfare State"? Fragments of Han Law Discovered in North-West China. *T'oung Pao*, 73, 265–285.
Ilbery, B. W. (1984). Core-Periphery Contrasts in European Social Well-Being. *Geography*, 69(4), 289–302.
Jolly, R. (1976). The World Employment Conference: The Enthronement of Basic Needs. *Development Policy Review*, 9(2), 31–44. doi:10.1111%2Fj.1467-7679.1976.tb00338.x.

Katz, M., & Sachsse, C. (1995). *The Mixed Economy of Social Welfare*. Baden-Baden: Nomos.
Knox, P. (1974). Social Indicators and the Concept of Level of Living. *The Sociological Review* (Sage), 22(2), 249–257.
Knox, P. (1975). *Social Well-being: A Spatial Perspective*. Oxford: Oxford University Press.
Korpi, W., & Palme, J. (1998). The Paradox of Redistribution and Strategies of Equality: Welfare State Institutions, Inequality, and Poverty in the Western Countries. *American Sociological Review*, 63(5), 661–687.
Kropotkin, P. (1899). *Memoirs of a Revolutionist*. New York: Houghton Mifflin Company.
Kropotkin, P., & Weigl, C. (2008). *The Conquest of Bread*. Oakland: AK Press.
Land, K. C. (1983). Social Indicators. *Annual Review of Sociology*, 9, 1–26.
Larson, J. S. (1996). The World Health Organisation's Definition of Health: Social Versus Spiritual Health. *Social Indicators Research*, 38(2), 181–192. doi:10.1007/BF00300458.
Lustig, N. (1995). *Coping With Austerity: Poverty and Inequality in Latin America*. Washington DC: The Brookings Institution.
Mackey, S. (2000). Towards a Definition of Wellness. *The Australian Journal of Holistic Nursing*, 7(2), 34–38.
Mairet, P. (1957). *Pioneer of Sociology: The Life and Letters of Patrick Geddes*. London: Lund Humphries.
Marshall, T. H. (1950). *Citizenship and Social Class: And Other Essays*. Cambridge: Cambridge: University Press.
Marx, K. (1850). Address of the Central Committee to the Communist League. Retrieved February 6, 2022, from Marxists.org.
Maslow, A. (1943). A Theory of Human Motivation. *Psychological Review*, 50(4), 370–396.
Maslow, A. (1954). *Motivation and Personality*. New York: Harper and Row.
Maslow, A. (1962). *Toward a Psychology of Being*. Princeton: D. Van Nostrand Company.
McCann, J. E. (2004). Best Places: Interurban Competition, Quality of Life and Popular Media Discourse. *Urban Studies*, 41, 1909–1929.
McCracken, K. (1983). Dimensions of Social Well-Being: Implications of Alternative Spatial Frames. 15(5), 579–592. doi:10.1068%2Fa150579.
McEwin, M. (1995). Social Indicators and Social Statistics in Australia. *Statistical Journal of the United Nations Economic Commission for Europe*, 12, 309–318.
Micholas, A. C. (2014). Mancur Olson. In A. C. Al (Ed.), *Encyclopedia of Quality of Life and Well-Being Research*. Dordrecht: Springer.
Mukherjee, R. (1989). *The Quality of Life: Valuation in Social Research*. London: SAGE Publications.
Noll, H.-H. (2004). Social Indicators and Quality of Life Research: Background, Achievements and Current Trends. In N. Genov (Ed.), *Advances in Sociological Knowledge: Over Half a Century* (pp. 151–181). Wiesbaden: Springer.
Noll, H.-H., & Wolfgang, Z. (1994). Social Indicators Research: Societal Monitoring and Social Reporting. In I. Borg, & P. P. Mohler (Eds.), *Trends and Perspectives in Empirical Social Research*. New York: Walter de Gruyter.
Orloff, A. (1993). Gender and the Social Rights of Citizenship: The Comparative Analysis of Gender Relations and Welfare States. American Sociological Review, 58(3), 303–328.
Papageorgiou, J. C. (1976). Quality of Life Indicators. *International Journal of Environmental Studies*, 9, 177–186.
Rangarajan, C. (2014). *Report of the Expert Group to Review the Methodology for Measurement of Poverty*. Planning Commission of India. Retrieved August 9, 2022, from https://niti.gov.in/planningcommission.gov.in/docs/reports/genrep/pov_rep0707.pdf.
Rapley, M. (2003). *Quality of Life Research: A Critical Introduction*. London: Sage.
Rose, N. (1999). *Powers of Freedom: Reframing Political Thought*. Cambridge: Cambridge University Press.

Roy, A. (2018). The Idea of Social Well-Being and Its Utility in Geographical Research. *Journal of Emerging Technologies and Innovative Research*, 5(7), 1019–1026.
Ryan, A. (2012). *The Making of Modern Liberalism*. Oxford: Oxford University Press.
Sastri, K. A. (1988). *Age of the Nandas and Mauryas*. Varanasi: Motilal Banarsidass.
Sen, A. (1985). *Commodities and Capabilities*. Amsterdam: North-Holland.
Sen, A. (1999). *Development as Freedom*. New York: Oxford University Press.
Smith, D. M. (1971). Radical Geography: The Next Revolution. *Area, 13*, 153–157.
Smith, D. M. (1973). *The Geography of Social Well-Being in the United States: An Introduction to Territorial Social Indicators*. New York: McBgraw-Hill.
Smith, D. M. (1977). *Human Geography: A Welfare Approach*. New York: St. Martin's Press.
Smith, D. M. (1994). *Geography and Social Justice*. Oxford: Blackwell.
Stoewen, D. L. (2017). Dimensions of Wellness: Change Your Habits, Change Your Life. *The Canadian Veterinary Journal*, 58(8), 861–862.
Swarbrick, M. (2006). A Wellness Approach. *Psychiatric Rehabilitation Journal*, 29(4), 311–314.
Titmuss, R. M. (1974). *Social Policy*. London: George Allen & Unwin.
Titmuss, R. M., & Abel-Smith, B. (1987). *The Philosophy of Welfare: Selected Writings of Richard M. Titmuss*. London: Allen & Unwin.
Tyrwhitt, J. (2021). *Patrick Geddes in India*. London: Lund Humphries.
Vila, C. B. (2018). An Enlightened Thinker's Critical Perspectives on Race, Slavery, and Globalisation. In P. H. Smith, J. N. Green, & T. E. Skidmore (Eds.), *Modern Latin America*. Oxford: Oxford University Press.
Walker, A., & Wong, C.-k. (2005). *East Asian Welfare Regimes in Transition: From Confucianism to Globalisation*. Bristol: Bristol University Press.
Ward, L. F., & Commager, H. S. (1950). *The American Mind: An Interpretation of American Thought and Character Since the 1880s*. New Haven, CT: Yale University Press.
Weir, M., Orloff, A., & Skocpol, T. (1988). *The Politics of Social Policy in the United States*. Princeton: Princeton University Press.
Wilkinson, R., & Pickett, K. (2010). The Spirit Level: Why Equality Is Better for Everyone. *Journal of Social Policy*, 42(4), 840–842. doi:10.1017/S0047279413000366.
Williamson, K. P. (1991). *The Community in Rural America*. Connecticut: Praegar.
Wolch, J. R. (1990). *The Shadow State: Government and Voluntary Sector in Transition*. New York: Foundation Center.
Woolley, C. M. (2009). Meeting the Mixed Methods Challenge of Integration in a Sociological Study of Structure and Agency. *Journal of Mixed Methods Research*, 3(1), 7–25. doi:10.1177/1558689808325774.
Zelinsky, W. (1970). *A Prologue to Population Geography*. New Jersey: Prentice-Hall International.

Chapter 3
Population

Introduction

The people of a nation are its most valuable resources. They contribute to its cultural and economic growth. The natural resources of a country become valuable when they are utilised by its people. People are the producers, distributors and consumers of resources. The total number of people living in a nation at a given point of time is known as its population. The management of population is very important from the perspective of national growth and development. A population that is well managed becomes invaluable human resource.

The official exercise of counting or enumeration of all the people living within the territory of a nation is known as census. It is usually done by the government agencies. It is defined as the procedure of systematically acquiring, recording and calculating information about the population. Such a type of census is known as population census. Apart from this, census of livestock, industries, wild animals, etc. is also conducted.

The essential attributes of a census, according to the United Nations Organisation are (a) individual enumeration, (b) universality within a defined territory, (c) simultaneity and (d) defined periodicity. Individual enumeration means that the information about the population is collected at the individual level. Universality within a defined territory means that all the individuals living within a territory are enumerated in the census without any exclusion. Simultaneity means that a particular census should have information about a population pertaining to a well-defined particular point in time. Defined periodicity means that census should be conducted regularly at defined intervals such as after every five or ten years to update the data regarding changes in population and make the information provided by census more meaningful.

Census is different from sample surveys as it involves the enumeration of all the members of the population and provides true information about all the population parameters. Sample surveys, on the other hand, enumerate only a small section of the population to estimate the population parameters. Census, as an exercise, is thus larger and more cumbersome than sample surveys.

The enumeration of the individuals in a population can be done by two methods: (a) de jure or (b) de facto method. In the de jure method, individuals are enumerated at their regular or legal residence while in the de facto method, individuals are enumerated at the geographical location where they were present at the time of enumeration. Enumeration, according to the de jure method has the risk of omission or double

DOI: 10.4324/9781003378006-3

count. On the other hand, de facto enumeration of population is difficult unless the movement of people is restricted at the time of census.

In a country as diverse as India, the census serves many purposes apart from enumeration of the population. It presents a reliable demographic, social, economic and cultural profile of the inhabitants at a particular point in time. Very often, it is the only source of comprehensive data at the ward and village level and other surveys use census for validating their results. It serves as a primary source for benchmark statistics related to demographic, social, economic and cultural attributes of the population (Chandramouli, 2011). It is used widely as a database for policy formulation, programme implementation and research by governments, academic institutions, think tanks, businesses, etc. The delimitation of constituencies for elections at the national, state and local levels is done based on the data provided by the census. The historical records of the census shed light on the progress and changes in the population and its attributes.

Census of India

The Census of India refers to the total process of collecting, compiling, evaluating, analysing and publishing or otherwise disseminating demographic, economic and social data pertaining, at a specified time, to all persons in the country.

In the ancient period of Indian history, the earliest reference to the census is found in *Arthashastra* (321–296 BCE) written by Kautilya during the Mauryan period. The *Ain-e-Akbari* (1595–1596 CE) written by Abul Fazl during the reign of the Mughal emperor Akbar in the medieval period also mentions about headcount of the population (Reich et al., 2009). During the colonial period, the headcount of the population was done in the North-western province in 1853 by the British. The first official population census was conducted non-synchronously between 1865 and 1872 in different regions of the British Indian territories. The first synchronous census was conducted in 1881 under Lord Ripon, who was then the Viceroy of India (Dyson, 2018). This census began the tradition of decennial census, which has been conducted consistently every ten years in India till 2011 for a period of 130 years. The first census after independence was conducted in 1951 (Samarendra, 2011). The census exercise of 2021 has got delayed due to the challenges of the Covid-19 pandemic.

In India, census is a union subject under Article 246 in the Seventh Schedule of the constitution. The Census of India Act, 1948 grants the statutory status and forms the legal basis for the conduct of the census. The Office of the Registrar General and Census Commissioner (ORGICC) under the Union Ministry of Home Affairs is the nodal agency responsible for the conception, planning and implementation of the census in India. It has field offices in different states and union territories headed by respective Directors of Census Operations who are responsible for conducting the census in their respective jurisdictions. At the district level, the District Magistrate (DM) or District Collector (DC) is responsible for conducting the census.

The census of India uses the extended de facto canvasser method for population enumeration. In this method, data from every individual is collected by visiting the household and canvassing the same questionnaire all over the country over a period of three weeks. It is followed by a revision round in which changes on account of births and deaths are incorporated.

The census till 1931 adopted the de facto method under which all individuals were enumerated in a single period of 24 hours, i.e. the census was conducted in a single day. However, due to the logistical issues of manpower and funds requirements, this method was discarded and the currently used extended de facto canvasser method was adopted in 1941 (Alborn, 1999).

Census enumerates the individuals in a particular territory at a particular point of time. For this purpose, the territory is represented by administrative units arranged in a hierarchy of states/union territories, districts, sub-districts, tehsils/talukas/Community Development (CD) blocks and villages/towns. Each of these units was given a unique eight-digit Permanent Location Code Number (PLCN) based on the hierarchical coding system in the Census of 2011. The status of these administrative units was frozen from 31 December 2009. The population figures are presented in a census with reference to a particular time, which is known as the reference time. In the 2011 Census, the reference time was 00:00 hours or 12:00 midnight on 1 March 2011.

The Census of India 2011 was the 15th continuous decennial census. It was conducted in two phases, namely (a) house-listing phase and (b) population enumeration phase. The house-listing phase was the first phase and collected information about all buildings. In this phase, information for National Population Register (NPR) was also collected, which will be used by the Unique Identification Authority of India (UIDAI) to issue a 12-digit unique identification number to all registered Indian residents. The second phase was the population enumeration phase in which the people were enumerated between 9 and 28 February 2011. This was the first census in which biometric information of individuals was collected. A total of 2.7 million officials were involved in conducting the census. The cost of conducting the census was ₹2,200 crores or ₹18.17 per person. Spread over 28 states and 7 union territories, the census covered 640 districts, 5,924 sub-districts, 7,935 towns and more than 600,000 villages. Along the border areas, India and Bangladesh conducted their first-ever joint census in 2011. The transgender population was counted in the population census in India for the first time in 2011 as in the section of sex in the population enumeration schedule, the value returned could be other than male or female (Chandramouli, Census of India 2011: Provisional Population Totals, 2011).

Questions in Population Enumeration: The population enumeration schedule contained 30 questions about:

1. Name of the person
2. Relationship to head
3. Sex
4. Date of birth and age
5. Current marital status
6. Age at marriage
7. Religion
8. Scheduled Caste
9. Scheduled Tribe
10. Disability
11. Mother tongue
12. Other languages known
13. Literacy status
14. Status of attendance (Education)
15. Highest educational level attained
16. Working any time during last year
17. Category of economic activity
18. Occupation nature of industry
19. Trade or service
20. Class of worker
21. Non-economic activity
22. Seeking or available for work
23. Travel to place of work
24. Birthplace
25. Place of last residence
26. Reason for migration
27. Duration of stay in the place of migration
28. Children surviving
29. Children ever born
30. Number of children born alive during the last one year

The population of India as per the 2011 Census was 1,210,854,977, which makes it the nation with the second highest population in the world after China. Since 2001, when the population was 1,028,737,436, India added 182,117,541 persons to its population, which translates into a decennial growth rate of 17.70 per cent. This addition was comparable to the population of Brazil. In the total population in 2011, there were 623,724,248 males and 586,469,174 females.

Salient Features of the Population of India

Some of the salient features that distinguish the population of India are:

- **Overpopulation**: According to the Census of 2011, the population of India was around 1,210 million. India with just 2.4 per cent of the total land area of the world supports 16.7 per cent of the world's population. This shows that India supports a larger population than the land resources it has. Hence, this definitely signifies overpopulation in the country (Sandu & Sukiasyan, 2018).
- **Uneven Spatial Distribution**: The population of India is not distributed uniformly in space. While on one hand, the National Capital Territory (NCT) of Delhi has a population density of 11,297 persons per sq. km, on the other hand, Arunachal Pradesh has only 17 persons per sq. km. The northern plains are highly populated, whereas the Himalayan states and semi-arid regions in western India have low populations.
- **Majority Rural Population**: In India, 68.84 per cent of the population lives in rural areas which means that two out of every three persons can be found in rural areas. The urban areas have only 31.16 per cent of the total population. However, according to the Census of 2011, the population growth in rural regions is less than that of urban regions.
- **High Percentage of Non-workers**: In India, the share of the population in the working age between 15 and 59 years is 60.5 per cent, whereas the dependent population constitutes 39.5 per cent of the total population. Hence, four out of every ten persons are dependent on the other six.
- **Skewed Sex Ratio**: The overall sex ratio of India as recorded in the Census of 2011 was 943 females per 1,000 males. Thus, there are more males in the population than females. The sex ratio in India has always been unfavourable for females in recorded census history.

Distribution of Population

Population by State: According to the Census of 2011, the states with the largest population were Uttar Pradesh (199 million), Maharashtra (112 million) and Bihar (104 million) while the smallest population was in Sikkim (6,10,577), Mizoram (10,97,206) and Arunachal Pradesh (13,83,727). The NCT of Delhi (16.7 million) recorded the maximum population while Lakshadweep (64,473) had the least population among the union territories (Figure 3.1(a)). Uttar Pradesh, Maharashtra and Bihar were the only three states with population exceeding 100 million and accounted for a little over one-third or 34.4 per cent of the total population of India. The top 11 states accounted for more than three-fourth of the Indian population. 15

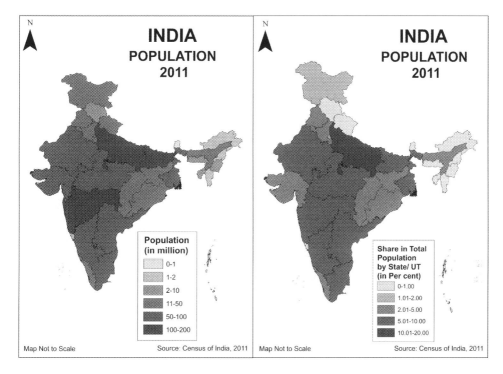

Figure 3.1 (a) Population of India (2011), (b) Share of State/UT in Population of India (2011)

states and union territories out of 35 in 2011 had less than 1 per cent of the total population of India. Rajasthan and Madhya Pradesh which are the two largest states in India by area accounted each only for about five per cent of the total population (Figure 3.1(b)).

Population Density: Population density is a parameter used to denote the concentration or relative distribution of people in a region. It is defined as the number of persons per square kilometre of land area. It is expressed by the following formula:

$$\text{Population Density} = \frac{\text{Number of Persons}}{\text{Land Area in sq. km}}$$

In 2011, the population density of India was 382 persons per square kilometre. In the previous census of 2001, the population density was 324 persons per square kilometre. Hence, for every square kilometre of land area, there has been an increase of 58 persons in the 2001–2011 decade. Since, the land area remains constant generally, an increase in the population results in an increase in population density and a greater concentration of people. In 1901, the population density of India was 77 persons per square kilometre. Between 1951 and 2011, the population density has increased very rapidly which has resulted in serious consequences. Since 1901, the population density

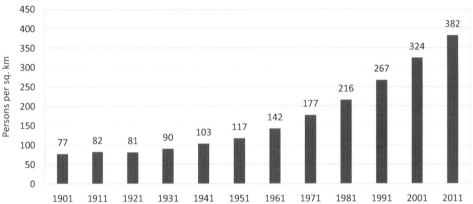

Figure 3.2 Population Density of India (1901–2011)

has increased continuously every decade except in 1921, when it decreased marginally. This population density, however, is not uniformly distributed and there are marked regional variations (Table 3.2).

In India, the population density in union territories is generally higher than in the states. Overall, the highest population density was in the NCT of Delhi (11,297 persons per sq. km) while it was lowest in Arunachal Pradesh (17 persons per sq. km) which shows the range of spatial variations. Among the states, the highest population density was in Bihar (1,102 persons per sq. km) and West Bengal (1,030 persons per sq. km). In the union territories, after the NCT of Delhi, the highest population density was in Chandigarh (9,252 persons per sq. km) and Puducherry (2,598 persons per sq. km) while the lowest was in Andaman and Nicobar Islands (46 persons per sq. km). Five union territories had a population density of more than 1,000 persons per sq. km. The population density generally is low in the hilly states in the Himalayan region and high in the region of northern plains (Figure 3.3(b)).

Factors of Population Distribution

The uneven spatial spread of the population in India is due to a wide variety of factors. These factors can be divided into two categories: (A) physical factors and (B) cultural factors, discussed below:

(A) **Physical Factors**: Physical factors play a primary role in the distribution of population. Historically, the population began settling and growing in regions which had a conducive physical environment with respect to landforms, climate, soil, etc. Some physical factors that affect the distribution of population include:
   a. **Topography**: The regions which have a difficult terrain such as mountainous, desert or plateau areas have low population compared to the plain areas

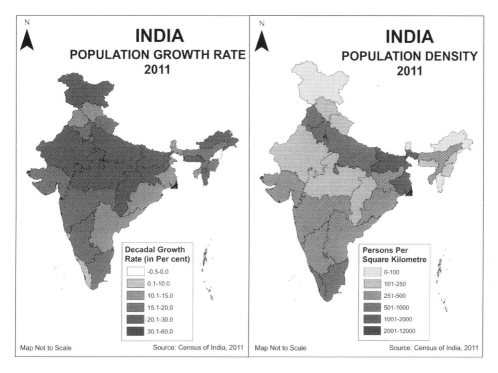

Figure 3.3 (a) Population Growth Rate of India (2001–2011) and (b) Population Density of India (2011)

which support a large amount of population. In India, the Himalayan and North-eastern states have low population, whereas the maximum concentration of population is found in the Indo-Gangetic plains.

b. **Climate**: Regions of moderate climate, without extremes of temperature, rainfall or humidity have greater populations such as in the northern or coastal plains. On the other hand, regions with climatic extremes such as hot or cold deserts in Rajasthan or Jammu and Kashmir have a comparatively low population.

c. **Soil**: The fertility and quality of the soil also influence the distribution of population. Fertile soil supports agriculture which provides food and fulfils one of the basic needs of the population. Regions which have high soil fertility, mainly the regions with alluvial soil are highly populated, which again includes the entire stretch of Indo-Gangetic plains. However, the regions having desert or montane soil or infertile soil as in the ravines of Bundelkhand region have low population.

(B) **Cultural Factors**: Cultural factors refer to the human factors that affect the distribution of population. It may include economic, political and social factors. While physical factors affect the spatial spread of population, the cultural factors determine the relative concentration of population. Some of these factors include:

a. **Historical Setting**: Regions which were populated early in history continue to grow due to momentum and agglomerative factors. For example, the northern plains have been continuously inhabited since the Vedic period dating around the first millennium BCE. Also, for example, the Pune–Mumbai region which is very densely populated has had a continuously increasing population since the colonial period, dating back to 17th century CE.

b. **Economic Opportunities**: Regions which have abundant economic opportunities in the form of either agriculture or industry have a high population concentration. It can be seen in the large population in the northern plains and the urban centres of Delhi, Mumbai, Kolkata, Bengaluru, etc.

c. **Political Centres**: Regions which serve or have served as the centres of political power have high population as they attract a lot of population due to administrative, political and economic opportunities, for example, Delhi, Patna, Kolkata.

d. **Peace and Harmony**: Regions which have general peace and harmony progress in terms of both population and economy. On the other hand, regions afflicted by war, invasions, and civil strife do not provide enough opportunity for the population to grow. For example, the North-West Frontier region of India has had a low population due to continuous war and invasions.

e. **Technology and Education**: Regions that are centres of technological innovation or education and industry have high population, for example, Bengaluru which is known as the Silicon Valley of India, Varanasi, Aligarh, Delhi.

f. **Religion**: Places which are religious centres tend to have high population due to various factors as pilgrimage services, economic opportunities, etc. such as Varanasi, Kamakhya, Madurai.

Population Regions

In India, the population does not have a uniform spatial distribution. Some regions have very high population while others are sparsely populated. On the basis of the density of population, there are five population regions in India:

1. **Regions of Extremely Low Density**: In these regions, the population density is less than 100 persons per sq. km. Such regions are found mainly in the remote, hilly and forested areas of the north-east and the islands. They include Arunachal Pradesh (17), Mizoram (52), Andaman and Nicobar Islands (46) and Sikkim (86).
2. **Regions of Low Density**: The regions which have a population density between 101 and 250 persons per sq. km are included in this category. Hilly regions with a notable population are included in this category, such as Nagaland (119), Manipur (122), Himachal Pradesh (123), Jammu and Kashmir (124), Meghalaya (132) and Uttarakhand (189). Plateau and forested regions of Chhattisgarh (189), Rajasthan (201) and Madhya Pradesh (236) and the arid and semi-arid state of Rajasthan (201) are included in this category.
3. **Regions of Moderate Density**: This category consists of regions where population density varies between 251 and 500 persons per square kilometre. This includes states with significant forest cover such as Odisha (269), Andhra Pradesh (308), Karnataka (319), Tripura (350), Maharashtra (345), Goa (394), Assam (397) and Jharkhand (414) along with Gujarat (308) that has a significant region in the Rann of Kutch, which is semi-arid in nature. By this category of classification,

India with a population density of 382 persons per sq. km is a region of moderate density.
4. **Regions of High Density**: This category includes the regions which have a population density between 501 and 1,000 persons per sq. km. High population density is found in regions which have large agricultural tracts such as states in the Indo-Gangetic plains of Uttar Pradesh (828), Haryana (573) and Punjab (550) along with regions that are agriculturally, industrially or commercially advanced such as Tamil Nadu (555), Dadra and Nagar Haveli (698) and Kerala (859).
5. **Regions of Very High Density**: These are the most densely populated regions and have a population density exceeding 1,000 persons per sq. km. These include the predominantly agricultural states with a high population growth rate such as West Bengal (1,029) and Bihar (1,102). West Bengal also has one of the largest industrial clusters in India located in the Hugli basin. Very high population density is also found in union territories that are industrial–commercial urban centres as Puducherry (2,548), Chandigarh (9,252) and Delhi (11,297) and those with small area but high population including Lakshadweep (2013) and Daman and Diu (2,169). The NCT of Delhi has the highest population density in India. It is also one of the most densely populated regions of the world. It is almost completely urbanised, with a very high population growth rate due to a large migrant influx as a result of the concentration of economic activities.

Change in Population

Population growth rate is the change in the number of people living in a particular area between two points of time, expressed in percentage. Change in population occurs mainly due to (a) natural change calculated by the difference between the total number of births and deaths and (b) induced change by migration of people which is the difference between the number of moving in and moving out. Population changes over time occur due to births, deaths and migration into or out of the area. Births and deaths are natural causes of population change. The natural increase in population is calculated by deducting the total deaths during a period from total births.

Natural Increase = Total Births – Total Deaths

The population will decline if the deaths are greater than births while it will increase if deaths are less than births.

Birth rate (annual) refers to the number of live births per 1,000 population per year. The mid-year population is generally used for calculation. Live births refer to the children who were born alive. The formula for calculating the birth rate is:

$$\text{Birth Rate} = \frac{\text{Number of Live Births in a Year}}{\text{Mid-Year Population}} * 1000$$

Death rate (annual) refers to the number of deaths per 1,000 population per year. The formula for calculating death rate is:

$$\text{Death Rate} = \frac{\text{Number of Deaths in a Year}}{\text{Mid-Year Population}} * 1000$$

The growth rate of the population is the difference between birth rates and death rates during a period, generally calculated on an annual or decadal basis. Thus, the annual natural population growth rate can be calculated by the difference in birth and death rates.

Natural Growth Rate = Birth Rate − Death Rate

Another phenomenon that causes a change in the population is migration or the movement of people from one place to another with the intention of taking up residence at the destination. Such a change in population is called induced change. If the persons moving in to a place are more than the persons moving out, then there is an induced increase in population. Persons who move into a place are known as immigrants if they are moving into another nation or in-migrants if they are moving to another place within the same nation. On the other hand, persons who move out of a place are known as emigrants if they are moving out from one nation to another or out-migrant if they are moving out from one place to another within the same nation.

Induced Increase =

Total Immigrants + Total Inmigrants − Total Emigrants − Total Outmigrants.

Hence, the total increase in the population during a period can be calculated as:

Increase in Population = Natural Increase + Induced Increase

or

Increase in Population

= Total Births − Total Deaths + Total Immigrants + Total Inmigrants

−Total Emigrants − Total Outmigrants

An important measurement of population growth is population doubling time. It is the time taken by the population to double itself at the current growth rate. The growth rate of population is calculated by the following formula:

Population 59

$$\text{Population Growth Rate} = \frac{P2 - P1}{P1} * 100$$

where P2 is the population of the current year and P1 is the population of the base year.

The statistics related to births and deaths are known as vital statistics. These are not included in the census but are published separately. In India, births and deaths are registered mandatorily under the Registration of Births and Deaths Act, 1969. This serves as the database for the calculation and estimation of birth and death rates. According to the latest estimates of 2019, the overall birth rate in India is 17.45 births per 1,000 population per year. The north Indian states of Bihar (26.2), Uttar Pradesh (25.6), Madhya Pradesh (24.6), Rajasthan (24) and Jharkhand (22.6) have the highest birth rates (Figure 3.4(a)). This is mainly due to the large and relatively young population as a result of which these states are still in the early stages of demographic transition. The regions which are developed, industrialised, have high migrant influx or are in the advanced stages of demographic transition that have low birth rates which include Andaman and Nicobar Islands (11.2), Goa (12.4) and Nagaland (12.9). The overall death rate in India is 5.74 deaths per 1,000 population per year. Death rates are high in regions which have high Schedule Caste and Schedule Tribe population, such as Chhattisgarh (8), Odisha (7.3), Himachal Pradesh (6.9) or have aged population as Kerala (6.9). Regions with high migrant influx and relatively satisfactory healthcare

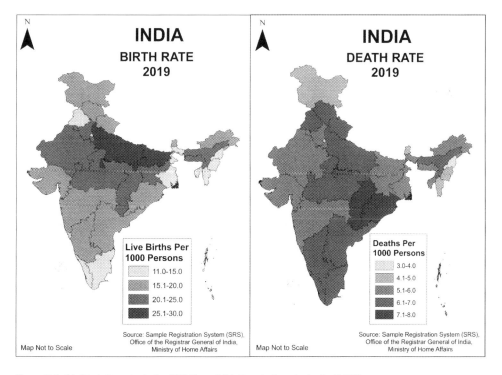

Figure 3.4 (a) Birth Rate in India (2019) and (b) Death Rate in India (2019)

services as the National Capital Territory (NCT of Delhi) (3.3) and Chandigarh (4.3), in advanced stages of demographic transition such as Nagaland (3.5), Mizoram (4.1) and Sikkim (4.5) have low death rates (Figure 3.4 (b)).

Population Growth in India

In the last 110 years between 1901 and 2011, the population of India has grown by more than five times, from around 238 million to 1,210 million. The population of India grew at a slow pace until 1921. In 1901, it was around 238 million. 1911–1921 was the only decade in recorded census history when there was an actual decline in the population, although marginal. Between 1931 and 1951, the population grew at a decadal rate exceeding ten per cent. Between 1961 and 2001, the decadal population growth rate was explosive exceeding 20 per cent (Kulkarni & Alagaraja, 2005). After 1961, more than 100 million people have been added to the population every decade. In the two decades between 1991 and 2011, the increase in population was nearly half a billion people. 2001–2011 was the only census period during which the addition in population was less than the previous decade. The trends in the historical growth of population can be divided into four phases (Table 3.1, Figure 3.5).

1. **Phase I or the Period of Stagnant Growth (1901–1921):** During 1901–1921, the growth in population was stagnant or stationary. The net addition during this period was only about 12 million persons. In fact, during 1911–1921, there was a net decrease of 772,177 persons in the population. During this period, India was in its first stage of demographic transition, with high birth and death rates. As a result, the net growth in population was low. The weak healthcare and food distribution system combined with frequent epidemic outbreaks, inefficient governance and World War I casualties inhibited the growth of population.
2. **Phase II or the Period of Steady Growth (1921–1951):** Between 1921 and 1951, the population of India experienced steady growth. The population increased

Table 3.1 India: Population Growth Rate (1901–2011)

Census	Persons	Growth Rate	Actual Variation
1901	238,396,327	–	0
1911	252,093,390	5.75	13,697,063
1921	251,321,213	–0.31	–772,177
1931	278,977,238	11.00	27,656,025
1941	318,660,580	14.22	39,683,342
1951	361,088,090	13.31	42,420,485
1961	439,234,771	21.51	77,682,873
1971	548,159,652	24.80	108,924,881
1981	683,329,097	24.66	135,169,445
1991	846,421,039	23.87	163,091,942
2001	1028,737,436	21.54	182,316,397
2011	1210,854,977	17.70	182,117,541

Source: Census Digital Library.

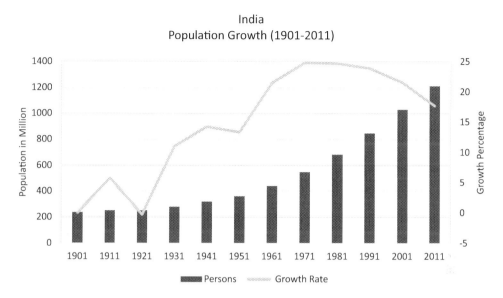

Figure 3.5 Population Growth Rate of India (1901–2011) (Source: Census Digital Library)

consistently with decadal growth rates in excess of ten per cent. Certain changes such as decentralisation of the governance system after Montague–Chelmsford reforms of 1921, the Government of India Act, 1935, greater representation of Indians in government along with the development of industry, commerce, transport and communication provided the impetus for steady population growth. Apart from this, no major epidemic was reported during this period. During this period, the population growth was mainly due to arresting of the mortality rates rather than an increase in fertility rates. Consequently, the population of India during these 30 years grew by more than a 100 million from 251 million to 361 million.

3. **Phase III or the Period of Population Explosion (1951–1981):** In the three decades following the independence of India in 1947, there was significant development and investment in the fields of agriculture, healthcare, medical services, education, public distribution, etc. As a result, the fertility rates shot up along with the already declining mortality rates. Food security, vaccination, economic growth and lack of family planning resulted in exponential population growth. Another factor which contributed to population growth during this period was the voluminous immigration from neighbouring regions of Bangladesh, Nepal and Tibet. From 361 million in 1951, the population almost doubled to 683 million in 1981. The population growth rate was more than 20 per cent every decade during this period.

4. **Phase IV or the Period of Rapid Growth with Signs of Slowing Down (1981-2011):** After 1981, the population has continued to grow due to the phenomenon known as population momentum, according to which, due to a high base population, even a small growth rate contributes to a large actual increase in population.

From 683 million in 1981, the population of India has almost doubled to 1,210 million in 2011. The growth rate has decreased from 23.87 per cent to 17.70 per cent. Due to improved healthcare and family planning services, educational attainment, standard of life, urban migration, etc., the fertility and growth rate have started declining.

State Population Growth Rate: Between 2001 and 2011, the decadal population growth rate of India was 17.70 per cent. The states with the highest growth rates were Meghalaya (27.8 per cent), Arunachal Pradesh (25.9 per cent) and Bihar (25.1 per cent) while the union territories that recorded the highest growth rates were Dadra and Nagar Haveli (55 per cent) and Puducherry (27.7 per cent). Nagaland was the only state with a negative growth rate of −0.5 per cent. Kerala (4.9 per cent) and Goa (8.2 per cent) were the states while Andaman and Nicobar Islands (6.7 per cent) and Lakshadweep (6.2 per cent) were the union territories with the lowest growth rates. Overall, 13 states and union territories recorded a decadal population growth rate in excess of 20 per cent (Figure 3.3 (a)).

Sex Ratio

Sex ratio is a qualitative attribute and represents the relative composition of females and males in the population. It is defined as the number of females per 1,000 males in the population. It is calculated by the following formula:

$$\text{Sex Ratio} = \frac{\text{Number of Females}}{\text{Number of Males}} * 1000$$

In 2011 the sex ratio in India was 943 females per 1,000 males. In India the sex ratio is generally unfavourable for women due to evident gender bias gender discrimination social practices such as female infanticide, female foeticide, son preference, poor access to healthcare education, etc. Consequently, the number of females has always been less than males in the population of India in the recorded census history of the past 110 years. According to the Census of 2011, the state and union territory with the highest sex ratio were Kerala (1,084) and Puducherry (1,037), respectively. The least sex ratio among the states was in Haryana (879) and Jammu and Kashmir (889) and in union territories was in Daman and Diu (618), Dadra and Nagar Haveli (774) and Chandigarh (818) (Figure 3.7(a)).

In 1901 the sex ratio of India was 972 females per 1,000 males. Since then the sex ratio has decreased significantly. In the last century, the lowest sex ratio was recorded in the census of 1991 when it reached 927 females per 1,000 males (Figure 3.6). After then, due to reasons such as growing awareness, government interventions, better educational and healthcare facilities, incentives for girl children, reduction in female foeticides and infanticides, the sex ratio has increased consistently but is still far from parity. In developed countries with adequate healthcare services, it is observed that the sex ratio is generally favourable for the females because of their high average life expectancy compared to males. However, in India there are 37,255,074 more males than females (Chandramouli, Status of Women in India, 2011).

Population 63

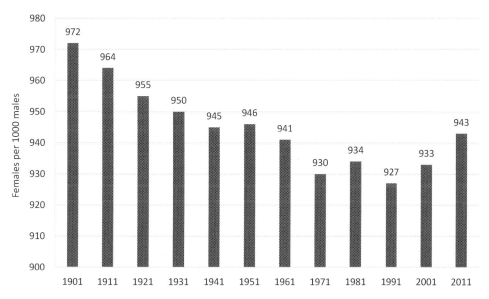

Figure 3.6 Sex Ratio of India (1901–2011) (Source: Status of Women in India, Census of India, 2011)

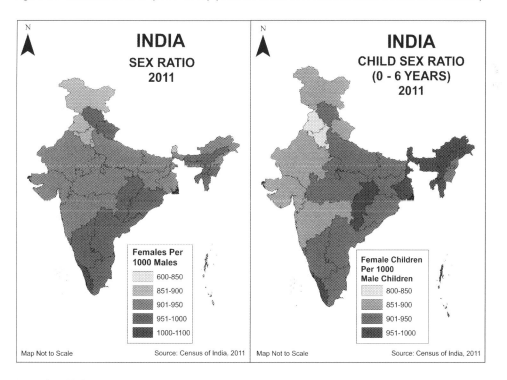

Figure 3.7 (a) Sex Ratio of India (2011) and (b) Child Sex Ratio of India (2011)

Child Sex Ratio

Child sex ratio is also a qualitative attribute of the population which represents the relative composition of females and males in the child population up to the age of six years. It is defined as the number of female children for every 1,000 male children in the age group of 0–6 years in the population. It is calculated by the following formula:

$$\text{Child Sex Ratio} = \frac{\text{Number of Females of age } 0-6 \text{ years}}{\text{Number of Males of age } 0-6 \text{ years}} * 1000$$

According to the Census of 2011, the child sex ratio in India was 914 females per 1,000 males. The highest child sex ratio was in Arunachal Pradesh (972), Meghalaya (970) and Mizoram (970) among states and Andaman and Nicobar Islands (968) and Puducherry (967) among the union territories. On the other hand, the lowest child sex ratio among states was in Haryana (834) and Punjab (846) and among union territories in the NCT of Delhi (871) and Chandigarh (880) (Figure 3.7 (b)). No state or union territory had parity in sex ratio or sex ratio favourable to female children. 13 states and union territories had child sex ratio lower than the overall child sex ratio. In the context of India, child sex ratio is an important attribute of the population due to the gender discrimination against the girl child and social practices such as female foeticide and infanticide that are used to deliberately reduce the population of female children and can be stopped by the right policy and programme implementation. It is also generally observed that the sex ratio at birth naturally tends to be unfavourable for females although it tends to attain parity at later stages as the mortality in male children is higher. However, if female children are not given adequate care, protection, nutrition and opportunities to grow, then their mortality rate increases and population gets reduced which has been observed in the case of India.

Literacy Rate

According to the census of India, a person aged seven and above who can both read and write with understanding in any language is considered to be literate. A person who can only read but cannot write is not literate. Formal education or any recognition is not required to be considered literate. Till the census of 1981, children below five years of age were treated as illiterates. However, from the 1991 Census, the definition of 'literate' was changed so as to automatically exclude the children less than seven years of age. Literacy rate is defined as the number of literate persons aged seven and above to the total population aged seven and above expressed in percentage. When literacy rate is calculated as the percentage of literate persons aged seven and above in the total population it is called Crude Literacy Rate which was used before the 1991 Census. The literacy rate used by the current census is the Effective Literacy Rate which is the per cent of literate persons in the population aged seven and above. Literacy is expressed by the following formula:

$$\text{Literacy Rate} = \frac{\text{Number of literate persons aged 7 and above}}{\text{Total Population aged 7 and above}} * 100$$

Literacy is an important indicator of socio-economic progress as a person who can read and write has greater capability than a person who is illiterate. For instance, a literate person can use banking services, mobile phones, read newspapers, do calculations, etc. However, literacy is still a very basic measure of educational attainment and should not be confused with education (discussed in Chapter 4).

From 1901 to 2011, the overall literacy rate has consistently increased by nearly 14 times from 5.4 per cent to 74.04 per cent. The female literacy rate has increased from 0.6 per cent to 65.46 per cent, and the male literacy rate has increased from 9.8 per cent to 82.14 per cent during the same period. Just after the independence of India in 1947, the census of 1951 recorded an overall literacy rate of 18.33 per cent with female and male literacy rates being 8.86 and 27.16, respectively (Figure 3.8).

In 2011 among the states the highest overall literacy rate was in Kerala (94 per cent) and Mizoram (91.33 per cent) and the lowest in Bihar (61.8 per cent) and Arunachal Pradesh (65.38 per cent). Among the union territories the highest literacy rate was in Lakshadweep (91.85 per cent) and the lowest in Dadra and Nagar Haveli (82 per cent) (Figure 3.9(a)). Among the males, the highest literacy rate was in Kerala (96.1 per cent) and Mizoram (93.4 per cent) among states and Lakshadweep (95.6 per cent) among union territories. The lowest male literacy rate in states was in Bihar (71.2 per cent) and Arunachal Pradesh (72.6 per cent) in states and Dadra and Nagar Haveli (76.2 per cent) in union territories (Figure 3.10(a)). In females, the highest literacy rate was in Kerala (92.1 per cent) and Mizoram (89.3 per cent) in states and Lakshadweep (88 per cent) in union territories. The states with the lowest female literacy rate were Bihar (51.5 per cent) and Rajasthan (52.12 per cent). The union territory that had the lowest female literacy rate was Dadra and Nagar Haveli (64.32 per cent) (Figure 3.10(b)).

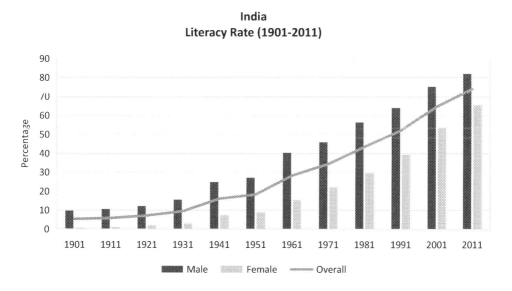

Figure 3.8 Overall Male and Female Literacy Rate of India (1901–2011) (Source: Census of India, 2011)

66 Population

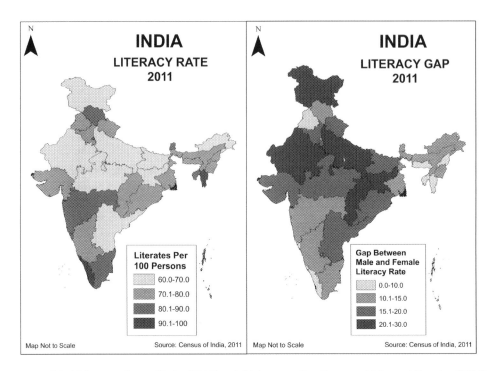

Figure 3.9 (a) Literacy Rate of India (2011) and (b) Literacy Gap Between Males and Females (2011)

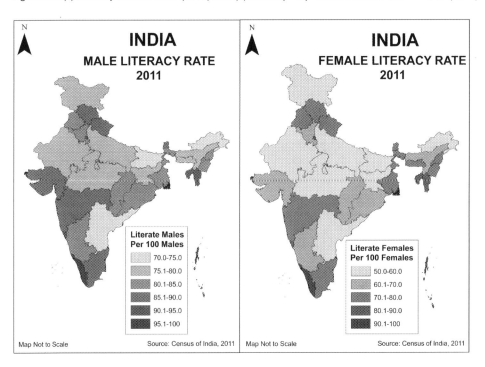

Figure 3.10 (a) Male Literacy Rate of India (2011) and (b) Female Literacy Rate of India (2011)

Gender gap in literacy is defined as the difference between male and female literacy rates. In 1901 the gender gap in literacy was 9.6 per cent although the educational opportunities for both males and females were dismal under the colonial rule. From 1961 to 2001, the gender gap in literacy was more than 20 per cent. The maximum gender gap was recorded in 1981 when it was 26.62 per cent. Since then, the gender gap in literacy has narrowed consistently and in 2011 it was 16.68 per cent. It was the narrowest gap after 1931 although both the male and female literacy rates in 2011 were the highest in recorded history (Figure 3.9(b)).

Scheduled Castes

Scheduled Castes (SC) refer to different deprived communities notified under Clause 1 of Article 341 of the constitution. These are the communities that have traditionally suffered from extreme social, educational and economic backwardness arising due to the practice of untouchability and discrimination. In the caste structure, these social groups have historically been placed at the bottom of the hierarchy. Special considerations have been made in the constitution for safeguarding their interests and for their accelerated socio-economic development.

In 2011, the total number of persons belonging to Scheduled Castes was 201,378,372 which amounted to 16.63 per cent of the total population. The highest population of Scheduled Castes were in Uttar Pradesh (41,357,608), West Bengal (21,463,270) and Tamil Nadu (14,438,445). Mizoram (1,218) and Daman and Diu (6,124) have the least number of SCs. Nine states had more than 10 million SCs in their population. No SC population was recorded in Arunachal Pradesh, Nagaland, Lakshadweep, and Andaman and Nicobar Islands. In terms of share in the population, the highest proportion of SCs in the total population was in Punjab (31.9 per cent), Himachal Pradesh (25.2 per cent) and West Bengal (23.5 per cent). Mizoram (0.11 per cent) and Meghalaya (0.58 per cent) had the least share of SCs in their population. 17 states recorded more than ten per cent of their population as SCs. The sex ratio in SCs was 945 females per 1,000 males, the highest being in Kerala (1,057) and Puducherry (1,056) and lowest in Mizoram (509) and Dadra and Nagar Haveli (853). Overall, the literacy rate among the SCs was 73.7 per cent which is marginally less than the national overall literacy rate. The highest literacy rate in SCs was recorded in Daman and Diu (92.6 per cent) and Mizoram (92.4 per cent) while the lowest was in Bihar (48.6 per cent) and Jharkhand (55.9 per cent) (Figure 3.11(a)).

Scheduled Tribes

Scheduled Tribes (STs) are tribal groups that have traditionally lived in geographically remote regions such as mountains, forest fringes, and are characterised by primitive traits distinct culture shyness of contact with the community at large economic backwardness, etc. They are listed in Article 342 of the constitution. The Scheduled Tribes are notified in 30 states and union territories, and there are total 705 Scheduled Tribes in India. The total population of STs in 2011 was 104,545,716 which was equal to 8.6 per cent of the total population of India. Madhya Pradesh (15,316,784) and Maharashtra (10,510,213) have the highest number of STs, whereas the least population of STs was in Daman and Diu (15,363), Andaman and Nicobar Islands

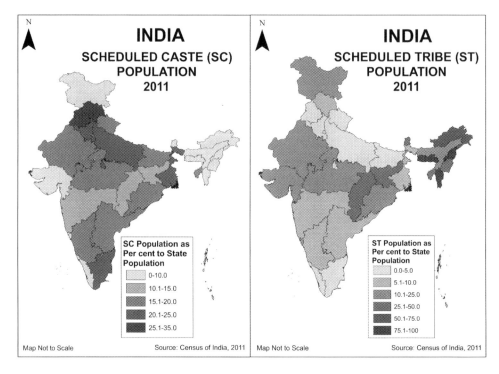

Figure 3.11 (a) Scheduled Castes Population in India (2011) and (b) Scheduled Tribes Population in India (2011)

(28,530) and Goa (149,275). Punjab, Chandigarh, Haryana, the NCT of Delhi and Puducherry have no recorded population of STs. In terms of share in the population, STs formed an overwhelmingly large chunk of population in Mizoram (94.4 per cent), Nagaland (86.5 per cent) and Meghalaya (86.2 per cent) while they form only around one per cent of the population of Kerala, Bihar, Tamil Nadu and Uttar Pradesh. More than half of the Scheduled Tribe population is concentrated in Central India, i.e. Madhya Pradesh (14.7 per cent), Chhattisgarh (7.5 per cent), Jharkhand (8.3 per cent), Andhra Pradesh (5.7 per cent), Maharashtra (10.1 per cent), Orissa (9.2 per cent), Gujarat (8.6 per cent) and Rajasthan (8.9 per cent) (Figure 3.11(b)). The other region of significant ST population is the North-eastern region consisting of Assam, Nagaland, Mizoram, Manipur, Meghalaya, Tripura, Sikkim and Arunachal Pradesh. More than two-thirds of the ST population is concentrated only in the seven States of the country, viz. Madhya Pradesh, Maharashtra, Orissa, Gujarat, Rajasthan, Jharkhand and Chhattisgarh. The sex ratio among the STs was 990 females per 1,000 males which was significantly higher than the overall sex ratio. The highest sex ratio was in Goa (1,046) and Kerala (1,035) while it was lowest in Jammu and Kashmir (924) and Andaman and Nicobar Islands (937). The literacy rate of the STs was 58.9 per cent significantly less than the overall literacy rate. Inadequate availability and access to educational facilities serve as the major hindrance in the literacy of STs. The highest literacy rate in STs was in Lakshadweep (91.7 per cent) and Mizoram (91.5

per cent) while it was lowest in Madhya Pradesh (50.6 per cent) and Andhra Pradesh (49.2 per cent).

Religious Composition

The population of India has a diverse religious profile. The religious community with the largest population is Hindus (966,257,353) followed by Muslims (172,245,158), Christians (27,819,588), Sikhs (20,833,116), Buddhists (8,442,972) and Jains (4,451,753). The maximum share in population was of Hindus (79.80 per cent) followed by Muslims (14.23 per cent) while the least share was of Jains and Buddhists who accounted for only around one per cent of the total population of India. Muslims form the majority population group in Jammu and Kashmir and Lakshadweep. Christians form the majority in four states namely Mizoram, Nagaland, Meghalaya and Arunachal Pradesh, while in Punjab Sikhs form the majority of the population. In the remaining 28 states and union territories, Hindus are in majority. The highest growth rate between 2001 and 2011 was of Muslims (24.6 per cent) followed by Hindus (16.8 per cent) while it was the least in Jains (5.4 per cent). The religious group with the maximum sex ratio was Christians (1,023) while the minimum sex ratio was observed in Sikhs (903). The literacy rate was the highest among the smallest religious group, i.e. Jains (94.9 per cent) while it was lowest in Muslims (68.5 per cent) (Table 3.2).

Table 3.2 India: Population Attributes by Religion (2011)

Religious Group	Population	Share in Population (in Per Cent)	Growth Rate	Sex Ratio (2011)	Literacy (2011)
Hindus	966,257,353	79.80	16.80	939	73.30
Muslims	172,245,158	14.23	24.60	951	68.50
Christians	27,819,588	2.30	15.50	1,023	84.50
Sikhs	20,833,116	1.72	8.40	903	75.40
Buddhists	8,442,972	0.70	6.10	965	81.30
Jains	4,451,753	0.37	5.40	954	94.90
Others/religion not specified	10,805,037	0.90	NA	959	NA

Table 3.3 India: Migrants by Reason for Migration (2011)

Reason for Migration	Persons	Males	Females
Work/employment	41,422,917	35,016,700	6,406,217
Business	3,590,487	2,683,144	907,343
Education	5,457,556	3,296,340	2,161,216
Marriage	211,186,431	5,346,733	205,839,698
Moved after birth	33,855,865	20,078,947	13,776,918
Moved with household	65,959,915	29,679,662	36,280,253
Others	94,314,450	50,044,441	44,270,009
Total	455,787,621	146,145,967	309,641,654

Age Structure

The population of a nation can be grouped conveniently into three categories on the basis of age groups. These categories are (i) the young (0–14 years), (ii) the adult (15–59 years) and (iii) the senile or old (60 and above). Dividing the population into these age groups provides estimates related to the workforce need for childcare and social security for the senior citizens and helps in the formulation of population policy. Generally, these three age categories are represented by the age-sex pyramid which is a graphical representation of the composition of the population based on age and sex. The population can be shown for every single year of age but is more conveniently represented in age cohorts spanning five years. Normally the age-sex composition of a population when plotted graphically appears in the form of a pyramid. For a developing country like India, the age-sex pyramid is upright with a wide base which indicates a large share of the young in the population. The pyramid tapers towards the top indicating that the population decreases with corresponding increase in age. In the case of India, males outnumber females towards the base of the pyramid which is due to the prevailing low sex ratio. However, towards the top, females outnumber males owing to their higher life expectancy. Another notable feature is that the base of the population pyramid of India in the age cohort 0–4 years and 5–9 years is narrower than the population cohort above it. This narrow base indicates a fall in fertility rates and slowing down of the population growth in the last ten years.

In India, the young population between 0 and 14 years of age comprises 30.9 per cent or nearly one-third of the total population. The adult population between 15 and 59 years of age is the largest population group forming around three-fifths or 60.5 per cent of the population. The senile population aged above 60 years constitutes less than one-tenth or 8.6 per cent of the population (Figure 3.12). Hence, the burden of the senior citizens is comparatively less on the nation. However, in a large country like India, even a meagre share of the old population amounts to 103,849,040 persons. The young and old population is known as dependent population. The ratio of the share of dependent population to the total population is known as dependency ratio. The dependency ratio for India is 39.5 which means for every 1,000 persons in the population there are 395 persons who are either young or old.

The majority of the Indian population is of working age. Currently, the population in the 15–59 years age group which is 60.5 per cent is expected to peak around 2036 when it will reach approximately 65 per cent. This advantage of young and economically active population is termed as a demographic dividend because if the potential of this workforce is utilised optimally India can transition from a developing to a developed nation within a matter of few decades (James, 2008). This demographic dividend started in 2005–2006 and is expected to last till 2055–2056. With consistently fewer births each year, the share of working-age population will grow larger relative to the dependent population. With more people in the workforce and fewer dependent people, there is a significant window of opportunity for economic growth. The period during which this window is available is known as the 'demographic window' which for India it is expected to last till 2055–2056. However, this demographic dividend window is available at different times in different states because of the differential behaviour of the population parameters (Chandrasekhar & Ghosh, 2006).

Population 71

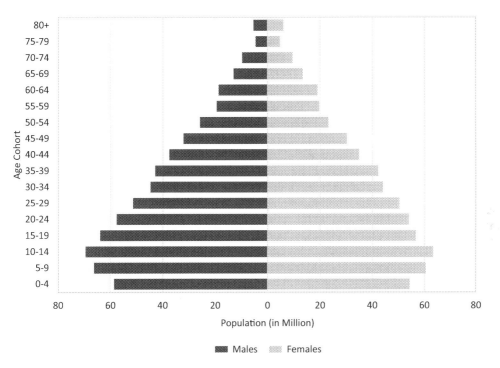

Figure 3.12 Age–Sex Structure of India

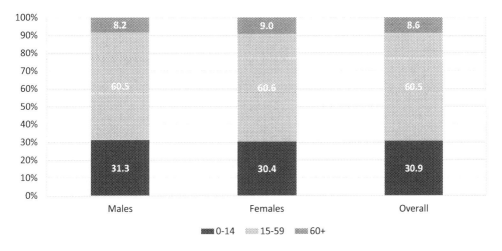

Figure 3.13 Overall Male and Female Age Structure of India

Demographic Transition of India

Demographic transition refers to the transition of population in a region that begins with high birth and death rates and low stationary population followed by a fall in the death rate, a phase of rapid population growth, a decrease in birth rate and concludes with a stable population and low stable birth and death rates. This change in population parameters is closely related to the change in the economy of the region that transitions from agrarian to industrialised. This theory was formulated by WS Thomson and FW Notestein and was subsequently modified by Karl Sax and CP Blacker. There are mainly four stages in demographic transition: (i) the stationary phase of high birth and death rates; (ii) the early expanding phase marked by high birth but rapidly declining death rates; (iii) the late expanding phase of declining birth rate and declining death rates; (iv) the low stationary phase of low and stable birth and death rates.

The demographic transition of India can be studied based on the census data. At the beginning of the 20th century, India was in the first stage of demographic transition between 1901 and 1921. During this period, both the birth and death rates were high above 40 per 1,000. The population was stationary and fluctuating due to high death rates as a consequence of frequent outbreaks of epidemics especially the Spanish Flu epidemic (1917–18), the First World War-related mortality (1914–1918), poor health facilities, etc. India transitioned into the second stage of demographic transition in the decade 1921–1931 when a marked reduction in death rates was observed although the birth rates continued to be high (Bose, 1996). As elsewhere in the less developed parts of the world, the decline in death rates was much more rapid in India than what had happened in the more developed countries earlier. This gap between birth and death rates meant a significant and rapid increase in population. This rapid increase in population lasted for around 50–60 years. During this period, India experienced a population explosion and an exponential growth in population. The third stage of demographic transition began between 1981 and 1991 when the death rate became less than 10 per 1,000 and the birth rate was also reduced to below 30 per 1,000. However, due to momentum, the population continued to increase substantially in the period following 1991 (Figure 3.14). Though it cannot be inferred with certainty whether India has entered the fourth stage of demographic transition, as per the data provided by the Sample Registration System (SRS) for 2019 both the birth and death rates have fallen to historically low levels of 17.4 and 5.8 per 1,000, respectively. Additionally, the period of 2001–2011 was the first decade when comparatively fewer people were added than in the previous decade. The annual population growth rate during this period was only 1.7 per cent. Thus, the reduction in population growth birth and death rates indicate that India will soon enter the fourth stage of demographic transition that will be marked by low birth and death rates along with a stable population.

Total Fertility Rate

The total fertility rate (TFR) in a specific year is defined as the total number of children that would be born to each woman if she were to live to the end of her childbearing years and give birth to children at the prevailing age-specific fertility rates (ASFR). It is calculated as the ratio between the number of live births in a year and the total female population of childbearing age, that is the average number of women between 15 and 49 years of age.

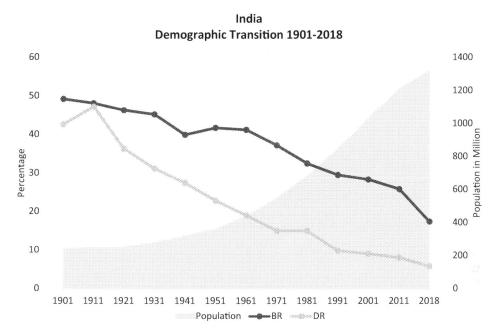

Figure 3.14 Demographic Transition in India (1901–2018)

Age-specific fertility rate (ASFR) is used to calculate the total fertility rate because the fertility in women varies during different ages; for instance, the fertility rate tends to be high during the twenties and thirties but is very low after the forties. On the basis of data on births by women of specific age groups in the reproductive span, 15–49 years age-specific fertility rates are calculated. The ASFR for women in the age group 15–19 is also known as the Adolescent Birth Rate (ABR). TFR is calculated from the ASFR using the following formula:

$$TFR = \frac{5 * \sum ASFR}{1000}$$

where

$$ASFR = (\frac{\text{Number of births by women in age group } 15-19 \text{ years}}{\text{Number of births by women in age group } 15-19 \text{ years}}$$

$$+ \frac{\text{Number of births by women in age group } 45-49 \text{ years}}{\text{Number of births by women in age group } 45-49 \text{ years}})$$

The multiplication by 5 is because a woman will spend 5 years of her life in each 5-year age group. We divide by 1,000 because the original rates were per 1,000 and we want to express the rate per woman. The TFR is interpreted as the number of births per

74 Population

woman. It can be compared across populations because it is not influenced by differences in age structure.

Another common concept is replacement level fertility. The rate of replacement level fertility is the TFR at which women have the number of births required to replace themselves and their partners but no more. If no children died before reaching adulthood, replacement level fertility would be two births per woman (one to replace the mother and one to replace her spouse). If death rates are low, replacement level fertility averages about 2.12 since not all children will survive to reach reproductive age. If mortality rates are high, replacement level fertility will be higher. Assuming no net migration and unchanged mortality, a total fertility rate of 2.1 children per woman ensures a broadly stable population. Together with mortality and migration fertility is an element of population growth reflecting both the causes and effects of economic and social developments.

Fertility is a simple measure of how many children are born of every woman on average. The fertility data in India are available consistently after 1971. However, based on the United Nations Population Division extrapolations, the total fertility rate of India can be estimated from 1950. In 1951 the fertility rate of India was 5.9 children per woman. India was in the second stage of demographic transition during this period and the population growth during this period was fertility-induced growth. The TFR continued to be high till 1981 after which it began reducing consistently. The low fertility rates between 1981 and 2011 have expressed definite signs of slowing down population growth. According to the UN projections, the TFR has reached a historically low level of 2.2 which is near replacement level fertility (Figure 3.15).

According to the latest estimates provided by the National Family Health Survey Round Five 2019–2021 (NFHS-5), the total fertility rate of India has dropped down to a historically low level of two children per woman which is below the replacement level (Figure 3.16(a)). While the rural fertility rate is 2.1 children per woman, the total

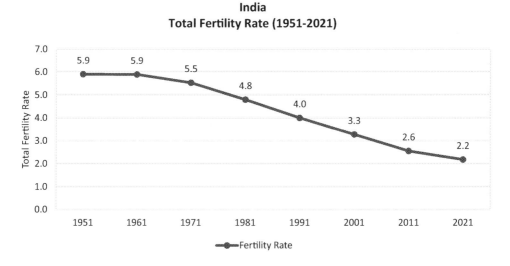

Figure 3.15 Total Fertility Rate (TFR) in India (1951–2021)

Population 75

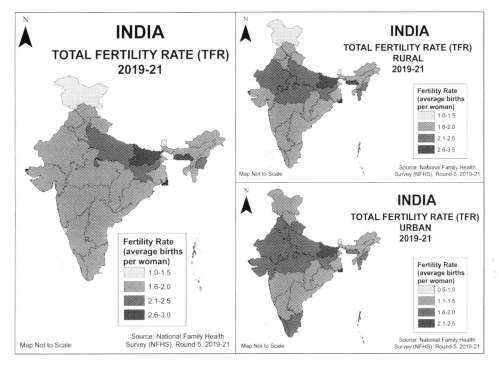

Figure 3.16 (a) Total Fertility Rate (TFR) in India (2019–2021), (b) Rural Total Fertility Rate (TFR) in India (2019–2021) and (c) Urban Total Fertility Rate (TFR) in India (2019–2021)

fertility rate recorded in urban areas is 1.6. Fertility trends in India exhibit much spatial variation with some regions reaching total fertility rates below 2.0 even as others lag far behind with levels above 3. The highest total fertility rate was recorded in Bihar (3), Meghalaya (2.9), Uttar Pradesh (2.4), Jharkhand (2.3) and Manipur (2.2), which are the only five states that have above replacement level fertility. Rest all of the states and union territories have recorded below replacement level fertility and the lowest being in Sikkim (1.1) and Ladakh (1.3). However, the two states Bihar (3) and Uttar Pradesh (2.4) with the highest fertility rate require special attention as they together comprise nearly a fourth of India's population (Figure 3.16(b,c)).

Population Policy

National Programme for Family Planning (1952)

India was the first country in the world to launch the National Programme for Family Planning in 1952. The central objective of the programme was family planning with an aim to reduce birth rates to stabilise the population at a level consistent with the requirement of national economy. After 1952 sharp declines in death rates were not accompanied by a similar drop in birth rates. The programme was based on five guiding principles:

1. The community must be prepared to feel the need for the services in order that when provided these may be accepted.
2. Parents alone must decide the number of children they want and their obligations towards them.
3. People should be approached through the media they respect and their recognised and trusted leaders and without offending their religious and moral values and susceptibilities.
4. Services should be made available to people as near their doorsteps as possible.
5. Services have greater relevance and effectiveness if made an integral part of medical and public health services and especially maternal and child health programmes.

The programme was tied to a series of five-year plans aimed at economic growth and restructuring which were carried out over 28 years from 1952 to 1979.

National Population Policy 2000 (NPP 2000)

The National Population Policy was introduced in 2000. It was based on the report of the National Population Commission chaired by renowned scientist MS Swaminathan. In alignment with the earlier National Programme for Family Planning (1952), the policy affirmed the commitment towards voluntary and informed choice and the consent of citizens while availing reproductive healthcare services along with the continuation of the target-free approach in the administration of family planning services. The policy sought to address the issues of child and infant mortality maternal health and contraception while increasing outreach and coverage of reproductive and child health services. It called for industry and voluntary non-government sector participation in the management of the population.

Objectives

The policy identified threefold objectives regarding the management of population. The immediate objective of the National Population Policy was to address the unmet needs for contraception healthcare infrastructure and health personnel and to provide integrated service delivery for basic reproductive and child healthcare. The medium-term objective was to bring the total fertility rate (TFR) to replacement levels by 2010. The long-term objective was to achieve a stable population by 2045 at a level consistent with the requirements of sustainable economic growth social development and environmental protection.

Goals

The policy identified certain national socio-demographic goals to be achieved by 2010:

1. Address the unmet needs for basic reproductive and child health services supplies and infrastructure.
2. Make school education up to age 14 free and compulsory and reduce dropouts at primary and secondary school levels to below 20 per cent for both boys and girls.

3. Reduce infant mortality rate to below 30 per 1,000 live births.
4. Reduce maternal mortality ratio to below 100 per 1,00,000 live births.
5. Achieve universal immunisation of children against all vaccine-preventable diseases.
6. Promote delayed marriage for girls not earlier than age 18 and preferably after 20 years of age.
7. Achieve 80 per cent institutional deliveries and 100 per cent deliveries by trained persons.
8. Achieve universal access to information/ counselling and services for fertility regulation and contraception with a wide basket of choices.
9. Achieve 100 per cent registration of births deaths marriage and pregnancy.
10. Contain the spread of Acquired Immuno-deficiency Syndrome (AIDS) and promote greater integration between the management of reproductive tract infections (RTI) and sexually transmitted infections (STI) and the National AIDS Control Organisation.
11. Prevent and control communicable diseases.
12. Integrate Indian Systems of Medicine (ISM) in the provision of reproductive and child health services and in reaching out to households.
13. Promote vigorously the small family norm to achieve replacement levels of TFR.
14. Bring about convergence in the implementation of related social sector programmes so that family welfare becomes a people centred programme.

The policy identified 12 strategic themes and laid down the operational strategies for their implementation:

(1) Decentralised Planning and Programme Implementation through Panchayats and Municipalities which should identify unmet needs for reproductive health services prepare need-based demand-driven socio-demographic plans at the local level and provide integrated basic reproductive and child health care.
(2) Convergence of Service Delivery at Village Levels through an integrated network of community health centres, primary health centres and subcentres along with the involvement of the voluntary sector and the non-government sector.
(3) Empowering women for improved health and nutrition by addressing the issues of malnutrition frequent pregnancies unsafe abortions.
(4) Child health and survival by addressing neonatal mortality, infant mortality and child mortality on account of inadequate care asphyxia during birth, premature birth, low birth weight, acute respiratory infections, diarrhoea, vaccine-preventable diseases, malnutrition and deficiencies of nutrients.
(5) Meeting the Unmet Needs for Family Welfare Services in both rural and urban areas by provision of contraceptive supplies and equipment for integrated service delivery, mobility of health providers and patients, and comprehensive information.
(6) Reaching under-served population groups in urban slums, Tribal Communities, Hill Area Populations, and Displaced and Migrant Populations and adolescents.
(7) Diversification of Health Care Providers and healthcare professionals
(8) Collaboration with and commitments from non-government organisations and the private sector by mobilising the private (profit and non-profit) sector to serve public health goals raise governance issues of contracting accreditation regulation

and referral besides the appropriate division of labour between the public and private health providers.
(9) Mainstreaming of Indian Systems of Medicine and Homeopathy to expand the pool of effective healthcare providers optimises utilisation of locally based remedies and cures and promotes low-cost healthcare along with proper regulation and standardisation.
(10) Contraceptive Technology and Research on Reproductive and Child Health and continuous applied research in the field of national demographics.
(11) Provisions for the older population by promoting old-age healthcare and support, sensitising training and equipping rural and urban health centres and hospitals for providing geriatric healthcare; encouraging NGOs to design and implement formal and informal schemes that make the elderly economically self-reliant; provision for and routinising screening for cancer osteoporosis and cardiovascular conditions.
(12) Information Education and Communication (IEC) of family welfare messages must be clear focused and disseminated everywhere including in local dialects.

Overall, the central objective of the policy was to address the unmet needs for basic reproductive and child health services supplies and infrastructure. The policy reiterated the voluntary and consent-based approach to family planning unlike China where a coercive one-child policy was implemented without exceptions. Other important aims of the policy included more comprehensive school education for girls, raising the age of marriage for females, reduction of mortality in new-borns, infants, children and mothers achieving universal immunisation of children against vaccine-preventable diseases. A major recommendation of the policy was to establish a permanent commission on population at the national and state levels to guide and review its implementation. Most of the goals set in the policy document could not be achieved by the targeted deadline in 2010. However, a decade later, India has achieved or is on the path to achieving major goals related to infant and maternal mortality, universal immunisation, institutional deliveries and containment of AIDS.

Migration

Migration refers to the movement of people from one place to another with the intention of taking up residence permanently or temporarily in the new location which may be within or outside the home country. Such people who migrate are known as migrants. Migration is the third factor responsible for changes in the population the other two being birth rate and death rate. Migration is commonly of two types: (a) temporary and (b) permanent. Temporary migration encompasses the annual or seasonal movement of population between two places. Compared to the birth rate and death rate, migration affects the size of the population differently as it is not a biological event like birth or death but is influenced by social, cultural, economic and political factors. Migration plays an important role in determining the distribution of population in the country.

There can be various reasons for people to migrate such as employment, business, education, marriage, war, drought, etc. All such factors can broadly be grouped into two categories, namely (a) push factors and (b) pull factors. Push factors are those factors that compel people to leave a place and migrate to some other place. Push factors include wars, civil strife, crime, pollution, drought, famine, floods, etc. Pull factors are those factors which attract migrants to a place. Availability of employment opportunities, healthcare, education, marriage, etc. can be considered as pull factors.

In the census of India, the collection of data related to migrants was based on the reference to the place of birth till 1961. However, this did not present a clear picture of migrants because the people moving for work or employment after marriage, etc. could not be assessed based on migration after birth. Since the 1971 census, a new reference of migration by the last place of residence was added. From 1991 the reasons for migration have also been recorded in the census. The reasons for migration as enumerated in the census are (1) work/employment, (2) business, (3) education, (4) marriage, (5) moved after birth, (6) moved with household and (7) others. Migrants by place of birth are those who are enumerated at a village/town at the time of census other than their place of birth. A person is considered as migrant by place of the last residence if he or she is residing at a place different from the place of residence enumerated in the previous census.

According to the Census of 2011 during the period 2001–2011, the total number of migrants in India were 455,787,621 which amounted to 37.64 per cent of the total population. The total number of male and female migrants was 146,145,967 and 309,641,654, respectively. Hence, in the migrant population, females outnumbered males, and the share of males being 32.1 per cent and females being 67.9 per cent.

The number of migrants to rural areas was 278,203,361 and that to urban areas was 177,584,260. Migrants to rural areas include migrants both from urban and rural areas. Similar is the case for urban areas. It can be observed that migrants to rural areas outnumbered the migrants to urban areas. In terms of share in the total migrant population, 61 per cent people of the migrants migrated to rural areas, whereas only 39 per cent of the migrants migrated to urban areas. Among the migrants to rural areas, 64,703,974 or 23.3 per cent were males and 213,499,387 or 76.7 per cent were females. Hence, more females migrated to rural areas than males. The migrants to urban areas were comprised of 81,441,993 or 45.8 per cent males and 96,142,267 or 53.2 per cent females.

The highest number of people migrated due to marriage which amounted to 211,186,431 (46.3 per cent), while the least number of people migrated for business around 3,590,487 (0.8 per cent). Among the males, the reason for maximum migration apart from other reasons was work/employment for which 35,016,700 males (24 per cent) migrated. The least number of males migrated for business numbering 2,683,144 (1.8 per cent). In females, the dominant reason for migration was marriage for which more than two-thirds or 205,839,698 (66.5 per cent) females migrated. The least migration in females was for business which was 907,343 (0.3 per cent) (Figure 3.17). The bulk of the migration in India is intra-state migration that is within the districts of the same state. Out of the total number of migrants in the 2011 Census, only 54.3 million (11.91 per cent) had moved to one state from another while nearly 395.7 million migrants had moved within their states. Just four states Uttar Pradesh, Bihar, Rajasthan and Madhya Pradesh accounted for half of India's total inter-state migrants. On the other side, Maharashtra, Delhi, Gujarat, Uttar Pradesh and Haryana received half of the country's inter-state migrants. Interestingly, Uttar Pradesh ranks high both in numbers of in-migrants and out-migrants.

80 Population

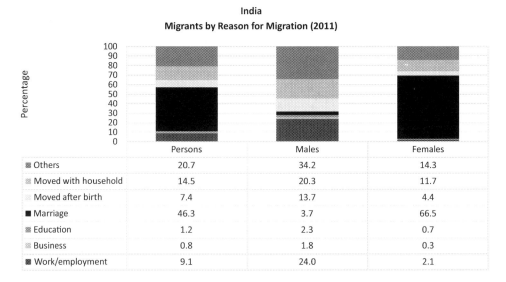

Figure 3.17 Migrants by Reason for Migration in India (2011)

The census also records information regarding the duration of migration of the migrants. This information is grouped into the following six categories based on the duration of migration: (1) less than one year, (2) 1–4 years, (3) 5–9 years, (4) 10–19 years, (5) 20 or more years and (6) duration not known. In 2011 the highest number of migrants recorded a duration of migration of 20 or more years numbering 146,421,501 (32.1 per cent) followed by 94,713,188 (20.8 per cent) migrants with a migration duration of 10–19 years. Among the male migrants whose duration of migration was known, the maximum number of males had a duration of migration exceeding 20 or more years amounting to 35,148,111 (24.1 per cent) followed by the males with a duration of migration between 10 and 19 years numbering 25,979,400 (17.8 per cent). An overwhelming amount of the female migrants had a duration of migration of 20 or more years their number being 111,273,390 (35.9 per cent) followed by female migrants with a duration of migration 10–19 years numbering 68,733,788 (22.2 per cent). In all three categories, the least number of migrants were those whose duration of migration was less than one year (Figure 3.18).

In 2011 among the states, the highest number of migrants was in Maharashtra at 57,376,776 (12.6 per cent) followed by Uttar Pradesh at 56,452,083 (12.4 per cent) and Andhra Pradesh at 38,360,644 (8.4 per cent). The states with the lowest number of migrants were Sikkim with 247,049 migrants (0.05 per cent), Mizoram with 387,370 migrants (0.08 per cent) and Nagaland with 549,618 migrants (0.12 per cent). The union territory with the highest number of migrants was the NCT of Delhi with 7,224,514 migrants (1.59 per cent) while the least number of migrants was in Lakshadweep at 20,401 (0.01 per cent).

The highest number of male migrants was in Maharashtra with 24,185,603 migrants (16.5 per cent), Andhra Pradesh with 14,594,644 migrants (10.0 per cent) and Tamil Nadu with 12,784,326 migrants (8.7 per cent), while the least male migrants were in Sikkim with 109,073 migrants (0.1 per cent), Mizoram

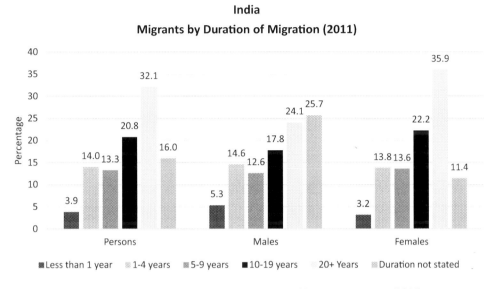

Figure 3.18 Overall Male and Female Migrants by Duration of Residence in India (2011)

with 193,388 migrants (0.1 per cent) and Manipur with 241,237 migrants (0.2 per cent). The union territory with the maximum number of male migrants was the NCT of Delhi with 3,751,348 migrants (2.6 per cent) and the minimum number was in Lakshadweep with 11,897 migrants (0.1 per cent). Female migrants were the highest in Uttar Pradesh with 45,260,222 migrants (14.6 per cent) followed by Maharashtra with 33,191,173 migrants (10.7 per cent) and Andhra Pradesh with 23,766,000 migrants (7.7 per cent). Lowest female migrants were recorded in Sikkim with 137,976 migrants (0.04 per cent), Mizoram with 193,982 migrants (0.06 per cent) and Nagaland with 268,499 migrants (0.08 per cent). The NCT of Delhi with 3,473,166 female migrants (1.1 per cent) and Lakshadweep with 8,504 migrants (0.003 per cent) were the union territories with the highest and lowest number of female migrants in 2011 (Figure 3.19).

Rural–Urban Composition

It is often said proverbially that India lives in its villages, meaning that the population of India is predominantly rural. For the Census of India 2011, the definition of urban area is as follows:

1. All places with a municipality corporation, cantonment board or notified town, area, committee, etc.
2. All other places which satisfied the following criteria:
    a. A minimum population of 5,000
    b. At least 75 per cent of the male main working population engaged in non-agricultural pursuits
    c. A density of population of at least 400 persons per sq. km

82 Population

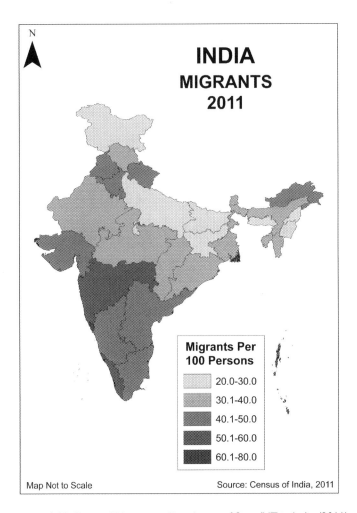

Figure 3.19 Share of Migrants in Population of State/UT in India (2011)

The first category of urban units is known as Statutory Towns which are towns notified under law by the concerned State or Union Territory (UT) Government and have urban local bodies such as municipal corporations, municipalities, etc. irrespective of their demographic characteristics. The second category of towns is known as Census Towns. These are identified on the basis of previous census data. All regions which are not urban are classified as rural.

According to the Census of 2011, the rural population was 83,37,48,852 while the urban population was 37,71,06,125. In terms of share in the population, 68.84 per cent of the population was rural while 31.16 per cent was urban. In the period between 2001 and 2011, for the first time since independence the absolute increase in population was more in urban than in rural areas. Since the last census of 2001, the urban population has increased from 27.81 per cent in 2001 to 31.16 per cent in 2011. On the other hand, the proportion of rural population has declined from 72.19 per cent to 68.86 per cent. The growth rate of urban population was 31.8 per cent while that of rural areas was 12.2 per cent. The states with the highest rural population in 2011 were Uttar Pradesh with 155,317,278 (18.6 per cent of total rural population), Bihar 92,341,436 (11.1 per cent) and West Bengal with 62,183,113 (7.5 per cent) persons. Sikkim with 456,999 (0.1 per cent), Mizoram with 525,435 (0.1 per cent) and Goa with 551,731 (0.1 per cent) persons had the least rural population. The NCT of Delhi with 419,042 (0.1 per cent) and Lakshadweep with 14,141 persons (0.002 per cent) had the highest and lowest rural population among the union territories. Urban population was the highest in Maharashtra with 50,818,259 (13.5 per cent) followed by Uttar Pradesh with 44,495,063 (11.8 per cent) and Tamil Nadu with 34,917,440 persons (9.3 per cent). Sikkim with a population of 153,578 (0.04 per cent) had the least urban population in India followed by Arunachal Pradesh with 317,369 persons (0.08 per cent) and Nagaland with 570,966 persons (0.15 per cent). The NCT of Delhi had the highest urban population with 16,368,899 persons (4.3 per cent) while Lakshadweep with 50,332 persons (0.01 per cent) had the lowest urban population.

In terms of state-wise share in the population, the most urbanised union territory was the NCT of Delhi (97.5 per cent) while the most urbanised state was Goa (62.2 per cent) followed by Mizoram (51.5 per cent) and Tamil Nadu (48.5 per cent). The least urbanised states were Himachal Pradesh (10.1 per cent) followed by Assam (14.1 per cent), and Bihar (11.3 per cent) while Andaman and Nicobar Islands (35.7 per cent) was the union territory with least urbanisation. Since urban and rural population are complementary to each other, hence Himachal Pradesh (90 per cent), Bihar (88.7 per cent) and Assam (85.9 per cent) were the states while Andaman and Nicobar Islands (64.3 per cent) was the union territory with the highest share of rural population. Similarly, Goa (37.8 per cent), Mizoram (48.5 per cent) and Tamil Nadu (51.6 per cent) had the minimum share among states and the NCT of Delhi (2.5 per cent) among union territories in terms of rural population (Figure 3.20).

Languages

Language is the medium through which people communicate with one another. It is an integral part of the culture of a social group and also lends cultural identity to the people. India is known for the plurality of languages spoken across different regions and cultures. People of India speak a large number of languages which can broadly be divided into four families as follows:

1) **Indo-European Family**: The Indo-European family of languages is spoken in north-central and eastern India. 78.07 per cent of the Indian population speaks different languages of the Indo-European family. This family can further be divided into the following four branches: (a) Indo-Aryan languages, (b) *Dardic* Aryan languages, (c) Iranian languages and (d) Germanic languages.
   i. **The Indo-Aryan Languages:** This sub-group consists of *Hindi, Bengali, Punjabi, Rajasthani, Gujarati, Sindhi, Kachchi, Marathi, Odia, Sanskrit, Assamese, Urdu*, etc. These languages can further be grouped into: **(a) Northern Aryan Languages:** These consist mainly of languages and dialects spoken by the people in the hilly regions of northern India such as *Nepali, Garhwali, Kumaoni*, etc.; **(b) North-Western Aryan Languages:** These are the languages spoken in

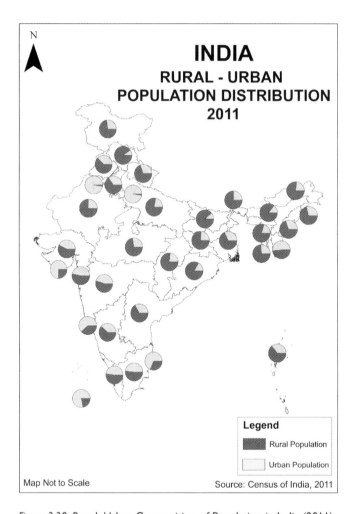

Figure 3.20 Rural–Urban Composition of Population in India (2011)

the north-western regions of Punjab, Haryana, Rajasthan such as *Kachchi*, *Khanda*, *Sindhi*, *Marwari*, etc.; **(c) Southern Aryan Languages:** These languages are spoken in the central Indian regions such as Maharashtra and Malwa such as *Marathi*, *Konkani*, etc.; **(d) Eastern Aryan Languages:** These are the languages spoken in Bihar, West Bengal, Assam such as *Bhojpuri*, *Maithili*, *Odia*, *Bengali*, *Assamese*, etc; and **(e) East Central Aryan Languages:** These languages are spoken in Madhya Pradesh, Chhattisgarh southern part of Uttar Pradesh such as *Avadhi*, *Bundeli*, *Bagheli*, etc.

ii. **Dardic Aryan Languages:** The languages of this group are spoken by the mountain communities of northern Jammu and Kashmir and Ladakh such as *Kashmiri*, *Shina*, *Kohistani*, *Nuristani*, *Chitrali*, etc.

iii. **Iranian Languages**: This sub-group consists of the languages that are mainly spoken by people of Afghanistan or the North-Western Frontier Province in Pakistan which include *Pashto, Afghani, Kabuli,* etc. and have a small population in India who speak these languages.

iv. **Germanic Language**: This sub-group consists of only one language in India, namely English, which is spoken by a large number of people and is an associate official language of India apart from being the lingua franca of higher education along with being a remnant of the colonial past.

2) **Dravidian Family**: Dravidian languages are considered to be older than the Aryan languages. They are spoken by 19.64 per cent of the Indian population. The Dravidian languages are spoken mainly in southern India and in some pockets of Central India. Based on the spatial distribution, Dravidian languages can be classified as: (a) **North Dravidian Languages**: These languages consist of various Gondi dialects *Oraoni, Malpahariya, Kui, or Kandh, Parji, Kolami,* etc. and (b) **South Dravidian Languages**: This sub-group includes *Tamil, Telugu, Kannada, Malayalam* apart from tribal dialects of *Tulu, Kota, Kedagu, Toda,* etc.

3) **Austro-Asiatic Family**: Austro-Asiatic family of languages is spoken mainly by small tribal groups of Central India in Jharkhand, Chhattisgarh, Madhya Pradesh and in certain other pockets. Just 1.11 per cent of the Indian population speaks this family of languages. This family of languages can be further classified into: (i) Mundari Languages: This sub-group is the largest within the Austro-Asiatic family and includes *Santhali, Mundari, Ho, Korwa, Birhor, Bhumiej,* etc. and (ii) Mon-Khmer Languages: This sub-group consists of the *Khasi* language spoken by the Khasi tribe of Meghalaya and *Nicobari* language spoken by the tribal people of the Nicobar Islands.

4) **Tibeto-Burmese Family**: The Tibeto-Burmese family of languages is spoken in the mountain regions of Ladakh, Lahaul and Spiti in Himachal Pradesh, Uttarakhand and the states of north-east India. Only 1.01 per cent of people in India speak languages of this family. It is the most diverse family of languages and the census has enumerated 66 languages of this family. This family can be sub-divided into: (a) **Tibeto-Himalayan Languages**: It consists of languages spoken in Ladakh, Himachal Pradesh and Uttarakhand such as *Chamba, Lahauli, Kannauri, Lepcha, Tibetan, Balti, Ladakhi, Lahauli,* etc.; (b) **Arunachal languages**: These languages are spoken by tribes in Arunachal Pradesh such as *Aka, Dafla, Abor, Miri, Mishmi, Mishing,* etc. and (c) **The Assam Myanmari Languages**: This group includes *Manipuri, Garo, Tripuri, Mikir* and *Lusai. Naga* is the most spoken language of this sub-group.

The census has been collecting data related to the language of the people for more than a century. In the Census of 2011 as in the previous censuses, the mother tongue as returned by each individual was collected. Mother tongue refers to the language spoken in childhood by the person's mother to him or her. If the mother of the person died in infancy the language mainly spoken in the person's home in childhood is regarded as the mother tongue. In the case of infants and deaf mutes, the language usually spoken by the mother should be recorded. The total number of languages in

India in 2011 was 121. These 121 languages are the languages which are spoken by at least 10,000 people. These languages have been classified into two categories by the census: (a) Part A languages include the 22 languages enlisted in the Eighth Schedule to the Constitution of India known as Scheduled Languages; and (b) Part B languages are those that are not included in the Eighth Schedule and are known as non-scheduled languages comprising 99 languages. In India, 96.71 per cent of people have one of the Scheduled Languages as their mother tongue while the remaining 3.29 per cent have other languages as their mother tongue. In India, 22 languages are recognised as Scheduled Languages. These languages are generally spoken by a large number of people and are called Scheduled Languages because they are listed in the Eight Schedule of the Constitution of India. These are the official languages of the Republic of India. The Government of India is under the obligation to take measures for the development of the Scheduled Languages so that 'they grow rapidly in richness and become effective means of communicating modern knowledge'. The Eighth schedule includes the recognition of the following 22 languages: (1) *Assamese*, (2) *Bengali*, (3) *Bodo*, (4) *Dogri*, (5) *Gujarati*, (6) *Hindi*, (7) *Kannada*, (8) *Kashmiri*, (9) *Konkani*, (10) *Maithili*, (11) *Malayalam*, (12) *Meitei* (Manipuri), (13) *Marathi*, (14) *Nepali*, (15) *Odia*, (16) *Punjabi*, (17) *Sanskrit*, (18) *Santhali*, (19) *Sindhi*, (20) *Tamil*, (21) *Telugu* and (22) *Urdu*. Uttar Pradesh (99.98 per cent), Haryana (99.94 per cent) and Tamil Nadu (99.93 per cent) have the maximum share of people who speak Scheduled Languages in their population. The least share of people speaking scheduled languages are in Nagaland (11.87 per cent), Mizoram (12.35 per cent) and Meghalaya (14.65 per cent). Twenty-five states and union territories have more than 90 per cent of the population speaking Scheduled Languages (Figure 3.22).

The five most spoken languages in India are *Hindi* with 528,347,193 (43.6 per cent) speakers followed by *Bengali* with 97,237,669 (8.3 per cent), *Marathi* with 83,026,680 (6.9 per cent), *Telugu* with 81,127,740 (6.7 per cent) and *Tamil* with 69,026,881 speakers (5.7 per cent). Along with *Gujarati* spoken by 4.6 per cent people, these languages are spoken by three-fourths or 75.8 per cent of the population of India. *Hindi* is the most spoken language in ten states and one union territory of the NCT of Delhi. These states are known as the *Hindi* belt and comprise Bihar, Chandigarh, Chhattisgarh, Haryana, Himachal Pradesh, Jharkhand, Madhya Pradesh, Rajasthan, Uttar Pradesh and Uttarakhand. Gujarati is the most spoken language in Gujarat, Dadra and Nagar Haveli, and Daman and Diu. Three languages are most spoken in two states or union territory each, namely *Malayalam* in Kerala and Lakshadweep, *Bengali* in West Bengal and Tripura, and *Tamil* in Tamil Nadu and Puducherry. Rest all the other states and union territories have different languages each as their most spoken language (Figure 3.21(a,b)).

Population Projections

The World Population Prospects report published in 2019 by the United Nations Population Division has made population projections of India for the 21st century. The report makes several types of projections by taking into account the variations in the long-term movement of the different population parameters such as fertility,

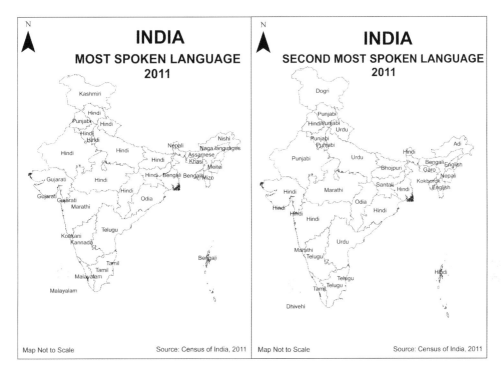

Figure 3.21 (a) Most Spoken Language by State/UT in India and (b) Second Most Spoken Language by State/UT in India

mortality and migration. The medium-variant population projection is used most frequently for comparison and demographic research. According to the projections by the United Nations Population Division, the population of India in 2020 stood at 1,380 million. India is expected to overtake China in 2027 and become the world's most populous nation. At this juncture, the population of India would be 1,461 million people while China would have 1,461 million people. The population of India is expected to grow consistently for the next few decades. The growth rate during this period would be slow. The population of India would peak between 2057 and 2060 when it would reach a total of 1,651 million people and the growth rate at this stage would come down to zero. India would thus become the country with the largest population ever in history, a record which would be unlikely to be surpassed. From 2061, the growth rate would become negative and the population would start declining henceforth. Around 2092 the population would fall down to 1,500 million, and at the turn of the 22nd century, the population is expected to be 1,447 million. From around 18 per cent of the share in world population currently, India would account only for 13.3 per cent of the global population in 2100. At the end of this century, the population would be the same as in 2025–2026 (Figure 3.23).

88 Population

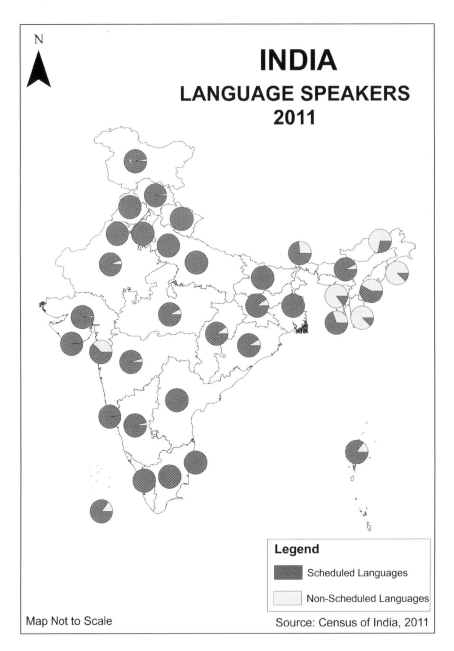

Figure 3.22 Speakers of Scheduled and Non-Scheduled Languages in India

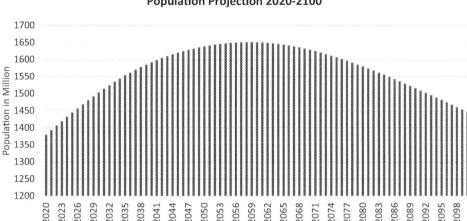

Figure 3.23 Projection of Population in India (2020–2100)

References

Alborn, T. L. (1999). Age and Empire in the Indian Census. *Journal of Interdisciplinary History*, *30*(1), 61–89.
Bose, A. (1996). Demographic Transition and Demographic Imbalance in India. *Health Transition Review*, 6, 89–99.
Chandramouli, C. (2011b). *Census of India 2011: Provisional Population Totals*. New Delhi: Government of India.
Chandrasekhar, C., & Ghosh, J. (2006). The Demographic Dividend and Young India's Economic Future. *Economic and Political Weekly*, *41*(49), 5055–5064.
Dyson, T. (2018). *A Population History of India: From the First Modern People to the Present Day*. Oxford: Oxford University Press.
James, K. S. (2008). Glorifying Malthus: Current Debate on 'Demographic Dividend' in India. *Economic and Political Weekly*, *43*, 63–69.
Kulkarni, P., & Alagaraja, M. (2005). Population Growth, Fertility, and Religion in India. *Economic and Political Weekly*, *40*, 403–410.
Reich, D., Thangaraj, K., Patterson, N., Price, A., & Singh, L. (2009). Reconstructing Indian Population History. *Nature*, *161*(7263), 189–194.
Samarendra, P. (2011). Census in Colonial India and the Birth of Caste. *Economic and Political Weekly*, *46*, 51–58.
Sandu, Z., & Sukiasyan, N. (2018). Overpopulation of India: Factors, Implications and Recommendations. *International Journal of Humanities, Art and Social Studies (IJHAS)*, *3*(2), 1–8.

Chapter 4

Education

Introduction

Education is the process of systematically imparting and acquiring knowledge, skills, values and development of personality through teaching and learning. Since education is a process, it continues lifelong. The term 'education' is rooted in the Latin word *educatio* which means bringing up or rearing. The ancient Indian text *Maitrayani Upanishada* states that *gyan* (knowledge) is the result of *vidya* (learning), *chintan* (reflection) and *tapas* (austerity).

Education has been recognised as fundamental to human development and 'an indispensable means of realising other human rights' (CESCR General Comment 13: The Right To Education, 1999). Article 13 of the International Covenant on Economic, Social and Cultural Rights (ICESCR), 1966 adopted by the United Nations Organisation (UNO) recognises the universal right to education for 'the full development of the human personality and the sense of its dignity' to enable individuals to participate effectively in the society. The Millennium Development Goals (MDGs) 2000–2015 had universal primary education enlisted as one of the eight international goals. In India, education was included in the Directive Principles of the State Policy (DPSP) in Article 45 under Part IV of the Constitution at its commencement. Article 21A inserted by the 86th Amendment, 2002 has granted the Right to Free and Compulsory Education to all children between 6 and 14 years of age in a manner as determined by the state through law. This article was operationalised by the enactment of the Right of Children to Free and Compulsory Education Act (RTE Act), 2009.

The Sustainable Development Goal Number 4 of the global initiative of 17 Sustainable Development Goals (SDGs) 2015–2030 adopted by the United Nations General Assembly is to 'ensure inclusive and equitable quality education and promote lifelong learning opportunities for all'. The three means of achieving targets are to build and upgrade inclusive and safe schools; expand higher education scholarships for developing countries and increase the supply of qualified teachers in developing countries. SDG 4 aims to provide children and young people with quality and easily accessible education plus other learning opportunities (Unterhalter, 2019). There are seven targets listed under this goal. These are (1) free primary and secondary education, (2) equal access to quality pre-primary education, (3) equal access to affordable technical, vocational and higher education, (4) increase the number of people with relevant skills for financial success, (5) eliminate all discrimination in education,

DOI: 10.4324/9781003378006-4

(6) universal literacy and numeracy and (7) education for sustainable development and global citizenship (Boeren, 2019).

Literacy and Education: Literacy refers to the ability to read and write, whereas education refers to the acquisition of knowledge, skills and values. According to the United Nations Educational, Scientific and Cultural Organisation (UNESCO), literacy is the "ability to identify, understand, interpret, create, communicate and compute, using printed and written materials associated with varying contexts" (Pahl & Rowsell, 2012; Gee, 2014). According to the Census of India, a person aged seven and above, who can both read and write with understanding in any language, is treated as literate.

Objectives of Education

The French philosopher Jean Jacques Rousseau believed that the objective of education was to direct the natural inclinations of the child wisely to train him properly. He was also in favour of popular education. Johann Heinrich Pestalozzi, a Swiss pedagogue, stated that the objective of education was the harmonious development of all the faculties and the improvement of the masses. John Dewy, the father of the movement of progressive education, held that education is the living of life, not a preparation of life. French sociologist Emile Durkheim believed that the purpose of education was the socialisation of the younger generation. Herbert Spencer was of the opinion that education should prepare individuals for a well-rounded life in society (Anderson, 2005).

Some of the major objectives of education are as follows:

1. **Mental Development**: Education should develop the mental and cognitive faculties of individuals and help them in comprehending the world around them. A healthy mental development is expressed in the ease of reading, writing, calculating and communicating. It helps to enhance the mental abilities of imagination, contemplation, memory, inspection, reasoning, judgement, etc. The development of critical thinking is considered to be an essential component of modern education.
2. **Social Development**: Education should make a person well-suited to living in harmony with society. It should make a person aware of the language, customs, lifestyles, religions, ethics, thinking, etc. of the social groups and individuals. Proper education helps people live comfortably and satisfactorily in the society they inhabit.
3. **Physical Development**: Education should aid in the physical development of one's body, as expressed in the adage *mens sana in corpore sano*, the Latin phrase meaning 'a healthy mind in a healthy body'. The physical development of the body is related to the development of mental faculties.
4. **Development of Character and Morality**: Education should help a person think and act responsibly and for the overall goodness of the people, society and nation they live in. It helps to develop qualities like honesty, compassion, kindness, responsibility, courage, etc.
5. **Transfer of Cultural Heritage**: The cultural attributes of a society such as lifestyles, traditions, customs, festivals, languages, literature, sports, etc. should be an integral component and objective of education. This helps to make students aware of their culture and appreciate other different cultures.

6. **Development of Vocational Skills**: Education should provide the skills to a person so as to serve society and hence earn a living. Hence, both academic and vocational components should be integrated in education. Vocation skills help children develop technical, administrative and organisational understanding and know-how to perform productive work. These skills should be developed in accordance with the interests, aptitude and abilities of the individual.
7. **Development of National Consciousness**: Education should create the awareness of responsibilities, civic duties and belongingness towards one's nation. The history of the motherland and the values associated with it should be integrated into education so as to make the students responsible citizens.
8. **Development of Spiritual Consciousness**: Education should cultivate and strengthen the inner spirit of individuals and prepare them for the different circumstances in life.

The **National Council of Educational Research and Training (NCERT)** in 1977 laid down the following objectives of elementary education:

1. Acquiring the tools for formal learning, namely literacy, numeracy and manual skills
2. Acquiring the habits of cooperative behaviours within the family, school and community
3. Developing social responsibility by inculcating habits
4. Appreciating the culture and lifestyles of persons of other religions, regions and countries

The Nobel-laureate economist Amartya Sen has listed the following purposes of education (Sen, 1992):

1. Education helps to make the world more secure and fair.
2. When people are illiterate, their ability to understand and invoke their legal rights can be very limited leading to their alienation.
3. Women's security is linked to their ability to read and write.
4. Literacy leads to higher political and economic participation of people in society.
5. Health problems and epidemics are better dealt with when people are educated.
6. The well-being of women is strongly influenced by their educated decision-making within and outside the house.

Types of Education: Based on the process by which education is imparted, it can be classified into two types, namely formal and informal education:

1. **Formal Education**: Formal education is imparted systematically within an organised structural framework of institutions with curriculum, teachers and assessment process, as in schools, colleges, training institutes and universities.
2. **Informal Education**: The learning that takes place in informal settings in daily lives such as homes, markets, playgrounds, etc. and influences thinking and development of a person is called informal education.

Levels of Education

The levels of education indicate the progress in knowledge and skills acquired by a person. These levels can be grouped into four stages (also see Table 4.1):

1. **Early Childhood or Pre-primary Education**: This is the preparatory stage for children below the age of six to seven years, and hence, it is also known as preparatory level. Teaching in this stage is generally not strictly formal and stresses on developing basic social, emotional, linguistic and cognitive skills. This stage initiates the process of education and provides the base for further school education. In India, only about 1 per cent of the child population under age six is enrolled in pre-primary education. This level can be further subdivided into four levels: (1) **Play**

Table 4.1 Levels of Education in India

Level	Grade	Ages	Comments
School Education			
Pre-primary level	Pre-kindergarten	2–5	This will cover children aged 3–8 years
Preschool (urban)/*Anganwadi* (rural)	Kindergarten	5–6	The focus of studies will be in activity-based learning
Primary school	Class I	6–7	
	Class II	7–8	
	Class III	8–9	It will gradually introduce subjects like speaking, reading, writing, physical education, languages, art, science and mathematics
	Class IV	9–10	
	Class V	10–11	
Middle school	Class VI	11–12	It will introduce students to the more abstract concepts in subjects of mathematics, sciences, social sciences, arts and humanities
	Class VII	12–13	
	Class VIII	13–14	
Secondary level	Class IX	14–15	These four years of study are intended to inculcate multidisciplinary study, coupled with depth and critical thinking. Multiple options of subjects will be provided
	Class X	15–16	
Higher secondary level	Class XI	16–17	
	Class XII	17–18	
Higher Education			
Undergraduate school	First year	18–19	1-year Vocational Certificate Course
	Second year	19–20	2-year Vocational or Technical Diploma Course
	Third year	20–21	3-year Bachelor's degree
	Fourth year	21–22	4-year Professional Bachelor's degree (mainly engineering)
	Fifth year	22–23	5-year Professional degree (mainly in medicine or law)
Graduate school	First year	21+	2-year Masters course in particular specialisation
	Second year	22+	
Doctorate		24+	
Postdoctorate			

Source: By author.

School or Pre-nursery: In this level, children learn basic activities such as eating food, dressing up and maintaining hygiene with minimal help. Children aged two to three years are enrolled. *Anganwadi* centres are pre-primary play schools funded by the government which provide free childcare and nutrition along with basic learning. (2) **Nursery**: At this level, children of the age three to four years learn to identify basic letters, words, numbers, colours, etc. (3) **Lower Kindergarten** (LKG): At this level, the children of the age four to five years are enrolled and learn basic sentences, games, rhymes, etc. (4) **Upper Kindergarten (UKG)**: It is also called the senior kindergarten with children aged five to six years. The LKG and UKG levels help in developing children emotionally, mentally, socially and physically

2. **Elementary Education**: This level consists of the first eight years of schooling that follows the kindergarten stage. In this stage, education is aimed to provide the fundamental reading, writing and mathematical skills to establish a solid foundation for learning. It provides the most critical literacy skills and abilities to a person. In most of the developed and developing nations, elementary education is compulsory and recognised as a right as well as the social welfare responsibility of the state. In India, elementary education is divided into two stages, namely (1) **Lower Primary** (Class I–V) and (2) **Upper Primary** (Middle school, Class VI–VIII). Eighty per cent of all the recognised schools at the elementary level are government run or aided; hence, the public sector is the largest provider of elementary education in the country.
3. **Secondary Education**: Secondary education is acquired after eight years of elementary education, typically between the age of 14–18 years. It is characterised by the learning of theoretical concepts and vocational skills across a broad range of subjects which can be developed further for higher education or vocational education or employment. In India, secondary education can be divided into two stages, namely (1) **Secondary Level** (Class IX–X) and (2) **Higher Secondary Level** (Class XI–XII). These two levels are very critical and educational qualification at this stage is given recognition via the standardised board exams conducted by national-level or state-level agencies. Students generally enter higher education after Class XII, but a lot of students also take up vocational or technical courses after Class X as well.
4. **Tertiary or Higher Education**: Tertiary or higher education level is after high school and is generally non-compulsory in nature. It is meant for acquiring higher skills and qualifications typically for white-collar or red-collar employment. In India, higher education includes graduate studies (bachelors), post-graduate studies (masters) going up to the doctorate level (PhD or Doctor of Philosophy).

The general levels of education in India are presented in Table 4.1. This pattern originated from the recommendation of the Education Commission (1964–1966), also known as the Kothari Commission. It is as follows:

Education in India

In ancient India, education was imparted through the institution of *Gurukulas* or *ashrams*, equivalent to modern-day schools or academies, where *shishyas* (students) cohabited with their *gurus* (teachers) during the period of their education. Teaching and learning were based on the tenets of the Vedas and Upanishads (Sharma &

Sharma, 1996). The purpose of education was to fulfil duties towards self, family, society, nature and religion and develop holistic knowledge and a strong character. Various disciplines such as *Itihas* (history), *Anviksiki* (logic), *Mimamsa* (interpretation), *Shilpashastra* (architecture), *Arthashastra* (polity), *Varta* (agriculture, trade, commerce, animal husbandry) and *Dhanurvidya* (archery) were taught. *Shastrartha* (learned debates) were organised to assess the students. Buddhist viharas (monasteries), Jain *Basadis* and universities were developed as centres of higher education. Takshashila, Nalanda, Vallabhi, Vikramshila, Odantapuri and Jagaddala had universities that were connected to viharas, whereas Benaras, Kanchipuram and Navadeep developed as centres of education in connection with temples in the period roughly between 500 BCE and 700 CE (Jayapalaa, 2005). Several of these archaic institutions have been declared to be World Heritage Sites by the UNESCO. Several travellers from different lands came to these institutions for education such as Faxian (337–422 CE), Xuan Zang (602–664 CE) and I-Qing (635–713 CE) from China. However, the organisation of the caste system determined the type and level of education. The *Brahmins*, or the priestly caste, were imparted knowledge of religion, philosophy, polity, administration, etc. and it was considered to be the duty of *Brahmins* to study. *Kshatriyas*, the warrior castes, were trained in various aspects of warfare such as archery, horse riding, etc. The *Vaishyas*, who were the trading caste, received training in business and accounts while the *Shudras*, who were ascribed the lowest position in the caste hierarchy and were considered untouchables, were largely deprived of education. This arrangement existed largely till the independence of India in 1947. During the medieval period, *maktabas* and *madrassas*, which were religious schools teaching Islamic scriptures became part of the education system. Educational institutions were known as *tols* in Bengal, *pathshalas* in western India and *chatuspadis* in Bihar. The modern school system was brought to India during the colonial period under the British rule. The famous minute by Thomas Babington Macaulay in 1833 paved the way for school education in the English medium so as to develop individuals in India as clerical workers for the British. The education was confined to disciplines such as science, mathematics, English, etc. while subjects like metaphysics, philosophy and literature which help to develop imagination and critical thinking were neglected (Nurullah & Naik, 1943). The traditional subjects were neglected altogether.

Constitutional Provisions

1. **Article 14** ensures that the State shall not deny to any person equality before law or equal protection of the laws, within the territory of India, which enables the reach of education to all.
2. **Article 15** prohibits discrimination on grounds of religion, race, caste, sex or place of birth by the State and ensures equality in educational opportunities in India.
3. **Article 15(4)** enables the government to make special provisions for the advancement of backward classes including the Scheduled Castes (SCs) and Scheduled Tribes (STs).
4. **Article 21A** provides Right to Free and Compulsory Education to all the children between the age of 6 and 14 years in a manner as the State may, by law, determine.

5. **Article 28** states that the institutions run by the State will not preach any religion or give religious education nor will they favour persons of any religion. It also provides that no person, attending State-recognised, aided school, can be compelled to take part in any religious instruction without parental consent.
6. **Article 29** states that no citizen shall be denied admission into any educational institution maintained by the State or receiving aid out of State funds on the grounds only of religion, race, caste, language or any of them.
7. **Article 30** provides that all minorities, whether based on religion or language, shall have the right to establish and administer educational institutions of their choice.
8. **Article 41** directs the State to make effective provisions for securing the right to work and right to education for all within the limits of its economic capacities and development.
9. **Article 45** provides that the State shall endeavour to provide early childhood education and care for all children up to six years of age. (Earlier it was up to 14 years of age but consequent upon the insertion of Article 21A in 2002, which made elementary education a fundamental right of all children between the age group of 6–14 years, the scope of Article 45 was limited to pre-primary education for children up to six years of age.)
10. **Article 46** provides that the State shall promote with the special case the educational and economic interests of the weaker sections of the people, and, in particular, of the SCs and the STs and shall protect them from social injustice and all forms of discrimination.
11. **Article 350A** states that it shall be the endeavour of every State and of every local authority within the State to provide adequate facilities for instruction in the mother tongue at the primary stage of education to children belonging to linguistic minority groups.

Right to Education

The Right of Children to Free and Compulsory Education Act or Right to Education (RTE) Act, 2009 was a landmark step in the implementation of the fundamental right to elementary education. With this act, India became one of the 135 countries that have made education a fundamental right for every child. This act has operationalised Article 21A of the Constitution inserted by the 86th Constitution Amendment Act, 2002, which states that the State shall provide free and compulsory education to all children of 6 to 14 years in such manner as the State may by law determine. The following are the key provisions of this act:

- **Free and Compulsory Elementary Education to All Children Between the Age of 6–14 Years**: Elementary education encompasses education from Class I to Class VIII. Free education means that there are no direct costs like school fees or indirect costs in the form of school uniforms, textbooks, school meals, transportation, etc. that have to be borne by the child or the parents. It is the duty of the state to provide schooling free of cost to the children until the completion of elementary level of education. Free education is applicable only to the government-run public schools and not private schools, either aided or unaided. Compulsory education

means that the appropriate state authorities have to ensure admission, attendance and completion of elementary education for all children in the age group of 6–14 years.
- **Pupil–Teacher Ratio (PTR)**: The act prescribes that at the primary level (Class I–V), the PTR should be 30:1 and at the upper primary level (Class VI–VIII) it should be 35:1.
- **Benchmarks**: The RTE Act has laid down norms and guidelines relating to students per classrooms, separate toilets for girls and boys, drinking water facility, number of school-working days, working hours of teachers, etc. All schools have the obligation to comply with these norms. The minimum number of working days for primary schools is 200 and for upper primary (Class VI–VIII) is 220. 800 instruction hours for primary and 1,000 instruction hours for upper primary classes have been prescribed. The minimum number of working hours per week for teachers is 45 hours. The act directs that every school should have a library providing newspapers, magazines and books. Sports equipment should also be provided to students.
- **Reservation for Economically Weaker Sections (EWS)**: Section 12 of the RTE Act has made it mandatory for all private schools to reserve 25 per cent of their seats for children who belong to socially disadvantaged and economically weaker sections (EWS) with the objective of promoting social inclusion. The costs borne by a private institution in this regard are reimbursed by the government.
- **Barriers to Admission**: No child can be denied admission to a school on the basis of lack of transfer certificate, age proof certificate, residence certificate, time of admission, etc.
- **Excluded Children**: The RTE Act has provided that children not attending school should be identified through surveys by local authorities and admitted to the age-appropriate class and provided with special training so as to enable them to match age-appropriate learning levels.
- **Expenditure**: Since education is a subject in the 'Concurrent List' of the Eighth Schedule of the Constitution of India, the expenditure incurred under this act is shared by the central and state governments.
- **Board Exams**: The RTE Act directs that no child can be held back, expelled or required to pass a board examination until elementary education is completed. The act introduced the Continuous Comprehensive Evaluation (CCE) system in 2009 to make the assessment of students holistic, grade-wise and independent of marks.
- **Prohibitions:** The RTE Act prohibits (a) physical punishment, mental harassment and discrimination on the grounds of gender, caste, class and religion; (b) screening procedures for admission of children; (c) capitation fee; (d) private tuition by teachers and (e) running of schools without recognition.
- **School Management Committees (SMCs)**: The act directs schools or clusters of schools to constitute School Management Committees (SMCs) comprising stakeholders that include officials from the local authority, parents, guardians and teachers. The function of the SMCs is to formulate School Development Plans along with monitoring the school environment and utilisation of government grants. The act has also mandated the inclusion of 50 per cent members of the SMC as women and parents of children from disadvantaged social groups.

- **Monitoring**: The National Commission for Protection of Child Rights (NCPCR), a statutory body set up by an act of Parliament in 2005 to monitor the rights and provide safeguards to children, has been designated as the nodal agency for monitoring provisions under the RTE Act at the national level. At the state level, this duty is performed by the State Commission for Protection of Child Rights (SCPCR).
- **Grievance Redressal**: The RTE act provides a Grievance Redressal (GR) mechanism for action against non-compliance of provisions of the Right to Education Act 2009.
- **Applicability to Minority Institutions**: The RTE Act does not apply to minority educational institutions established under Article 30 of the Constitution. The Supreme Court had exempted minority schools from the purview of the RTE Act in the Pramati Education and Cultural Trust vs. Union of India case (2014).

The RTE Act has been criticised on several counts for its provisions and operations. It does not make pre-primary or early childhood education a fundamental right; thus, the state does not have the obligation to make provisions for children up to the age of six years. A large number of children face problems in getting admissions under the EWS category in private schools. The RTE Act does not address gender inequalities in its provisions. The need of the children with special needs (CWSN) is also not addressed as their education is governed by the Persons with Disabilities Act, 2016. The act does not provide the norms for salaries of teachers. Teachers in the rural areas and private sector are often overworked and underpaid which affects their performance. The School Managing Committees as prescribed by the act are advisory in nature and hence mostly inefficient. The Act also protects the government from legal proceedings for any act done in 'good faith' for its implementation.

Organisation of School Education

Education in India is managed mainly by the state-run public education system. Schools are managed and controlled variously by the central, state and local governments. The 42nd Constitutional Amendment, 1976 made education a 'concurrent subject', after which the responsibility of administering and funding education has come to be shared between the central and state governments. The framework of education is guided by education policies designed from time to time. Notably, national educational policies were introduced in 1968, 1986, 1992 and 2020. The educational achievement of India has increased multifold since independence and this has often been considered as one of the driving factors behind the economic development of the nation. The progress in higher education and scientific research has been credited to various public institutions.

Types of Schools

1. **Government Schools**: The school education in India is mainly the responsibility of government-run public schools. Of the total number of schools, 68.5 per cent are public schools under the management of the government, in which 51.1 per cent of all the students are enrolled. These schools are managed completely by the government. The construction, curriculum, recruitment, funding and management are all under the control of government. These schools can be under central government such as Kendriya Vidyalayas, Sainik Schools, Kasturba Balika Schools,

Eklvaya Schools, Jawahar Navodaya Schools, etc. They are managed and controlled completely by the agencies of the central government. Other schools are under state government and local governments. These schools bear the greatest responsibility of educating children from economically and socially backward and vulnerable backgrounds. There are a total of 12.81 lakh government schools and this wide network is credited for the increase in literacy rates across the country.
2. **Government-Aided Private Schools**: These schools are usually managed by charitable trusts and receive partial funding from the government. For example, the Dayanand Anglo-Vedic (DAV) schools are aided by the government. Ten per cent of schools in India are government-aided private schools which number around 2.7 lakh. The curriculum, study materials, syllabus, examinations, etc. for each class of education are done according to the government rules and regulations.
3. **Private Schools (Unaided)**: These schools are owned and controlled by private management. They are still subject to government regulations in aspects of fee structure, curriculum framework and total intake. However, these schools can design their own entrance process, dress code, etc. They can be divided into two types: recognised and unrecognised schools. For government recognition, a private school is required to fulfil a number of conditions. There are a total of 8.89 lakh private schools in India which account for 35.4 per cent of the total schools.
4. **Other Schools**: These schools include Islamic *madrassas*, either autonomous or controlled by state governments, or autonomous schools such as Woodstock School, Sri Aurobindo International Centre of Education, Puducherry; *Patha Bhavan* and *Ananda Marga Gurukula*, etc. These schools have varying levels of control and management and generally follow their own curriculum. There are around 69,000 such schools which constitute 2.8 per cent of all schools in India.

Curriculum Framework: The National Council of Educational Research and Training (NCERT) is the apex institution established in 1961 as a literary, scientific and charitable society under the Societies' Registration Act, 1860. It is autonomous in nature and functions under the Ministry of Education, Government of India. Its main function is to design and support a common system of education and deal with curriculum-related matters of school education, i.e. from pre-primary to higher secondary level. It provides support, guidance and technical assistance to a number of schools in India and oversees many aspects of the enforcement of education policies. It introduced the National Curriculum Framework for School Education in 2005. Apart from this, it also publishes standard textbooks from time to time for the different grades of school education. In many states, curriculum frameworks and textbooks are designed by the respective State Council of Educational Research and Training (SCERT).

School Boards: School boards assess students by conducting exams at various levels, mainly in Class X and Class XII. The examination is based on prescribed syllabus and courses, a predetermined assessment method and an organised schedule. Following are the major school boards in India:

1. **Central Board of Secondary Education (CBSE)**: It is a national-level board of education in India for both public and private schools, controlled and managed by the Ministry of Education. It was established in 1929. The headquarters of CBSE is in New Delhi with 15 regional offices across India. Schools affiliated to CBSE

follow the NCERT curriculum. CBSE conducts exams at Class X, known as the All-India Secondary School Examination (AISSE), and Class XII, known as the All-India Senior School Certificate Examination (AISSCE) at the all-India level. There are several schools outside India, as in Nepal, Yemen, Bangladesh, Japan, etc. affiliated with CBSE.

2. **Council for the Indian School Certificate Examinations (CISCE)**: It is a privately held national-level board of school education in India. It conducts the Indian Certificate of Secondary Education (ICSE), Indian School Certificate (ISC) and the Certificate in Vocational Education (CVE) examination for Class X and Class XII. It was established in 1958. Its headquarter is in New Delhi and almost 2,500 schools are affiliated with CISCE. Its curriculum is considered to be more rigorous than CBSE. The CBSE and CISCE are recognised internationally.

3. **National Institute of Open Schooling (NIOS)**: The NIOS is a national board of education under the Ministry of Education established in 1989. It conducts all Indian examinations at the Secondary and Senior Secondary levels along with courses in Vocational Education, similar to CBSE and CISCE. Its objective is to provide education to all segments of society, especially to students from sections that are unable to attend regular schools. It is the largest open schooling system in the world. NIOS has its own curriculum and the students are provided flexibility in completing their exams.

4. **State Boards of Education**: Most states have their own state boards of secondary school education. Some states like Andhra Pradesh have more than one school board. The boards set the curriculum for school education which varies from state to state. These boards generally have greater local appeal with examinations in regional languages. The curriculum is often less rigorous than CBSE or CISCE. Most of these boards conduct exams at Class X and Class XII levels, but some even conduct at the Class VIII level.

5. **International Baccalaureate (IB)**: It is a privately run multinational academic organisation with headquarters in Geneva, Switzerland. It offers three major programmes: the Primary Programme up to Class V, the Middle Year Programme from Class VI to Class X and the Graduation Programme for Class XI–XII. Schools affiliated under IB are private schools that have dual affiliations, also being affiliated with one of the school education boards in India. The education is costly and meant for the elite and expat class. The main characteristics of this organisation include innovative curriculum, unique teaching methods, emphasis on all-round development and wide global acceptance. The management is shared by international organisations and embassies.

6. **Cambridge International Exams (CIE)**: This board offers globally accredited certificates and conducts examinations that are accepted for entry by universities such as Oxford and Cambridge, Ivy League Universities in the USA, Canada, the European Union, New Zealand, Australia, etc. It is also one of the highly preferred Education Boards in India by the elite and expat classes. The curriculum is less rigorous, promoting creativity and encouraging student understanding outside classrooms. The examinations are conducted at two levels, the AS level and the A level.

7. **Autonomous Schools**: There are a few schools that have their own curriculum and assessment method such as Sri Aurobindo International Centre of Education in Puducherry, Woodstock School and *Ananda Marga Gurukula*.

8. **Islamic *Madrassas***: *Madrassas* are controlled by boards established by local or state governments, or they are affiliated with recognised educational institutions as *Darul Uloom Deoband* or *Nadwtul Ulama*.

School Education in India

Schools: There are a total of 15,09,136 (15 lakh) schools in India, of which 12.5 lakh (83.4 per cent) schools are in rural areas whereas the remaining 2.5 lakh (14.6 per cent) schools are in urban areas. Of these 15 lakh schools, 12.22 lakh (81 per cent) are elementary schools consisting of Class I–VIII, 1.51 lakh (10 per cent) are secondary schools up to Class X and the remaining 1.33 lakh (9 per cent) are higher secondary schools up to Class XII. In terms of management, 68.5 per cent schools are public schools under the management of the government, 28 per cent are either private or government-aided private schools. Of all the schools in India, 97.2 per cent are co-ed schools, meaning that both boys and girls get education in these schools; 1.9 per cent schools are only-girl schools while the remaining 0.9 per cent are schools meant only for boys. In spatial terms, Uttar Pradesh has the highest number of schools among the states with 2,54,352 schools, followed by Madhya Pradesh with 1,33,379 schools. Among the Union Territories, the highest number of schools is in Jammu and Kashmir with 28,863 schools, followed by the National Capital Territory (NCT) of Delhi with 5,669 schools. The state with the least number of schools is Sikkim with 1,277 schools while the union territory with the least number of schools is Lakshadweep with 45 schools (Figure 4.1(a)).

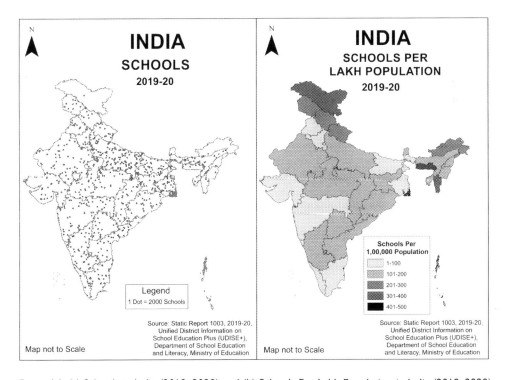

Figure 4.1 (a) Schools in India (2019–2020) and (b) Schools Per Lakh Population in India (2019–2020)

When adjusted for population, the state with the highest number of schools per lakh population is Meghalaya with 438 schools for every 1 lakh people whereas the union territory of Ladakh has the highest 365 schools per lakh population. Among the states and union territories with least number of schools per lakh population, Bihar and Chandigarh rank the lowest with only 72 and 20 schools. All the Himalayan states and the northeastern states have a high number of schools per lakh population. The states in which there are less than 100 schools per lakh population include Bihar, West Bengal, Punjab, Haryana, Gujarat, Maharashtra, Kerala, Tamil Nadu and Goa, some of which such as Bihar are economically backward while others like Gujarat and Tamil Nadu have high industrial development (Figure 4.1(b)).

Students and Teachers: The total number of students in India is 26.45 crore, out of which 12.71 crore (48 per cent) are girls and 13.74 crore (52 per cent) are boys. Thus, there are more boy students than girls, which is in accordance with the sex ratio of India, skewed in favour of males. Fifty-one per cent of the students are enrolled in government schools, whereas the other 49 per cent are in private or government-aided private schools. Nearly three-fourths or 74.3 per cent of the students are in the elementary level, whereas the secondary and higher secondary levels have 15.3 and 10.3 per cent of the students, respectively. When the mean enrolment per school is considered, Chandigarh has the highest number of students per schools at 1,040, followed by Delhi at 737 among the union territories. Kerala has 351 whereas Bihar has 272 students per school. This partly explains the low number of schools per lakh population in these states because the intake per school is very high. On the other hand, Meghalaya and Ladakh have the least number of students per school at just 64 and 44 among the states and union territories, respectively. Thus, there is an inverse relationship between schools per lakh population and mean enrolment per school (Figure 4.2(a)).

There are 96.87 lakh teachers in India, of which females constitute 49.12 lakh (50.7 per cent) while male teachers form the rest 47.71 lakh (49.3 per cent). Thus, female teachers outnumber male teachers in India at the school level. 55.7 per cent (53.97 lakh) teachers teach at the elementary level, 17.2 per cent (16.6 lakh) at the secondary and 27.1 per cent (26.2 lakh) at the higher secondary level. Fifty-one per cent of the total teachers are employed in government schools, while the rest 49 per cent are in private or government-aided private schools. Kerala has the highest number of teachers per school on average with 17 teachers per school among the states, while Chandigarh has the highest 44 teachers per school among the union territories. The least number of teachers per school among the states and union territories is in Meghalaya and Ladakh with four and six teachers per school, respectively (Figure 4.2(a)). However, this small ratio is due to the small number of students per school in these regions. On the other hand, Chandigarh has the highest number of teachers per school because of the high number of students per school. The average number of teachers per school is low in Jharkhand, Madhya Pradesh, Odisha, Chhattisgarh and Andhra Pradesh. These states have substantial tribal areas in which student intake per school is low and the schools are small. This may be the reason why these states have low teacher per school ratio.

Pupil–Teacher Ratio (PTR): The pupil–teacher ratio or the student–teacher ratio is the number of students per teacher. It is calculated by dividing the total number of students by the total number of teachers. PTR for a level of education can be expressed using the following formula:

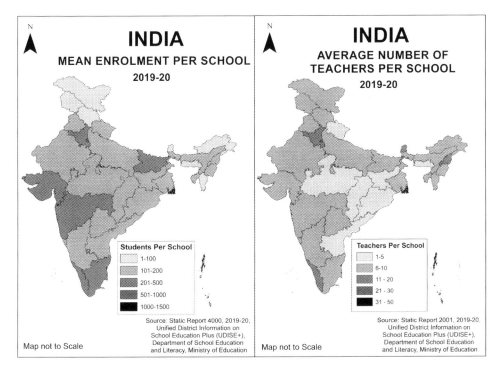

Figure 4.2 (a) Mean Enrolment Per School (2019–2020) and (b) Average Number of Teachers Per School (2019–2020)

$$\text{PTR} = \frac{\text{Number of Enrolled Students}}{\text{Number of Teachers}}$$

This ratio is often considered a good indicator of measuring educational achievement. The New Education Policy 2020 has recommended a pupil–teacher ratio of 30 at the school level. It means that there should be at least one teacher for every 30 students in a school or region. In the elementary school, comprising primary and upper primary levels, a small PTR value is desirable so that teachers can give the required attention to the students, in both academic and other curriculum activities. As the level of education increases, the PTR also increases because in secondary and senior secondary levels, it becomes relatively easier for a teacher to teach a large number of students. A low PTR is often considered as a proxy for higher educational achievement. The PTR at the elementary level is 23 at the all India level. The state and union territories with the lowest PTR are Sikkim, Lakshadweep and Ladakh, each with eight students per teacher. In terms of PTR, Bihar has the highest 38 students per teacher while Delhi has 32 at the elementary level. The mean PTR at the secondary and senior secondary levels for all India is 20. Himachal Pradesh and Lakshadweep have the lowest PTR of 9 and 8, respectively, whereas Bihar has a PTR of 56 and Jharkhand 45 at this level. Dadra and Nagar Haveli and Daman and Diu and the NCT of Delhi, both have the highest PTR among union territories at 23 each (Figure 4.3(a–c)).

104 Education

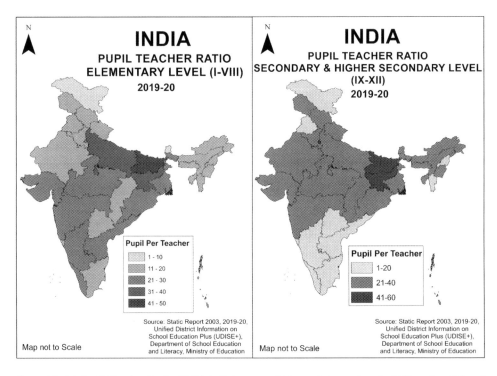

Figure 4.3 (a) Pupil–Teacher Ratio (PTR) in Primary and Upper Primary Level of Education (Class I–VIII) (2019–2020) and (b) Pupil–Teacher Ratio (PTR) in Secondary and Higher Secondary Level of Education (Class IX–XII) (2019–2020)

Schools with WASH Facilities: WASH stands for Water, Sanitation and Hygiene. WASH facilities comprise handwashing facilities, access to toilets and safe drinking water. These are recognised by the United Nations International Children's Fund (UNICEF) as essential to the right of every child to grow up in a clean and hygienic environment. These facilities not only make the school environment healthy but also help to prevent various infectious diseases in school-going children. Seventeen states and union territories have more than 90 per cent school with WASH facilities. The lowest number of schools with WASH facilities are in Meghalaya, having just 19.8 per cent schools and Ladakh with 38.5 per cent such schools. The schools in the Himalayan region have less coverage of WASH facilities in their schools, for example, Arunachal Pradesh, Nagaland, Tripura and Manipur apart from Meghalaya and Ladakh. Andhra Pradesh has only 62.9 per cent schools having WASH facilities. Andaman & Nicobar Islands, Dadra & Nagar Haveli and Daman & Diu, the NCT of Delhi, Tamil Nadu, Chandigarh, Goa, Lakshadweep and Punjab have nearly all of the schools with such facilities. Overall, 82.3 per cent schools in India have coverage of WASH facilities. However, efforts should be made to achieve universal coverage of WASH facilities across all schools (Figure 4.4 (a)).

Schools for CWSN (Children with Special Needs): Schools for CWSN make education inclusive by providing opportunities to disabled children. Such schools have

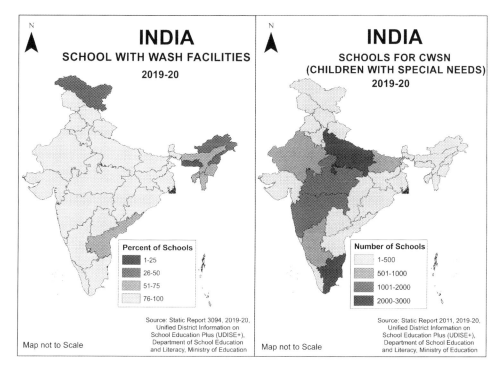

Figure 4.4 (a) Per cent of Schools with WASH Facilities (2019–2020) and (b) Schools for CWSN (Children with Special Needs) (2019–2020)

specially designed curriculum and adopt different pedagogical methods for teaching. The number of schools for CWSN is an indicator of educational achievement and represents equality of opportunity for marginalised and disabled students. Uttar Pradesh and Tamil Nadu have the highest number of schools for CWSN, with 2,409 and 2044 schools, respectively. Andhra Pradesh, Karnataka, Rajasthan and Bihar each have more than 500 such schools. Some states and union territories have no such schools such as Andaman & Nicobar Islands, Goa, Ladakh and Lakshadweep which is due to lack of commercial viability and required demand (Figure 4.1(b)).

Gross Enrolment Ratio (GER): Gross Enrolment Ratio (GER) or the Gross Enrolment Index (GEI) is the ratio of the number of children enrolled in a particular level of education to the total number of children in that age or age-group, expressed in percentage. GER for a level of education can be expressed by the following formula:

$$GER = \frac{Number\ of\ Enrolled\ Students\ in\ a\ level\ of\ Education}{Number\ of\ Children\ in\ the\ corresponding\ age\ group}$$

The age group corresponding to a level of education can be known from Table 4.1. The United Nations Educational, Scientific and Cultural Organisation (UNESCO) has defined GER as the total enrolment within a country in a specific level of education, regardless of age, expressed as a percentage of the population in the official age group corresponding to this level of education. It is used as a statistical indicator of educational achievement. Every level of education corresponds to a particular age group, for example, children between 6 and 14 years of age are in the elementary level, 15–16 years in the secondary level and 17–18 years in the higher secondary level. GER is calculated by dividing the total number of children enrolled at a particular level to the total number of children in the corresponding age group and multiplying it by 100. A GER of 100 means that all the children in a particular age group are enrolled in the corresponding education level; a GER less than 100 means a few children are excluded and not enrolled in schools at the particular level of education where as a GER greater than 100 indicates that there more children enrolled in a particular education level than there are children in the corresponding age group. This is due to the enrolment of overaged or underaged children, for instance, GER can be higher in regions where children begin their education late or dropout and re-enrol due to various reasons. In India, the GER at the elementary level is 97.78 per cent, whereas at the secondary level, it is 77.97 per cent. The GER is higher at the elementary level in India due to various reasons: (i) Article 21A of the Constitution of India has made elementary education a fundamental right of all children aged 6–14 years and made it obligatory for the parents and guardians to ensure that their children receive elementary education, (ii) the Right to Education Act, 2009 and the Sarva Shiksha Abhiyan that operationalised this right had an overwhelming emphasis on free elementary education through government-owned schools and (iii) programmes like the Mid-day Meal scheme have encouraged the poorer sections of the society to enrol their children in schools (Figure 4.5(a)).

In India, the Gross Enrolment Ratio was 97.8 per cent at elementary level; 77.9 per cent at the secondary level; and 51.4 per cent at the higher secondary level in 2019–2020. At the elementary level, Mizoram had the highest GER of 143.5, followed by Nagaland at 124.4 among the states while the NCT of Delhi had the highest GER of 121.3 among the union territories. The least GER at this level was in Madhya Pradesh at 71.1 among states and Lakshadweep at 77.1 among union territories. The GER for males at the elementary level was the highest in Mizoram at 139.3 and the NCT of Delhi at 119.2 while the lowest was 73.1 in Madhya Pradesh and 73.2 in Lakshadweep. The GER for females was the highest in Mizoram at 147.8 and Delhi at 123.7 and the lowest in Madhya Pradesh at 69.1 and Andaman and Nicobar Islands at 80.8. Madhya Pradesh, Bihar, Jharkhand, Odisha and Punjab have more than 10 per cent of students of eligible children not enrolled in schools at the elementary level (Figure 4.5(b)).

At the secondary level, the GER tends to drop due to various reasons. Some children move into the workforce from education for earning, and the number and density of secondary schools reduces, so the increased distance forces some students to dropout, especially among girls. The highest overall GER at the secondary level among states was in Himachal Pradesh at 103.3, followed by Rajasthan at 103.1 and among union territories in Delhi at 110.3. The lowest was in Odisha at 58.14, followed by Bihar at 58.49 among states and in Lakshadweep at 58.23, among union territories. Only Himachal Pradesh, Rajasthan and Delhi have GER greater than 100 at the secondary level. The GER for males at the secondary level is the highest in Himachal Pradesh at

Education 107

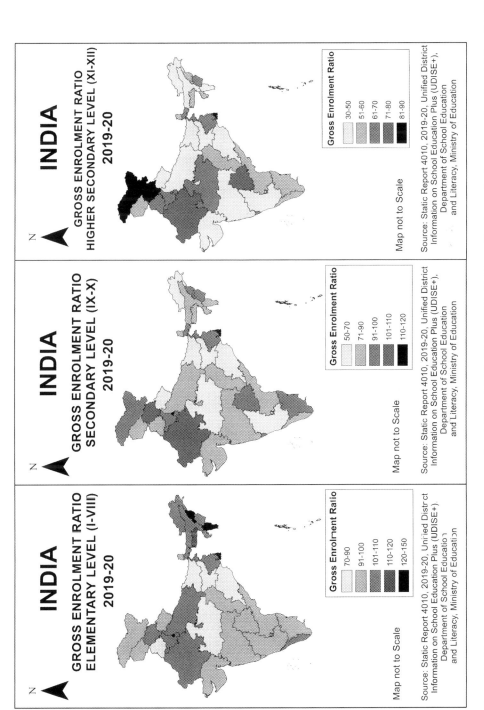

Figure 4.5 (a) Gross Enrolment Ratio at Elementary Level (Class I–VIII) (2019–2020), (b) Gross Enrolment Ratio at Secondary Level (Class IX–X) (2019–2020) and (c) Gross Enrolment Ratio at Higher Secondary Level (Class XI–XII) (2019–2020)

103.24 among states and Delhi at 108.09 among union territories. The lowest is in Odisha at 54.7 and Lakshadweep at 53.67. On the other hand, the GER for females is the highest in Tamil Nadu at 105.33 and Delhi at 112.92, while it is lowest in Jharkhand at 59 and Lakshadweep at 63.1. At the secondary level, Himachal Pradesh, Rajasthan, Tamil Nadu and Delhi have GER for females greater than 100. At the higher secondary level, the GER tends to drop even further. The overall GER at the higher secondary level is in Himachal Pradesh at 83.4 and Ladakh at 83 and lowest in Bihar at 30.8 and Lakshadweep at 39.2. For males, the GER at the higher secondary level is the highest in Himachal Pradesh at 80.3 and Ladakh at 79.1 while it is the lowest in Assam at 30.4 and Lakshadweep at 33.2. For females, it is the highest in Himachal Pradesh at 87 and Ladakh at 87.1 while it is the lowest in Bihar at 31 per cent and Lakshadweep at 45.7 per cent. Bihar, Assam, Jharkhand, Odisha, Uttar Pradesh, Uttarakhand, Arunachal Pradesh, Tripura, Gujarat, Maharashtra and Karnataka have very low GER, less than 50 per cent which means that more than half of the eligible students are not receiving education at this level in these states (Figure 4.5(c)).

Dropout Rate: Dropout rate is defined as the percentage of students who fail to complete a particular level of education. A student who leaves school before the completion of a school stage or leaving at some intermediate or non-terminal point of a given level of education is termed as dropout. The dropout rate increases with the level of education as more students join the workforce or have to leave education due to various socio-economic reasons. The formula for dropout rate, say, at the primary level is:

Dropout Rate at Primary Level

$$= \frac{\text{No. of Students in Class I} - \text{No. of Students in Class V}}{\text{No. of Students in Class I}} * 100$$

The dropout rate can be conveniently measured at three levels, mainly primary, upper primary and secondary levels. It is difficult to measure the dropout rate at the higher secondary level because in the education system in India, the students get scattered across different careers or education domains after this level. In 2019–2020, at the primary level, after Class V, the overall dropout rate is 1.91 per cent whereas for males and females it is 2.15 and 1.68 per cent, respectively. Twelve states and union territories reported zero dropout rate overall including Andhra Pradesh, Chandigarh, Dadra & Nagar Haveli and Daman & Diu, Delhi, Haryana, Kerala, Ladakh, Lakshadweep, Puducherry, Punjab, Sikkim and Telangana, whereas another eight had dropout rate less than 1 per cent that included Maharashtra, Goa, Andaman & Nicobar Islands, West Bengal, Madhya Pradesh, Odisha, Himachal Pradesh and Gujarat. The highest dropout rate was in Manipur at 8.77 per cent and Jammu and Kashmir at 3.91 per cent. For males at the primary level, 12 states and union territories had zero dropout rate while eight had dropout rate less than 1 per cent. For females, at this level, the dropout rate was zero in Andhra Pradesh, Chandigarh, Delhi, Haryana, Kerala, Ladakh, Lakshadweep, Puducherry, Punjab, Sikkim, Telangana and less than 1 per cent in Maharashtra, Dadra & Nagar Haveli and Daman & Diu, Goa, Andaman & Nicobar Islands, West Bengal, Chhattisgarh, Madhya Pradesh, Himachal Pradesh,

Odisha, Tamil Nadu, Gujarat and Karnataka. The highest dropout rate was in Manipur for both males and females. The dropout rate for males is higher than females at the primary level. At the upper primary level, i.e. after Class 8, the overall dropout rate is 2.38 per cent, the male dropout rate is 2.45 per cent while the female dropout rate is 2.38 per cent. Even at the upper primary level, the dropout rate is less for females than males. The overall dropout rate and female dropout rate are the highest in Bihar, whereas the highest male dropout rate is in Meghalaya. 9 states and union territories reported zero dropout rate overall and for females each while 10 reported zero dropout rate for males. At the secondary level, i.e. after Class X, the overall dropout rate was 15.55 per cent, while for males and females, it was 17.01 and 14.01 per cent, respectively. The lowest dropout rate was in Punjab overall as well as for males and females. The highest dropout rate overall was in Arunachal Pradesh at 34.26 per cent, for males in Arunachal Pradesh at 37.64 per cent and for females in Assam at 32.87 per cent (Figure 4.6 (a–c)).

Gender Parity Index (GPI): The Gender Parity Index (GPI) is an indicator of educational achievement that measures the relative access to education of males and females. The formula of GPI at a level of education is:

$$GPI = \frac{Number\ of\ Enrolled\ Female\ Students}{Number\ of\ Enrolled\ Male\ Students}$$

A GPI equal to 1 signifies an equal number of males and females at a level. A GPI less than 1 indicates a fewer number of females compared to males while a GPI greater than 1 signifies gender parity that favours females. The closer GPI is to 1, the closer a country is to achieving equality of access to education between males and females. At the elementary level, the GPI is 1.02, which means that there are 102 female students for every 100 male students. Andhra Pradesh, Haryana, Karnataka, Madhya Pradesh, Sikkim, Lakshadweep, Mizoram, Odisha and Rajasthan have GPI of less than 1, i.e. these states and union territories have lesser females. Twenty-seven states and union territories have parity or higher females than males in the elementary stage. Similarly, the GPI at the secondary level is 1.06. Eight states have fewer females than males including Gujarat, Rajasthan, Madhya Pradesh, Uttar Pradesh, Haryana, Maharashtra, Karnataka and Kerala, whereas the other 28 states and union territories have GPI equal to or higher than 1. At the higher secondary level, GPI is 1.24. Only five states have a lesser number of females compared to males that include Rajasthan, Uttar Pradesh, Gujarat, Manipur, Madhya Pradesh and Maharashtra. Rajasthan and Madhya Pradesh have GPI of less than 1 across all education levels. Hence, GPI is in favour of females at the higher secondary level. The GPI indicates the level of gender parity that most regions have been able to achieve across all levels of school education (Figure 4.7 (a–c)).

Social Profile: At the elementary level, 44.8 per cent of enrolled students are from Other Backward Classes (OBC) category, 25.7 per cent from the unreserved category, 19.2 per cent from the Scheduled Castes (SCs) and 10.4 per cent from the Scheduled Tribes (STs). At the secondary level, the share of respective categories remains the same, with 45.7 per cent students being OBCs, 27.5 per cent unreserved, 18.3 per cent SCs and 9.2 per cent STs. This proportion remains similar at the higher secondary level with 44.8 per cent being OBCs, 30.6 per cent unreserved, 17.3 per cent SCs and

110 Education

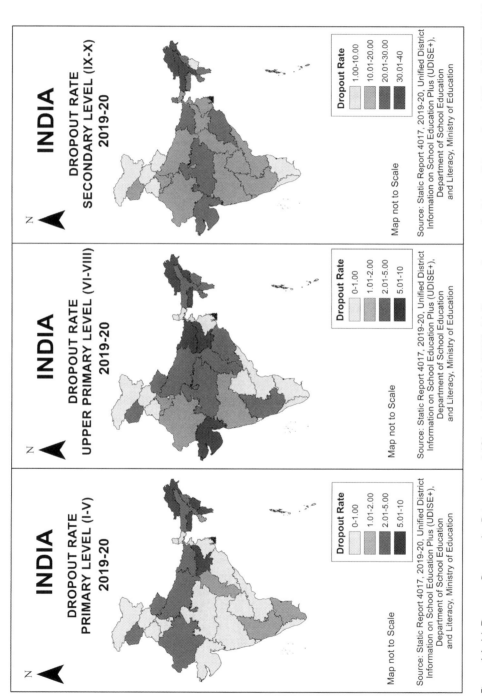

Figure 4.6 (a) Dropout Rate at the Primary Level (Class I–V) (2019–2020), (b) Dropout Rate at the Upper Primary Level (Class VI–VIII) (2019–2020) and (c) Dropout Rate at the Secondary Level (Class IX–X) (2019–2020)

Education 111

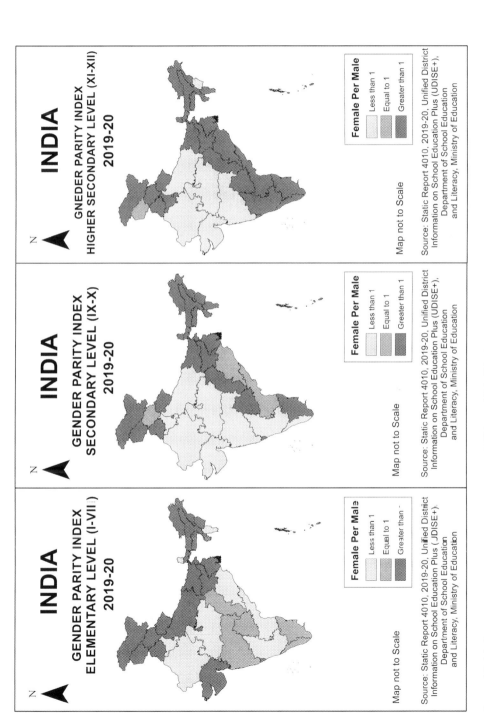

Figure 4.7 (a) Gender Parity Index at Elementary Level (Class I–VIII) (2019–2020), (b) Gender Parity Index at Secondary Level (Class IX–X) (2019–2020) and (c) Gender Parity Index at Higher Secondary Level (Class XI–XII) (2019–2020)

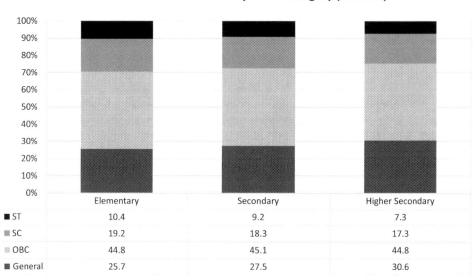

Figure 4.8 Enrolment by Social Category in School Education in India (2019–2020) (Source: Unified District Information on School Education Plus 2019–2020)

7.3 per cent STs. With the progression in school education, the share of SCs and STs in total students reduces consistently, thus, proving the barriers that exist in access to education for the socially disadvantaged groups of SCs and STs (Figure 4.8).

Organisation of Higher Education

After passing the Higher Secondary Examination of Class XII, students enrol in undergraduate programmes for bachelor's degree in arts, commerce or science, or professional courses such as engineering, medicine, nursing, pharmacy, or law. The main governing body at the tertiary level is the University Grants Commission (UGC) whose function is to enforce standards and advise the government on matters related to higher education. Accreditation for higher learning is overseen by several autonomous institutions established by the University Grants Commission.

Regulatory Bodies

1. **University Grants Commission (UGC):** UGC is a statutory body set up under the University Grants Commission (UGC) Act, 1956 under the administrative control of the Department of Higher Education, Ministry of Education. Its headquarters are in New Delhi, and it has six regional centres. The main functions of UGC are to determine and maintain standards of teaching, examination and research in universities, frame regulations on minimum standards of education, monitor developments in the field of college and university education, and disburse grants

to the universities and colleges. The New Education Policy 2020 has proposed to replace it with a new regulatory body Higher Education Commission of India (HECI). UGC grants recognition to universities and disburses funds as well as doctoral scholarships. The National Accreditation and Assessment Council (NAAC) functioning under the aegis of UGC assesses universities and colleges based on an alphabetical ranking system.

2. **All India Council for Technical Education (AICTE)**: AICTE is a statutory body established under All India Council for Technical Education (AICTE) Act, 1987 of the Parliament of India. It functions under the administrative control of the Department of Higher Education, Ministry of Education. It is headquartered in New Delhi with 12 regional offices. The main role of AICTE is planning, formulation and maintenance of norms and standards, quality assurance through school accreditation, funding in priority areas, monitoring and evaluation, maintaining parity of certification and awards and ensuring coordinated and integrated development and management of technical education in the country.

3. **National Council for Teacher Education (NCTE)**: NCTE is a statutory body set up under the National Council for Teacher Education Act, 1993 of the Parliament of India. It functions under the administrative control of the Department of Higher Education, Ministry of Education. Its main function is to regulate standards, procedures, qualifications and processes relating to teacher education and Teacher Training Institutes in India.

4. **Distance Education Bureau (DEB)**: DEB is a bureau of the University Grants Commission (UGC) based in New Delhi, in charge of regulating distance education in India. It is responsible for the promotion and coordination of open and distance learning (ODL) in India.

5. **National Medical Commission (NMC)**: NMC is a regulatory body that regulates medical education and medical professionals set up under National Medical Commission Act, 2019. It replaced the Medical Council of India in 2020. The commission is comprised of 33 members and four autonomous boards: (1) Undergraduate Medical Education Board (UGMEB), (2) Post-Graduate Medical Education Board (PGMEB), (3) Medical Assessment and Rating Board and (4) Ethics and Medical Registration Board that serve various functions as granting recognition to medical qualifications, providing accreditation to medical schools, granting registration to medical practitioners, and monitoring medical practice and carrying out the assessment of medical infrastructure in India.

Types of Universities: The higher education system in India includes both private and public universities. Public universities are controlled, funded and managed by the central and state governments while private universities are mostly under various bodies, corporations or societies. University Grants Commission (UGC) grants recognition to the universities in India. There are 1,043 universities in India as reported in the All-India Survey of Higher Education (AISHE) 2019–2020. Among 1,043 universities, 408 universities are privately managed while 736 are under government control. Seven hundred twenty-three universities are in urban areas while the remaining 420 universities are located in rural areas. 17 universities are exclusively for women. The AISHE released by the Department of Higher Education, Ministry of Education uses 'university' as an umbrella term for 13 types of institutions namely: (1) Central

University, (2) Central Open University, (3) Institute of National Importance, (4) State Public University, (5) Institutes established under acts of State Legislature, (6) State Open University, (7) State Private University, (8) State Private Open University, (9) Government Deemed University, (10) Government-Aided Deemed University and (11) Private Deemed University. Some of the important types of universities are as follows:

1. **Central Universities**: These are established by an Act of Parliament and are under the purview of the Department of Higher Education in the Union Education Ministry and granted recognition by UGC. They are also regulated by the Central Universities Act, 2009, which lays down norms related to purpose, powers, governance, etc. Most of these universities and their affiliated colleges offer a full range of courses from the undergraduate to the doctorate level. There are 54 central universities in India. Most of the universities have affiliated colleges.
2. **State Universities**: They are established by an act of the State Legislature and are managed and controlled by the state government agencies. These universities are also affiliating universities because they have a large number of affiliated colleges, mainly located in small towns and cities that serve as the backbone of higher education in India. They generally offer undergraduate and post-graduate courses. There are 426 state universities in India.
3. **Private Universities**: These are established by non-government institutions such as trusts, societies or corporations. They are granted recognition by the UGC and regulated as per the UGC (Establishment and Maintenance of Standards in Private Universities) Regulations, 2003. UGC approval is necessary for recognition as a private university. They can grant degrees but are not allowed to have affiliated colleges off the campus. There are 397 private universities in India.
4. **Deemed University or Deemed-to-be-University**: It is an accreditation granted to a higher educational institution in India by the Department of Higher Education, Ministry of Education. An Institution of Higher Education, other than universities, working at a very high standard in a specific area of study, can be declared by the Central Government on the advice of the University Grants Commission (UGC), as an Institution 'Deemed-to-be-university'. These institutions have the academic status and privileges of a university. However, they cannot affiliate with colleges and are not officially termed as 'universities'.
5. **Open Universities**: These universities are set up by acts of Parliament at the central level or by the state legislatures at the state level and are granted recognition by UGC. These universities follow the distance mode of education in which the students do not have to attend classes regularly but only appear for exams and assessments.
6. **Institute of National Importance (INI)**: It is a status that is conferred on a premier higher education public institution by an act of the Parliament of India. These institutions receive special recognition, greater autonomy and funding from the government. There are 161 Institutes of National Importance which include Indian Institutes of Technology (IITs), the National Institute of Design (NID), the All India Institute of Medical Sciences (AIIMS), etc.
7. **Autonomous Institutes**: These are institutes established by acts of the Parliament and have considerable autonomy in deciding their curriculum, course structure, fees, entrance process, etc. They do not affiliate with colleges and are not officially

Education 115

referred to as 'universities'. They are called autonomous institutes and are under the control of the Department of Higher Education, Ministry of Education. Autonomous institutes include the Indian Institutes of Technology (IITs), the National Institutes of Technology (NITs), the Indian Institutes of Science Education and Research (IISER), the Indian Institutes of Management (IIM), the All India Institute of Medical Sciences (AIIMS), etc.

8. **Institute under State Legislature Act**: These are institutions established by an act of the State Legislature. These institutes receive the academic status and privileges of state universities.

Higher Education in India

Universities: Rajasthan has the highest number of universities at 89 followed by Uttar Pradesh at 81 and Gujarat at 76. Goa, Mizoram, Puducherry, Tripura, Nagaland, Manipur, Sikkim, Arunachal Pradesh and Meghalaya, Chandigarh all have 10 or fewer universities. The union territory of Ladakh has one central university established recently. Andaman & Nicobar Islands, Dadra & Nagar Haveli and Daman & Diu and Lakshadweep have no university. The NCT of Delhi has 28 universities. States with large population but small number of universities are Bihar, Jharkhand, West Bengal and Odisha (Figure 4.9(a)).

Colleges: There are 42,343 colleges in India. Most of the colleges run only undergraduate-level programmes. Only about 2.7 per cent of colleges run doctorate-level

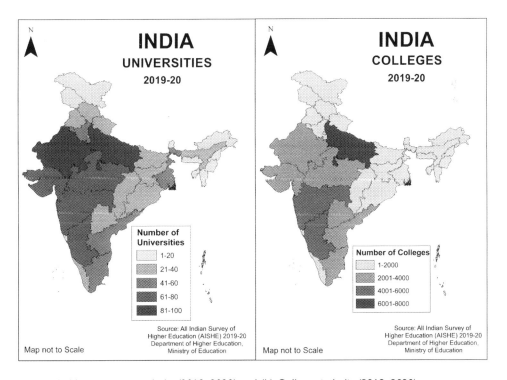

Figure 4.9 (a) Universities in India (2019–2020) and (b) Colleges in India (2019–2020)

programmes and 35.04 per cent of colleges run post-graduate-level programmes. 32.6 per cent colleges, which run only single programme, of which 84.1 per cent are privately managed colleges. Among the privately managed colleges, 37.4 per cent colleges run Bachelors of Education (B.Ed) courses for teachers. Uttar Pradesh has the largest number of colleges at 7,788, followed by Maharashtra with 4,494 and Karnataka with 4,047 colleges. Lakshadweep, Ladakh and Andaman & Nicobar Islands have fewer than ten colleges. Just five states Uttar Pradesh, Maharashtra, Karnataka, Rajasthan and Andhra Pradesh have more than 50 per cent of the total colleges in India (Figure 4.9(b)). Sikkim, Chandigarh, Mizoram, Arunachal Pradesh, Tripura, Goa, Meghalaya, Nagaland and Puducherry have less than 100 colleges. Punjab, Haryana, Odisha, West Bengal and Kerala have 1,000–2,000 colleges (Table 4.2).

More than one-fifth of the districts have less than ten colleges. 80.7 per cent districts have less than 100 colleges. Only Bangalore has more than 1,000 colleges. The districts with the highest number of colleges are (1) Bengaluru Urban (1,009 colleges), (2) Jaipur (606), (3) Hyderabad (482), (4) Pune (467) and (5) Prayagraj (363). According to the nature of **Management,** the majority of the colleges, around 65.2 per cent are private colleges; 13.4 per cent are private aided; and the remaining 21.4 per cent are government colleges. As per the size of colleges, the majority of colleges are smaller in terms of enrolment. In terms of enrolment per college, 16.6 per cent of the colleges have enrolment of less than 100 students and 48.9 per cent of the colleges have student strength of 100–500, which means 65.5 per cent of the colleges enrol less than 500 students. Only 4 per cent of Colleges have enrolment more than 3,000. Nearly one-third of the colleges have enrolment less than 200 students. 81.8 per cent of the colleges have less than 1,000 students enrolled. 16.6 per cent of the colleges are very small and have fewer than 100 students enrolled. A majority of the colleges have less than 500 students. Just about 8 per cent of the colleges have more than 2000 students (Table 4.3).

Stand-Alone Institutions: There are 11,779 Stand-Alone Institutions which are categorised into seven categories as described below:

Table 4.2 Number of Colleges in Districts

Number of Colleges	Districts	Per Cent of Total Colleges	Cumulative Per Cent
1–10	149	21.3	21.3
11–19	95	13.6	34.9
21–49	186	26.6	61.5
51–99	134	19.2	80.7
101–199	97	13.9	94.6
201–299	28	4.0	98.6
301–399	6	0.9	99.4
401–499	2	0.3	99.7
501–999	1	0.1	99.9
More than 1,000	1	0.1	100.0
Total	699	100	100.0

Source: All India Survey of Higher Education 2019–2020.

Table 4.3 Enrolment in Colleges

College Enrolment	Number of Colleges	Per Cent	Cumulative Per Cent
0–50	2,795	7.0	7
51–100	3,821	9.6	16.6
101–200	8,032	20.1	36.7
201–500	11,506	28.8	65.5
501–1,000	6,520	16.3	81.8
1,001–2,000	4,138	10.4	92.1
2,001–3,000	1,553	3.9	96
>3,000	1,590	4.0	100
Total	39955	–	–

Source: All India Survey of Higher Education 2019–2020.

1. **Type I** – Diploma Level Technical Institutes: These include Polytechnics, which are generally recognised by the All India Council for Technical Education (AICTE) and administered by the State Directorate of Technical Education.
2. **Type II** – Diploma Level Teacher Training Institutes: These include the District Institute of Education and Training (DIETs) recognised by the National Council for Teacher Education (NCTE) and generally administered by the State Council for Education Research and Training (SCERT).
3. **Type III** – Diploma Level Nursing Institutes recognised by Indian Nursing Council (INC) and generally administered by State Nursing Council/Boards.
4. **Type IV** – Post Graduate Diploma in Management (PGDM) Institutes: They are recognised by AICTE.
5. **Type V** – Institutes directly under the control of various Central Ministries
6. **Type VI** – Paramedical Institutes
7. **Type VII** – Hotel Management & Catering Institutes

Only 23.8 per cent stand-alone institutions are in public sector while majority of them are under private management. 56.1 per cent stand-alone Institutions are located in rural areas.

Gross Enrolment: In higher education, the highest number of students are enrolled at the undergraduate level across India. Out of the total enrolment of 3,85,36,359 students, a vast majority of 3.06 crore students are undergraduates constituting 79.5 per cent of the total enrolment. 11.2 per cent of students in higher education are enrolled in post-graduation, approximately 43.1 lakh students. There are 2.02 lakh students who are enrolled at the doctorate or PhD level. In terms of Programme-wise enrolment, ten programmes cover more than 79 per cent of the total students enrolled in higher education. Bachelor of Arts (BA) has 96.55 lakh students enrolled in it which is the highest enrolment. The percentage share of students enrolled in BA programme is 47.1 per cent for male and 52.9 per cent for female. Bachelor of Science (B.Sc) has 47.07 lakh students enrolled in total and out of them 47.7 per cent are male students and 52.3 per cent are female students. There are 41.6 lakh students enrolled in B.Com. and out of them 51.2 per cent are male and 48.8 per cent are female. B.Tech. has 21.48 lakh enrolled students out of which 71.5 per cent are male, whereas the percentage of female is 28.5 per cent. Bachelor of Engineering (BE) has 14.9 lakh students enrolled out of which 71 per cent students are males. Master of Arts (MA) has 16.02 lakh total number of students enrolled with 62.3 per cent female students. BA (Hons) has 17.7 lakh students with 43.8 per cent male and 56.2 per cent female students. B.Ed has a total number of 13.7 lakh students and out of them 66 per cent are females. M.Sc. has a total number of 7.84 lakh students with 37.5 per cent male and 62.5 per cent female. MBA has a total number of 6.09 lakh students with 57.4 per cent male students. B.Sc. (Hons) has a total number of 6.40 lakh students with 54.8 per cent male students. In terms of state-share of enrolment, Maharashtra tops in the enrolment of students in universities (including constituent units) with 9,67,034 students. This is followed by Tamil Nadu with 9,26,490 students and Delhi with 8,16,110 students. There are 92,831 PWD (Persons with Disabilities) students enrolled in higher education out of which 47,830 are male and 45,001 are female students.

Pupil–Teacher Ratio (PTR): PTR is considered to be an indicator of educational achievement. Generally, higher the PTR, lower the quality of education. Puducherry has the best PTR in higher education with 13 students for every teacher among union territories and while among the states Karnataka and Goa have only 15 students for every teacher. Jharkhand has a PTR of 60, followed by Bihar with 59, Delhi 52, Uttar Pradesh 40. In these states and union territories, there is a greater burden of students per teacher. Andhra Pradesh, Kerala, Nagaland, Mizoram, Punjab, Tamil Nadu and Telangana have a PTR below 20 (Figure 4.10(a)).

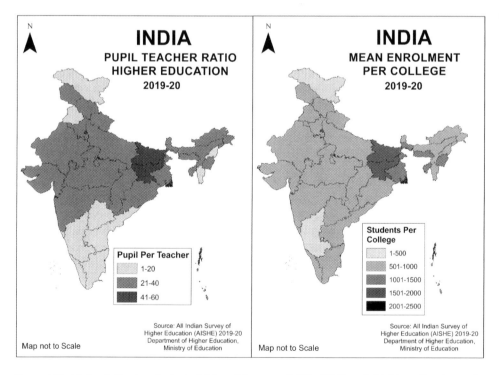

Figure 4.10 (a) Pupil–Teacher Ratio in Higher Education (2019–2020) and (b) Mean Enrolment Per College (2019–2020)

Mean Enrolment Per College: Ladakh and Karnataka with 480 and 415 students per college have the lowest enrolment per college among union territories and states. Chandigarh with 2022 students per college and Jharkhand with 1938 students per college have the highest mean enrolment. Bihar, Delhi, West Bengal, Tripura, Meghalaya and Manipur have on average more than 1,000 students per college. 28 states and union territories have less than 1,000 students per college on average (Fig 4.10(b)).

Gross Enrolment Ratio: In higher education, the estimated Gross Enrolment Ratio (GER) in Higher education in India is 29.5 per cent, calculated for 18–23 years of age group. GER for the male population at the all-India level is 28.5 per cent, whereas for female population it is 30.9 per cent. The highest GER among states is in Sikkim overall and for both male and female categories. The lowest overall GER is in Lakshadweep at 7.5, for males and for females in Ladakh at 3.6 and 11.3, respectively. Chandigarh, Tamil Nadu, Delhi, Puducherry and Uttarakhand have GER higher than 40, which means that more than 40 per cent of eligible students are enrolled in higher education in these regions. Overall, West Bengal, Chhattisgarh, Nagaland, Assam and Bihar have GER between 10 and 20 per cent and Ladakh, Dadra & Nagar Haveli and Daman & Diu and Lakshadweep have GER less than 10 per cent. For males, Sikkim has GER of 83.8 followed by Tamil Nadu with 51.1. Only Delhi, Chandigarh, Puducherry and Uttarakhand have GER higher than 40 while Andaman & Nicobar Islands, Assam, Chhattisgarh, Nagaland, Bihar, Dadra & Nagar Haveli and Daman & Diu, Ladakh and Lakshadweep have very low GER for males less than 20. For females, the highest GER is in Sikkim at 67.6 per cent, followed by Chandigarh at 65.6 per cent and Puducherry at 52.6 per cent. Apart from these, Delhi, Tamil Nadu, Himachal Pradesh, Kerala and Uttarakhand have GER higher than 40 per cent. Chhattisgarh, Gujarat, West Bengal, Tripura, Assam, Bihar, Dadra & Nagar Haveli and Daman & Diu, Lakshadweep and Ladakh have female GER less than 20 per cent (Figure 4.11(a)).

Gender Parity Index: Female participation in higher education for all groups is 101 females per 100 males. Overall, the GPI is 1.1. The highest GPI is in Lakshadweep at 3.2, Ladakh at 2.3 and Dadra & Nagar Haveli and Daman & Diu at 2.2. The state with the highest GPI is Goa with 1.5. The lowest GPI is in Tripura at 0.80, Sikkim at 0.81 and Bihar at 0.83. States that have GPI less than 1 include Assam, Tamil Nadu, Rajasthan, West Bengal, Arunachal Pradesh, Maharashtra, Mizoram, Odisha, Gujarat and Andhra Pradesh. The percentage of male students in higher education is higher than females in almost every level, except MPhil, Post-Graduate and Certificate. Student enrolment at Under Graduate level has 50.8 per cent males and 49.2 per cent females. PhD level has 55 per cent males and 45 per cent females (Figure 4.11(b)).

Social Profile: In higher education, in the overall category, nearly 42.7 per cent students are from unreserved (UR) category, 37 per cent are from the Other Backward Classes (OBC), 14.7 per cent from the Scheduled Castes (SCs) and 5.6 per cent from the Scheduled Tribes (STs). Similar distribution exists along the male and female categories (Figure 4.12).

National Education Mission: National Education Mission or the *Samagra Shiksha Abhiyan* was launched in 2018 for the development of school education from the pre-primary to the higher secondary level. Its main objective is to improve school effectiveness measured via equal opportunities and equitable learning outcomes. It has four components, namely (1) *Saakshar Bharat* (Literate India), (2) *Sarva Shiksha Abhiyan*,

120 Education

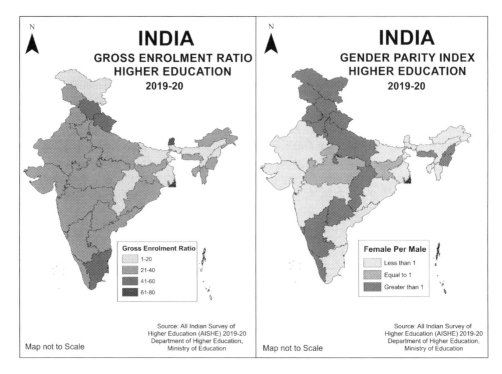

Figure 4.11 (a) Gross Enrolment Ratio in Higher Education (2019–2020), (b) Gender Parity Index in Higher Education (2019–2020)

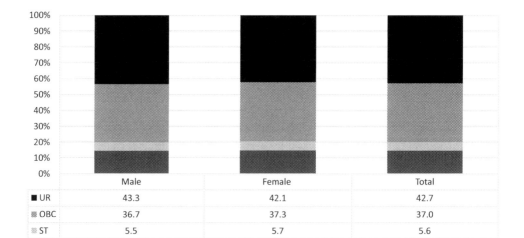

Figure 4.12 Male, Female and Total Enrolment by Social Category in Higher Education in India (2019–2020)

(3) *Rashtriya Madhyamik Shiksha Abhiyan* and (4) Centrally Sponsored Scheme on Teacher Education (CSSTE). The mission covers 11.6 lakh schools, over 15.6 crore students and 57 lakh teachers of the government and government-aided schools. Some of the major characteristics of this mission are a holistic approach to education, integrated administration, enhanced funding for education, emphasis on the improvement of learning outcomes, enhanced capacity building of teachers, focus on strengthening teacher education institutions, focus on digital education through the provision of Information and Communication Technology (ICT) labs, smart classrooms including support for digital boards, increased allocation for school infrastructure, specific provisions for *swachhta* (cleanliness) activities and maintaining *swachh vidyalaya* (clean schools), focus on girl education, allocation for uniforms, textbooks, etc. under RTE act, strengthening of vocational education at the secondary level as an integral part of the curriculum, focus on sports and physical education and promotion of balanced educational development of students.

Education Policy in India

(1) **National Education Policy (1968)**: This policy was introduced during the Prime Ministership of Mrs Indira Gandhi, based on the report of the Kothari Commission (1964–1966). It called for a 'radical restructuring' of the education system. It suggested equal educational opportunities for cultural and economic development and achieving national integration and unity. It emphasised on the implementation of the Directive Principle listed in Article 45 of the Constitution which directs the state to endeavour to provide free and compulsory primary education to all children up to the age of 14 years, with special emphasis and provisions for socially and educationally backward classes, minority children, girls and the children with special needs. It also recommended a greater focus on specialised training and qualification of teachers along with greater academic freedom to them for writing and speaking on national and international issues. The policy introduced the 'three-language formula' as a part of the secondary education curriculum whereby the students were to receive instruction in three languages that would include the English language, the official language of the state, and Hindi, to promote unity in the form of a pan-India lingua franca. The policy introduced the uniform educational structure in the 10+2+3 pattern encompassing elementary and secondary (Class I–X), higher secondary (Class XI–XII) and college level (three-year undergraduate programme) education. It recommended that the government should review the progress of education in the country from time to time and make provisions for future development (Ayyar, 2017).

(2) **National Education Policy (1986)**: This policy was introduced during the tenure of Rajiv Gandhi as the Prime Minister. The special emphasis of this policy was to remove disparities and equalise educational opportunities, especially for women, Scheduled Castes (SCs) and the Scheduled Tribes (STs) in India. It suggested several measures for the achievement of social integration through education, which included expanding scholarships, adult education, recruitment of more teachers from disadvantaged backgrounds, incentives for poor families to enable the education of their children, development of new institutions, etc. This policy adopted the welfare approach to education. With a child-centred

focus, 'Operation Blackboard' was launched to improve primary education across the nation. The Indira Gandhi National Open University (IGNOU) was launched in 1985 to provide benefits of university education through distance learning mode. The policy suggested establishing rural universities following the Gandhian approach to education and promoting socio-economic development at the grassroots level. It recommended expenditure on education to be 6 per cent of the Gross Domestic Product (GDP). This policy was modified with the National Policy on Education (1992) that mandated a common entrance examination for admission to professional and technical programmes on all India basis following which the Joint Entrance Examination (JEE) and the All India Engineering Entrance Examination (AIEEE) were introduced for engineering courses.

(3) **National Education Policy (2020)**: The New Education Policy (NEP) was introduced in 2020 to provide a comprehensive framework for education as well as vocational training in both rural and urban India. It is aligned with the 2030 Agenda for Sustainable Development and aims to transform the education system of India by 2040 (Aithal & Aithal, 2020).

Vision: The NEP 2020 'envisions an India-centric education system that contributes directly to transforming our nation sustainably into an equitable and vibrant knowledge society by providing high-quality education to all'.

Foundational Pillars: The NEP is built on the five foundational pillars of (1) Access, (2) Equity, (3) Quality, (4) Affordability and (5) Accountability.

Expenditure on Education: NEP has recommended increasing public expenditure on education from around 3 per cent at the present to 6 per cent of the GDP, as suggested by the earlier policies.

Language Policy: NEP has suggested educational instruction up to Class V in the mother tongue or local language and recommended continuing it till Class VIII and beyond. Special emphasis has been given on teaching of Sanskrit and foreign languages. The three languages should be the choices of states, regions and students, as long as at least two of the three languages are native to India.

Recommendations of the NEP 2020 School Education

- **School Structure:** NEP has recommended replacing the 10 + 2 school structure with a new pedagogical and curricular restructuring of 5+3+3+4 model between ages 3–18. Currently, children in the age group of 3–6 are not covered in the 10+2 structure as Class I begins at age 6. In the new 5+3+3+4 structure, a strong base of Early Childhood Care and Education (ECCE) from age 3 is also included, which is aimed at promoting better overall learning, development and well-being. This 5+3+3+4 structure is as follows:
    1) **Foundational Stage**: This stage is of 5 years subdivided into two levels: (a) three years of pre-primary schooling or *Anganwadi*, followed by (b) two years of primary school (Class I–II). This will cover children in the age of 3–8 years and the emphasis will be on activity-based learning.
    2) **Preparatory Stage**: This stage will be of three years from Class III to Class V, in the age of 8–11 years. In this stage, subjects and skills of reading, writing,

speaking, physical education, languages, art, science and mathematics will be introduced.
3) **Middle Stage**: This stage will also be of three years from Class VI to Class VIII, for children aged between 11 and 14 years. Abstract concepts in subjects such as of mathematics, sciences, social sciences, arts and humanities will be taught at this stage.
4) **Secondary Stage**: This will be the final stage of schooling, from Class IX to Class XII, covering students aged between 14 and 18 years. There are two stages: (a) secondary level of Class IX and Class X and (b) higher secondary level of Class XI and Class XII. This stage will have multidisciplinary courses along with in-depth and critical thinking. The stream-wise distinction of humanities, science and commerce will be replaced with multidisciplinary courses, even combining vocational and academic courses, that can be chosen by the students. Thus, students will be provided with increased flexibility and a wider choice of subjects.

- **Early Childhood Care and Education (ECCE)**: NEP has laid great emphasis on ECCE which will be provided through the network of *Anganwadis* and pre-schools that will have teachers and *Anganwadi* workers trained in the ECCE pedagogy and curriculum. The planning and implementation of ECCE will be through inter-ministerial effort of the Ministries of Education, Women and Child Development (WCD), Health and Family Welfare (HFW), and Tribal Affairs. In this regard, NCERT is required to develop a National Curricular and Pedagogical Framework for Early Childhood Care and Education (NCPFECCE).
- **Foundational Literacy and Numeracy (FLN)**: NEP has called for the setting up of a National Mission on Foundational Literacy and Numeracy. In this regard, the Ministry of Education has launched the National Initiative for Proficiency in Reading with Understanding and Numeracy (NIPUN Bharat) programme, for ensuring that every child in the country attains foundational literacy and numeracy (FLN) by the end of Grade 3, by 2026–2027.
- **School Curriculum**: NEP has called for reformation in the school curricula and pedagogy for the holistic development of students by teaching them key skills required for the 21st century, reduction in the volume of curricular content, enhancement of critical thinking and greater emphasis on experience-based learning. The rigid distinction between streams of humanities, arts, sciences and commerce and between curricular and extra-curricular activities will be done away with. NEP has recommended vocational education and internships to start from Class VI. In this regard, the National Curricular Framework for School Education (NCFSE) will be developed by the NCERT.
- **Assessment Reforms**: NEP has called for the replacement of the present summative assessment method with regular and formative assessment. This assessment is to be based on competency, learning and development which should test higher-order skills as analysis, critical thinking and conceptual clarity. NEP has recommended mandatory examinations for all students at three stages in Class III, Class V and Class VIII to be conducted by the appropriate authority. The policy has recommended the continuation of the Board exams in Class X and Class XII but with substantial redesigning. All students will be allowed to take

the board exam twice if unable to clear it in the first instance. In this regard, a new National Assessment Centre, PARAKH (Performance Assessment, Review, and Analysis of Knowledge for Holistic Development) will be set up for prescribing related standards.

- **Equity and Inclusion**: Greater emphasis is given to Socially and Economically Disadvantaged Groups (SEDGs) which can be social groups based on gender, caste, religion, geographical identities or disabilities for providing them equal opportunities and making education inclusive. In this regard, NEP has recommended establishing Gender Inclusion Fund and Special Education Zones for disadvantaged and backward regions and groups. This policy has suggested universalisation of education from preschool to secondary level by extending The Right of Children to Free and Compulsory Education (RTE) Act, 2009, for children between 3 and 18 years. Children with benchmark disabilities should have the choice of regular or special schooling.
- **Teacher Recruitment and Career Path**: NEP has called for teachers to be recruited through robust, regular and transparent processes and promotions to be based on merit and periodic performance appraisals. By 2030, the four-year integrated B.Ed programme will be the minimum qualification for teaching. In this regard, a new and comprehensive National Curriculum Framework for Teacher Education (NCFTE) 2021 will be formulated by the National Council for Teacher Education (NCTE) in consultation with NCERT.
- **School Governance**: NEP has suggested schools to be organised into clusters for governance and to ensure the availability of resources such as infrastructure, academic libraries, professional teacher community etc.
- **Standard Setting and Accreditation for School Education**: NEP has suggested establishing State School Standards Authority (SSSA) for policy making, regulation, operations and academic matters of schools. In this regard, the SCERT will develop a School Quality Assessment and Accreditation Framework (SQAAF) through consultations with the stakeholders.
- **Scholarships**: All scholarships and other opportunities and schemes available to students from SEDGs will be coordinated and announced by a single agency and website to ensure that all students are aware of, and may apply in a simplified manner on such a 'single window system', as per eligibility.

Higher Education

- **Increase GER to 50 per cent by 2035**: NEP aims to increase the Gross Enrolment Ratio (GER) in higher education, including vocational education to 50 per cent by 2035. The policy has recommended the addition of 3.5 crore new seats in Higher Education Institutions (HEIs).
- **Multiple Entry Exit System**: The policy envisions multidisciplinary, holistic higher education with flexible curricula providing flexibility in the choice of subjects and integration of academic with vocational education. The Multiple Entry-Exit System has been proposed for greater convenience and flexibility for students. The undergraduate education has been proposed to be of three to four years with permissible exit options after every year. Students will get the following recognition corresponding to the exit at different stages: (1) Certificate after one year,

(2) Advanced Diploma after two years, (3) Bachelor's degree after three years and (4) Bachelor's with research after four years.
- **Abolition of M.Phil**: NEP has recommended the abolition of the Masters of Philosophy (M.Phil) programme of research. Research will be conducted only through the Doctor of Philosophy (PhD) programme which will be interdisciplinary in nature.
- **Academic Bank of Credit**: NEP has suggested establishing an Academic Bank of Credit to be established for digitally storing academic credits earned from education in different HEIs. These credits will be transferable and will count towards the attainment of the final degree.
- **Multidisciplinary Education and Research Universities (MERUs)**: NEP has recommended setting up of Multidisciplinary Education and Research Universities (MERUs) as models of premier multidisciplinary education institutions adhering to global standards.
- **National Research Foundation (NRF)**: NEP has suggested establishing a National Research Foundation (NRF) as an apex body for fostering a strong research culture and capacity building of research across higher education.
- **Regulation**: For regulation of higher education, Higher Education Commission of India (HECI) will be set up as a single overarching umbrella body. Its scope will be regulation of the entire higher education, excluding medical and legal education. HECI will be comprised of four independent institutions: (1) National Higher Education Regulatory Council (NHERC) for regulation, (2) General Education Council (GEC) for standard setting, (3) Higher Education Grants Council (HEGC) for funding, and (4) National Accreditation Council (NAC) for accreditation of HEIs.
- **Rationalisation of Higher Education Institutions**: NEP has suggested that the definition of university should include a spectrum of institutions from Research-intensive Universities to Teaching-intensive Universities and Autonomous degree-granting Colleges. The process of affiliation of colleges will be phased out in 15 years and they would be granted graded autonomy. Ultimately, every college should be classified into either of the two categories, (1) autonomous degree-granting college, or (2) a constituent college of a university.
- **National Mentoring Mission**: NEP has suggested establishing a National Mission for Mentoring consisting of senior or retired faculties with the ability to teach in Indian languages to provide mentorship to college teachers.
- **Open and Distance Learning**: NEP has suggested the greater utilisation and application of online courses, digital libraries, improved student services, credit-based recognition of Massive Online Open Courses (MOOCs), etc. for strengthening distance learning.
- **Online and Digital Education**: In the wake of the Covid-19 pandemic, NEP has recommended the promotion of online education for ensuring access to quality education when traditional and in-person education is not possible. The Ministry of Education should create a specialised agency for building digital infrastructure and online content to cater to the e-education needs of students. The Government of India announced the setting up of a digital university to make education accessible.
- **Technology in Education**: NEP has recommended setting up of an autonomous body in the form of the National Educational Technology Forum (NETF) for the

use of technology to enhance learning, assessment, planning and administration. Classroom teaching should be adequately supplemented with technological tools. Technology in education should be used to enhance educational access for disadvantaged social groups.
- **Collaboration with International Institutions**: Education should be internationalised through institutional collaborations, and student and faculty mobility. Foreign universities should be allowed to set up campuses in India.
- **Professional Education**: Professional education will be an integral part of the higher education curriculum. Specialised stand-alone technical universities along with health science, legal and agricultural universities should aim to become multidisciplinary institutions.
- **Adult Education**: NEP aims to achieve 100 per cent youth and adult literacy.
- **National Entrance Test**: NEP has recommended for a single university exam to be conducted under the aegis of National Testing Agency (NTA). Students will be relieved of appearing for different entrance exams of different universities.

Expenditure on Education

The National Education Policy, 2020 (NEP) has recommended public expenditure on education to be 6 per cent of GDP. In 2020–2021, according to the budget estimates, the combined expenditure on education by the central and all state governments was 6,75,000 crores. This amounted to 3.5 per cent of the GDP. In the last five budget years, the total expenditure on education has grown steadily although not in accordance with the rate of GDP growth. The expenditure on education as a percentage of the GDP has remained almost constant at around 3 per cent. This is just half of the expenditure recommended by the National Education Policy in 1968 as well as the most recent policy in 2020. The expenditure on education as a per cent of total expenditure has also hovered only around 10 per cent (Table 4.4, Figure 4.13).

Contemporary Issues

Research and Development (R&D) Funding: Funding or expenditure on research and development (R&D) is used for systematically increasing knowledge of humans, culture, science and society, and the application of such knowledge for new innovations.

Table 4.4 India: Expenditure on Education

Budget Year	GDP (at Current Prices at Factor Cost) in Crore Rupees	Expenditure on Education (Centre + States) in Crore Rupees	Education Expenditure as Per Cent of GDP	Education Expenditure as Per Cent to Total Expenditure
2016–2017	15,391,669	428,011	2.8	10.2
2017–2018	17,090,042	486,164	2.8	10.7
2018–2019	18,886,957	539,351	2.8	10.4
2019–2020	20,351,013	613,000	3	10.4
2020–2021	19,745,670	675,000	3.5	10.4

Source: Economic Survey 2021–2022.

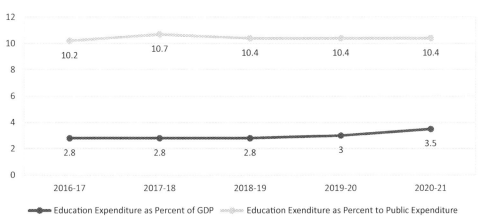

Figure 4.13 Expenditure on Education in India (Source: Economic Survey 2021–2022)

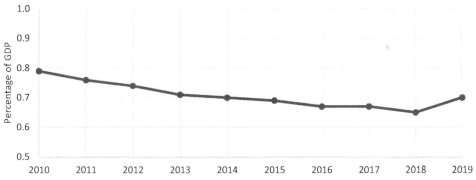

Figure 4.14 Public Expenditure on Research and Development (R&D) in India as Per Cent of the GDP (2010–2019) (Source: Economic Survey 2021–2022)

R&D encompasses basic research, applied research and experimental development. Several studies have proved that learning at the higher education level is enhanced in environments when there is a strong emphasis on research and knowledge creation. The Science and Technology Policy of 2003 fixed the threshold of devoting 2 per cent of GDP to research and development (R&D). In India, research and development has been pioneered mainly by government-funded Higher Education Institutions and specialised institutions such as the Indian Space Research Organisation (ISRO), the Council for Scientific and Industrial Research (CSIR), Defence Research and

Development Organisation (DRDO), IITs, etc. In 2018–2019, the estimated public expenditure on R&D in India was Rs 1,23,847.7 crore which amounted to 0.6 per cent of the GDP. The total public expenditure on scientific research and development has increased steadily over the years. However, this funding is extremely small when compared to the developed or rapidly developing nations such as Israel (4.6 per cent), South Korea (4.5 per cent), Japan (3.2 per cent) and Germany (3.0 per cent). Among the BRICS nations, China spends 2.1 per cent, Brazil 1.3 per cent and Russia spends around 1 per cent of their GDP on R&D. According to the Economic Survey 2019–2020, the private sector contributes about 37 per cent of the total R&D expenditure in India. According to the UNESCO Science Report 2018, India had 253 full-time equivalent (FTE) researchers per 10 lakh people, with a consistent increase from 2011 (157 per 10 lakh) and 2015 (216 per 10 lakh). Atal Innovation Mission (AIM), launched under the aegis of the National Institute for Transforming India (NITI) Aayog in 2016, has the objective of developing innovation culture at the grassroots level in schools, universities and businesses. Research has found that when the private sector funds research in universities, the number of patents filed increases. The Economic Survey in 2020–2021 has called for increased expenditure on R&D by the private sector.

Brain Drain: Brain drain is defined as the emigration of highly qualified and skilled persons such as surgeons, physicians, scientists and engineers, from low-income countries to more prosperous and developed countries. Primary external brain drain refers to human resources emigrating from their country to work abroad in developed countries such as Europe, North America and Australia. The secondary external brain drain is the emigration of human resources to countries in the nearby region. Brain drain has been observed to be a major issue in India as highly educated professionals emigrate from India and take up citizenship in developed nations, thus depriving their homeland of valuable human resources and economic activity. According to the information provided by the Ministry of Home Affairs (MHA) in 2019, more than 6 lakh Indians renounced their citizenship in the period from 2015 to 2019. According to the 'International Migration Highlights 2020', published by the Population Division of the United Nations Department of Economic and Social Affairs (UN DESA) in 2021, nearly 10 million or one crore Indians migrated overseas between 2000 and 2020. The United Nations World Migration Report 2020 has estimated the size of Indian diaspora to be 1.75 crore or 17.5 million. India has the largest transnational population, with around 35 lakh people living in the United Arab Emirates, 27 lakh in the USA and 25 lakh in Saudi Arabia. According to the Organisation for Economic Cooperation and Development (OECD), around 69,000 Indian-trained doctors were working in the UK, the USA, Canada and Australia in 2017. In these four countries, 56,000 Indian-trained nurses were working in the same year. There are several reasons for brain drain that include both pull and push factors. Some of the pull factors include high salaries, better standard of life, the requirement for skilled professionals, better research facilities, better environment and health facilities, etc. Push factors include structural unemployment, inadequate health and education facilities, low incomes, inadequate research environment, etc. In developed nations, the welfare state provides essential services to the migrants and their families reducing their social burden (Romer, 2022). India needs systematic change in sectors of education, health, academics and economy and constructs an overall environment that is beneficial and attractive enough for the highly skilled people to stay in the country.

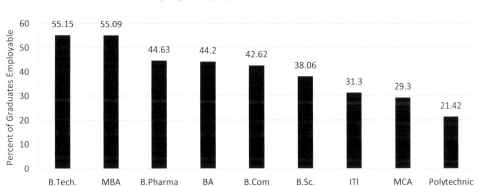

Figure 4.15 Employability of Graduates by Domain of Education in India (Source: India Skills Report 2022)

Employability: Employability refers to the attributes of a person that include skills, knowledge and character that enable a person to gain and maintain employment. According to the India Skills Report 2022 prepared by private thinktank Wheebox in collaboration with several institutions such as the All India Council of Technical Education (AICTE) and the United Nations Development Programme (UNDP), only 46.3 per cent of the graduates in India are employable. 55.44 per cent of women are employable whereas only 45.97 per cent males are employable. Maharashtra, Uttar Pradesh and Kerala have the most employable graduates. The states with the highest job supply are Maharashtra, Karnataka and Tamil Nadu. The states which have graduates with the highest employability are (1) Maharashtra, (2) Uttar Pradesh, (3) Kerala, (4) West Bengal, (5) Karnataka, (6) Delhi, (7) Andhra Pradesh, (8) Tamil Nadu, (9) Gujarat and (10) Haryana. The domains with the highest employability are B.Tech. (55.15 per cent) followed by MBA (55.09 per cent). Polytechnic graduates are the least employable with only about one in five persons with a polytechnic degree having skills to be employable (Figure 4.15).

References

Aithal, P. S., & Aithal, S. (2020). Analysis of the Indian National Education Policy 2020 Towards Achieving Its Objectives. *International Journal of Management, Technology, and Social Sciences*, 5(2), 19–41.

Anderson, L. W. (2005). Objectives, Evaluation, and the Improvement of Education. *Studies in Educational Evaluation*, 31(2–3), 102–113.

Ayyar, R. V. (2017). *History of Education Policymaking in India 1947–2016*. Oxford: Oxford University Press.

Boeren, E. (2019). Understanding Sustainable Development Goal (SDG) 4 on "Quality Education" From Micro, Meso and Macro Perspectives. *International Review of Education*, 65(2), 277–294.

CESCR General Comment 13: The Right to Education. (1999, December 8). UN Economic and Social Council.

Gee, J. P. (2014). *Literacy and Education*. New York, NY: Routledge.
Jayapalaa, N. (2005). *History of Education in India*. New Delhi: Atlantic Publishers & Dist.
Nurullah, S., & Naik, P. J. (1943). *History of Education in India During the British Period*. Bombay: Macmillan.
Pahl, K., & Rowsell, J. (2012). *Literacy and Education*. Thousand Oaks: SAGE Publications Ltd.
Romer, F. (2022). How Immigration Affects the Welfare State in the Short and Long Run: Differences Between Social Spending and Policy Generosity. *European Policy Analysis*, 00, 1–22. https://doi.org/10.1002/epa2.1140.
Sen, A. (1992). *Inequality Re-Examined*. Oxford: Clarendon Press.
Sharma, R., & Sharma, R. (1996). *History of Education in India*. New Delhi: Atlantic Publishers & Distributors.
Unterhalter, E. (2019). The Many Meanings of Quality Education: Politics of Targets and Indicators in SDG 4. *Global Policy, 10*, 39–51.

Chapter 5
Health

Introduction

Health is defined by the World Health Organization (WHO) (1948) as "the state of complete mental, social and physical well-being, not merely the absence of disease or infirmity". The health of people is not only essential to their well-being but is also fundamental to the progress and development of a nation. Healthy individuals and healthy societies become assets for the nation. A society with unhealthy people will find it very difficult to develop. Historically, scientific progress in the field of health has played a defining role in the development of nations across the world. Only when people have good health can they live a good quality of life, fulfil their aspirations and contribute productively to the development of the nation (Hazen & Anthamatten, 2011).

The role of health is so important in determining the well-being of the individual and society that it is considered to be a fundamental and universal human right. Article 25(1) of the Universal Declaration of Human Rights (UDHR) adopted by the United Nations Organisation (UNO) in 1948 states, "Everyone has the right to a standard of living adequate for the health and well-being of himself and of his family, including food, clothing, housing and medical care", while Article 25(2) proclaims, "Motherhood and childhood are entitled to special care and assistance". The International Covenant on Economic, Social and Cultural Rights (ICESCR) adopted by the United Nations Organisation (UNO) in 1966 in Article 12 recognises "the right of everyone to the enjoyment of the highest attainable standard of physical and mental health". Several other international instruments recognise the right to health and its importance which include the International Convention on the Elimination of All Forms of Racial Discrimination (1965), United Nations Convention on the Elimination of All Forms of Discrimination against Women (1979), Convention on the Rights of the Child (1989), Convention on the Rights of Persons with Disabilities (2006), etc. The Alma-Ata Declaration (in Alma-Ata in former USSR) adopted in 1978 at the International Conference on Primary Health Care identified primary healthcare as fundamental to the attainment of the goal of 'Health for All' across the world. This was followed by the Astana Declaration adopted in 2018 at the Global Conference on Primary Health Care in which more than 120 nations affirmed their 'commitment to the fundamental right of every human being to the enjoyment of the highest attainable standard of health without distinction of any kind; to prioritise, promote and protect people's health and well-being, at both population and individual levels, through strong health

DOI: 10.4324/9781003378006-5

systems and work towards achievement of universal health care (UHC).' Among the eight goals of the Millennium Development Goals (MDGs) set by the UNO for the period 2000–2015, three goals were directly related to health, namely (i) to reduce child mortality, (ii) to improve maternal health and (iii) to combat HIV/AIDS, malaria and other diseases. The Sustainable Development Goal 3 (SDG 3), as adopted by the UNO for the period 2015–2030, is "To ensure healthy lives and promote well-being for all at all ages". There are 13 targets listed under SDG 3 which include (1) reduction of maternal mortality (Target 3.1), (2) ending all preventable deaths under five years of age (Target 3.2), (3) fight communicable diseases (Target 3.3), (4) ensure a reduction of mortality from non-communicable diseases and promote mental health (Target 3.4), (5) prevent and treat substance abuse (Target 3.5), (6) reduce road injuries and deaths (Target 3.6), (7) grant universal access to sexual and reproductive healthcare, family planning and education (Target 3.7), (8) achieve universal health coverage (Target 3.8), (9) reduce illnesses and deaths from hazardous chemicals and pollution (Target 3.9), (10) implement the WHO Framework Convention on Tobacco Control (Target 3.a), (11) support research, development and universal access to affordable vaccines and medicines (Target 3.b), (12) increase health financing and support health workforce in developing countries (Target 3.c) and (13) improve early warning systems for global health risks (Target 3.d).

Principles of Health: The Constitution of the World Health Organization (1948) has laid down the following principles regarding health (Constitution of the World Health Organization, 1946):

1. Health is a state of complete physical, mental and social well-being and not merely the absence of disease or infirmity.
2. The enjoyment of the highest attainable standard of health is one of the fundamental rights of every human being without distinction of race, religion, political beliefs, economic or social condition.
3. The health of all peoples is fundamental to the attainment of peace and security and is dependent upon the fullest co-operation of individuals and States.
4. The achievement of any State in the promotion and protection of health is of value to all.
5. Unequal development in different countries in the promotion of health and control of disease, especially communicable diseases, is a common danger.
6. Healthy development of the child is of basic importance; the ability to live harmoniously in a changing total environment is essential to such development.
7. The extension to all peoples of the benefits of medical, psychological and related knowledge is essential to the fullest attainment of health.
8. Informed opinion and active cooperation on the part of the public are of the utmost importance in the improvement of the health of the people.
9. Governments have a responsibility for the health of their people which can be fulfilled only by the provision of adequate health and social measures.

Earlier, health was considered to be a disease-free state of an individual. This was the negative concept of health as it implied health to be the absence of disease or disability. As a result, lack of health was limited to being understood as a disruption in the everyday functioning of an individual by the occurrence of disease. However, in the present-day context, the state of health represents the overall well-being of a person across different aspects of life. Hence, even a physically fit person can be unhealthy if they are suffering from mental stress, etc. This is a positive concept which has expanded health to be a state of physical, mental, intellectual, emotional and social health and well-being.

Aspects of Health

Health is a broad and multidimensional concept as it is a state of physical, mental, emotional and social well-being. The different dimensions of health are discussed as follows:

1. **Physical Health**: It refers to the state of the normal functioning of the human body and the capability of an individual to carry out physical activities properly. It consists of strength, flexibility, endurance, coordination, etc. The necessary conditions for maintaining physical health include balanced diet, sleep, exercise, nutrition, avoidance of harmful substance consumption and fulfilment of basic physical needs. It can be measured through various parameters such as Body Mass Index (BMI), bone density, body weight, cholesterol level, etc. The absence of diseases and disabilities is essential for optimum physical health.
2. **Mental Health**: It refers to the proper cognitive functioning of an individual which involves significant mental activities of thinking, reasoning, remembering, imagining, decision-making, problem-solving and learning. Healthy brain functioning is essential to having good mental health which implies the ability of individuals to observe, think, reason, criticise and process information and act properly. Severe stress or physical injury can impair mental health. Activities such as problem-solving, reading, critical reasoning and creative work help to optimise mental health.
3. **Social Health**: It refers to the state of having proper relationships and interactions with other people. The ability to cultivate healthy relationships with family, neighbours, friends, peers, teachers, and community members and social life in accordance with socially acceptable norms represent good social health. Humans are social animals; hence, having a healthy social life is significant to the well-being of a person. An individual who is socially healthy contributes positively to society while an individual who does not enjoy good social health may suffer from isolation, stress and ostracisation.
4. **Emotional Health**: It refers to the state of having well-balanced emotions and feelings and the ability to cope with failures and setbacks. Hope, enthusiasm, healthy communication and positive thinking contribute to good emotional health.
5. **Spiritual Health**: It refers to the state of having a sound inner spirit, value-system and a purpose in life. An individual may find participation in community or religious activities, reading, writing or creating art to be spiritually healthy. Spiritual health is closely related to emotional health.

Perspectives of Health

There are various perspectives on understanding the concept of health. They are discussed as follows:

1. **Biomedical Perspective**: The biomedical perspective lays emphasis on physical health and views health as the absence of disease and disability. Hence, an individual who is free from any disease is considered to be healthy. However, this perspective fails to account for health issues which are not related to the incidence of disease or injury, such as malnutrition, obesity, allergy, depression, etc.
2. **Ecological Perspective**: The ecological perspective views health to be a result of the harmonious relation between the individual and the environment. Hence, environmental conditions are considered to be of primary importance in maintenance of the health of an individual. While this perspective is suitable for understanding communicable diseases, it is inadequate to understand non-communicable diseases such as hereditary diseases (Zhu et al., 2020).
3. **Psychological Perspective**: From the psychological perspective, health is considered to be a result of psychological conditions which are affected by social, emotional, mental and behavioural factors. This perspective is suitable for understanding health issues such as hypertension, diabetes, cardiovascular diseases, peptic ulcers but is inadequate for understanding communicable diseases, epidemics, etc.
4. **Holistic Perspective**: The holistic perspective considers health to be a result of the holistic functioning of body, mind and environment. Physical, social, economic, cultural, environmental and psychological factors are considered to influence the health of an individual.

Determinants of Health

There are various factors that influence health. These factors are known as the determinants of health. Some major determinants of health include:

- **Heredity**: The transmission of physiological characteristics from parents to the offspring is known as heredity. Physiological characteristics are transmitted through genes present in the chromosomes of the cell which determine physical appearance, immunity, eyesight, blood group, etc. of the offspring. Sometimes, variations in genes result in physiological abnormalities, disabilities, mental disorders, cancers and genetic diseases such as Down syndrome, infantile diabetes, haemophilia, etc.
- **Nutrition**: For the growth and healthy functioning of an individual, adequate nutrition is necessary. A balanced diet containing the required nutrients in the form of carbohydrates, proteins, fats, vitamins, minerals and fibres in the correct proportion helps to keep a person healthy. Undernutrition can result in nutrition-related diseases such as anaemia, night blindness, scurvy, etc., whereas excess nutrition leads to obesity, diabetes, arteriosclerosis, etc.
- **Physical Activity and Rest**: Regular exercise and physical activity help to maintain the strength, endurance and flexibility of the human body and ensure its proper functioning. In the absence of physical activity, several diseases like sclerosis can occur. Regular sleep patterns and rest help in the proper functioning of the human body and recovery from diseases.
- **Personal Hygiene**: Personal hygiene refers to having a clean internal and external environment which prevents the spread of germs. WASH (Water, Sanitation and Hygiene) activities such as having clean drinking water and access to toilets help to

prevent the spread of communicable diseases such as diarrhoea, cholera, typhoid, worm infections, jaundice, skin diseases, tuberculosis, etc.
- **Lifestyle**: Lifestyle factors refer to food and consumption habits, activity, work, addiction, etc. and non-modifiable factors such as age and heredity. These factors influence the general level of health and may lead to certain types of diseases.
- **Socio-economic Conditions**: Socio-economic conditions refer to the social group, educational level, community and the economic-occupational status of an individual. These conditions determine the consumption patterns of individuals, access to healthcare and resources which affect their health (Marmot & Wilkinson, 2005).

Other determinants of health include social support networks, education levels, personal health practices, coping skills, gender, etc.

Healthcare in India

In ancient India, archaeological evidences of well-developed sewage systems and bathrooms have been found in the sites of the Harappan Civilisation dating back to 2300–1700 BCE which signify the importance accorded to hygiene and health. The traditional medicine system of *Ayurveda* developed during 1000–500 BCE in the Later *Vedic* Period. The *Atharva Veda* or the book on science of life describes several body parts such as bones and internal organs. *Charaka Samhita* (200 BCE–100 CE) by *Charaka* (third century CE) on medicine, *Sushruta Samhita* (300–500 CE) by *Sushruta* (800–700 BCE) on surgery and *Astanga Hridaya* (7th century CE) by *Vagbhata* (600–650 CE) on medicinal practices are known as the *Great Triad* or the three seminal texts on Ayurveda. King *Ashok*a (273–232 BCE) established hospitals for the treatment of people.

Al-Biruni (973–1048 CE), the traveller from Khorasan (in Uzbekistan), wrote about the treatment using herbal medicines during his visit to India in the 11th century CE in the book *Kitab-ul Hind* (Banerji, 2004). However, up until the 19th century, medical practices and treatment of diseases were based mainly on the traditional indigenous system of medicine which include the AYUS (Ayurveda, Yoga and Naturopathy, Unani, Siddha) system. The medicinal system of Ayurveda and the Yoga system developed indigenously in India, the Unani system was brought into India as a result of the cultural interactions with the Arabian and Iranian civilisations around the 10th century CE while the Siddha system is said to have been developed by saints in southern India.

The Royal Hospital in Goa was set up between 1510 and 1515 CE by the Portuguese. During the colonial period beginning around the 17th century CE, the British established medical services and institutions along the lines of the modern medicine system of allopathy. The first hospital during British rule in India was the Madras General Hospital established in 1679 while the Presidency General Hospital, Calcutta was established in 1796. The first medical department was established in Bengal in 1764. Medical departments were set up in Madras, and Bombay presidencies in 1785. However, this was utilised mainly to cater to the health needs of British sepoys, military officials, civil servants, etc. Just like other public services like railways and posts, medical services were established essentially for the furtherance of colonial needs and industries (Pati & Harrison, 2009).

The record-keeping of vital statistics at the local level, mainly of births and deaths, began with the enactment of the Birth and Death Registration Act, 1873. In 1896, with the abolition of the Presidency system, the three medical departments were unified as the Indian Medical Services (IMS). The Epidemic Diseases Act, 1897 conferred special powers upon the local authorities to implement the necessary measures in the event of epidemics, which included forced segregation of infected persons, disinfections, evacuation and even demolition of infected places (Mushtaq, 2009).

The apathy of the public healthcare system towards the general public was evident in the occurrence of frequent epidemics of communicable diseases such as malaria, tuberculosis, cholera, smallpox. Major outbreaks of epidemics during the colonial period include the cholera epidemic during 1817–1824, 1826–1837, 1863–1875 and 1899–1923, the Bombay plague epidemic during the late 19th century and the Spanish flu epidemic of 1918 (Swetha, Eashwar, & Gopalakrishnan, 2019). Under the Indian Councils Act of 1919, popularly known as the Montagu–Chelmsford reforms, provincial health departments were established in provinces (Roy, 1985). Public health, sanitation and vital statistics became provincial subjects. In 1920–1921, Municipality and Local Board Acts were passed containing legal provisions for the advancement of public health in provinces. Under the Government of India Act, 1935, the Central Advisory Board of Health was established in 1937 with the Public Health Commissioner as secretary to coordinate the public health activities in the country. The Quarantine Act 1825, Vaccination Act 1880, Medical Act 1886, Epidemic Diseases Act 1897, Indian Factories Act 1911, Poisons Act 1919, Indian Red Cross Act 1922, Dangerous Drugs Act 1930, and Indian Port Health Rules 1938 were some of the major legislations in the field of health during the colonial period.

The Nehru Report published in 1928 under the chairmanship of Motilal Nehru included public health as a constitutional right. The National Planning Committee (NPC) of the Indian National Congress was set up in 1938 during the tenure of Subhash Chandra Bose as President which had a sub-committee on National Health chaired by Major General Sir Santok Singh Sokhey. The report of the committee in 1940 pointed out the lacunae in the existing healthcare system of the nation and recommended measures for addressing them. At the time of independence, there were total 7,400 hospitals and dispensaries in India with 1,13,000 beds with 0.24 hospital beds per 1,000 population, 47,000 doctors, 7,000 nurses, 19 medical schools and 28 medical colleges.

The report of the National Development Committee chaired by Joseph Bore, also known as the Bhore Committee Report, published in 1946 laid the foundations for the organisation of healthcare in India (Duggal, 1991). It laid emphasis on primary and universal healthcare, irrespective of the capacity of the patient to pay. The model of health infrastructure later adopted by the Government of India, composed of Primary Health Centres (PHCs) at the village level, Secondary Health Centres at the sub-division or Taluka level and district hospitals at district headquarters, was suggested by this report. It also recommended a provision of 500 beds in every district hospital. The Health Survey and Planning Committee set up in 1959 also known as the Mudaliar Committee published its report in 1961 recommended 300–500 beds for every district hospital, 50 beds per Taluka Secondary Health Centre and 6 beds per Primary Health Centre (PHC) at the village level. Health was made an integral component of the socio-economic planning incorporated within the Five-year Plans

(Goel, 2008). Primary Health Centre (PHC) system was established in 1952 as a component of the Community Development Programme (CDP) that emphasised the community approach to healthcare at the grassroots level. Historically the Indian commitment to health has been guided by two principles. The first principle is 'state responsibility' for healthcare and the second is free universal medical care for all, and not merely for those unable to pay.

Constitutional Provisions

1. **Article 21** in Part III of the Constitution, dealing with Fundamental rights, states that 'no person shall be deprived of his/her life or personal liberty except according to the procedure established by law'. The term 'life' has been accorded a broad-based meaning and the right to health is inherent to life with liberty. In the State of Punjab vs MS Chawla case (1996), the Supreme court of India affirmed that the right to life under Article 21 included the fundamental right to healthcare.
2. **Article 38** in Part IV under Directive Principles of State Policy (DPSP) of the Constitution directs the state to secure a social order for the promotion of welfare of the people. The provision of welfare inherently includes public health.
3. **Article 39(e)** under DPSP directs the state to ensure that the health and strength of workers irrespective of whether men, women or children should not be abused or manipulated.
4. **Article 39(f)** under DPSP directs the state to ensure that children are given opportunities and facilities to develop in a healthy manner and in conditions of freedom and dignity.
5. **Article 41** makes it the duty of the state to provide assistance in case of sickness and disablement. It states that the state shall within the limits of its economic capacity and development, make effective provisions for securing the right to work, to education and to public assistance in case of unemployment, old age, sickness and disablement and in other cases of undeserved want.
6. **Article 42** states that the State shall make provisions for securing just and humane conditions of work and for maternity relief.
7. **Article 47** makes it the duty of the State to raise the level of nutrition and the standard of living and to improve public health The State shall regard the raising of the level of nutrition and the standard of living of its people and the improvement of public health as among its primary duties and, in particular, the State shall endeavour to bring about prohibition of the consumption except for medicinal purposes of intoxicating drinks and of drugs which are injurious to health.
8. **Article 48A** ensures that State shall endeavour to protect and impose the pollution-free environment for good health.
9. In **Article 246** and the **Seventh Schedule** of the Constitution of India, 'Public health and sanitation; hospitals and dispensaries' is listed as an entry within the State List, meaning that the responsibility to legislate on this matter and implement such legislations lies with the respective state governments.
10. The local governments at the level of **Panchayats** and **Municipalities** also have the duty to improve and protect public health. **Article 243G** and **Article 243W** of the Constitution provide that the legislature of a state may endow the panchayats and municipalities with necessary power and authority in relation to matters listed

in the 11th and 12th Schedules, respectively. 'Health and sanitation, including hospitals, primary health centres' is listed as an entry in the 11th Schedule regarding which the responsibility and powers lie with the Panchayats. Similarly, in the 12th Schedule, 'public health and sanitation' has been made the responsibility of the Municipalities.

Legal Judgements on the Right to Health: The Supreme Court of India in various judgements has held the right to health to be integral to the fundamental right to life and liberty as conferred by Article 21 of the Constitution on every citizen (Mathiharan, 2003). In the *Bandhua Mukti Morcha* vs Union of India (1984) case, the Supreme Court ruled that dignity and health were part of the right to life under Article 21. In *Paschim Banga Khet Mazdoor Samiti* vs State of West Bengal (1996), the court held that the duty of the welfare state in India is to provide adequate medical aid to every person to secure the welfare of the people. The responsibility of the state is to ensure basic necessities such as food, nutrition, medical assistance, hygiene and contribute to the improvement of health. Hence, the right to life including the right to health was observed by the apex court in the State of Punjab vs. *Mohinder Singh Chawla* (1997) case. In a similar judgement in the Consumer Education and Research Centre vs Union of India (1995), the court explicitly held that the right to health was an integral part of the right to life. The Supreme Court in the State of Punjab vs. *Ram Lubhaya Bagga* (1998) case affirmed that the responsibility of the state is to maintain health services for the welfare of the public. Hence, the judgements of the highest court have incorporated the right to health within the right to life and also cast the duty upon the government to provide and maintain adequate medical facilities for the people.

Health Status in India

Life Expectancy at Birth: Life expectancy at birth is defined as how long a newborn can expect to live, on average, at the existing age-specific death rates. It is measured in years and is one of the most frequently used health status indicators. The different determinants of health influence life expectancy at birth and accessibility to healthcare is the most crucial factor influencing it. It is generally observed that life expectancy is higher in females than males and higher in developed than developing regions. Average life expectancy data in India is based on the life tables of the Sample Registration System (SRS). Births and deaths are compulsorily and officially registered in India under the Registration of Births & Deaths Act, 1969. SRS is published by the Office of the Registrar General of India (ORGI), Ministry of Home Affairs.

According to the SRS life tables, Life Expectancy of Life at Birth has increased from 49.7 years in 1970–1975 to 69 years in 2016–2020. The life expectancy for females is 70.4 years and it is 67.8 years for males. Overall highest life expectancy observed among the states is in Kerala (75.2 years) and in the union territories in the National Capital Territory (NCT) of Delhi (74.7 years). The lowest life expectancy is in Chhattisgarh (65.2 years) and Uttar Pradesh (65.4 years). For males, the highest life expectancy is in the NCT of Delhi (73.5 years) and Kerala (73 years) while the lowest is in Madhya Pradesh (65.2 years) and Assam (65.5 years). For females, the highest life expectancy is in Kerala (78.7 years) and Delhi (76.2 years). The lowest female life expectancy is in Uttar Pradesh (67.6 years) and Assam (68.2 years) (Figure 5.1(a–c)).

Health 139

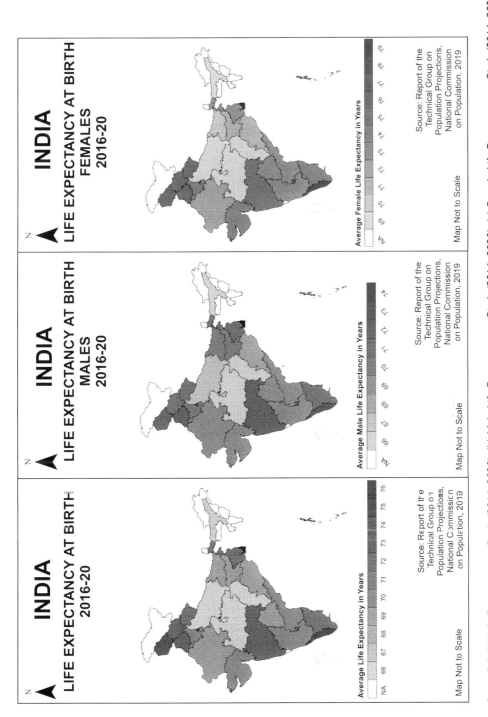

Figure 5.1 (a) Life Expectancy at Birth (2016–2020), (b) Male Life Expectancy at Birth (2016–2020), (c) Female Life Expectancy at Birth (2016–2020)

Infant Mortality Rate (IMR): Infant mortality is the death of children under the age of one year. It is considered an important indicator of the status of health in a geographic region. Infant mortality rate (IMR) is defined as the number of infant deaths per 1,000 live births. It is calculated using the following formula:

$$\text{IMR} = \frac{\text{Total Number of Infant Deaths}(0-12\text{ months}) \text{during a specific period}}{\text{Total Number of Live Births during a specific period}} * 1000$$

Some of the factors that influence IMR include access to healthcare, type of delivery, premature birth, congenital malformations, low birth weight, malnutrition, vaccinations, diseases such as malaria, diarrhoea, measles, jaundice, sanitation conditions, etc. As per the Sample Registration System (SRS), the overall IMR has reduced from 37 per 1,000 live births in 2015 to 30 per 1,000 live births in 2019. The highest IMR was registered in Uttar Pradesh (46) while the states with the lowest IMR are Nagaland (3) and Mizoram (3). Manipur (10), Goa (8), Lakshadweep (8), Andaman and Nicobar Islands (7), Kerala (6) and Sikkim (5) have IMR below 10 (Figure 5.2(a)).

Under-Five Mortality Rate (UFMR or U5MR): Under-Five Mortality or Child Mortality refers to the death of children below the age of five years. It includes within it infant mortality. Under-Five Mortality Rate (UFMR or U5MR) or Child Mortality Rate is defined as the number of child deaths under the age of five years per 1,000 children in the age group of zero to five years. It is calculated using the following formula:

$$\text{UFMR} = \frac{\text{Total Number of Child Deaths}(0-60\text{ Months}) \text{During a Specific Period}}{\text{Total Number of Live Births During a Specific Period}} * 1000$$

The child mortality rate in India in 2020 was 35.7 child deaths per 1,000 live births. The factors influencing the child mortality rate are similar to the IMR. The state with the highest UFMR is Madhya Pradesh (56) while the lowest UFMR was recorded in Tamil Nadu (17) and Delhi (19). Assam (47), Uttar Pradesh (47), Chhattisgarh (45), Odisha (44) and Rajasthan (40) have recorded high levels of UFMR (Figure 5.2(b)).

Maternal Mortality Rate: Maternal death is the death of a woman while pregnant or within 42 days of termination of pregnancy, irrespective of the duration and site of the pregnancy, from any cause related to or aggravated by the pregnancy or its management but not from accidental or incidental causes. Maternal mortality rate (MMR) is the number of maternal deaths per 1,00,000 births during a specified time period, usually in a year. Complications during pregnancy and childbirth are leading causes of death and disability among women of reproductive age in developing countries. Maternal mortality rate (MMR) represents the risks associated with each pregnancy and is known as obstetric risk. Maternal mortality in a region is a measure of the reproductive health of women. It is measured using the following formula:

Health 141

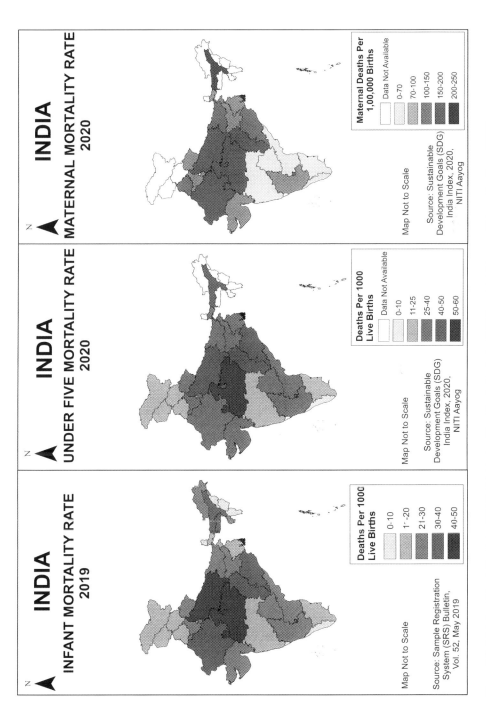

Figure 5.2 (a) Infant Mortality Rate (2019), (b) Under Five Mortality Rate (2020) and (c) Maternal Mortality Rate (2020)

$$\text{MMR} = \frac{\text{Total Number of Maternal Deaths During a specific Period}}{\text{Total Number of Births During a Specific Period}} * 1,00,000$$

The MMR data in India is made available through the Sample Registration System (SRS), and it is also used as an indicator under SDG 4 of the Sustainable Development Goals (SDG) India Index published by the NITI Aayog. Overall, the MMR of India is 113 maternal deaths per lakh live births during 2016–2018. MMR in India has declined to 113 in 2016–2018 from 122 in 2015–2017 and 130 in 2014–2016. The highest MMR in India is in Assam (215) while the lowest is in Kerala (43). Bihar (149), Madhya Pradesh (173), Chhattisgarh (159), Odisha (150), Rajasthan (164), Uttar Pradesh (197) and Uttarakhand (99) are the states with high MMR. The target set for MMR under the SDG framework is 70 or fewer maternal deaths per 1,00,000 live births. Andhra Pradesh (65), Telangana (63), Tamil Nadu (60), Maharashtra (46) and Kerala are the states that have achieved this target. Overall, MMR is higher in the northern states compared to the southern states (Figure 5.2 (c)).

Prevalence of Anaemia in Females: Anaemia is a nutritional deficiency disease, a condition in which the number of red blood cells (RBCs) and their oxygen-carrying capacity through haemoglobin are insufficient to meet physiological needs. Iron deficiency is the most common cause of anaemia, apart from vitamin B_{12} and vitamin A deficiencies or inheritance (Kumar, 1999). In females, anaemia prevalence is higher than males due to menstrual blood losses and the high iron demands of a growing foetus during pregnancies, aggravated by the deficiency of iron in the diet. Anaemia results in fatigue, weakness, dizziness and drowsiness, impaired cognitive development of children and increased morbidity in both mother and children. The prevalence rate of anaemia is high among females in India due to reasons such as insufficient nutrition, lack of access to healthcare and medicine, inadequate pre-natal care, etc. Females in the menstruating years, from the beginning of teenage to about 50 years, are more likely to suffer from anaemia. So, the prevalence of anaemia is taken to be an indicator of health of women. In India, 53.9 per cent females in the age group 15–49 years suffer from anaemia. Ladakh (92.8 per cent) and West Bengal (71.4 per cent) have the highest prevalence of anaemia in females in this age group. Overall, 25 states and union territories out of 36 have more than half of females suffering from anaemia. Manipur (29.4 per cent), Nagaland (28.9 per cent) and Lakshadweep (25.8 per cent) have the least prevalence of anaemia in women.

Institutional Delivery: Institutional delivery refers to the birth of a child in a medical institution under the overall supervision of trained health personnel. It is used as an important health indicator because it signifies the availability of amenities and care during childbirth for responding to complications or diseases. Poverty, education, expenditure on health and exposure to community health workers are some of the factors that help in achieving an institutional delivery (Kesterton et al., 2010). The higher the share of institutional deliveries, the greater the care provided to the mother and newborn and the higher the chances of dealing with childbirth complications. Hence, the chance of neonatal death is reduced significantly. According to the National Family Health Survey, Round 5 conducted during 2019–2021, 94.5 per cent of the total deliveries in India were institutional deliveries. Puducherry recorded 100 per cent institutional deliveries while Chandigarh, Goa, Karnataka, Kerala, Tamil Nadu,

Telangana, Dadra & Nagar Haveli and Daman & Diu, Lakshadweep, Andhra Pradesh, Gujarat, Sikkim and Maharashtra had more than 99 per cent institution deliveries. Meghalaya with 60.4 per cent had the least amount of institutional deliveries. All other states recorded more than 80 per cent of institutional deliveries (Figure 5.3(b)).

Out-of-Pocket Expenditure (OOPE) on Health: In order to avail healthcare facilities such as medicines, lab tests, consultation, etc., certain expenditure has to be made by the people. In a market-led economy, most of this expenditure has to be made privately by the person availing these facilities. The constitution of India proclaims India to be 'socialist' and directs the state to ensure the welfare of the people and in various judgements of the Supreme Court, the right to health has been included implicitly in the right to life. In India, healthcare is comprised of both the public and private sectors. Most of the healthcare services provided by the public sector are either free or subsidised. Out-of-pocket expenditure on health is used as an indicator of the status of healthcare because it is less when the public healthcare system is well developed and easily accessible. If the public healthcare system is not well developed, then people have to spend on health from the private purse. In such a scenario, a large number of people who are socially and economically disadvantaged may not be able to avail healthcare facilities. As a result, OOPE on health has also been included as a target in the Sustainable Development Goals (SDG) India Index under SDG 4. In 2020, the average out-of-pocket expenditure on health as percentage of monthly consumption

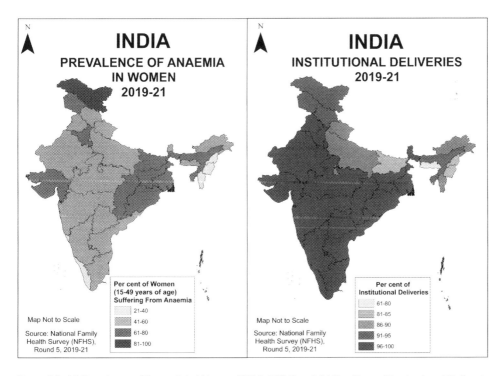

Figure 5.3 (a) Prevalence of Anaemia in Women (2019–2021) and (b) Per Cent of Institutional Deliveries

expenditure in India is 12 per cent. In Chhattisgarh (6.6 per cent) and Dadra & Nagar Haveli and Daman & Diu (5.55 per cent), the OOPE on health is the least. The highest OOPE on health as per cent of monthly consumption expenditure is in Jammu & Kashmir (18.6 per cent) and Ladakh (18.6 per cent) (Figure 5.4(a)).

Health Insurance: Health insurance refers to a contract whereby a third party which is generally an insurance company covers the expenditure incurred on health by a person or household. The range and type of medical expenditure differ from plan to plan. In India, health insurance can be bought from private or public companies. The government employees and the poorest 1,00,00,000 families, as identified under the Socio-Economic Caste Census (SECC) 2011, are provided health insurance cover by the government, as a form of social protection. Private sector employees in the organised sector are provided health insurance cover by their respective employer organisations. Health insurance requires regular payment of a fee which is known as a health insurance premium. This premium is paid by the person buying the health insurance. While employed persons contribute to the premium from their salary, the premium burden for the Below Poverty Line (BPL) families is borne by the government. Health insurance provides protection from unexpected expenditure on health, especially when availing secondary and tertiary healthcare services such as surgery, hospitalisation, transplant, etc. A person or household having health insurance cover is more resilient from falling below the poverty line or reducing consumption of essential goods and services. In India, 39.6 per cent of households have at least one member covered under

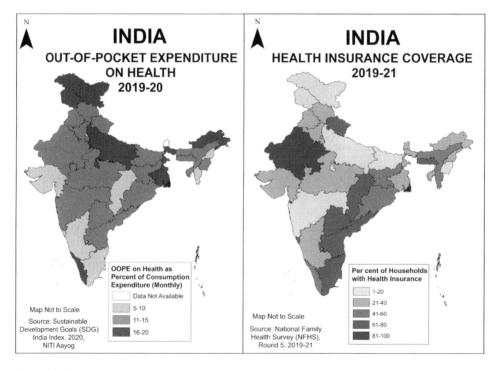

Figure 5.4 (a) Out-of-Pocket-Expenditure on Health (2020) and (b) Per Cent of Households with at least One Member under Health Insurance Cover

health insurance. In rural regions, 38.1 per cent while in urban regions 42.4 per cent households have at least one member covered under health insurance. Rajasthan (87.8 per cent) and Chhattisgarh (71.4 per cent) have high coverage of health insurance while Jammu & Kashmir (12.7 per cent) and Andaman & Nicobar Islands (1.6 per cent) have the least coverage. 13 states and union territories have more than 50 per cent households covered under health insurance (Figure 5.4(b)).

Immunisation: Immunisation programme is one of the key interventions for the protection of children from life-threatening conditions and diseases, which are preventable. The National Health Mission of the Ministry of Health and Family Welfare is responsible for the immunisation of children in India. The Universal Immunisation Programme (UIP) launched in 1985 is India's largest initiative to vaccinate children and pregnant women. The vaccines are administered under the immunisation programme in several phases, primarily over the course of first two years. These include vaccines for tuberculosis (BCG, or bacillus Calmette– Guérin), oral polio vaccine (OPV) and Injectable Polio Vaccine (IPV) for polio, hepatitis A and hepatitis B, diphtheria, tetanus and pertussis (DTP), influenza type B, pneumonia and meningitis (PCV – pneumococcal conjugate vaccine), rotavirus, measles, mumps and rubella (MMR) and chickenpox. According to the National Family Health Survey, Round 5 conducted during 2019–2021, 85.9 per cent of the children aged up to two years are fully vaccinated. Jammu & Kashmir (109 per cent), Ladakh (109 per cent) and Maharashtra (100 per cent) have the highest percentage of fully vaccinated children. Figures in excess of 100 per cent indicate vaccination of overaged children or immigrant children. The least percentage of vaccinated children are in Nagaland (54 per cent) and Puducherry (54 per cent) (Figure 5.5(a)).

Immunisation under Mission Indradhanush: Mission Indradhanush was launched by the Ministry of Health in 2014 to ensure full immunisation with all available vaccines for children up to two years of age and pregnant women, with a targeted regional focus. This mission was upgraded in the form of Intensified Mission Indradhanush (IMI) and IMI 2.0 with emphasis on selected backward districts. Under this programme, vaccination is provided against ten vaccine-preventable diseases that include (1) diphtheria, (2) whooping cough, (3) tetanus, (4) polio, (5) measles, (6) tuberculosis, (7) hepatitis B, (8) pneumonia and meningitis (PCV – pneumococcal conjugate vaccine), (9) rotavirus diarrhoea and (10) Japanese encephalitis. Vaccines related to Toxoid Tetanus (TT) and diphtheria are administered to pregnant women. The objective of this mission is to achieve the target of Sustainable Development Goal 4 of ending preventable child deaths by 2030. The programme includes the conduction of four rounds of immunisation annually and continuously, enhanced immunisation sessions with flexible timing, mobile sessions, enhanced emphasis on excluded and resistant families and hard-to-reach areas, focus on urban, underserved population and tribal areas. In 2019–2020, 97 per cent children up to two years of age in the target regions were vaccinated under Mission Indradhanush 2.0. Uttar Pradesh (116 per cent) had the maximum vaccination coverage while Meghalaya (58 per cent) had the least percentage of vaccinated children. Himachal Pradesh, Jammu & Kashmir, Madhya Pradesh, Telangana, Rajasthan, Bihar, Andhra Pradesh, Chhattisgarh, Tamil Nadu, Gujarat, Jharkhand and Odisha achieved more than 100 per cent vaccination coverage (Figure 5.5(b)). Arunachal Pradesh, Assam, Haryana, Maharashtra, Nagaland, Karnataka, Manipur and West Bengal had more than 95 per cent of the children vaccinated. During the

146 Health

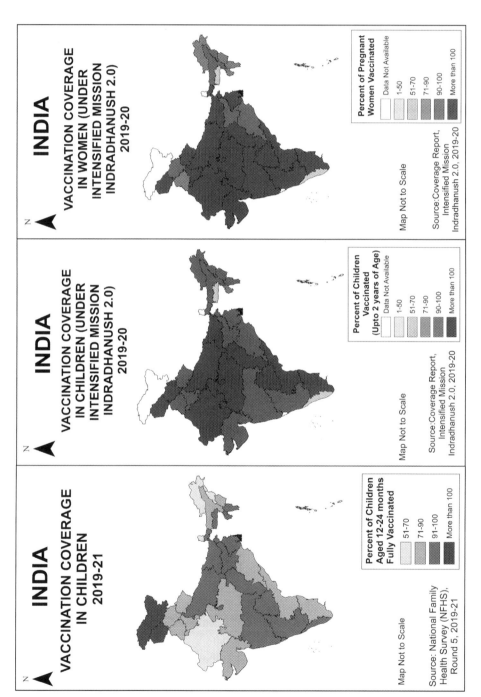

Figure 5.5 (a) Fully Vaccinated Children of Age 12–24 months (2019–2021), (b) Vaccination Coverage in Children under Mission Indradhanush 2.0 (2019–2020) and (c) Vaccination Coverage in Women under Mission Indradhanush 2.0 (2019–2020)

same period, 98.5 per cent of pregnant women were vaccinated. West Bengal (129 per cent) had the maximum while Meghalaya (67 per cent) had the minimum percentage of vaccinated pregnant women. Uttar Pradesh, Bihar, Rajasthan, Andhra Pradesh, Delhi, Gujarat, Maharashtra, Tamil Nadu, Telangana, Haryana, Madhya Pradesh, Uttarakhand, Karnataka, Jammu & Kashmir, Chhattisgarh and Odisha achieved more than 100 per cent vaccination coverage of women (Figure 5.5 (c)).

Healthcare Infrastructure

Sub-Health Centres (SHCs), Primary Health Centres (PHCs) and Community Health Centres (CHCs) form the rural healthcare infrastructure in India. SHCs and PHCs constitute the primary-level healthcare infrastructure while CHC serves secondary healthcare functions (Chokshi et al., 2016). Since 68.4 per cent of the Indian population or about 810 million people live in rural areas, these centres form essential components of public healthcare in India. The standards for these institutions are prescribed under the Indian Public Health Standards (IPHS). The three-tier infrastructure is based on the following population norms:

Sub-Health Centre (SHC): The Sub-Health Centre is the first contact point between the primary healthcare system and the community. SHCs are assigned the role of interpersonal communication between healthcare workers and the rural population to engender behavioural change and provide services relating to maternal and child health, family welfare, nutrition, immunisation, diarrhoea control and control of communicable diseases programmes. Each SHC has at least one auxiliary nurse midwife (ANM) or female health worker and one male health worker. ANM perform the functions related to maternal and child health services, family planning, immunisation services, facilitating Accredited Social Health Activists (ASHA) and maintenance of health registers. One Health Assistant who is female commonly known as Lady Health Visitor (LHV) and one Health Assistant who is male located at the Primary Health Centre (PHC) level are entrusted with the task of supervising all the Sub-centres (generally six sub-centres) under a PHC. An SHC should have its own building apart from spaces that include a labour room, clinic room, examination room, toilet and residential accommodation for the health workers. The total number of SHCs in India is 1,57,921. Uttar Pradesh (20,778) has the largest number of SHCs while Lakshadweep (11) and Sikkim (153) have the least number of SHCs. In terms of per 1,00,000 population, Dadra & Nagar Haveli and Daman & Diu (58) and Mizoram (30) have the highest number of SHCs, whereas Bihar (8) and Puducherry (6) have the lowest number of SHCs. Haryana (9), Uttar Pradesh (9) and Maharashtra (9) have very low number of SHCs per 1,00,000 population. In terms of distribution, southern states have a higher number of SHCs compared to northern states (Figure 5.6(a)).

Primary Health Centre (PHC): PHC is the first contact point between village community and the medical officer. The PHCs are envisaged to provide integrated curative and preventive healthcare to the rural population with emphasis on preventive and promotive aspects of health as recommended by the *Bhore* Committee (1946). A typical Primary Health Centre covers a population of 20,000 in hilly, tribal, or difficult areas and 30,000 populations in plain areas with six indoor or observation beds. It acts as a referral unit for six SHCs and refers out-cases to Community Health Centres which are 30 bedded hospitals and higher-order public hospitals located at

148 Health

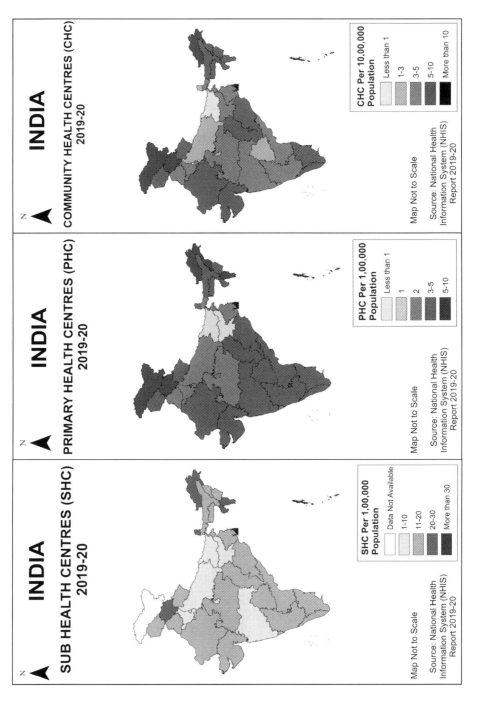

Figure 5.6 (a) Distribution of Sub-Health Centres (SHC) (2019–2020), (b) Distribution of Primary Health Centres (PHC) (2019–2020) and (c) Distribution of Community Health Centres (CHC) (2019–2020)

sub-district and district levels. The activities of PHC involve curative, preventive, promotive and family welfare services. PHCs are generally classified into two types: (1) Type-A PHC: PHC with a delivery load of less than 20 deliveries in a month and (2) Type-B PHC: PHC with a delivery load of 20 or more deliveries in a month. The services available at a PHC include maternal and child health care including family planning, medical termination of pregnancies, nutrition services, management of Reproductive Tract Infections (RTIs), prevention and control of locally endemic diseases like dengue, malaria, encephalitis, etc., collection and reporting of vital events, i.e. births and deaths, health education and Behavioural Change and Communication (BCC). The facilities available at a PHC include waiting area, Out Patient Department (OPD), labour room, Operation Theatre (OT), laboratory, computerised Management Information System (MIS) and referral transport. IHPS has recommended at least three staff nurses on a 24×7 basis in a PHC. The National Health Policy, 2017 recommended strengthening the delivery of Primary Health Care, by transforming them into 'Health and Wellness Centres' to deliver Comprehensive Primary Health Care. There are a total of 28,265 PHCs in India in 2020. Uttar Pradesh (3,415) has the largest number of PHCs, whereas Lakshadweep (4) and Sikkim (25) have the least number of PHCs. In terms of distribution of PHCs per 1,00,000 population, Ladakh (11) and Arunachal Pradesh (8) have the highest while Bihar (0.4), Uttar Pradesh (1), West Bengal (1) and Jharkhand (1) have the least number of PHCs (Figure 5.6 (b)).

Community Health Centre (CHC): The Community Health Centre (CHC) constitutes the secondary level of healthcare and provides referral as well as specialist healthcare to the rural population. CHCs serve the function of making modern healthcare services accessible to the rural population and secondly, ease the crowding in the district hospital (DH). Community Health Centre (CHC) typically act as the referral centre for every four PHCs covering 80,000 to 1,20,000 lakh population. The CHCs are mandated to have six specialists in the areas of medicine, surgery, paediatrics, gynaecology, anaesthetist and public health specialist; 30 beds for indoor patients; operation theatre, labour room, X-ray machine, pathological laboratory, standby generator, etc., along with the complementary medical and para-medical staff. It is mandatory for every CHC to have a functional *Rogi Kalyan Samiti* (RKS) and the Charter of Patients' Rights to be displayed prominently at the entrance. In India, the total number of CHCs is 5,593 in 2020. Uttar Pradesh (680) has the highest number of CHCs while the least number of CHCs is in Chandigarh (2) and Sikkim (2). In terms of per 1,00,000 population, Lakshadweep (4) and Arunachal Pradesh (4) have the highest number of CHCs while Telangana (0.2), Chandigarh (0.2) and Bihar (0.1) have the least number of CHCs (Figure 5.6(c)).

Hospital Beds: Hospital beds are used as an indicator of public health as they represent the availability of specialised healthcare services. Hospital beds include beds in SHCs, PHCs, CHCs and District Hospitals. The total number of hospital beds in India in 2020 is 7,39,024. Tamil Nadu (72,616) has the highest number of hospital beds, whereas Lakshadweep (250) and Sikkim (1,145) have the least number of hospital beds. In terms of per 1,00,000 population, Mizoram (187) has the highest number of beds while Jharkhand (19) and Bihar (14) have the lowest number of beds (Figure 5.7(a)).

Medical Colleges: Medical Colleges in India provide medical education and are recognised by the statutory National Medical Commission under the National Medical

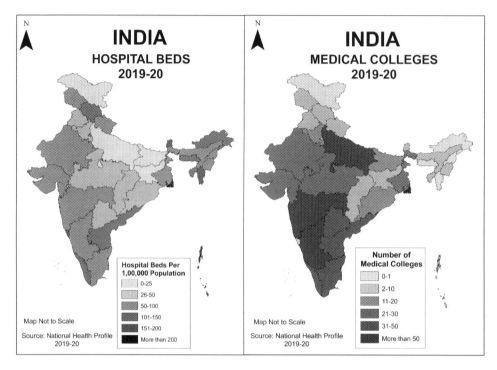

Figure 5.7 (a) Hospital Beds per Lakh Population (2019–2020) and (b) Medical Colleges in India (2019–2020)

Commission Act, 2019. These colleges grant the entry-to-practice degree in modern medicine known as the Bachelor of Medicine and Bachelor of Surgery (MBBS) apart from other advanced and specialised degrees. The total number of medical colleges in India in 2019–2020 is 542. Karnataka (60), Maharashtra (57), Uttar Pradesh (55) and Tamil Nadu (50) have the highest number of medical colleges. Arunachal Pradesh, Chandigarh, Dadra & Nagar Haveli and Daman & Diu, Goa, Meghalaya and Mizoram have just one medical college while Ladakh, Lakshadweep and Nagaland have no medical college (Figure 5.7(b)).

Doctors: Doctors are health professionals trained in medicine having a recognised professional degree. Doctors play an essential role in treating diseases of people and maintaining their well-being and health. World Health Organization has recommended a ratio of 100 doctors per 1,00,000 persons by 2024. In 2019, the total number of doctors trained in modern allopathic medicine and registered in the Indian Medical Register of the National Medical Commission (NMC) was 11,81,539. Maharashtra (1,83,843), Tamil Nadu (1,44,737), Karnataka (1,26,567) and Andhra Pradesh (1,02,924) have the highest number of doctors, being the only states having more than 1,00,000 doctors. Nagaland (134) and Mizoram (97) have the least number of doctors. In terms of doctors per 1,00,000 population, Goa (245) and Sikkim (205) have the highest number of doctors. Mizoram (8) and Nagaland (6) have the least number of doctors per lakh population (Figure 5.8(a)).

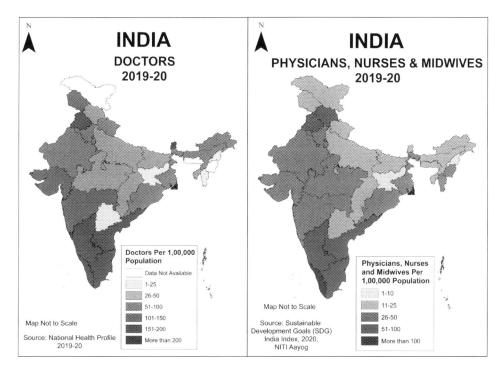

Figure 5.8 (a) Doctors in India (2019–2020) and (b) Physicians, Nurses and Midwives in India (2019–2020)

Health Workers: With regard to health workers, there are three major categories namely physicians, nurses and midwives (PNMW). Health workers are essential to the functioning of a healthcare system. World Health Organization has recommended 445 health workers per 1,00,000 population. India has, on average, only 35 health workers per 1,00,000 population, 410 less than the WHO recommended standards. Kerala (115) has the highest number of health workers per 1,00,000 population while Jharkhand (4), Chandigarh (1) and Nagaland (1) have the least ratio of health workers per lakh population (Figure 5.8(b)).

Illness and Diseases

Disease refers to abnormal functioning or dysfunctioning of the body or any part of the body. Illness refers to the subjective experience of a disease. On the basis of the mode of acquisition, diseases can be classified into the following two types:

1) Congenital Disease: The disease which is present from birth caused by some genetic abnormality or malfunctioning of an organ due to any defect in inherited genes.
2) Acquired Disease: The disease which occurs after birth during the lifetime of a person is called acquired disease. Acquired diseases can be classified into two types, (a) communicable and (b) non-communicable diseases.

Communicable Disease

Communicable disease is caused by the interaction of agent, host and environment. It occurs when the host is weak, but the agent is strong and enters the host in a sufficient amount through the right channel, for instance, poor sanitation and contaminated water and malnutrition can cause diarrhoea in a child. They are caused by microorganisms known as germs. This type of disease can get transferred from one host to another via different means. On the basis of causative organisms, communicable diseases can be classified into:

1. **Bacterial Disease**: It is caused by bacteria which are unicellular organisms, e.g. plague, typhoid, cholera, tuberculosis.
2. **Viral Disease**: It is caused by virus which are semi-living microbes that reproduce only when they enter a host, e.g. common cold, influenza, AIDS-HIV, dengue.
3. **Protozoal Disease**: It is caused by protozoa are transmitted either through contaminated medium or a vector, e.g. malaria, kala-azar.
4. **Fungal Disease**: It is caused by fungi, e.g. athlete's foot, jock itch, mycosis.
5. **Parasitic Disease**: It is caused by parasites which are organisms that derive nutrition from the host, e.g. infections of roundworm, lice.

On the basis of mode of transmission, communicable diseases can be classified into:

1. **Directly Transmitted Disease**: It can be transmitted directly from one host to another directly through close contact via blood or serum transfer, touch and sneeze droplets. e.g. Covid-19, flu.
2. **Indirectly Transmitted Disease**: It is transmitted from one host to another through some medium such as contaminated medium as water, food, air, surface or vector. Indirectly transmitted diseases are transferred in the following ways:

    2.1. **Transmission by Vehicle**: Such diseases are transmitted through an already infected or contaminated medium like food, water, air, surface, fomites, e.g. jaundice spreads through contaminated water.
    2.2. **Transmission by Vector**: Such diseases are transmitted through a vector which is normally an organism that carries the germ or pathogen and transmits it to the host without itself getting affected by it. e.g. dog acts as a vector for the rabies virus which gets transferred to humans after a dog bite; anopheles mosquito is the vector of the parasite *Plasmodium vivax* which causes malaria.

Non-Communicable Diseases (NCDs)

A disease which cannot be communicated from one person to another and generally occurs due to lifestyle habits, nutritional deficiency, allergy, malfunctioning of an organ, etc. is known as a non-communicable disease. There are several types of non-communicable diseases:

1. **Degenerative Disease**: It is caused by the malfunctioning or dysfunctioning of some vital organs or organ systems of the body, mainly due to old age, e.g. osteoarthritis, osteoporosis, Alzheimer's disease.

2. **Deficiency Disease**: This is caused due to nutritional deficiency of essential vitamins and minerals due to an imbalanced diet, e.g. anaemia is caused due to deficiency of iron in the diet, beriberi occurs due to vitamin B deficiency in the diet.
3. **Cancer**: It is the uncontrolled and unwanted growth of cells in the body. The actual cause of cancer is still not known, but some materials in diet and environment are known to increase the chances of getting cancer. They are known as carcinogens, for instance, cigarette smoke, alcohol, tobacco, etc. The cell growth in cancer is manifested in the form of tumours, which are of two types: (a) Benign tumour which remains confined to the place of origin and does not spread easily to other regions and (b) Malignant tumour which spreads to other parts of the body and grows rapidly and generally ends with the death of the diagnosed person.
4. **Chronic Respiratory Disease**: It refers to a group of diseases that affect the respiratory system consisting of lung structures and airways. It may occur due to genetic or environmental factors. Some examples of chronic respiratory diseases include chronic obstructive pulmonary disease (COPD), asthma, bronchitis, etc.
5. **Diabetes**: Diabetes occurs when enough insulin is not produced in the body. Insulin is a hormone produced in the pancreas that regulates blood sugar levels. Diabetes can lead to heart disease, vision loss, kidney injury, etc. It is generally of two types: (1) Type 1 diabetes which results due to immune system dysfunction and is diagnosed during childhood, (2) Type 2 diabetes occurs due to poor diet, inactivity, obesity, and other lifestyle and environmental factors and is diagnosed during adulthood.
6. **Cardiovascular Disease**: It is caused by the malfunctioning of the cardiovascular system which consists of hearts and blood vessels. Some common cardiovascular diseases include coronary heart disease, heart attack, stroke, arteriosclerosis.
7. **Allergy**: It refers to a group of non-communicable diseases that occur due to hypersensitivity to certain foreign matter known as allergens such as pollen grains, feathers, odour. Its symptoms include sneezing, gasping, bloodshot eyes, irritation of throat.

Morbidity in India

The India State-Level Disease Burden Initiative 2016–2017 which is a collaborative effort between the Indian Council of Medical Research, Public Health Foundation of India, Institute for Health Metrics and Evaluation provides the data for morbidity in India (Indian Council of Medical Research, 2017). Five of the ten individual leading causes of disease burden in India are diarrhoeal diseases, lower respiratory infections, iron-deficiency anaemia, preterm birth complications and tuberculosis. Major non-communicable disease groups include cardiovascular diseases, diabetes, chronic respiratory diseases, mental health and neurological disorders, cancers, musculoskeletal disorders and chronic kidney disease. Three of the five leading individual causes of disease burden in India were non-communicable, that include ischaemic heart disease, chronic obstructive pulmonary disease and stroke. Road injuries and self-harm, which include suicides and non-fatal outcomes of self-harm, are the leading contributors to the injury burden of morbidity.

The report stated that the health system in India is facing a dual challenge. On one hand, morbidity and mortality due to communicable, maternal, neonatal and nutritional diseases (CMNNDs) have declined substantially, yet it remains high. On the other hand, the share of non-communicable diseases (NCDs) and injuries have increased in the overall disease burden. The proportion of morbidity-related deaths in India due to CMNNDs was 27.5 per cent and due to NCDs was 61.8 per cent in 2016. 10.7 per cent deaths were caused due to injuries. The death rate due to NCDs was more than twice that of CMNNDs. CMNNDs (80.8 per cent) caused the predominant proportion of deaths in the age group 0–14 years in all the states. The majority of morbidity-related deaths in the 15–39 years age group were caused by injuries (36.5 per cent), 40–69 years and more than 70 years age group by NCDs (73.2 per cent and 71.6 per cent, respectively) (Figure 5.9).

The disease categories among CMNNDs that caused the highest proportion of death were diarrhoea, lower respiratory infections and other common infectious diseases, HIV-AIDS and tuberculosis and neonatal disorders. Among NCDs, the category of cardiovascular diseases was the leading cause of death, followed by chronic respiratory diseases, cancers and the category containing diabetes and urogenital disorders. In India, 30 out of 36 states and union territories had ischaemic heart disease as the leading cause of death. Among the other states, Jharkhand and Odisha had diarrhoeal diseases, Mizoram and Rajasthan had chronic obstructive pulmonary disease and Assam reported stroke as the leading cause of morbidity-related deaths.

Cardiovascular diseases (28.1 per cent); diarrhoea, lower respiratory and other common infectious diseases (15.5 per cent); chronic respiratory diseases (10.9 per cent); cancer (8.3 per cent); and diabetes, urogenital, blood and endocrine diseases (6.5 per cent) were the five leading individual causes of deaths in India. Neglected tropical diseases and malaria, maternal disorders, nutritional deficiencies, mental and substance use disorders and musculoskeletal disorders, each accounted for less than 1 per cent of morbidity-related deaths in India (Table 5.2).

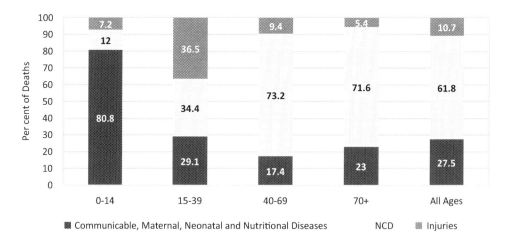

Figure 5.9 Distribution of Diseases by Categories and Age-Groups in India (Source: Health of the Nation's States – The India State-Level Disease Burden Initiative 2016–2017)

Table 5.1 Population Norms for Public Healthcare Facilities

Healthcare Facility	Population Cut-off	
	Plain Area	Hilly/Tribal/Difficult Area
Sub-Health Centre (SHC)	5,000	3,000
Primary Health Centre (PHC)	30,000	20,000
Community Health Centre (CHC)	120,000	80,000

Table 5.2 Causes of Morbidity-Related Deaths

S. No.	Disease	Per Cent of Total Deaths
1	Cardiovascular diseases	28.1
2	Diarrhoea, lower respiratory and other common infectious diseases	15.5
3	Chronic respiratory diseases	10.9
4	Cancers	8.3
5	Diabetes, urogenital, blood and endocrine diseases	6.5
6	HIV/AIDS and tuberculosis	5.4
7	Unintentional injuries	4.9
8	Neonatal disorders	3.8
9	Transport injuries	2.9
10	Suicide and interpersonal violence	2.8
11	Digestive diseases	2.2
12	Cirrhosis and other chronic liver diseases	2.1
13	Neurological disorders	2.1
14	Other non-communicable diseases	1.1
15	Other communicable, maternal, neonatal and nutritional diseases	0.9
16	Neglected tropical diseases and malaria	0.8
17	Maternal disorders	0.5
18	Nutritional deficiencies	0.5
19	Mental and substance use disorders	0.4
20	Musculoskeletal disorders	0.1
	Total	100

Source: Health of the Nation's States – The India State-Level Disease Burden Initiative 2016–2017.

Public Expenditure on Health

Total expenditure on health as a percentage of gross domestic product (GDP) is the level of total expenditure on health expressed as a percentage of annual GDP and is used as an indicator of health as it provides information on the level of resources channelled to health, relative to a country's wealth. In 2020–2021, the expenditure on health was Rs 3,50,000 crores which amounted to 1.8 per cent of the GDP according to the revised budget estimates. In the period between 2016 and 2021, health expenditure was 1.3–1.4 per cent of the GDP. Per cent of the public expenditure on health is the Gross Public Health Expenditure (GPHE) expressed as a percentage of total government expenditure. It represents the resources channelled through government

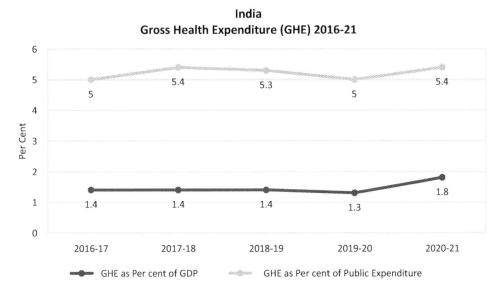

Figure 5.10 Public Expenditure on Health in India (2016–2021) (Source: Economic Survey 2021–2022)

budgets on health. In 2020–2021, 5.4 per cent of the total public expenditure was on health. In the last five years, in the period of 2016–2021, the expenditure on health has remained between 5 and 5.4 per cent of the total public expenditure and between 1 and 2 per cent of the GDP (Figure 5.10).

Health Policy in India

National Health Policy (1983): The first National Health Policy of India was released by the Ministry of Health and Family Welfare in 1983, 36 years after independence, during the tenure of Smt. Indira Gandhi as the Prime Minister. It recognised the success of the healthcare system in eradication of smallpox and the reduction in cases of diseases that were responsible for a large number of deaths before independence, namely, malaria, cholera and plague. Among the health issues to be addressed as identified by the policy were high population growth rate, mortality rate, infant mortality rate, malnutrition, communicable diseases such as leprosy, tuberculosis and diarrhoeal diseases and lack of sanitation in rural areas. The policy called for developing universal, comprehensive primary healthcare and criticised the curative western-oriented medical treatment system, with special emphasis on preventive, promotive and rehabilitative aspects of healthcare. The primary goal listed by the policy was to achieve 'Health for All' by 2000. It recommended the formulation of a separate National Population Policy in the direction of population stabilisation and a National Medical and Health Education Policy to produce skilled medical professionals and for conducting research. The policy also drew attention to the existing regional imbalances in terms of medical facilities, especially in the tribal, hilly and other backward regions. It also called for the promotion of health volunteers and decentralisation of healthcare services along with encouragement to the private sector so that the public healthcare system could be used by the needy. It recommended that the municipalities and local authorities should be given greater responsibility in the decentralisation of healthcare. The policy suggested taking steps for the organisation of the traditional system of medicine and health professionals in the AYUSH (*Ayurveda, Unani, Siddha, Sowa Rigpa*, Homeopathy, Naturopathy) system. Necessary measures for prevention of food adulteration and legislations for production and distribution of quality drugs were recommended by the policy. With regard to immunisation, the policy recommended a nationwide vaccination programme with complete coverage of the target groups. It called for the union and the state governments to take measures to ensure occupational health of workers to boost labour productivity. For the monitoring of the healthcare system, a Management Information System was recommended to be established. The policy also set goals with respect to (1) Infant Mortality Rate, (2) Crude Mortality Rate, (3) Under-Five Mortality Rate, (4) Maternal Mortality Rate, (5) Life Expectancy, (6) Crude Birth Rate, (7) Effective Couple Protection, (8) Net Reproduction rate, (9) Population growth Rate, (10) Family Size, (11) Pregnant women receiving Antenatal Care and (12) Deliveries by skilled professionals, (13) Immunisation for several diseases, (14) Tuberculosis Incidence, (15) Leprosy Incidence, etc. to be achieved in a phased manner by 2000.

National Health Policy (2002): The second health policy was released by the Ministry of Health and Family Welfare 19 years later during the tenure of Atal Bihari Vajpayee as the Prime Minister in 2002. The main objective of the policy was the organisational restructuring of the national public healthcare system to make access to health facilities more equitable. It recognised the low public expenditure on health as a percentage of the GDP, the rural-urban divide persisting across the health sector and the lack of access faced by women, children and the socially disadvantaged sections of society. Primacy was given to preventive and first-line curative initiatives at the primary health level along with emphasis on rational use of drugs. The policy acknowledged that the implementation of a national health programme can only be carried out through the decentralised public health machinery of the state governments, with the role of the central government being to design broad-based public health initiatives. It suggested entrusting some limited public health functions to nurses, paramedics, homoeopathic doctors and other personnel from the extended health sector after adequate training. The policy called for initiatives to encourage doctors and other professionals to serve in backward and rural regions. It recommended research in speciality disciplines and issues of anaesthesiology, radiology, forensic medicine along with biomolecular science and gene manipulation, along with greater emphasis on public health and family medicine. It directed adequate attention to manufacturing of generic drugs and vaccines for ensuring the health security of the country. It suggested greater adoption of Information, Education and Communication (IEC) strategies for monitoring diseases and health of the population. The policy said that medical research needed to lay emphasis on therapeutic drugs and vaccines for tropical diseases, genetics, genome-based drug and vaccine development, molecular biology, etc. It addressed the need for a regulatory mechanism for the maintenance of adequate standards by private diagnostic centres and medical institutions. Further, it recommended a programme for putting in place a modern and scientific health statistics database along with a system of national health accounts. It recognised the ethical issues existing in the health sector and the potential of medical tourism in India. To maintain the health of the people, with regard to adequate nutrition, safe drinking water, basic sanitation, a clean environment and primary education, especially for the girl child, the policy called for inter-sectoral cooperation and synergy among government departments. It envisaged programme implementation through autonomous bodies at state and district levels with the participation of elected political representatives. It recommended vertical programmes for control of major diseases like tuberculosis, malaria, HIV/AIDS, along with the Reproductive and Child Health (RCH) and Universal Immunisation Programme. The goals enumerated included (1) increase health sector expenditure to 6 per cent of GDP, with 2 per cent of GDP being contributed as public health investment, by the year 2010, (2) allocation of 55 per cent of the total public health investment for the primary health sector; the secondary and tertiary health sectors being targeted for 35 per cent and 10 per cent, respectively, (3) eradicate polio and yaws by 2005, (4) eliminate leprosy by 2005, (5) eliminate kala-Azar by 2010, (6) Eliminate lymphatic filariasis by 2015, (7) achieve zero-level growth of HIV/AIDS by 2007, (8) reduce mortality by 50 per cent due to tuberculosis, malaria and other vector and water-borne diseases by 2010, (9) reduce prevalence of blindness to 0.5 per cent by 2010, (10) reduce infant mortality rate to 30 and maternal mortality rate to 100 by 2010, (11) increase utilisation of public health facilities from current level of 75 per cent by 2010, (12) establish an integrated system of surveillance, National Health Accounts etc.

National Health Policy (2017): The third health policy of India was brought in 2017 under the tenure of Narendra Modi as the Prime Minister. It acknowledges the need for the modification of health policy. (i) First, the health priorities are changing, for instance, even though maternal and child mortality have rapidly declined, the burden of non-communicable diseases has increased, (ii) second is the emergence of a robust healthcare industry estimated to be growing rapidly, (iii) third is the growing incidence of expenditure on healthcare costs contributing majorly to poverty and (iv) fourth, the need for greater fiscal expenditure on health.

Objective: The primary aim of the policy is to inform, clarify, strengthen and prioritise the role of the government in shaping health systems in all its dimensions – investments in health, organisation of healthcare services, prevention of diseases and promotion of good health through cross-sectoral actions, access to technologies, developing human resources, encouraging medical pluralism, building a knowledge base, developing better financial protection strategies, strengthening regulation and health assurance.

Goal: The policy envisages the attainment of the highest possible level of health and well-being for all at all ages, through a preventive and promotive health care orientation in all developmental policies, and universal access to good quality health care services, pivoted around Sustainable Development Goals (SDGs).

Principles: The main principles enlisted by the policy include professionalism, integrity and ethics, equity, affordability, universality, patient-centric and quality of care, accountability, inclusive partnerships, pluralism, decentralisation, dynamism and adaptiveness.

Priority Areas: There are seven priority areas listed by the policy:

1. *Swachh Bharat Abhiyan* (Clean India Campaign)
2. Balanced, healthy diet and regular exercise

3. Addressing tobacco, alcohol and substance abuse
4. *Yatri Suraksha* (Passenger Safety) – preventing deaths due to rail and road traffic accidents
5. *Nirbhaya Nari* (Fearless Women) – action against gender violence
6. Reduced stress and improved safety in the workplace
7. Reducing indoor and outdoor air pollution

Targets: Several targets have been set regarding health outcomes by the National Health Policy 2017:

1. **Life Expectancy and Healthy Life**
   a. Increase Life Expectancy at birth from 67.5 to 70 by 2025.
   b. Establish regular tracking of Disability Adjusted Life Years (DALY) Index as a measure of the burden of disease and its trends by major categories by 2022.
   c. Reduction of total fertility rate (TFR) to 2.1 at national and sub-national levels by 2025.
2. **Mortality by Age**
   a. Reduce Under-Five Mortality to 23 by 2025 and MMR from current levels to 100 by 2020.
   b. Reduce infant mortality rate to 28 by 2019.
   c. Reduce neonatal mortality to 16 and still birth rate to a single digit by 2025.
3. **Reduction of disease prevalence/incidence**
   a. Achieve the global target of 2020 which is also termed as the target of 90:90:90, for HIV/AIDS, i.e. 90 per cent of all people living with HIV know their HIV status, – 90 per cent of all people diagnosed with HIV infection receive sustained antiretroviral therapy and 90 per cent of all people receiving antiretroviral therapy will have viral suppression.
   b. Achieve and maintain the elimination status of leprosy by 2018, kala-azar by 2017 and lymphatic filariasis in endemic pockets by 2017.
   c. To achieve and maintain a cure rate of >85 per cent in new sputum-positive patients for tuberculosis and reduce the incidence of new cases, to reach elimination status by 2025.
   d. To reduce the prevalence of blindness to 0.25/1,000 by 2025 and disease burden by one third from current levels.
   e. To reduce premature mortality from cardiovascular diseases, cancer, diabetes or chronic respiratory diseases by 25 per cent by 2025.
4. **Coverage of Health Services**
   a. Increase utilisation of public health facilities by 50 per cent from current levels by 2025.
   b. Ante-natal care coverage to be sustained above 90 per cent and skilled attendance at birth above 90 per cent by 2025.
   c. More than 90 per cent of newborns will be fully immunised by one year of age by 2025.
   d. Meet the need for family planning above 90 per cent at national and sub-national levels by 2025.
   e. 80 per cent of known hypertensive and diabetic individuals at the household level maintain 'controlled disease status' by 2025.

5. Cross-sectoral goals related to health
   a. Relative reduction in the prevalence of current tobacco use by 15 per cent by 2020 and 30 per cent by 2025.
   b. Reduction of 40 per cent in the prevalence of stunting of under-five children by 2025.
   c. Access to safe water and sanitation to all by 2020 (Swachh Bharat Mission).
   d. Reduction of occupational injury by half from current levels of 334 per lakh agricultural workers by 2020.
   e. National/State-level tracking of selected health behaviour.
6. Health finance
   a. Increase health expenditure by the Government as a percentage of GDP from the existing 1.15–2.5 per cent by 2025.
   b. Increase State sector health spending to > 8 per cent of their budget by 2020.
   c. Decrease in the proportion of households facing catastrophic health expenditure from the current levels by 25%, by 2025.
7. Health Infrastructure and Human Resource
   a. Ensure the availability of paramedics and doctors as per the Indian Public Health Standard (IPHS) norm in high-priority districts by 2020.
   b. Increase community health volunteers to population ratio as per IPHS norm, in high-priority districts by 2025.
   c. Establish primary and secondary care facilities as per norms in high-priority districts (population as well as time to reach norms) by 2025.
8. Health Management Information
   a. Ensure district-level electronic database of information on health system components by 2020.
   b. Strengthen the health surveillance system and establish registries for diseases of public health importance by 2020.
   c. Establish federated integrated health information architecture, Health Information Exchanges and National Health Information Network by 2025.

Key Features

- **Health Mission**: It advocates scaling up National Urban Health Mission (NUHM) to cover the entire urban population within the next five years with sustained financing.
- **Primary Healthcare**: This policy calls for change from very selective to comprehensive primary healthcare package which includes geriatric health care, palliative care and rehabilitative care services in the form of 'Health and Wellness Centres'. Health centres should be established on geographical norms apart from population norms. Free primary care provision by the public sector, supplemented by the strategic purchase of secondary care hospitalisation and tertiary care services from both public and from the non-government sector would be utilised to address critical gaps in healthcare services.
- **Secondary Healthcare**: The policy recommends secondary care at the district level which is currently provided at medical college hospitals. Basic secondary care services, such as caesarian section and neonatal care would be made available at the least at sub-divisional level. It affirms to expand the network of blood banks across the country to ensure improved access to safe blood.

- **Tertiary Healthcare**: The policy endorses that public hospitals would provide universal access to a progressively wide array of free drugs and diagnostics.
- **Urban Healthcare**: Given the large presence of the private sector in urban areas, the policy recommends exploring the possibilities of developing sustainable models of partnership with for-profit and not-for-profit sectors for urban healthcare delivery. An important focus area of the urban health policy will be achieving convergence among the wider determinants of health – air pollution, better solid waste management, water quality, occupational safety, road safety, housing, vector control and reduction of violence and urban stress.
- **Child and Adolescent Health**: The policy envisages school health programmes as a major focus area as also health and hygiene being made a part of the school curriculum. The scope of Reproductive and Sexual Health should be expanded to address issues like inadequate calorie intake, nutrition status and psychological problems interalia linked to misuse of technology, etc.
- **Malnutrition and Micronutrient Deficiencies**: The policy focus would be on reducing micronutrient malnourishment and augmenting initiatives like micronutrient supplementation, food fortification, screening for anaemia and public awareness.
- **Integrated Disease Surveillance Programme**: The policy advocates the need for districts to respond to the communicable disease priorities, well-equipped laboratories backed by tertiary care centres and enhanced public health capacity to collect, analyse and respond to disease outbreaks.
- **Non-Communicable Diseases**: Screening for oral, breast and cervical cancer and for chronic obstructive pulmonary disease (COPD) will be focused on in addition to hypertension and diabetes.
- **Mental Health**: This policy will take into consideration the provisions of the National Mental Health Policy 2014 with simultaneous action on the following fronts: Increase the creation of specialists through public financing and develop special rules to give preference to those willing to work in public systems; create a network of community members to provide psycho-social support to strengthen mental health services at primary-level facilities and leverage digital technology in a context where access to qualified psychiatrists is difficult.
- **Population Stabilisation**: The National Health Policy recognises that improved access, education and empowerment would be the basis of successful population stabilisation.
- **Reproductive Health**: There will be enhanced provisions for reproductive morbidities and health needs of women beyond the reproductive age group (40 or more years), making public hospitals more women-friendly and ensuring that the staff have orientation to gender-sensitivity issues.
- **Disaster Management**: The policy supports the development of earthquake and cyclone-resistant health infrastructure in vulnerable geographies. Creation of a unified emergency response system, trauma management centres – one per 30 lakh population in urban areas and one for every 10,00,000 population in rural areas.
- **AYUSH**: Policy recognises the need to nurture AYUSH system of medicine, through the development of infrastructural facilities of teaching institutions, improving quality control of drugs, capacity building of institutions and professionals.
- **Regional Disparities**: Regional disparities in the distribution of medical institutions must be addressed: regional, zonal and apex referral centres. It recommends

that the government should set up new medical colleges, nursing institutions and AIIMS in the country following this.
- **Training**: This policy recommends that medical and para-medical education be integrated with service delivery systems so that the students learn in the real environment and not just in the confines of the medical school.
- **Medical Education**: common entrance exam is advocated on the pattern of NEET for UG entrance at the all-India level; a common national-level Licentiate/exit exam for all medical and nursing graduates; a regular renewal at periodic intervals with Continuing Medical Education (CME) credits accrued, are important recommendations.
- **Accredited Social Health Activists (ASHA)**: The policy recommends the revival and strengthening of the Multipurpose Male Health Worker cadre, in order to effectively manage emerging infectious and non-communicable diseases at the community level. A certification programme for ASHAs for their preferential selection into ANM, nursing and para-medical courses is recommended.
- **Financing**: A robust National Health Accounts System would be operationalised to improve public sector efficiency in resource allocation and payments.
- **Corporate Social Responsibility (CSR)**: CSR is an important area which should be leveraged for filling health infrastructure gaps in public health facilities across the country. The private sector could use the CSR platform to play an active role in awareness generation through campaigns on occupational health, blood disorders, adolescent health, safe health practices and accident prevention, micronutrient adequacy, anti-microbial resistance, screening of children and ante-natal mothers, psychological problems linked to misuse of technology, etc.
- **Private Sector**: Immunisation, organ transplant, strengthening disease surveillance, the private sector laboratories could be engaged for data pooling and sharing, customised indigenous medical devices.

Contemporary Issues

Covid-19 Pandemic: Coronavirus disease (Covid-19) is a communicable and highly contagious disease caused by the severe acute respiratory syndrome coronavirus 2 (SARS-CoV-2). It is believed to have a zoonotic origin. The first known case of Covid-19 was identified in Wuhan, China, in December 2019. Thereafter, it has turned into the deadliest pandemic of the 21st century due to its contagious nature. SARS-CoV-2 is a single-strand RNA virus that primarily attacks the respiratory system. The virus of Covid-19 spreads from one infected person to another by direct contact through small liquid particles ejected from the mouth and nose while coughing, sneezing, speaking, etc. The World Health Organization (WHO) initially declared Covid-19 a 'Public Health Emergency of International Concern' on 30 January 2020, and a 'pandemic' on 11 March 2020. Symptoms of Covid-19 often include fever, dry cough, headache, fatigue, breathing difficulties, loss of smell and taste. Symptoms generally begin between 1 and 14 days after exposure to the virus. People of old age or with existing morbidities are more likely to develop serious illnesses and die. Most people, however, develop only mild symptoms but they are still capable of transmitting the virus. Preventive measures for Covid-19 include physical distancing, quarantine, ventilation of indoor spaces, covering coughs and sneezes with mask, hand washing and avoiding movement without masks in public (Ghosh et al., 2020). No treatment has yet been developed for the disease even though several vaccines have been approved by the World Health Organization (WHO) and national governments to prevent and reduce its impact.

The total Covid-19 cases in India as on 1 May 2022 were 43,082,180. Maharashtra (7,877,901), Kerala (6541728) and Karnataka (3947726) were states with the highest number of cases. The least number of cases were in Andaman and Nicobar Islands (10,035) Lakshadweep (11,402) among the union territories and Nagaland (35,488) and Sikkim (39153) among the states. The NCT of Delhi (1,884,560) was the union territory with the highest number of cases. In terms of per 1,00,000 population, the highest number of cases were in Mizoram (18,357 cases per 1,00,000 persons), Kerala (18,324) and Lakshadweep (15,580) while the least were in Bihar (666), Uttar Pradesh (872) and Jharkhand (1,128). Overall, the Covid-19 cases per lakh population were high in states of south and central India (Figure 5.11(a)).

The total number of cases of Covid-19 deaths in India on 1 May 2022 were 523,798. However, the figures related to Covid-19 deaths have been questioned by experts. Maharashtra (147,843), Kerala (69,068) and Karnataka (40,102) reported the highest number of deaths, while the least number of deaths were in Dadra & Nagar Haveli and Daman & Diu (4), Lakshadweep (52) in the union territories. The state with the least death toll due to Covid-19 was Arunachal Pradesh (296 deaths). In terms of Covid-19 deaths per lakh population, the highest number of deaths were in Goa

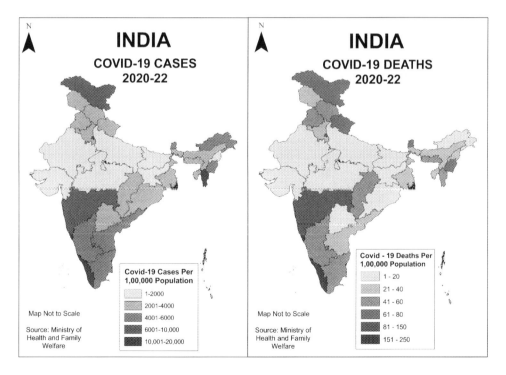

Figure 5.11 (a) Distribution of Covid-19 Cases (2020–2022), (b) Distribution of Covid-19 deaths (2020–2022)

(242 deaths per 1,00,000 persons), Kerala (193) and Delhi (140). The least number of deaths per lakh population were in Dadra & Nagar Haveli and Daman & Diu (1), Bihar (10) and Uttar Pradesh (10) (Figure 5.11(b)).

India began administering Covid-19 vaccines on 16 January 2021. As of 2 April 2022, India has administered a total of around 1.8 billion doses overall, which includes first, second and precautionary or booster doses. Persons aged 12 and above are eligible for receiving the Covid-19 vaccine. The vaccines were made available in a phased manner, first to health workers, followed by persons aged 60 or more, followed by adults over 45 years of age and so on. The vaccines approved by the Government of India for Covid-19 are (a) Covishield, (b) Covaxin, (c) Sputnik V and (d) Corbevax. Of the total population eligible for vaccination, 91.17 per cent have been partially vaccinated with the first dose of the Covid-19 vaccine; 76.88 per cent of the eligible population have received both doses of the vaccine and are, thus, fully vaccinated.

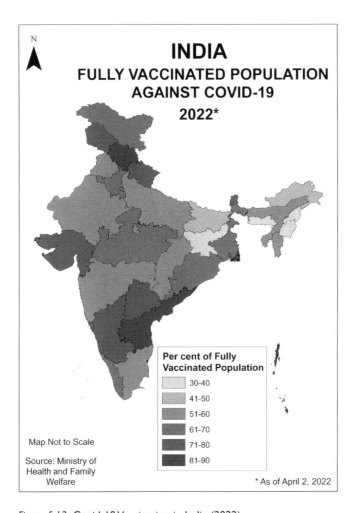

Figure 5.12 Covid-19 Vaccination in India (2022)

Uttar Pradesh (141 million), Maharashtra (72 million) and West Bengal (63 million) had the highest number of eligible people fully vaccinated. The states with the highest population of eligible population fully vaccinated are in Andhra Pradesh (86 per cent), Lakshadweep (84 per cent), Andaman & Nicobar Islands (81 per cent) and Himachal Pradesh (81 per cent). Meghalaya (30 per cent), Nagaland (31 per cent) and Manipur (37 per cent) had the least share of population that were fully vaccinated with both doses of the vaccine (Figure 5.12).

References

Banerji, D. (2004). The People and Health Service Development in India: A Brief Overview. *International Journal of Health Sciences*, 34(1), 123–142.

Chokshi, M., Patil, B., Khanna, R., Neogi, S. B., Sharma, J., Paul, V. K., & Zodpey, S. (2016). Health Systems in India. *Journal of Perinatology*, 36(3), 9–12.

Constitution of the World Health Organization. (1946). *American Journal of Public Health*, 36(11).

Duggal, R. (1991). Bhore Committee (1946) and Its Relevance Today. *The Indian Journal of Pediatrics*, 58(4), 395–406.

Ghosh, A., Nundy, S., & Mallick, T. K. (2020). How India is Dealing With Covid-19 Pandemic. *Sensors International*, 1, 100021.

Goel, S. (2008). From Bhore Committee to National Rural Health Mission: A Critical Review. *The Internet Journal of Health*, 7(1), 1–4.

Hazen, H., & Anthamatten, P. (2011). *An Introduction to the Geography of Health*. London: Routledge.

Indian Council of Medical Research. (2017). *India: Health of the Nation's States — The India State-Level Disease Burden Initiative*. New Delhi: Indian Council of Medical Research.

Kesterton, A. J., Cleland, J., Sloggett, A., & Ronsmans, C. (2010). Institutional Delivery in Rural India: The Relative Importance of Accessibility and Economic Status. *BMC Pregnancy and Childbirth*, 10(1), 1–9.

Kumar, A. (1999). National Nutritional Anaemia Control Programme in India. *Indian Journal of Public Health*, 43, 3–16.

Marmot, M., & Wilkinson, R. (2005). *Social Determinants of Health*. Oxford: Oxford University Press.

Mathiharan, K. (2003). The Fundamental Right to Health Care. *Issues Med Ethics*, 11(4), 123.

Mushtaq, M. U. (2009). Public Health in British India: A Brief Account of the History of Medical Services and Disease Prevention in Colonial India. *Indian Journal of Community Medicine: Official Publication of Indian Association of Preventive & Social Medicine*, 34(1), 6.

Pati, B., & Harrison, M. (2009). *The Social History of Health and Medicine in Colonial India*. London: Routledge.

Roy, S. (1985). Primary Health Care in India. In *Health and Population: Perspectives and Issues*, 8(3), 135–167.

Swetha, G., Eashwar, V. A., & Gopalakrishnan, S. (2019). Epidemics and Pandemics in India throughout History: A Review Article. *Indian Journal of Public Health Research & Development*, 10(8), 1503–1509.

Zhu, Y.-G., Gillings, M., & Penuelas, J. (2020). Integrating Biomedical, Ecological, and Sustainability Sciences to Manage Emerging Infectious Diseases. *One Earth*, 3(1), 23–26.

Chapter 6

Income and Employment

Introduction

Economy refers to the social domain which involves the activities related to the production, distribution, exchange and consumption of resources by different agents. Resources, here, refer to the goods and services required for the fulfilment of needs and wants of the agents. These needs and wants can be required to be fulfilled in short term or long term. The agents operating within the economy include individuals, households, firms, governments. The term economy originated from the ancient Greek term *oikonomia* which means management or administration of the household (Mankiw, 2016).

The sum total of all interrelated activities comprising production, distribution, exchange and consumption of resources are referred to as the economic system. The academic discipline that studies the production, distribution, exchange and consumption of resources is called economics. Adam Smith (1723–1790), the Scottish philosopher and economist wrote the famous book titled *An Inquiry into the Nature and Causes of the Wealth of Nations* in 1776 which laid the foundation of the discipline of economics.

Resources, as said earlier, refer to goods and services that fulfil the needs and wants of economic agents. Anything which is useful for humans is a resource. According to Erich Zimmermann (1888–1961),

> The word resource does not refer to a thing or a substance but to a function which a thing or a substance may perform or to an operation in which it may take part, namely, the function or operation of attaining a given end such as satisfying a want.
>
> (Zimmerman, 1951)

As resources provide utility, they have value and their value is conveniently measured in terms of money. Measurement of resources in monetary terms helps to assess their value and facilitate distribution and exchange (Phillips, 1995).

Some resources are ubiquitous and may not be valued monetarily, for instance, sunlight and air. They are also known as renewable resources because their quantity is not affected by consumption. However, most of the resources are non-ubiquitous and hence limited. Resources which are consumed faster than they are replenished are known as non-renewable resources, which are limited in their quantity. This property

DOI: 10.4324/9781003378006-6

is known as scarcity. The relative scarcity of a resource often determines its monetary value. For instance, petroleum which is a non-renewable resource is valued highly due to its scarce nature. Land in urban regions is often scarce due to high demand and hence tends to have high value. Nature is the ultimate source of all resources. Some resources can be consumed directly, such as fruits. However, not every substance or material present in nature can be utilised directly and may need to be processed or transported before they can be consumed. They may need to be collected, organised, processed, assembled, transported, exchanged before they fulfil needs and wants. The activities by which goods and services are produced, distributed, exchanged and consumed are known as economic activities. All economic activities can be measured in monetary terms (Gregori, 1987). Activities which are not valued monetarily are not considered to be economic activities. For example, the care of an infant by the mother is not considered to be an economic activity.

Economic Activities

Economic activities are activities by which goods and services are produced, distributed, exchanged and consumed. Economic activities can be classified into the following five types:

1. **Primary Sector Activities**: These activities involve the extraction and production of natural resources along with the reproduction and development of living organisms, plants, etc. They may be (i) extractive industries in which natural resources are obtained directly from nature, such as lumbering, mining, etc. or (ii) genetic industries in which plants and animals are bred and reproduced for their further usage, such as agriculture, animal husbandry, etc.
2. **Secondary Sector Activities**: These activities involve the value addition of resources obtained from primary sector activities. The value addition in primary products is known as manufacturing which can be done by (i) analytical process in which simpler materials are extracted from complex products, e.g. iron from iron ore, (ii) synthetic process in which simple materials are combined to form new products, e.g. cement from limestone, clay, slate, blast furnace slag, silica sand, etc., (iii) analytical-synthetic process in which primary products undergo processing that involves both analytical and synthetic processes, for instance, in the production of iodised cooking salt, salt is first obtained from seawater and then processed in factory where iodine and other elements are added to it, (iv) assembly process where different components are combined to make a finished product, for instance, mobile phone or automobile assembly units, (v) construction process which involve construction of structures such as buildings, dams, tunnels.
3. **Tertiary Sector Activities**: These activities involve providing services and facilities, and hence, such activities are also known as service sector activities. They may be related or unrelated to primary and secondary sector activities. For instance, electric repair service is related to secondary sector activity, while teaching is an activity unrelated to the primary or secondary sector.
4. **Quaternary Sector Activities**: These activities involve a specialised form of services, which require significant levels of skills and knowledge. Consequently, this

sector is also called the 'knowledge sector'. For instance, surgery, research, auditing, software development are quaternary sector activities.
5. **Quinary Sector Activities**: These activities involve highly specialised managerial services which require experience along with highly developed skills and knowledge. This sector is referred to as the 'management sector'. For instance, the services provided by bureaucrats, diplomats, corporate directors, managers, CEOs, etc. are quinary sector activities.

Workers involved in different economic activities are also denoted by collar colours which provide an informal classification of economic activities as follows:

1. **Blue-Collar Workers**: They perform manual unskilled or semi-skilled labour and generally earn hourly wages.
2. **Black-Collar Workers**: They work in the mining or petroleum industry, which is mainly primary sector activities.
3. **Pink-Collar Workers**: They work in low-end service jobs such as receptionists, waiters, domestic servants, etc.
4. **White-Collar Workers**: They are regular salaried persons who perform clerical, administrative and managerial functions.
5. **Gold-Collar Workers**: They are highly-skilled and knowledgeable persons such as doctors, lawyers and scientists who receive high salaries. They are mainly involved in quaternary sector activities.
6. **Green-Collar Workers**: They are employed in activities related to alternate energy sources like solar energy, hydroelectric energy, etc.
7. **Gray-Collar Workers**: They are workers who are working beyond the age of retirement such as senior professors, elected parliamentarians etc.
8. **Open-Collar Workers**: They are workers who work remotely from home via the internet.
9. **Red-Collar Workers**: Red-collar workers refer to government workers of all types.
10. **New-Collar Workers**: They are persons who have new-age skills such as soft skills and technical skills such as yoga teachers, software developers, etc.
11. **No-Collar Workers**: These are artists and freelance workers who do not work in the traditional sense and value freedom over job security.

Measuring National Income

Gross Domestic Product: One of the most globally accepted and popular ways of measuring national income is the Gross Domestic Product (GDP). GDP is defined as the value of final goods and services produced in each sector during a particular year in a region or country. Final goods refer to items that are meant for final consumption and once sold, go out of the economic flow. They do not undergo any further production and transformation by the producer, though they may be modified by the buyer but not with the intention of selling it further (Dynan & Sheiner, 2008). For instance, shirts, cars, packaged bread, mobile phones and canned milk are final goods. The inputs used in the manufacture of final goods are called intermediate goods. The value of intermediate goods is included in the value of final goods.

For instance, bread is made from wheat, so wheat is an intermediate good, whereas bread is a final good. Similarly, final services are services which are consumed directly, for instance, the service provided by a plumber, electrician or tuition teacher who visits home is final services. Intermediate services are used in the production of a final good or providing a final service. For example, the services provided by a plumber or electrician in the construction of a ready-to-move apartment, or the service provided by a school teacher is intermediate services. Only the final goods and services produced by both domestic and international agents within the domestic territory of a nation are included in the calculation of the GDP. GDP denotes the amount of economic production and consumption taking place across all the sectors within the domestic territory of an economy. GDP is well accepted because it generally correlates well with a lot of other socio-economic indicators like poverty, unemployment, material attainments, etc. (Moyer & Dunn, 2020). Hence, it is used as a statistical tool for measuring economic growth. For the purpose of calculating GDP, the domestic territory of a nation includes the following:

a) Territory lying within the geographical boundaries of a country including airspace and territorial waters. Territorial water is the belt of coastal waters that go at most 12 nautical miles from the coast.
b) Ships including fishing vessels, and aircrafts operated by residents of the country across different parts of the world. Thus, if a person is inside an Indian aeroplane or ship outside India, it will be considered to be inside the domestic territory of India. It will also include Indian aircrafts and shipping vessels plying completely outside India because they are included in the property of India.
c) Diplomatic missions such as embassies, consulates and military establishments of a country located abroad. Thus, the Indian Embassy in any other country is considered to be the domestic territory of India. The domestic territory of India does not include the properties of individuals or private companies in foreign countries.

American economist Simon Smith Kuznets (1901–1985) developed the modern concept and method of measuring GDP in 1934 in a report presented to the US Congress. After the Bretton Woods conference in 1944, which laid the foundation of the World Bank and International Monetary Fund, GDP became the primary tool for the measurement of the income of a country. Each nation publishes its own GDP data regularly. In India, the National Accounts Division in the National Statistical Office (NSO) under the Ministry of Statistics and Programme Implementation prepares and publishes quarterly and annual estimates of GDP. These estimates are usually published with a lag of two months. Since the financial year in India runs from 1 April to 31 March, the annual estimate of GDP and related indicators is released on 31 May. In addition, the World Bank and the International Monetary Fund publish and maintain historical GDP data for many countries periodically. **GDP potential** refers to the maximum output that can be produced in a country using the available labour and capital at a constant inflation rate.

Methods of GDP Calculation: Three approaches are used for the calculation of GDP, namely (i) production approach, (ii) expenditure approach and (iii) income approach. These are discussed below:

1. **Production Approach**: In the production approach, gross value added of all firms across all sectors is taken to be the value of GDP. It is close to the actual definition of GDP which is the value of final goods and services produced in a country. Gross Value Added (GVA) is calculated by deducting the value of intermediate goods and services from the gross output value. Hence,

   GVA = Gross Output Value – Value of Intermediate Goods and Services

2. **Income Approach**: This approach takes into consideration the fact that the final goods and services produced in a country are completely sold which must equal the total income of all the agents in the economy. The total income in an economy can be divided into four types, namely (i) remuneration earned by human labour, which may be called wage (W), (ii) remuneration earned from capital which may be called interest (In), (iii) remuneration earned from entrepreneurship and business which may be called profit (P) and (iv) remuneration earned from fixed natural resources as land, which may be called rent (R). Hence, GDP from income approach is given by the following formula:

   GDP = W + In + P + R

3. **Expenditure Approach**: This approach calculates GDP from the demand side of the economy. It takes into consideration that the final goods and services produced in a country are bought which amounts to the total expenditure incurred in the economy. The total expenditure in the economy can be divided into the following types, namely (i) private consumption expenditure by individuals and households, which may be called consumption expenditure (C), (ii) investment expenditure made by the firms and households in the form of capital goods, savings, etc. which may be called investment (I), (iii) expenditure made by the government which includes both consumption and investment expenditure of government, which may be called government expenditure (G) and (iv) the net export revenues earned by firms by selling goods and services abroad, which may be called export revenues (X). From this total expenditure, the expenditure incurred on consumption goods import (C_m), government imports (G_m) and foreign investment goods and services (I_m) is deducted because this value goes out of the domestic territory. ($C_m + G_m + I_m$) can be called aggregate import expenditure (M). X–M can be called net exports. Hence, GDP according to the expenditure method is expressed as:

   $$GDP = C + I + G + X - (Cm + Gm + Im) \text{ or } GDP = C + I + G + X - M$$

   This formula of GDP gives GDP at current prices. In reality, consumption expenditure (C) is measured by Private Final Consumption Expenditure (PFCE), investment expenditure (I) is measured by the summation of Gross Fixed Capital Formation (GFCF) and Change in Stocks (CIS), government expenditure (G) is measured by Government Final Consumption Expenditure (GFCE).

Factor Cost and Market Price: When the Gross Value Added of all firms of all sectors is added, then it is known as GDP at factor cost. GDP at factor cost expresses only the cost price of a good which includes the payments made to the factors of the production. Land, labour, capital and entrepreneurship are referred to as the factors of production. Hence, factor cost is also known as the factory price.

GVA at basic prices is calculated by adding the production taxes and deducting the production subsidies from GDP at factor cost.

GVA at Basic Prices = GDP at Factor Cost + Production Taxes – Production Subsidies

When product taxes are added and product subsidies deducted from GVA at basic prices, it becomes GDP at market prices.

GDP at Market Prices = GVA at Basic Prices + Product Taxes – Product Subsidies

The difference of product taxes and product subsidies is known as Net Taxes. Hence, GDP at market prices can be expressed as,

GDP at Market Prices = GVA at Basic Prices + Net Taxes

Production taxes refer to taxes that are imposed even when the products are not produced and are independent of the volume of actual production, such as property tax. However, taxes paid on the product such as excise duty, Goods and Services Tax (GST), etc. are product taxes. Production subsidies include subsidies to railways, petroleum companies, input subsidies to farmers, subsidies to village and small industries. Product subsidies are received per unit of product such as food, petroleum and fertiliser subsidies, interest subsidies given to farmers, households, etc. through banks.

Constant Price and Current Price: Inflation or the general increase in the prices of goods and services is considered to be a natural phenomenon in the economy. Hence, over a period of time, the price of goods and services in the economy increases. As a result, the increase in GDP of nation may not be due to increase in output but due to increase in prices of the goods and services. Inflation diminishes the value of money and reduces the amount of goods and services that can be purchased over a period of time for a given amount of money. Hence, it is essential to measure the GDP of a nation with reference to a base year to factor out the effect of inflation on the prices of output. Usually, the national accounting agency selects a base year. The prices of goods and services during the base year are used as a reference for measuring the GDP during any succeeding year. In India, 2011–2012 is used as the base year. The GDP measured during any year at the current level of prices is known as GDP at current price. This is also known as nominal GDP. When the value of goods and services are adjusted for the effects of inflation, the value of GDP obtained consequently is known as GDP at constant price or real GDP. Since January 2015, nominal GDP at market prices is reported as the GDP of India by the National Statistical Office (NSO). GDP at constant price presents a better picture of the economic growth of a nation.

GDP Deflator: The ratio of GDP at current price to GDP at constant price is called GDP deflator. It is a unitless ratio which represents the effect of inflation on the growth of GDP.

$$\text{GDP Deflator} = \frac{\text{GDP at Current Price}}{\text{GDP at Constant Price}} \quad \text{or} \quad \text{GDP Deflator} = \frac{\text{Nominal GDP}}{\text{Real GDP}}$$

Nominal GDP and GDP at Purchasing Power Parity: Nominal GDP refers to the GDP at current prevailing market prices. However, by this measure, the GDP of different countries are not comparable because the cost of living varies across countries. GDP at Purchasing Power Parity (PPP) is used to compare the GDP of different nations which is based on the law of one price, according to which the price of a good should be the same at every location if there are no transaction costs or trade barriers for a particular good. The PPP is calculated with the formula: $E = P1/P2$, where E = exchange rate of currency 1 to currency 2, P1 = cost of a good in currency 1, P2 = cost of a good in currency 2. For instance, if the price of a mobile phone is 500 US dollars in the USA and the same mobile phone costs 10,000 rupees in India, then according to the PPP terms, the exchange rate should be 20 Indian Rupees for every 1 US dollar. The value of the PPP exchange rate depends on a selected basket of goods and services. The PPP exchange rate is different from the nominal exchange rate which is affected by demand-supply forces of the market and actions of the central bank. PPP exchange rates are relatively stable and do not take into account tariffs and they are used for many international comparisons. The International Comparison Programme (ICP) of the World Bank collects and compares price data across nations and estimates GDP by PPP of the economies of different countries.

Per Capita Gross Domestic Product: When the GDP of a country is divided by its total population, then the per capita Gross Domestic Product is obtained.

$$\text{Per Capita GDP} = \frac{\text{GDP During a Specific Period}}{\text{Total Population During a Specific Period}}$$

Other Related Concepts

Gross National Product (GNP): GNP is calculated by adding the Net Factor Income from Abroad (NFIA) to the Gross Domestic Product (GDP) of a nation. NFIA is calculated by subtracting the income earned by the factors of production of the rest of the world employed in the domestic economy from the income earned by the domestic factors of production employed in the rest of the world. For instance, the income of a non-Indian citizen working and earning in India is considered to be the income earned by a factor of production from the rest of the world. On the other hand, an Indian citizen working abroad will be considered to be a domestic factor of production employed abroad. Hence, GNP can be expressed as:

GNP = GDP + Net Factor Income from Abroad

where Net Factor Income from Abroad (NFIA) = Factor income earned by the domestic factors of production employed in the rest of the world − Factor income earned by the factors of production of the rest of the world employed in the domestic economy.

Net National Product (NNP): When depreciation is deducted from the GNP, then NNP is obtained. Depreciation refers to the gradual reduction in value of a good due to wear and tear. It is mainly an accounting concept. Depreciation does not result in any actual outflow of money but just means that a particular good is not worth as much as it used to be. The rates of depreciation are fixed by the national governments differently for different goods and also vary across different nations. NNP can be expressed as:

$$NNP = GNP - Depreciation$$

National Income (NI): Generally, NNP is expressed at market prices. However, when NNP is expressed at factor cost that is, by deducting the net taxes from NNP at market prices, then National Income (NI) is obtained. Hence,

$$National\ Income = NNP\ at\ Market\ Prices - Net\ Taxes\ or$$

$$National\ Income = NNP\ at\ Market\ Prices - (Indirect\ Taxes - Subsidies)$$

Personal Income (PI): To obtain personal income, undistributed profits, net interest payments made by households and corporate tax paid by companies are deducted from National Income (NI) and transfer payments to the households from the government and firms added to it. Hence,

Personal Income = National Income − Undistributed profits − Net interest payments made by households − Corporate tax + Transfer payments to the households from the government and firms.

Personal Disposable Income (PDI): Personal income is not the real income available to the households. From personal income, tax and non-tax payments have to be made. After deducting these payments from personal income, Personal Disposable Income is obtained. It is the real in-hand income available to the households or individuals. Hence,

$$Personal\ Disposable\ Income = Personal\ Income - Tax\ Payments - Non\ Tax\ Payments$$

Gross State Domestic Product (GSDP): GSDP is the value of all final goods and services produced within the domestic territory of a state or union territory (Table 6.1).

Limitations of GDP

Even though GDP is recognised internationally as an indicator of economic growth, it has certain limitations which include the following:

Table 6.1 Economic Indicators of Measuring Income

GDP	Total Value of All Final Goods and services Produced Within the Domestic Territory of Nation
GNP	GDP + NFIA
NNP (at market price)	GNP − Depreciation
National Income	NNP (at factor cost) + Indirect Taxes - Subsidies
National Disposable Income	Net National Product at market prices
Personal Income	National Income − Undistributed profits − Net interest payments made by households − Corporate tax+ Transfer payments to the households from the government and firms
Personal Disposable Income	National Income − Tax Payments − Non-Tax Payments

- GDP is an aggregate statistical measure. Hence, it does not consider how the goods and services produced within the economy are distributed across the population. Consequently, even though the GDP of a country may be increasing while the overall standard of life or income of the people may not be growing. GDP can also increase when the increase in income is concentrated in the hands of a few people. Hence, GDP is not a holistic measure of economic development.
- GDP does not take into account non-monetary activities and social transactions, even if they are significant in the functioning of the economy. Such activities may include barter exchanges or activities in the care economy. For instance, the care provided to a child by parents or to senior citizens in the family is not accounted in GDP even though it is essential to the social well-being of individuals and families. Similarly, many activities performed for family or relatives or friends are also kept out of GDP (Costanza et al., 2009).
- GDP does not account for externalities that arise out of economic activities. For example, the pollution generated by industries which is detrimental to the environment can result in significant economic loss in the long run, yet any deduction is not made from the GDP on this count.
- GDP does not take into consideration the underground economy, which includes activities which are not officially recorded or may be taking place in the process of criminal acts.
- GDP measures the value of final goods and services from the point of view of production in the economy but where the profits from these goods and services accrue to are not counted in GDP. For instance, the profits from production and manufacturing of MNCs (Multi-National Companies) accrue to other nations.
- GDP does not express the educational, health or standard of life attainments of the people of the nation. It also fails to measure whether economic growth is accompanied by social progress. Notable economists such as Amartya Sen and Martha Nussbaum have worked on Quality-of-Life and capability approach to measure economic development while Mahbub-ul-Haq devised the Human Development Index (HDI) as a measure of development.
- The measurement of GDP in a large economy such as India is a cumbersome process as it requires measuring the value of all final goods and services produced, and hence, it is subject to over- and underestimation. Also, the concepts such as

inflation, Gross Value Added, etc. involved in measuring GDP can be tampered with by the governments to tweak the statistics in their favour.
- The base effect is generally known to present misleading figures for GDP growth. The base effect occurs when the GDP increases due to a rise in inflation or low production or any economic shock in the base year or the year used in the denominator for calculating GDP growth. For instance, economic growth was severely inhibited in India in 2020–2021 due to the effects of the Covid-19 pandemic and resulting lockdowns. On the other hand, economic growth has shown recovery during 2021–2022 post the easing of Covid-19-related curbs and restrictions. Hence, the year-on-year GDP growth between 2020–2021 and 2021–2022 will be positive because the GDP during the base year was low. However, in reality, this growth does not represent the damage suffered by the economy.

GDP of India

The official GDP of India is calculated by two methods: (a) by Gross Value Added (GVA) at basic prices using the production method and (b) by expenditure method. In the production method, the GVA is reported for eight types of economic activities across the three economic sectors, where gross value added is defined as the final value of output minus the value of intermediate consumption. The net taxes are added to GVA to obtain the gross domestic product (GDP). GDP is reported at both constant and current prices. The GDP at current prices or nominal GDP is used to quote the official GDP figure of India. The GDP at constant prices is represented with reference to a base year. The base year is generally updated from time to time in order to inculcate changes related to new types of goods and services and accounting methods. In 2015, a new GDP series was announced with upgraded methodology and data sources aligned with the United Nations' System of National Accounts (SNA) introduced in 2008. In the latest series, the base year was changed from 2004–2005 to 2011–2012. Among other changes introduced in the new GDP series include data for the organised private sector from the database of the Union Ministry of Corporate Affairs known as MCA-21, the inclusion of final service value of financial institutions and regulatory bodies like the Securities and Exchange Board of India (SEBI), the Pensions Fund Regulatory and Development Authority (PFRDA), the Insurance Regulatory and Development Authority (IRDA), etc.

The economy of India is the world's sixth-largest economy by nominal GDP and the third largest by Purchasing Power Parity (PPP). According to the estimates provided by the National Statistical Office (NSO), the GDP of India in 2020–2021, nominal GDP or GDP at current prices is Rs 198.01 lakh crore. The real GDP or GDP at constant prices (base year 2011–2012) for 2020–2021 is Rs 135.58 lakh crore. Nominal Net National Income (NNI) or NNI at current prices for the year 2020–2021 stands at Rs 171.94 lakh crore. Per Capita Net National Income at current prices is estimated at Rs 1,26,855 for the year 2020–2021.

GVA Using Production Method: The GVA figure of India's economy is arrived at by calculating the net change in value for eight types of economic activities across the three economic sectors over the designated time period of one year. These economic activities are listed in Table 6.2.

176 Income and Employment

Table 6.2 Economic Activities used in Calculating GDP by Gross Value Added (GVA) Method

Economic Sector	Economic Activity	Economic Activity Group (as used by NSO)
Primary Sector	Agriculture, Forestry and Fishing	**Agriculture**
	Mining and Quarrying	**Industry**
Secondary Sector	Manufacturing	
	Electricity, Gas, Water Supply and Other Utility Services	
	Construction	**Services**
Tertiary Sector	Trade, Hotels, Transport, Communication and Services Related to Broadcasting	
	Financial, Real Estate and Professional Services	
	Public Administration, Defence and Other Services	

Table 6.3 GVA at Current Price 2020–2021 (in Crore Rupees)

Economic Sector	GVA	Economic Activity	GVA	Economic Activity Group	GVA
Primary Sector	3,908,643	Agriculture, Forestry and Fishing	3,616,523	Agriculture	3,616,523
		Mining and Quarrying	292,120	Industry	4,644,385
Secondary Sector	4,352,265	Manufacturing	2,585,740		
		Electricity, Gas, Water Supply and Other Utility Services	484,477		
		Construction	1,282,048	Services	9,654,259
Tertiary Sector	9,654,259	Trade, Hotels, Transport, Communication and Services Related to Broadcasting	2,941,477		
		Financial, Real Estate and Professional Services	3,950,786		
		Public Administration, Defence and Other Services	2,761,996		
GVA	17,915,167		17,915,167		17,915,167

According to the estimates of 2020–2021 provided by the National Statistical Office (NSO), the GVA at current prices was Rs 179.15 lakh crore while at constant prices (base year 2011–2012) was Rs 124.53 lakh crore. In terms of the economic activity type, the maximum Gross Value Added was by Financial, Real Estate & Professional Services (Rs 39.5 lakh crore) while the least GVA was by Mining & Quarrying (Rs 2.9 lakh crore) in current prices. This trend was also visible in GVA at constant prices. In terms of economic sector, the GVA at current prices was the maximum by tertiary sector (Rs 96.5 lakh crore) followed by secondary (Rs 43.52 lakh crore) and primary sector (Rs 39 lakh crore) (Tables 6.3 and 6.4). The GVA added by tertiary sector was greater than that of both the primary and secondary sectors combined which shows the importance of the tertiary sector in the economy of India.

Table 6.4 GVA at Constant Price (2011–2012) 2020–2021 (in Crore Rupees)

Economic Sector	GVA	Economic Activity	GVA	Economic Activity Group	GVA
Primary Sector	2,334,723	Agriculture, Forestry and Fishing	2,040,079	Agriculture	2,040,079
Secondary Sector	3,359,718	Mining and Quarrying	294,644	Industry	2,707,966
		Manufacturing	2,107,068		
		Electricity, Gas, Water Supply and Other Utility Services	306,254		
Tertiary Sector	6,758,989	Construction	946,396	Services	7,705,385
		Trade, Hotels, Transport, Communication and Services Related to Broadcasting	2,208,388		
		Financial, Real Estate and Professional Services	2,872,815		
		Public Administration, Defence and Other Services	1,677,786		
GVA at Basic Prices	12,453,430		12,453,430		12,453,430

When the share of different economic activities in GVA is considered, Financial, Real Estate & Professional Services (22.1 per cent) contributed the maximum to GVA, followed by Agriculture, Forestry and Fishing (20.2 per cent) while Mining & Quarrying (1.6 per cent) made the least contribution to GVA. Sector-wise, the highest contribution to GVA was by tertiary sector (53.9 per cent) followed by the secondary sector (24.3 per cent) and primary sector (21.8 per cent) (Figure 6.2). In 2020–2021, the contribution of Agriculture, Forestry and Fishing at current prices was 20.2 per cent while at constant prices it was 16.4 per cent, which expresses the effect of inflation on the prices of agricultural commodities. The share of different economic activities in GVA was agriculture (16.4 per cent), industry (21.7 per cent) and services (61.9 per cent) (Figure 6.1). When the indirect taxes are added and subsidies deducted from GVA, which is known as net taxes, then the value of GDP is obtained.

GDP by Expenditure Method: Another method which is officially used by the National Statistical Office (NSO) to estimate the GDP is the expenditure method. According to the expenditure method, GDP is equal to (C + I + G + X − M), where C is the consumption expenditure, I is the investment expenditure, G is the aggregate government expenditure, X is the total exports, M is the total imports. The different components are measured using parameters such as (1) Private Final Consumption Expenditure (PFCE), (2) Gross Fixed Capital Formation (GFCF), (3) Changes in Stocks (CIS), (4) Valuables, (5) Government Final Consumption Expenditure (GFCE), (6) Exports of Goods and Services (Exports), (7) Import of Goods and Services (Imports). Among these components, at current prices, the maximum contribution is by Private Final Consumption Expenditure (PFCE) (58.6 per cent) followed by Gross Fixed

178 Income and Employment

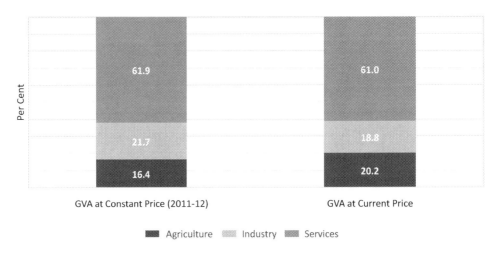

Figure 6.1 GVA (Gross Value Added) of Economic Activities (Source: National Statistical Office)

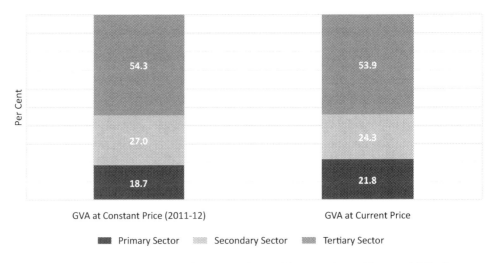

Figure 6.2 GVA (Gross Value Added) of Economic Sector (Source: National Statistical Office)

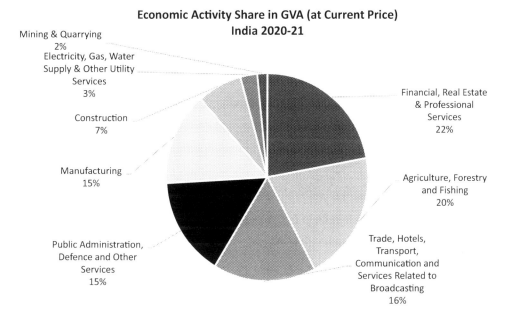

Figure 6.3 GVA (Gross Value Added) by Individual Economic Activity (Source: National Statistical Office)

Capital Formation (GFCF) (27.1 per cent) which is a measure of investment expenditure. The pattern is similar with respect to constant prices (Tables 6.5 and 5.6).

GDP Growth: The Gross Domestic Product (GDP) of India in 2020–2021, according to the estimates of the National Statistical Office (NSO) was Rs 197.45 lakh crore at current prices and Rs 135.12 lakh crore at constant prices. At current prices, the GDP of India is roughly equal to 2.59 trillion US dollars. In the last 10 years, from 2011 to 2021, the decadal GDP growth of India has been 126 per cent which amounts to 12.6 per cent year-on-year growth on average, at the current prices. However, when the prices are adjusted for inflation, then the real GDP growth of India during the same decade has been 54.7 per cent, which translates into 5.47 per cent year-on-year growth on average. The GDP of India crossed the Rs 100 lakh crore mark in 2013–2014. The GDP deflator in 2011–2012 was one as it is the base year in which the current and constant prices are the same. However, in 2020–2021, the value of GDP deflator is 1.5 which means that the GDP at current prices is inflated by 1.5 times due to the effect of inflation. The GDP of India in absolute terms has grown consistently between 2011 and 2020, except for 2020–2021, during which the economic growth was affected severely due to the effects of the Covid-19 pandemic which included restrictions and curbs, lockdown, reduction in demand and global trade, etc. (Table 6.7, Figure 6.4).

The growth rate of the GDP of India has been inconsistent during the last ten years, according to the estimates of the NSO. For most part of the decade, the nominal GDP growth rate has been greater than 10 per cent annually. However, during 2019–2020, the growth rate fell to 7.8 per cent while in 2020–2021, the growth rate was negative

Table 6.5 Components of GDP by Expenditure Method

Component of Expenditure	Components	Constant Prices (2011–2012)	Current Prices
C	Private Final Consumption Expenditure	7,560,985	11,568,231
I	Gross Fixed Capital Formation	4,220,508	5,349,875
	Changes in Stocks	154,276	195,411
	Valuables	167,784	235,782
G	Government Final Consumption Expenditure	1,586,745	2,467,415
X	Exports of Goods and Services	2,694,386	3,685,170
M	Import of Goods and Services	2,865,827	3,792,712
	Discrepancies	-6117	36,499
Gross Domestic Product		**13,512,740**	**19,745,670**

where C = consumption expenditure, I = investment expenditure, G = aggregate government expenditure, X = total exports, M = total imports and GDP = C + I + G + X - M

Discrepancies are added or subtracted to match with the GDP figure obtained by the production method using GVA

Table 6.6 Components of GDP by Expenditure Method (in Per cent)

Component of Expenditure	Components	Constant Prices (2011–2012)	Current Prices
C	Private Final Consumption Expenditure	56.0	58.6
I	Gross Fixed Capital Formation	31.2	27.1
	Changes in Stocks	1.1	1.0
	Valuables	1.2	1.2
G	Government Final Consumption Expenditure	11.7	12.5
X	Exports of Goods and Services	19.9	18.7
M	Import of Goods and Services	21.2	19.2
	Discrepancies	0.0	0.2
Gross Domestic Product		**100**	**100**

where C = consumption expenditure, I = investment expenditure, G = aggregate government expenditure, X = total exports, M = total imports and GDP = C + I + G + X - M

Discrepancies are added or subtracted to match with the GDP figure obtained by the production method using GVA

at −3 per cent, where the total GDP value was actually reduced. The real GDP growth of India during the same decade was much lower, averaging around only 5.1 per cent annually. The highest real GDP growth was during 2016–2017 (8.3 per cent) and 2015-2016 (8 per cent). However, as a consequence of a slew of economic restructuring measures such as demonetisation in 2016 and the introduction of the Goods

Table 6.7 Gross Domestic Product (in Crore Rupees) of India 2011–2021

Year	GDP at Current Price	GDP at Constant Price (2011–2012)	GDP Deflator
2011–2012	8,736,329	8,736,329	1.0
2012–2013	9,944,013	9,213,017	1.1
2013–2014	11,233,522	9,801,370	1.1
2014–2015	12,467,959	10,527,674	1.2
2015–2016	13,771,874	11,369,493	1.2
2016–2017	15,391,669	12,308,193	1.3
2017–2018	17,090,042	13,144,582	1.3
2018–2019	18,886,957	14,003,316	1.3
2019–2020	20,351,013	14,569,268	1.4
2020–2021	19,745,670	13,512,740	1.5

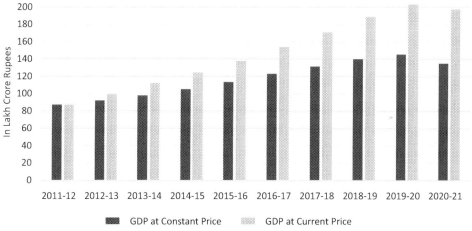

Figure 6.4 Gross Domestic Product of India (2011–2021)

and Services Tax (GST) in 2017, the real GDP growth has contracted consistently ever since. In 2020–2021, the real GDP growth rate was –7.3 per cent which was only the fifth time in history when the GDP of India registered negative growth. The other instances when the GDP recorded negative growth were in 1957–1958 (–1.2 per cent), 1965–1966 (–3.66 per cent), 1972–1973 (–0.32 per cent) and 1979–1980 (–5.2 per cent). While the negative GDP growth rate in 2020–2021 can be attributed to the Covid-19 pandemic, earlier contractions were mainly due to war, agricultural droughts, energy crisis, etc. (Table 6.8).

Per Capita Gross Domestic Product: The Per Capita Gross Domestic Product is obtained by dividing the GDP by the total population of the country. The Per Capita

182 Income and Employment

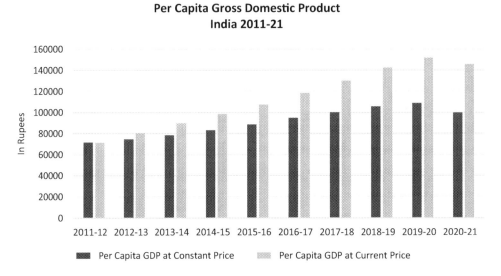

Figure 6.5 Per Capita Gross Domestic Product of India (2011–2021)

Table 6.8 Gross Domestic Product (GDP) Year-on-Year Growth (in Per Cent)

Year	GDP Growth at Current Price or Nominal GDP Growth	GDP Growth at Constant Price (2011–2012) or Real GDP Growth
2011–2012	14.4	5.2
2012–2013	13.8	5.5
2013–2014	13.0	6.4
2014–2015	11.0	7.4
2015–2016	10.5	8.0
2016–2017	11.8	8.3
2017–2018	11.0	6.8
2018–2019	10.5	6.5
2019–2020	7.8	4.0
2020–2021	−3.0	−7.3

Gross Domestic Product in 2020–2021 at current prices was Rs 1,45,680 and at constant prices was Rs 99,694. The decadal growth of per capita GDP at the current price between 2011 and 2021 has been 103.4 per cent which is equal to 10.34 per cent average annual growth. On the other hand, the per capita GDP decadal growth at constant prices has been only 39.2 per cent which is 3.9 per cent average annual growth. During 2020–2021, the per capita GDP registered negative growth, that is it contracted compared to the previous year. As with GDP, the per capita GDP growth was the highest in 2016–2017 (11.8 per cent at current prices and 6.9 per cent at constant prices) (Table 6.9).

Table 6.9 Per Capita Gross Domestic Product and Growth (in Rupees)

Year	Per Capita GDP at Current Price	Per Capita GDP at Constant Price	Per Capita GDP Growth at Current Price	Per Capita GDP Growth at Constant Price
2011–2012	71,609	71,609	14.4	2.3
2012–2013	80,518	74,599	13.8	4.2
2013–2014	89,796	78,348	13.0	5.0
2014–2015	98,405	83,091	11.0	6.1
2015–2016	107,341	88,616	10.5	6.6
2016–2017	118,489	94,751	11.8	6.9
2017–2018	130,061	100,035	11.0	5.6
2018–2019	142,328	105,526	10.5	5.5
2019–2020	151,760	108,645	7.8	3.0
2020–2021	145,680	99,694	−3.0	−8.2

Employment

People who are actively participating in an economic activity are said to be employed. According to the Periodic Labour Force Survey 2019–2020, in India, the maximum proportion of employed persons were in primary sector (45.6 per cent), followed by tertiary sector (42.3 per cent) and secondary sector (12.1 per cent). Even though the economic contribution of the primary sector in GDP was the least (21.8 per cent), it employed the maximum number of persons. The secondary sector contributes more than double to the economy (24.3 per cent) than the share of persons employed in it (12.1 per cent). The tertiary sector contributes the maximum to the GDP and employs the second highest share of persons. Among males, the maximum employment is in tertiary sector (47.7 per cent), followed by primary (40 per cent) and secondary sector (12.5 per cent) while the majority of females are employed in primary sector (59.9 per cent), followed by tertiary (28.8 per cent) and secondary sector (11.3 per cent) (Figure 6.6). In the primary sector, most of the females are employed mainly as agricultural and casual labourers. The gender bias and the barriers faced by women in education, skill enhancement due to various socio-economic obstacles is visible in the employment figures. Majority of women do not get opportunity to work in industries or the service sector and remain confined to agricultural fields.

Gross State Domestic Product

At current prices, the highest GSDP in 2019–2020 was of Maharashtra (Rs 28.18 lakh crore) followed by Tamil Nadu (Rs 17.97 lakh crore) and Uttar Pradesh (Rs 16.88 lakh crore) while the least GSDP was of Mizoram (Rs 25,148.57 crore) and Arunachal Pradesh (Rs 28,046.13 crore). Apart from Maharashtra, Tamil Nadu, Uttar Pradesh, the states with GSDP exceeding Rs 10 lakh crore are Gujarat, Karnataka and West Bengal. Among the union territories, the highest GSDP was of the National Capital Territory (NCT) of Delhi (Rs 8.3 lakh crore) and the least was of Andaman and Nicobar Islands (Rs 9,719 crore). At constant prices, the highest real GSDP was

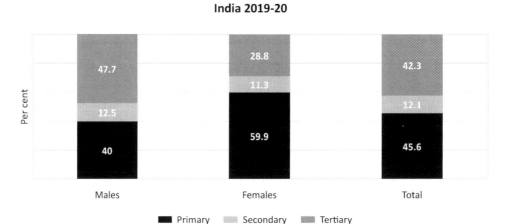

Figure 6.6 Employment by Economic Sector in India (2019–2020)

of Maharashtra (Rs 21.34 lakh crore), Tamil Nadu (Rs 12.78 lakh crore) and Gujarat (Rs 12.68 lakh crore) and the least real GSDP was of Andaman & Nicobar Islands (Rs 7,1984.4 crore) and Arunachal Pradesh (Rs 17,916.4 crore) (Figure 6.7(a,b)).

Per Capita Gross State Domestic Product (GSDP): When the GSDP is divided by the population of the state or union territory, then per capita Gross State Domestic Product (GSDP) is obtained. It is a better measure of the economic activity in a state as it expresses the value of goods and services being produced per head. In India, at current prices, in 2019–2020, the highest per capita Gross State Domestic Product (GSDP) was of Goa (Rs 4,71,731), Sikkim (Rs 4,46,345), Delhi (Rs 4,44,057) and Chandigarh (Rs 3,76,999) while the lowest was in Bihar (Rs 47,597), Uttar Pradesh (Rs 70,952) and Jharkhand (Rs 83,214). Uttar Pradesh which has the third-highest nominal GSDP also has the second lowest per capita GSDP. In terms of constant prices during the same period, the highest per capita GSDP was in Gujarat (Rs 85,042), Uttarakhand (Rs 84,352) and Odisha (Rs 82,759) while the lowest was in Arunachal Pradesh (Rs 70,905), Sikkim (Rs 69,361) and Nagaland (Rs 68,310) (Figure 6.8(a,b)).

GSDP Growth Rate: During 2019–2020, at the current prices, the highest annual GSDP growth rate was of Madhya Pradesh (15.19 per cent), Mizoram (14.94 per cent), Manipur (14.07 per cent) and Bihar (12.51 per cent) while the lowest annual GSDP growth was of Goa (4.14 per cent), Jharkhand (5.06 per cent) and Punjab (5.30 per cent). Tripura, Andhra Pradesh, Nagaland, Telangana, Puducherry, Arunachal Pradesh, Haryana, the NCT of Delhi and Tamil Nadu were the other states and union territories with annual GSDP growth rate exceeding 10 per cent. At constant prices, the highest annual GSDP growth rate was of Mizoram (12.20 per cent), Madhya Pradesh (9.63 per cent) and Tripura (9.40 per cent) while the lowest growth rate was of Jammu & Kashmir and Ladakh (2.31 per cent), Assam (2.95 per cent) and Kerala (3.45 per cent) (Figure 6.9 (a), (b)).

Income and Employment 185

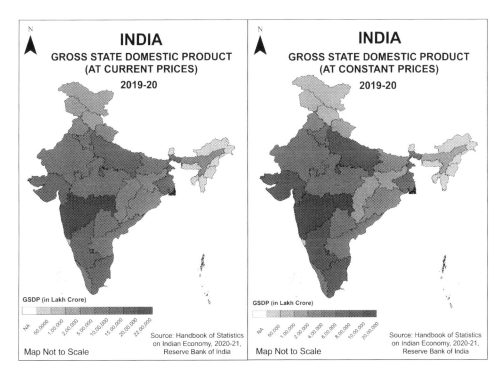

Figure 6.7 (a) Gross State Domestic Product (GSDP) at Current Prices (2019–2020) and (b) Gross State Domestic Product (GSDP) at Constant Prices (2019–2020)

Labour Force Participation Rate (LFPR)

The Labour Force Participation Rate (LFPR) is used as a statistical measure of the proportion of a country's working-age population that is engaging actively in the labour market and is either working or looking for work. The people employed in the economy or looking for work is known as the labour force. LFPR provides an indication of the size of the supply of labour available for working in the economy. The Labour Force Participation Rate is calculated by dividing the labour force by the total working-age population. The working-age population refers to people aged between 15 and 59 years. It is calculated using the following formula:

$$\text{Labour Force Participation Rate} = \frac{\left(\begin{array}{c}\text{Number of Employed Persons} \\ +\text{Number of Unemployed Persons}\end{array}\right)}{\text{Population in the Age 15}-59\,\text{years}} * 100$$

or

186 Income and Employment

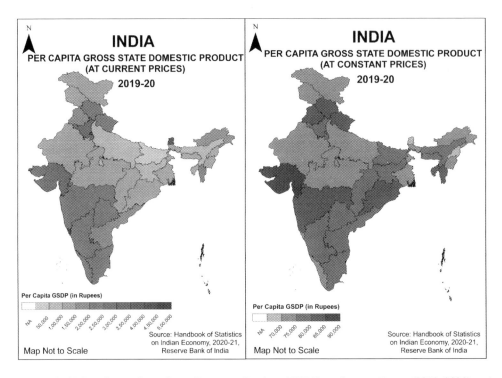

Figure 6.8 (a) Per Capita Gross State Domestic Product (GSDP) at Current Prices (2019–2020) and (b) Per Capita Gross State Domestic Product (GSDP) at Constant Prices (2019–2020)

$$\text{Labour Force Participation Rate} = \frac{\text{Labour force}}{\text{Working Age Population}} * 100$$

According to the Periodic Labour Force Survey (PLFS) 2019–2020, the highest male LFPR was recorded in Himachal Pradesh (77.6 per cent), Dadra & Nagar Haveli and Daman & Diu (72.5 per cent), Sikkim (72.4 per cent) and Chhattisgarh (70.7 per cent) while the lowest LFPR was recorded in Bihar (42.5 per cent) and Arunachal Pradesh (48 per cent). Apart from these states, Uttar Pradesh and Assam had less than 50 per cent of the working-age population in the labour force. Among the males, the highest LFPR was recorded in Lakshadweep (90.6 per cent), Dadra & Nagar Haveli and Daman & Diu (89.9 per cent), Himachal Pradesh (85.2 per cent), West Bengal (85 per cent) and Chhattisgarh (84.7 per cent) while the lowest LFPR was in Arunachal Pradesh (70 per cent), Manipur (74.9 per cent) and Bihar (75.1 per cent). The female LFPR in India during 2019–2020 was 36.75 per cent, much less than males. Himachal Pradesh (70.3 per cent), Sikkim (61.8 per cent), Chhattisgarh (56.8 per cent) and Ladakh (56.6 per cent) recorded the highest female LFPR and were the only states and union territories having more than 50 per cent of women involved in the labour force. Bihar (9.7 per cent), Assam (17.4 per cent) and Delhi (17.4 per cent) had the lowest female participation in labour force (Figure 6.10(a,b)).

Income and Employment 187

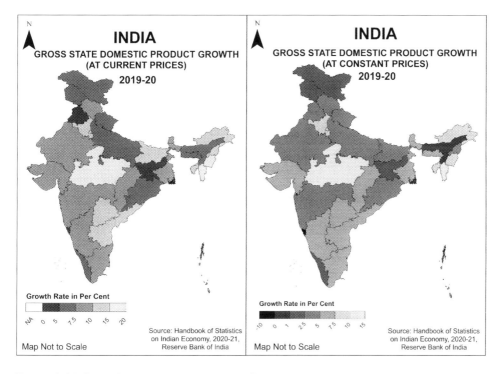

Figure 6.9 (a) Gross State Domestic Product (GSDP) Growth at Current Prices (2019–2020), (b) Gross State Domestic Product (GSDP) Growth at Constant Prices (2019–2020)

Main and Marginal Workers: In the Census of India, work is defined as participation in any economically productive activity with or without compensation, wages or profit which may be physical and/or mental in nature. Apart from manual labour, work can involve (i) effective supervision and direction of work, (ii) part time help or unpaid work on farm, family enterprise and (iii) cultivation or milk production even solely for domestic consumption. Accordingly, all persons who are engaged in 'work' which is participation in any economically productive activity with or without compensation, wages or profit are termed as workers. The reference period for determining a person as worker or non-worker is one year preceding the date of enumeration. Consequently, the Census identifies two types of workers: (a) Main Workers and (b) Marginal Workers. Main Workers are those workers who worked for the major part of the reference period, i.e. six months or more or for 180 or more days in the preceding year. On the other hand, those workers who did not work for majority of the reference period, i.e. for less than six months or 180 days are termed as marginal workers. The main workers are further classified on the basis of category of work into (1) Cultivators, (2) Agricultural Labourers, (3) Household Industry Workers and (4) Other Workers. This classification is suitable considering the nature of employment in India which is largely in the primary sector. Main and marginal workers together constitute the total workers in the economy. When the unemployed persons who actively

188 Income and Employment

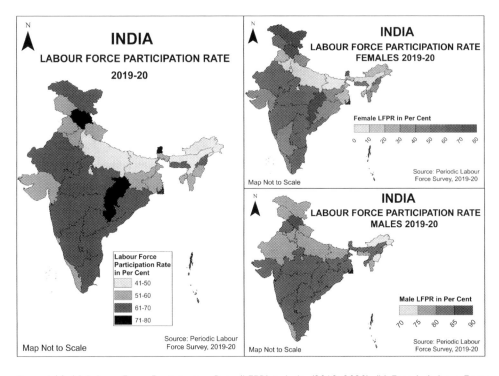

Figure 6.10 (a) Labour Force Participation Rate (LFPR) in India (2019–2020), (b) Female Labour Force Participation Rate (LFPR) in India (2019–2020), (c) Male Labour Force Participation Rate (LFPR) in India (2019–2020)

sought but did not find 'work' at all during the reference period of preceding one year are added to total workers, then we get the total labour force.

Total Workers = Main Workers + Marginal Workers

Labour Force = Main Workers + Marginal Workers + Unemployed Persons

The proportion of main workers points towards the regularity of employment. In 2011, the total number of main workers were 39,82,47,098 which equalled 30.45 per cent of the total population. The highest number of main workers were in Uttar Pradesh (4,46,35,492), Maharashtra (4,37,62,890) and Andhra Pradesh (3,30,37,378) while the least were in Lakshadweep (10,804), Andaman & Nicobar Islands (1,25,910) and Sikkim (2,30,397). In terms of share in the state population, the highest share of main workers was in Dadra & Nagar Haveli and Daman & Diu (42 per cent) and Andhra Pradesh and Telangana (39.1 per cent). The least share of main workers in the total population was in Lakshadweep (16.8 per cent), Bihar (20.5 per cent) and Jharkhand (20.7 per cent). Twenty-two states and union territories had a higher share of workers in their population compared to the national average. In 2011, the total marginal workers in India were 12,73,87,389 which was roughly equal to 9.74 per cent of the total population. The highest number of marginal workers were in Uttar Pradesh (1,24,26,463), Bihar (79,51,499) and West Bengal (50,37,768) while the least was in Lakshadweep (6,181) and Chandigarh (10,969) among union territories and Mizoram (27,435) and Sikkim (33,845) among the states. In percentage terms, Himachal Pradesh (21.8 per cent) and Jharkhand (19.0 per cent) had the highest while Delhi (1.7 per cent), Chandigarh (1.7 per cent), Puducherry (3.6 per cent) and Maharashtra (5 per cent) have the lowest share of marginal workers in the population (Figure 6.11 (a), (b)).

Workers and Non-Workers: Main and marginal workers are together known as total workers, according to the Census of India. The rest of the population apart from main and marginal workers is referred to as non-workers. Non-workers include the following persons: (a) persons who did not work at all during the reference period of the past one year, (b) students who did not participate in any economic activity, paid or unpaid, (c) those who were attending to daily household chores like cooking, cleaning utensils, looking after children, fetching water, etc. and are not even helping in the unpaid work in the family farm or cultivation or milching, (d) dependants such as infants or very elderly people not included in the category of worker, (e) those who are drawing pension after retirement and are not engaged in any economic activity, (f) beggars, vagrants, prostitutes and persons having unidentified

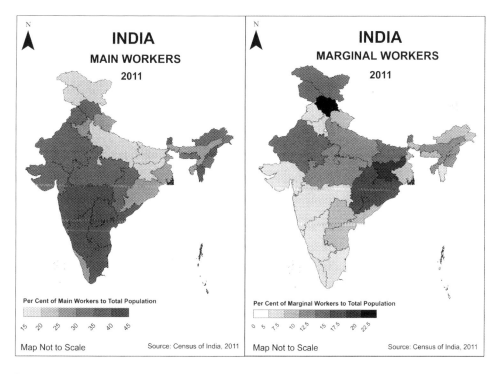

Figure 6.11 (a) Distribution of Main Workers in India (2011), (b) Distribution of Marginal Workers in India (2011)

source of income and with unspecified sources of subsistence and not engaged in any economically productive work during the reference period, (g) persons who may not come under the above categories such as rentiers, persons living on remittances, agricultural or non-agricultural royalty, convicts in jails or inmates of penal, mental or charitable institutions doing no paid or unpaid work and persons who are seeking/available for work.

The total number of workers during 2001–2011, according to the Census of India, was 48,18,88,868 which amounted to 36.84 per cent of the total population. Uttar Pradesh (6,58,14,715), Maharashtra (4,94,27,878) and Andhra Pradesh (3,94,22,906) have the highest while Lakshadweep (18,753), Andaman & Nicobar Islands (1,52,535) and Sikkim (3,08,138) had the least number of workers. In terms of share of workers in the total population, Himachal Pradesh (52 per cent), Sikkim (50 per cent) and Nagaland (49 per cent) have the highest share while the least share of workers is in Lakshadweep (29 per cent), Uttar Pradesh (33 per cent) and Delhi (33 per cent). The number of non-workers between 2001 and 2011 in India was 72,89,66,109. The highest non-workers were in Uttar Pradesh (13,39,97,626), Bihar (6,93,74,465) and Maharashtra (6,29,46,455) while the lowest number of non-workers were in Lakshadweep (45,720), Andaman & Nicobar Islands (2,28,046) and Sikkim (3,02,439). In terms of share in total population, Lakshadweep (70.9 per cent), Uttar Pradesh (67.1 per cent) and Delhi (66.7 per cent) had the maximum while Himachal Pradesh (48.1 per cent), Sikkim (49.5 per cent) and Nagaland (50.8 per cent) had the least share of non-workers (Figure 6.12).

Formal and Informal Workers: The workers in the economy who have regular and specific working hours get a regular wage or salary, have job security and generally have a written work contract are known as formal workers. Informal workers generally do not have job security and the income they earn is erratic and irregular. For instance, employees in banks, corporate houses and factories are formal while agricultural labourers, casual labourers and waste pickers are informal workers. The data on formal and informal workers is provided by the Periodic Labour Force Survey (PLFS) conducted by the NSO. The PLFS groups workers into three categories, namely (1) self-employed, (2) regular wage/salary workers and (3) casual labourers. The category of self-employed workers is further classified into (a) own account worker or employer, (b) helper in household enterprise and (c) all self-employed workers. Out of these categories, the workers earning regular wage/salary are formal workers while self-employed workers and casual labourers are informal workers. The regularity of income can be the only criterion for classifying formal workers according to this data. Overall, in 2019–2020, only 22.9 per cent or just about one-fifth of the workers in India were formal workers while the remaining 77.1 per cent were informal workers. Of the 77.1 per cent informal workers, 23.6 per cent were casual labourers, while 53.5 per cent workers were self-employed. The highest proportion of formal workers are in Chandigarh (67.3 per cent), Delhi (66 per cent) and Goa (60.3 per cent) while the least is in Bihar (9.6 per cent), Jharkhand (14.1 per cent) and Odisha (14.9 per cent). On the other hand, the maximum share of informal workers was in Bihar (90.4 per cent), Jharkhand (85.9 per cent) and Odisha (85.1 per cent) while the least share is in Chandigarh (32.7 per cent), Delhi (34 per cent) and Goa (39.7 per cent) (Figure 6.13).

Income and Employment 191

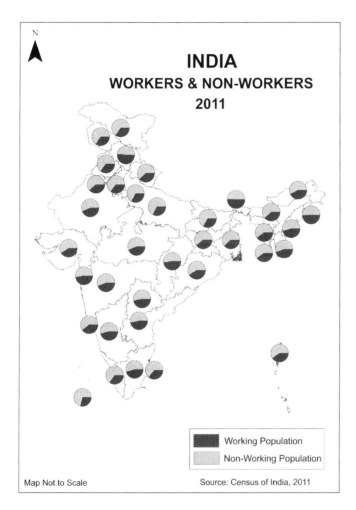

Figure 6.12 Distribution of Working and Non-working Population in India (2011)

Poverty

Poverty is a situation in which a person does not have enough money to fulfil his or her basic needs and wants. A person who suffers from poverty is a poor person. Poverty rate is defined as the number of poor persons to the total population of the nation, expressed in percentage. This is also known as the poverty headcount rate.

$$\text{Poverty Rate} = \frac{\text{Number of Poor Persons in Population}}{\text{Total Population}} * 100$$

There are different measures used to estimate poverty and poverty rates. The method used in India is the Poverty Line Method. In the poverty line method, a person earning

192 Income and Employment

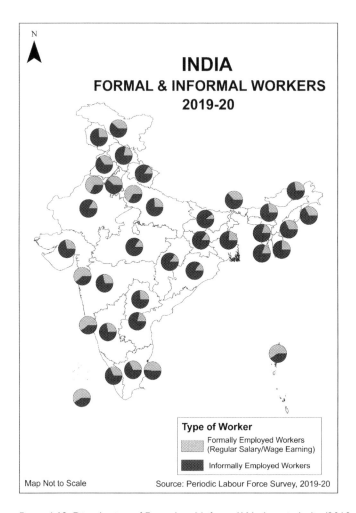

Figure 6.13 Distribution of Formal and Informal Workers in India (2019–2020)

less than a certain amount of money during a designated period is considered to be poor. The poverty line is decided by different governments and international agencies. Persons whose incomes are less than this amount are said to be below poverty line (BPL) and those having higher incomes than this amount are said to be above poverty line (APL). The poverty rate estimated by this method is called absolute poverty because any person earning less than the designated amount of money falls into the poverty bracket. The proportion of the population below the poverty line is called the poverty ratio or headcount ratio (HCR) (Monitoring Global Poverty, 2020). According to the World Bank, a person earning less than 1.90 US dollars a day is poor and less than 1.25 US dollars a day is extremely poor (Ravallion, 1992). A problem with this method is that poverty is not an absolute economic status but represents a spectrum, so, for instance, a person earning 1.91 US dollar per day will not be considered poor while a person earning 1.89 US dollar per day will be considered poor while in reality, the real difference between their incomes is just 0.02 dollars per day.

One of the earliest estimates of poverty in India was made by Dadabhai Naoroji in the book 'Poverty and the Un-British Rule in India' where he estimated poverty line ranging from Rs 16 to Rs 35 per capita per year, based on 1867–1868 prices. In 1938, the National Planning Committee (NPC) under the chairmanship of Jawaharlal Nehru set up by Indian National Congress (INC) estimated a poverty line ranging from Rs 15 to Rs 20 per capita per month. Another effort at estimating poverty line was by VM Dandekar and N Rath in 1971 (Deaton & Kozel, 2005). In India, governments and government agencies have set up committees from time to time to estimate the poverty line. In 1979, the YK Alagh committee was set up by the Planning Commission, which estimated the poverty line separately for rural and urban areas taking calorie consumption requirements as the criterion for estimating poverty line. A person who consumed less than the stipulated calories per day was considered poor. The DT Lakdawala Committee (1993) established again by the Planning Commission estimated poverty line using multiple indicators such as calorie requirements, consumption expenditure adjusted for inflation, etc. (Manna, 2007).

The current poverty line estimates used officially were made by the Suresh Tendulkar Committee (2009) set up by the Planning Commission. It recommended four major changes to the former methods of poverty estimation, namely (i) marked shift away from calorie consumption-based poverty estimation, (ii) a uniform poverty line basket (PLB) separately for rural and urban India, (iii) spatial and temporal correction of prices, (iv) incorporation of private expenditure on health and education while estimating poverty. The Committee recommended using Mixed Reference Period (MRP) which measures consumption of five low-frequency items (clothing, footwear, durables, education and institutional health expenditure) over the previous year, and all other items over the previous 30 days (Alagh, 2010). The Mixed Reference Period was used by the National Sample Survey Office (NSSO) in its regular surveys for measuring poverty rate. The poverty line varies from state to state due to varying price levels.

The C Rangarajan Committee was set up in 2012 by the Planning Commission mainly used per capita nutritional fulfilment, consumption expenditure to estimate poverty. It recommended a poverty line of Rs 22 per head per day for rural areas and Rs 36 per head per day for urban areas. The recommendations of this committee were not accepted due to uproar and protests against the defined poverty line (Ray & Sinha, 2014). Another method of poverty estimation was used by the Socio-Economic Caste Census (SECC) 2011 which used multi-criteria deprivations. According to it, nearly 44 per cent of the rural population was poor. The estimates of this census are used for providing welfare services as housing under PMAY (Prime Minister *Awas Yojana*), etc. but the complete figures of this census have not been published yet.

The last estimate of poverty was done in 2011–2012 by the NSSO using the Tendulkar committee methodology based on a Mixed Reference Period. The poverty line was defined as Rs 816 per capita per month for rural areas and Rs 1,000 per capita per month for urban areas. According to this estimate, 26,97,83,000 persons were below poverty line in India which amounted to 21.92 per cent of the total population being poor. Chhattisgarh (39.93 per cent), Dadra & Nagar Haveli and Daman & Diu (39.62 per cent), Jharkhand (36.96 per cent) and Manipur (36.89 per cent) had the highest while Andaman & Nicobar Islands (1 per cent), Lakshadweep (2.77 per cent),

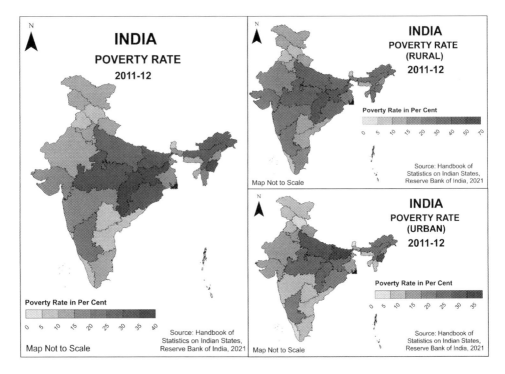

Figure 6.14 (a) Poverty Rate in India (2011–2012), (b) Rural Poverty Rate in India (2011–2012) and (c) Urban Poverty Rate in India (2011–2012)

Goa (5.09 per cent) and Kerala (7.05 per cent) had the least proportion of poor people. Uttar Pradesh (5,98,19,000), Bihar (3,58,15,000), Madhya Pradesh (2,34,06,000) and Maharashtra (1,97,92,000) have the highest number of poor people.

The number of persons below poverty rate in rural areas was 21,66,58,000 or 25.7 per cent of the rural population. The number of urban poor was 5,31,25,000 which is roughly equal to 13.7 per cent of the urban population. The highest urban poverty was in Manipur (32.6 per cent), Bihar (31.2 per cent) and Uttar Pradesh (26.1 per cent) and lowest in Lakshadweep (3.4 per cent), Sikkim (3.7 per cent) and Goa (4.1 per cent). In rural areas, the highest poverty rate was in Dadra & Nagar Haveli and Daman & Diu (62.6 per cent), Chhattisgarh (44.6 per cent), Jharkhand (40.8 per cent) and lowest in Andaman & Nicobar Islands (1.6 per cent), Chandigarh (1.6 per cent) and Goa (6.8 per cent) (Figure 6.14 (a), (b)).

Unemployment

Unemployment refers to a situation in which individuals who are employable and are actively seeking a job but are unable to find a job. Unemployment rate refers to the number of unemployed persons who are willing to work and are actively looking for a job expressed as a per cent of the labour force.

$$\text{Unemployment Rate} = \frac{\text{Number of Unemployed Persons}}{\text{Total Persons in Labour Force}} * 100$$

where

Total Persons in Labour Force = Number of Employed Persons
+ Number of Unemployed Persons

Persons who are not actively looking for work are not included in the definition of unemployed persons. These may include students, homemaker women, etc. Unemployment serves as one of the important indicators of the status of economic growth of a country. Unemployment causes workers to suffer financial hardships and impacts families and communities. It also reduces consumer spending and may result in slowing of economic growth leading to recession or even a depression if not addressed (Nepram et al., 2021). Unemployment results in reduced demand, consumption and buying power, which in turn causes lower profits for businesses and leads to budget cuts and workforce reductions. There are different types of unemployment based on causative factors:

1. **Structural Unemployment**: It occurs when the skills set of a worker does not match the skills demanded in the job market, or when workers are available but are unable to reach the geographical location of the jobs.
2. **Demand-Deficient Unemployment**: It occurs during economic slowdown or recession when the demand of workers in the economy goes down or firms are forced to reduce their workforce.
3. **Frictional Unemployment**: It occurs during the period when a person is unemployed after leaving one job and searching for another.
4. **Voluntary Unemployment**: It occurs when a worker voluntarily decides to leave a job due to any reason which may include further studies, disease, etc. and does not intend to join the labour force soon.
5. **Open Unemployment**: It occurs when a large section of the labour force does not get a job that yields regular income, mainly because the labour force expands at a rate faster than the growth of jobs in economy.
6. **Disguised Unemployment**: It occurs when more persons are employed in the economy than required. Disguised unemployment refers to a situation when the marginal productivity of the additional worker is zero.
7. **Seasonal Unemployment**: It occurs when there is no employment during certain seasons of the year. It generally occurs in sectors such as agriculture, tourism etc.
8. **Cyclical Unemployment**: It occurs due to the boom-and-bust cycle in the economy. It is normally a shot-term phenomenon.
9. **Casual Unemployment**: When a person who is a casual labourer or is employed on a day-to-day basis, casual unemployment can occur when such a person is unable to find employment. It is generally short term.
10. **Underemployment**: It occurs when a person is employed in a job that has wages less than their qualifications and capacity.

11. **Natural Unemployment**: It refers to the natural rate of unemployment that is always going to exist in the economy as a result of changing jobs, outdated skills etc.

In India, unemployment-related data is recorded and published by the Periodic Labour Force Survey (PLFS). This survey defines an unemployed person as a person 'not working, but making tangible efforts to seek "work" or being available for "work" if "work" is available'. Consequently, unemployment rate is defined in this survey as the per cent of persons 'not working, but seeking/available for work' in the labour force. The unemployment rate is derived from the Usual Principal Status and Subsidiary Status (PS+SS) according to which a person is considered unemployed if he or she did not engage in any economic activity for a period of 30 days or more during the preceding 365 days. The unemployment rate according to this approach expresses a problem of chronic unemployment.

In 2019–2020, according to the Usual Principal Status and Subsidiary Status, the overall unemployment rate in India was 6.6 per cent. The male employment rate was 6.4 per cent and female unemployment rate was higher at 7.6 per cent. The highest unemployment rate was in Nagaland (27.8 per cent), Lakshadweep (14 per cent), Kerala (11.6 per cent) and Manipur (10.1 per cent). Along with Andaman and Nicobar Islands, these states and union territories had an unemployment rate exceeding ten per cent. The least unemployment rate was in Ladakh (0.1 per cent), Gujarat (2.2 per cent) and Sikkim (2.4 per cent). Nagaland (30.1 per cent), Andaman & Nicobar Islands

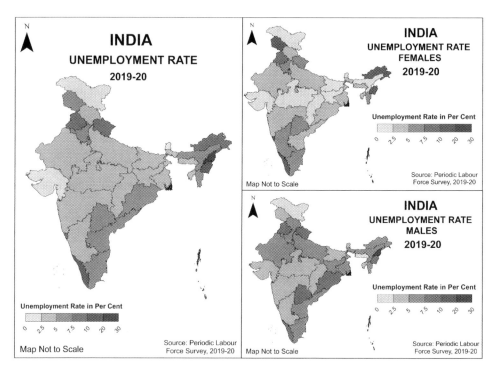

Figure 6.15 (a) Unemployment Rate in India (2019–2020), (B) Female Unemployment Rate in India (2019–2020), (c) Male Unemployment Rate in India (2019–2020)

(28.2 per cent) and Kerala (17.1 per cent) had the highest while Gujarat (1.1 per cent), Jharkhand (1.3 per cent) and Madhya Pradesh (1.4 per cent) had the lowest female unemployment rate. On the other hand, the highest male unemployment rate was in Nagaland (26.7 per cent), Lakshadweep (11 per cent) and Manipur (9.7 per cent) while the lowest was in Ladakh (0.2 per cent), Meghalaya (2.2 per cent) and Gujarat (2.6 per cent) (Figure 6.15(a,b)).

References

Alagh, Y. K. (2010). The Poverty Debate in Perspective: Moving Forward With the Tendulkar Committee. *Indian Journal of Human Development*, 4(1), 33–44.
Costanza, R., Hart, M., Posner, S., & Talberth, J. (2009). *Beyond GDP: The Need for New Measures of Progress*. Boston: Pardee Center for the Study of the Longer-Range Future.
Deaton, A., & Kozel, V. (2005). Data and Dogma: The Great Indian Poverty Debate. *The World Bank Research Observer*, 20(2), 177–199.
Dynan, K., & Sheiner, L. (2008). *GDP as a Measure of Economic Well-Being*. Brookings: Hutchins Center on Fiscal and Monetary Policy.
Gregori, T. R. (1987). Resources Are Not; They Become: An Institutional Theory. *Journal of Economic Issues*, 21(3), 1241–1263.
Mankiw, N. G. (2016). *Macroeconomics*. New York: Worth Publishers.
Manna, G. C. (2007). On Calibrating the Poverty Line for Poverty Estimation in India. *Economic and Political Weekly*, 42(30), 2108–3115.
Moyer, B. C., & Dunn, A. (2020). Measuring the Gross Domestic Product (GDP): The Ultimate Data Science Project. *Harvard Data Science Review*, 2(1). https://doi.org/10.1162/99608f92.414caadb
Nepram, D., Singh, S. P., & Jaman, S. (2021). The Effect of Government Expenditure on Unemployment in India: A State Level Analysis. *The Journal of Asian Finance, Economics and Business*, 8(3), 763–769.
Phillips, R. (1995). *Economic Mavericks: The Texas Institutionalists*. Bingley: Emerald Group Publishing.
Ravallion, M. (1992). *Poverty Comparisons: A Guide to Concepts and Methods*. Washington DC: The World Bank.
Ray, R., & Sinha, K. (2014). Rangarajan Committee Report on Poverty Measurement: Another Lost Opportunity. *Economic and Political Weekly*, 49, 43–48.
World Bank. (2020). *Monitoring Global Poverty*. Washington DC: World Bank.
Zimmerman, E. (1951). *World Resources and Industries*. New York: Harper & Bros.

Chapter 7
Measuring Social Well-Being

Introduction

The concept of social well-being is broad, subjective and multidimensional. Its various components have been discussed in earlier chapters. There are various indicators that can be used to measure social well-being. However, the challenge in using individual indicators is that it presents only a particular aspect of social well-being. This challenge can be addressed by using a combination of several indicators in the form of a statistical function which represent social well-being (Bandura, 2008). For instance, the Human Development Index (HDI) expresses human development as a function of health, education and income.

These functions which combine or aggregate a set of indicators are known as composite indicators or composite indices. They are used to represent a broad or subjective concept, generally in the form of a single score which is mostly unit free. These composite indicators are simplistic numerical representations widely used in the field of social sciences. Composite indicators aim to represent subjective concepts like social well-being or poverty by reducing them to a statistic or score (Booysen, 2022). The subjective concepts are thus measured objectively through certain indicators and variables.

One of the main advantages of composite indicators is multidimensionality, i.e. indicators related to different dimensions can be aggregated into a single value or score, which can include economic, social and political dimensions (Nagar & Basu, 2004). For instance, a single HDI score is representative of indicators related to health, education and income. Some other advantages of composite index are: flexibility as variables can be included or excluded without significantly altering the theoretical framework of the index; wide applicability since it becomes easy to compare a single score across national or sub-national units (McGranahan, 1972).

Creation of Composite Index: There are four steps involved in the creation of composite indicators (Mazziotta & Pareto, 2016). These are discussed as follows:

1. **Defining the Phenomenon**: The foremost step in creating a composite index should be to define the phenomenon being measured, as accurately and precisely as possible. The definition should be able to make a clear sense of what is being measured. It should be inclusive in nature, with adequate regard to the theoretical framework and clear enough so as to be reduced to component indicators.
2. **Selection of Indicators**: The first step is to select the indicators that would make up the composite index. This selection can be done arbitrarily, randomly, on intuitive

DOI: 10.4324/9781003378006-7

appeal without any justification or a priori, based on a survey of the previous research literature. The indicators can also be selected a posteriori by empirically observing the impact of different variables in relation to the phenomenon being studied. Some important selection criteria for indicators include reliability, comparability, simplicity and data availability. To make the composite indicator meaningful and effective, such variables should be selected which truly represent the concept being objectified. If the variables are universally significant and acceptable across cultures, the relevance and applicability of the composite index are increased.

3. **Normalisation of Data**: The second step is to normalise the different variables. The data relating to different variables selected in the first step can vary in range and dimension and may be bidirectional, i.e. either positive or negative in nature. Hence, it is essential to reduce the variables to a scale that is comparable across variables, is preferably of the same dimension or dimensionless in nature and is in the same direction, i.e. an increase in the value of the variable increases the overall value of the composite index. Normalisation can be done using different techniques such as decimal place normalisation, z-score normalisation, linear normalisation, standard deviation normalisation, etc. The normalised value of data is within a fixed range, such as between 0 and 1, or 1 and 10 or 1 and 100, etc.

4. **Weighting of Indicators**: Different indicators may impact the phenomenon under study equally or differently. Hence, the indicators are assigned weights in proportion to the impact they have on the phenomenon. The weights can be assigned a priori or a posteriori. The normalised data are multiplied by the weight in order to arrive at the scores that are finally aggregated to get the composite index value.

5. **Aggregation of Indicators**: The different normalised indicator values are multiplied by their weights to calculate the weighted value of indicators. Finally, the weighted values of different indicators are combined or aggregated through some function to arrive at the final composite index value. This function can be additive, in which the different weighted values are simply added together or multiplicative or any other complex function (Saltelli, 2006). For instance, the HDI uses a geometric mean of the weighted values of the different indicators to calculate the HDI score.

Human Development Index

The Human Development Index (HDI) is a composite statistical index measuring the level of human development of a country or region. Human development refers to development that enlarges the freedom and choices of people and thus, improves their lives. The nations of the Western world experienced unprecedented growth for a period of more than two decades from the 1950s to the 1970s. The size of economy and its growth rate came to be popularly used as a measure of development in the post-war period. However, the benefits of this phase of development were distributed unequally. Inequalities in terms of income persisted not only between countries at the international level but also within countries across different classes. While on one hand, the economic production expanded greatly, on the other hand, this did not result into a high quality of life and social well-being for the masses in general. A global economic crisis occurred in the mid-1970s during which high levels of unemployment were experienced, especially in the developed world. Thus, it became clear that the concept of development centred around economic growth was inadequate to measure and assess the social well-being of the people. The conceptual shift was brought about by human development, which sought to measure the social well-being of the people using indicators that were not centred on economic growth but represented the distribution of resources and the individual capabilities of people (Stanton, 2007).

The concept of human development to measure the development of a region was developed mainly by the economists Mahbub-ul-Haq and Amartya Sen. Both the economists strived to devise a composite indicator which could present a better picture of the level of development by measuring the capabilities of the people, going beyond the metric of GDP and GNP. The vision of Haq was to come up with a measure which was "not as blind to social aspects of human lives as the GNP is" (Haq, 1999).

Human Development Index measures attainments across three dimensions of income, health and education, which are considered to be the *sine qua non* for developing the capabilities of individuals by which they can enjoy a wide range of choices and enhance their freedom. The rationale of devising this index is that if people are well educated, healthy and have sufficient income, then they will have the capability to live a life of good quality (Sen, The Standard of Living, 1987). The indicators used by Human Development Index are life expectancy as a measure of health, Mean Years of Schooling completed by adults aged 25 years and more and Expected Years of Schooling upon entering the education system as a measure of education and per capita Gross National Income (GNI) in Purchasing Power Parity (PPP) terms as a measure of income.

The HDI is the composite statistical score expressed as a geometric mean of normalised indices for indicators across each of the three dimensions of health, education and income. Its value ranges between 0 and 1, with 0 representing the least and 1 representing the highest level of human development. A country with a high HDI score represents a high average life expectancy, high level of educational attainment and a high income per capita. The HDI is a globally accepted statistic for estimating the real level of development enjoyed by the people of a nation. Even nations or regions that have a small size of economy can also have a high level of human development if the income generated is well distributed and the healthcare and educational facilities are well developed and accessible to the people. HDI scores can be used to assess the welfare services of the government in the sectors of health and education, scrutinise the relative concentration or distribution of wealth, question national policy choices and development outcomes. The Human Development Index is published on an annual basis as a part of the Human Development Report (HDR) by the Human Development Report Office of the United Nations Development Programme (UNDP). The UNDP borrowed the concept of human development developed by Mahbub-ul-Haq and the capabilities approach developed by Amartya Sen. This report was first published in 1990 and has since been published continuously every year.

Calculation of HDI

The method used for the calculation of the HDI currently was introduced in 2010. As mentioned earlier, the HDI uses four indicators across three dimensions, as mentioned in Table 7.1.

Table 7.1 Dimensions and Indicators of the Human Development Index

Dimension	Indicator	Weight	Measured By	Source of Data	Minimum Value	Maximum Value
Health	Average Life Expectancy	1/3	Life Expectancy Index (LEI)	UN Population Division, UN Department of Economic and Social Affairs (UNDESA)	20	85
Education	Mean Years of Schooling (MYS) for adults above 25 years of age	1/6	Mean Years of Schooling Index (MYSI)	UNESCO Institute for Statistics (UIS) Educational Attainment Data	0	15
	Expected Years of Schooling (EYS) for children under 18 years of age	1/6	Expected Years of Schooling Index (EYSI)		0	18
Income	Gross National Income Per Capita (GNIPC) in Purchasing Power Parity terms at constant rates	1/3	Income Index (II)	World Bank, International Monetary Fund and United Nations Statistics Division	$100 Rs 2000 (in India for state-level computation of HDI)	$75,000 Rs 4,00,000 (in India for state-level computation of HDI)

The data for each of the four indicators are obtained for each country. These indicators have different units which need to be normalised. Normalisation is done by using the following general formula:

$$\text{Normalised Index} = \frac{\text{Actual value} - \text{Minimum Value}}{\text{Maximum value} - \text{Minimum Value}} \quad \text{...............(Eq. 7.1)}$$

The maximum and minimum values are known as goalposts and act as the aspirational targets and natural zeros, respectively, which helps in the normalisation of the components of HDI. In reality, the normalisation is done by the calculation of the respective indices for the different dimensions in the following manner:

Life Expectancy Index (LEI): It is calculated by the following formula:

$$\text{LEI} = \frac{\text{LE} - 20}{85 - 20} \quad \text{...............(Eq. 7.2)}$$

where LE is the average life expectancy at birth in a given country. When the life expectancy at birth is 85 years, LEI is equal to 1 and it is 0 when the life expectancy at birth is 20 years. The justification for placing the minimum value for life expectancy at 20 years is based on the historical evidence that no nation for the last 100 years has had a life expectancy of less than 20 years. The maximum life expectancy is set at 85 years because it is considered to be a realistic target to be achieved by the countries. In several nations, the life expectancy is already close to 85 years as a result of constantly improving living conditions and advances in the medical field such as 84.7 years in Hong Kong and 84.5 years in Japan.

The HDI uses the logarithm of income to reflect the diminishing importance of income with increasing GNI. The scores for the three HDI dimension indices are then aggregated into a composite index using the geometric mean.

Education Index (EI): It is calculated by the following formula:

$$\text{EI} = \frac{\text{MYSI} + \text{EYSI}}{2} \quad \text{...............(Eq. 7.3)}$$

Mean Years of Schooling Index (MYSI) is calculated by using the following formula:

$$\text{MYSI} = \frac{\text{MYS} - 0}{15 - 0} = \frac{\text{MYS}}{15} \quad \text{...............(Eq. 7.4)}$$

The minimum Mean Years of Schooling is zero years because people can live without any formal education, i.e. with zero years of schooling. The maximum Mean Years of Schooling is set at 15 years until the period of 2025 based on previously recorded data.

Expected Years of Schooling Index (EYSI) is calculated by the following formula:

$$\text{EYSI} = \frac{\text{EYS} - 0}{18 - 0} = \frac{\text{EYS}}{18} \quad \text{...............(Eq. 7.5)}$$

The minimum Expected Years of Schooling (EYS) is set at zero years. The maximum value for the Expected Years of Schooling is set at 18 which is equivalent to achieving a postgraduate degree in most of the countries.

Income Index (II): It is calculated by the following formula:

$$II = \frac{\ln(GNIPC) - \ln(100)}{\ln(75000) - \ln(100)} \quad \text{(Eq. 7.6)}$$

When GNI per capita is $75,000, II is equal to 1 and it is 0 when GNI per capita is $100. The logarithm of GNI per capita is used because each additional dollar of income has a smaller effect on human development. The approach is to value each year of age or education equally, and therefore the principle has been applied only to the income indicator (Sen & Anand, Human Development and Economic Sustainability, 2000).

The GNI in Purchasing Power Parity (PPP) terms is calculated at a constant rate using 2017 as the base year. The official PPP conversion rates are obtained from the International Comparison Program of the World Bank, which collects periodic data related to thousands of matched goods and services in many countries. For the calculation of GNI per capita, the latest population data from 'The World Population Prospects' Report of 2019 by the United Nations Population Division is used. The minimum value for Gross National Income (GNI) per capita is set at $100, which is justified by the minimum amount of GNI as captured in the data previously recorded. The maximum value of GNI per capita is set at $75,000 per capita which is justified as empirical studies have shown that there is little marginal improvement in human development when the annual GNI per capita exceeds $75,000. Currently, there are only four countries, namely Brunei Darussalam, Liechtenstein, Qatar and Singapore which have GNI per capita exceeding $75,000 (Kahneman & Deaton, 2010).

Finally, the HDI is calculated as the geometric mean of the three normalised indices:

$$HDI = \sqrt[3]{LEI \cdot EI \cdot II} \quad \text{(Eq. 7.7)}$$

Categories: Upon computation, the HDI score returns a value between 0 and 1. Since 2014, the Human Development Report has categorised the nations on the basis of the distribution of the HDI score averaged over 2004–2013 in the following categories (Table 7.2).

Table 7.2 Categories of the Human Development Index (HDI)

HDI Category	HDI Score
Very High Human Development	0.800–1
High Human Development	0.700–0.799
Medium Human Development	0.550–0.699
Low Human Development	0–0.549

Calculating the HDI score of India: According to the UNDP, the following are the values of different indicators for India, used in the HDI: (a) Life Expectancy (LE) at Birth is 69.7 years, (b) Expected Years of Schooling (EYS) is 12.2 years, (c) Mean Years of Schooling (MYS) is 6.5 years and (d) the Gross National Income (GNI) per capita (GNIPC) at constant rate in 2017 at Purchasing Power Parity terms is 6,681 dollars. Now, we shall calculate the HDI according to the formulae listed above:

$$\text{LEI} = \frac{\text{LE} - 20}{85 - 20} = \frac{69.7 - 20}{65} = \frac{49.7}{65} = 0.765 \quad \text{............(from Eq. 7.2)}$$

$$\text{MYSI} = \frac{\text{MYS}}{15} = \frac{6.5}{15} = 0.433 \quad \text{............(from Eq. 7.3)}$$

$$\text{EYSI} = \frac{\text{EYS}}{18} = \frac{12.2}{18} = 0.677 \quad \text{............(from Eq. 7.4)}$$

$$\text{EI} = \frac{\text{MYSI} + \text{EYSI}}{2} = \frac{0.433 + 0.677}{2} = 0.555 \quad \text{............(from Eq. 7.5)}$$

$$\text{II} = \frac{\ln(\text{GNIPC}) - \ln(100)}{\ln(75000) - \ln(100)} = \frac{\ln(6681) - \ln(100)}{\ln(75000) - \ln(100)} = 0.634 \quad \text{............(from Eq. 7.6)}$$

Calculating the HDI value from the three indices LEI, EI and II, we get:

$$\text{HDI} = \sqrt[3]{\text{LEI.EI.II}} = \sqrt[3]{0.765 * 0.555 * 0.634} = 0.645 \quad \text{............(from Eq. 7.7)}$$

Hence, the HDI score of India in 2019–2020 was 0.645 and as per the categorisation of HDI score, there is a medium level of human development in the country. India ranked 131 out of 189 countries in the UNDP Human Development Index this year and registered a slide of two ranks from the previous year. The nations that performed the best in terms of HDI were (1) Norway (0.957), (2) Ireland and Switzerland (0.955) and (3) Hong Kong and Iceland (0.949). These countries reported very high levels of human development. The three bottom most countries among the 189 countries were Niger (0.389), Central African Republic (0.397) and Chad (0.396) which are all located in the Sahel region of Africa. Kerala (0.782), Chandigarh (0.776) and Goa (0.763) have the highest level of human development in India while Bihar (0.574), Uttar Pradesh (0.596) and Jharkhand (0.599) have the lowest human development (Figure 7.1).

The Human Development Index (HDI) provided an alternate paradigm for measuring development. Since it was introduced in 1990, it has gained global acceptance and reputation as a composite indicator of human development. However, over the years, this index has also been criticised on several grounds. The HDI provides a simplified and

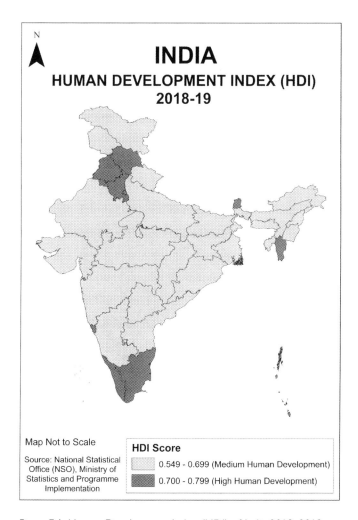

Figure 7.1 Human Development Index (HDI) of India 2018–2019

limited perspective of human development (McGillivray, 1991). It is crude in the sense that it limits human development only to life expectancy, years of schooling and per capita GNI without considering the access to opportunities and quality of services related to health and education. The per capita GNI represents the mean income distribution per person, which can be skewed by extreme values (Noorbaksh, 1998). The three dimensions of health, education and income are weighted equally even though income level can significantly affect access and attainment of health and education (Lugo & Decancq, 2013). Other factors affecting social well-being such as environmental quality, gender disparity, racial inequality, internal security, etc. are not considered within HDI. For several countries, some of the data related to life Expectancy and Mean Years of Schooling are based on estimation, which may not represent the ground reality.

Multidimensional Poverty Index

The Multidimensional Poverty Index (MPI) was developed in alignment with the broad framework of the Human Development Index (HDI) of measuring human development using indicators related to health, education and standard of living or income. The drawbacks in measuring human development via the HDI became obvious in the decades following its inception in 1990. Human development is a broad and multidimensional concept. When the index was first devised, the availability and comparability of data was a major challenge and consequently, the HDI remained a crude measure of human development. The MPI was developed as an expansion of the HDI.

Multidimensional measures complement monetary measures by capturing information they lack – such as broader qualitative aspects of life such as child mortality, housing conditions, and other basic services such as water and sanitation (Greeve, 2020). This is of significance to policy formulation and targeted interventions in the context of intra-country or intra-region heterogeneity in development. The rationale behind developing MPI was that human development cannot be limited to a few indicators limited to income, life expectancy and years of schooling. Hence, the initiative of measuring human development should be expanded to include several more indicators related to nutrition, school attendance, cooking fuel, sanitation, drinking water, electricity, housing, assets, etc. Another reason was that the HDI scores of the developed nations of the western world had already reached an optimum level and hence, remained more or less at similar levels over the years. Hence, most of the changes were observed in developing nations. Also, the inequality of distribution within developing nations has remained a persistent challenge. Hence, it was natural that the efforts for human development should be relatively concentrated in developing nations. With these considerations in mind, the MPI was conceptualised. The MPI uses the concept of multidimensional poverty to estimate the level of human development in a region.

HDI uses indicators at the aggregate level while MPI uses micro-data and all indicators must come from the same survey. This, amongst other reasons, has led to the MPI only being calculated for just over 100 countries, where data are available for all these diverse indicators, while HDI is calculated for almost all countries. The global MPI was developed by the Oxford Poverty Human Initiative (OPHI) in collaboration with the UN Development Programme (UNDP) and is published along with the UNDP flagship Human Development Report. It was first published in 2010 and has been published annually ever since. In the MPI, the assessment of poverty is done at the individual level. If a person is deprived in a third or more of ten weighted indicators, then they are considered to be as multidimensionally poor. The percentage of deprivations also represents the intensity of poverty being experienced as the multidimensional poor people (Walker & Godinot, 2020).

Just like the HDI, the indicators of the MPI are spread across three dimensions (a) health, (b) education and (b) standard of living, which represents the level of income. Each dimension is assigned equal weight and each indicator within a dimension is further weighted equally so that the sum of their weights equals the weight of the dimension. However, the indicators used in the MPI are radically different from the HDI. While the HDI uses only four indicators, there are ten indicators used in MPI. The ten indicators of MPI include two for health, two for education and six for living standards. The indicators of the MPI have been selected on the basis of expert guidance and availability of nation-wise data related to the three dimensions. The indicators in MPI are objective in nature and the value returned by a deprivation criterion is either in the form of yes or no, i.e. 0 or 1. These indicators are related to the Sustainable Development Goals (SDGs). The list of indicators, deprivation criteria, weights and the related SDGs are listed in Table 7.3.

The method used for the calculation of the MPI is known as the Alkire–Foster Method developed by Sabina Alkire and James Foster (Foster & Alkire, Counting and Multidimensional Poverty Measurement, 2011). This method measures the overlapping or simultaneous deprivations experienced by a person or household in different indicators of poverty. A person or household which does not fulfil the deprivation criteria is identified as deprived in that indicator. The MPI is calculated by multiplying the incidence of poverty (H) with the average intensity of poverty (A):

$$MPI = H*A \quad \quad \quad \quad \quad \quad \quad \quad \quad \quad \quad \quad \quad \quad \quad \text{(Eq. 7.8)}$$

where H is the proportion of the population that experiences multidimensional poverty and A is the average per cent of dimensions in which poor people are deprived. MPI, thus, helps to estimate the share of people multidimensionally poor along with the intensity of poverty they experience (Foster, Alkire, & Seth, 2013).

Sources of Data: The MPI uses data from a number of sources such as Demographic and Health Survey (DHS) for nutritional information on children and women of reproductive age, Multiple Indicator Cluster Surveys (MICS) for nutritional information on children, and World Health Survey (WHS) for nutritional information on adult household members. The indicators related to living standards are 'means rather than ends'. They are closely related to the end or 'functionings' and secondly, most of the indicators are related to the Millennium Development Goals (MDGs), which provide the justification for inclusion in the index.

In the MPI a person or household is identified as (a) 'multidimensionally poor' or if they experience deprivation in at least one-third of the weighted MPI indicators, (b) as 'vulnerable' if they are deprived in 20 – 33.3 per cent of the weighted indicators and (c) living in 'severe poverty' if they are deprived in 50 – 100 per cent of the weighted indicators.

Example: Let us consider a hypothetical example of two households and their MPI score (Table 7.4).

Censored Deprivation Score: If the deprivation experienced by a household is less than one-third of the sum of all weighted indicators, then the deprivation score is censored to be zero because such a household is not poor and, hence, it is not meaningful to proceed ahead and calculate the headcount ratio as well as intensity of poverty.

Headcount Ratio: From the Deprivation score, it can be observed that Household-2 is multidimensionally poor because the deprivation experienced is in more than one-third of the weighted value of the deprivation criteria. If we consider that there are only two households, then the headcount ratio (H) of the multidimensionally poor would be:

$$H = \frac{\text{Number of Multidimensionally Poor Persons}}{\text{Total Number of Persons}} \quad \quad \quad \quad \text{(Eq. 7.9)}$$

Table 7.3 Dimensions and Indicators of the Multidimensional Poverty Index (MPI)

Dimensions of Poverty (Weight)	Indicator	Deprivation Criteria (Deprived if Living in a Household Where …)	Weight of Indicator	Related SDG
Health (1/3)	Nutrition	Any person under 70 years of age for whom there is nutritional information is **undernourished**.[1]	1/6	SDG 2: Zero Hunger
	Child mortality	A child **under 18** has **died** in the household in the five-year period preceding the survey.	1/6	SDG 3: Health and Well-being
Education (1/3)	Years of schooling	**No** eligible household member has completed **six years of schooling**.	1/6	SDG 4: Quality Education
	School attendance	Any school-aged child is **not attending** school **up to** the age at which he/she would complete **class 8**.	1/6	SDG 4: Quality Education
Living Standards (1/3)	Cooking fuel	A household cooks using **solid fuel**, such as dung, agricultural crop, shrubs, wood, charcoal or coal.	1/18	SDG 7: Affordable and Clean Energy
	Sanitation	The household has **unimproved** or **no** sanitation **facility** or it is improved but **shared** with other households.[2]	1/18	SDG 6: Clean Water and Sanitation
	Drinking water	The household's source of **drinking water** is **not safe** or safe drinking water is a **30-minute** or **longer walk** from home, roundtrip.[3]	1/18	SDG 6: Clean Water and Sanitation
	Electricity	The household has **no electricity**.	1/18	SDG 7: Affordable and Clean Energy
	Housing	The household has **inadequate** housing materials in **any of the three** components: **floor, roof,** or **walls**.[4]	1/18	SDG 11: Sustainable Cities and Communities
	Assets	The household does **not own more than one** of these **assets**: radio, TV, telephone, computer, animal cart, bicycle, motorbike, or refrigerator, and does not own a car or truck.	1/18	SDG 1: No Poverty

Table 7.4 Calculation of the MPI

Dimensions of Poverty (Weight)	Indicator	Deprivation Criteria (Deprived if Living in a Household Where …)	Weight of Indicator	Household 1	Household 2	Household-1 Weighted Value	Household-2 Weighted Value*
Number of Persons				4	5	Household Deprivation Value * Weight of Indicator	
Health (1/3)	Nutrition	Any person under 70 years of age for whom there is nutritional information is **undernourished**.	1/6 = 0.167	0	1	0	0.167
	Child mortality	A child **under 18** has **died** in the household in the five-year period preceding the survey.	1/6 = 0.167	0	1	0	0.167
Education (1/3)	Years of schooling	**No** eligible household member has completed **six years of schooling**.	1/6 = 0.167	0	0	0	0
	School attendance	Any school-aged child is **not attending** school **up to** the age at which he/she would complete **class 8**.	1/6 = 0.167	1	1	0.167	0.167
Living Standards (1/3)	Cooking fuel	A household cooks using **solid fuel**, such as dung, agricultural crop, shrubs, wood, charcoal or coal.	1/18 = 0.056	0	1	0	0.056
	Sanitation	The household has **unimproved or no** sanitation **facility** or it is improved but **shared** with other households.	1/18 = 0.056	0	0	0	0
	Drinking water	The household's source of **drinking water** is **not safe** or safe drinking water is a **30-minute or longer walk** from home, roundtrip.	1/18 = 0.056	0	1	0	0.056
	Electricity	The household has **no electricity**.	1/18 = 0.056	0	0	0	0

(Continued)

Table 7.4 Continued

Dimensions of Poverty (Weight)	Indicator	Deprivation Criteria (Deprived if Living in a Household Where …)	Weight of Indicator	Household 1	Household 2	Household-1 Weighted Value	Household-2 Weighted Value
	Housing	The household has **inadequate** housing materials in **any** of the three components: **floor, roof,** or **walls.**	1/18 = 0.056	1	1	0.056	0.056
	Assets	The household does **not own more than one** of these **assets**: radio, TV, telephone, computer, animal cart, bicycle, motorbike, or refrigerator, and does not own a car or truck.	1/18 = 0.056	0	1	0	0.056
Deprivation Score (sum of each deprivation multiplied by its weight)						= (0.167 + 0.056) = 0.223	= (0.167 + 0.167 + 0.167 + 0.056 + 0.056 + 0.056 + 0.056) = 0.725
Censored Deprivation Score						0	0.725
Is the household poor? (MPI Score >= 0.333)						No	Yes

Hence, here,

$$H = 5 / (5+4) = 5/9 = 0.556$$

Since the headcount ratio is 0.556, it means that 55.6 per cent of the people are multidimensionally poor.

Intensity of Poverty: Further, the intensity (A) of multidimensional poverty can be calculated for a household H_i (only for households that have a deprivation score equal to or more than 0.333) using the following formula:

$$A_i = (\text{Censored Deprivation Score of } H_i * \text{ Number of Persons in } H_i)$$
$$/ (\text{Total Number of Persons}) \quad \ldots\ldots\ldots\ldots(\text{Eq. 7.10})$$

Here, we know that only Household-2 is multidimensionally poor and its censored deprivation score is 0.725, the number of persons in the household is five and the total number of persons is nine. Therefore, the intensity (A) of multidimensional poverty will be:

$$A = (0.725 * 5) / 9 = 0.402$$

It means that on average, the poor people are deprived in 40.2 per cent of the deprivation criteria.

MPI Score: The MPI score is finally calculated by multiplying the headcount ratio (H) with intensity (I) of multidimensional poverty. In this case, the MPI score will be:

$$\text{MPI} = H * A \quad \ldots\ldots\ldots\ldots\ldots\ldots\ldots\ldots\ldots\ldots\ldots\ldots\ldots\ldots(\text{from Eq. 7.8})$$

MPI = 0.556 * 0.402 = 0.223

The value of MPI score ranges between 0 and 1 and is rounded off up to three places of the decimal. The closer the MPI score is to 1, the higher the level of multidimensional poverty.

The National Institute for Transforming India (NITI) Aayog is the nodal agency for the Multidimensional Poverty Index (MPI). It publishes the MPI in collaboration with the United Nations Development Programme (UNDP) and Oxford Poverty and Human Development Initiative (OPHI) and other specialised agencies such as the International Institute for Population Sciences (IIPS) under the Ministry of Health and Family Welfare which conducts the National Family Health Survey (NFHS). Globally, the data for MPI indicators are taken from the Demographic and Health Surveys (DHS) conducted by various nations. The DHS for India is the National Family Health Survey (NFHS) conducted by the International Institute for Population Sciences (IIPS). This survey has not been conducted regularly. Beginning with the first round in 1992–1993, only four subsequent rounds of this survey have been conducted, Round 2 (1998–1999), Round 3 (2005–2006), Round 4 (2015–2016) and Round 5 (2019–2021). The first report on MPI in India, also known as the baseline report released by the NITI Aayog in 2021, has been computed using the data from the NFHS Round 4 (2015–2016). The NFHS Round 4 had a sample size of 28,69,043 individuals across 6,28,892 households at the national, state and

Table 7.5 India: Multidimensional Poverty Index 2021

Area	MPI Score	Headcount (H) in Per cent	Intensity (A) of Deprivation in Per Cent	Share of Population
National	0.123	27.9	43.9	100
Rural	0.163	36.8	44.1	32.3
Urban	0.039	9.2	42.6	67.7

district levels. The entity identified and analysed as multidimensional poor or non-poor according to the national MPI is the household. The information of all members in a household is considered together, and thus, all members in a household are given the same deprivation scores.

According to the Global MPI 2021 report by the UNDP, the MPI score of India was 0.123 and it ranked 66 out of the 109 developing countries assessed. The MPI score was higher in rural areas at 0.163 and lower in urban areas at 0.039. In terms of the headcount rate, 27.9 per cent of the total population of India experienced multidimensional poverty. In rural areas, 36.8 per cent and in urban areas 9.2 per cent people faced multidimensional poverty. In terms of intensity of deprivations, overall, the multidimensional poor faced deprivation in 43.9 per cent of the indicators. This intensity was higher for rural areas at 44.1 per cent and lower for urban areas at 42.6 per cent. Overall, in India, nearly one-third or 32.3 per cent of the multidimensional poor are in urban areas while the rest two-thirds are in rural areas (Table 7.5).

According to the first Multidimensional Poverty Index (MPI) report of 2021 by the NITI Aayog, Bihar, Jharkhand and Uttar Pradesh have emerged as the states with the highest number of multidimensional poor people in India. In Bihar, 51.91 per cent population is multidimensional poor, followed by 42.16 per cent in Jharkhand, 37.79 per cent in Uttar Pradesh. Madhya Pradesh (36.65 per cent) has been placed fourth while Meghalaya (32.67 per cent) is at the fifth spot. Kerala (0.71 per cent), Goa (3.76 per cent), Sikkim (3.82 per cent), Tamil Nadu (4.89 per cent) and Punjab (5.59 per cent) have registered the lowest poverty across India. Among union territories (UTs), Dadra & Nagar Haveli (27.36 per cent), Jammu & Kashmir and Ladakh (12.58) had the highest share of poor in their population while Puducherry (1.72 per cent) and Lakshadweep (1.82 per cent) had the least share of poor. Of all the people experiencing multidimensional poverty, 15.7 per cent were in Uttar Pradesh, 8.9 per cent in Bihar and 7.8 per cent in West Bengal. Together, these three states accounted for one-third of the poor in India. In terms of the intensity of deprivations faced by the poor, the maximum intensity was in Rajasthan (45.3 per cent), Mizoram (45.2 per cent), Jharkhand and Assam (both 44.7 per cent). This means that even though the headcount of the poor in these states was not very high, yet the poor living here faced more severe deprivations. The least deprivation intensity was in Puducherry (36.6 per cent), Goa (37.2 per cent) and Kerala (37.3 per cent) (Figure 7.2).

Several studies have shown that people may experience deprivations in certain areas of their lives, such as education, health, safety or employment, without being income poor (Bourguignon et al., 2008). Furthermore, there are many more indicators which can be included in the Multidimensional Poverty Index (Cavapozzi et al., 2015).

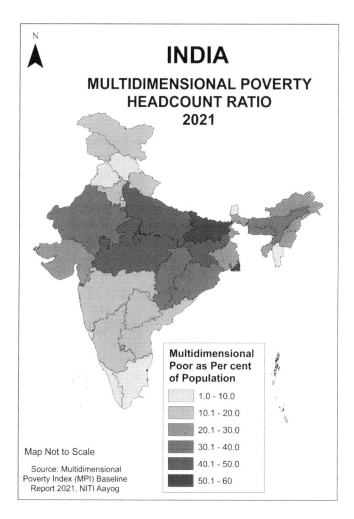

Figure 7.2 Headcount Ratio of Multidimensional Poor in India (2021) Based on Data from NFHS Round 4 (2015–2016)

Sustainable Development Goals (SDG) Index

Sustainable Development Goals (SDGs) are a set of 17 goals adopted by 193 member countries of the United Nations in 2015. The objective of the SDGs is to stimulate developmental actions by local, national and global actors in areas such as ending poverty and hunger, ensuring healthy lives and quality education, achieving gender equality, providing renewable energy, sustainable economic growth, reducing inequality, etc. The time period for achieving these goals is of 15 years between 2016 and 2030. Hence, they are also referred to as the 2030 Agenda for Sustainable Development. SDGs have been developed as the successor to the Millennium Development Goals (MDG) 2000–2015 which were also adopted by the United Nations for achieving critical goals of development relating to poverty, hunger, health, etc. The SDGs aim to transform the lives and livelihoods of people globally. SDGs are based on the growing realisation that the process of development cannot remain limited to national boundaries, but require efforts with international collaboration. The essential philosophy of the SDGs is the interconnectedness of global problems.

The framework of SDGs is comprised of 17 goals further elaborated into 169 targets. SDGs follow a multidimensional approach and the 17 SDGs are spread across the various dimensions of sustainable development, with six predominantly social goals (SDG 1 to 6), five economic goals (SDG 7 to 11) and four environmental goals (SDG 12 to 15). The SDG 17 on global partnership emphasises the role of international collaboration for the achievement of the SDGs.

An annual report on the global progress of the SDGs is published annually by the Sustainable Development Solutions Network (SDSN). All the UN member countries are ranked based on their performance. Nations are given a score between 0 and 100, on the basis of their achievements in the various SDGs. A score near 100 means higher achievement with regard to the SDGs. In the sixth edition of the report, India ranked India at 120th out of 165 countries with a country score of 60.1 out of 100. India has showed consistent progress in the achievement of the SDGs. The SDG framework also encourages member nations of the United Nations to take steps to assess progress towards the achievement of the SDGs across the sub-national units. In India, the NITI (National Institute for Transforming India) Aayog is the nodal agency responsible for the preparation of the Sustainable Development Goals (SDG) report and SDG India Index. The first edition of the SDG India Index was launched in 2018. In 2020–2021, the third edition of the report was published. The SDG India Index assesses the performance of the 36 states and union territories (UTs) in India across 16 SDGs and 115 indicators. The SDG 17, which is about international partnership for achieving the goals, is assessed qualitatively in the report.

The SDG India Index is a composite index in which the States/UTs are ranked based on their overall performance across multiple goals. Like the international SDG Index, the SDG India Index has a range of scores between 0 and 100, in which a score close to 100 represents a high level of achievement. The objective of the SDG India Index is to promote healthy competition among the States/UTs in their journey towards achieving the SDGs and to support them in the identification of priority areas of the SDGs which demand more attention.

The methodology of the SDG India Index has been developed in close association with the Ministry of Statistics and Programme Implementation (MoSPI), on the lines of the International Sustainable Development Goals (SDG) Report. Based on the 17 goals and 169 targets, 115 indicators have been selected. These indicators are chosen based on their relevance to the SDG framework, alignment with the National Indicator Framework (NIF), data availability at the national level for States and UTs from official statistical systems, etc.

After the selection of indicators, they are normalised using the same formula as used in the HDI, as follows:

$$\text{Normalised Value} = \frac{\text{Actual value} - \text{Minimum Value}}{\text{Target value} - \text{Minimum Value}} \quad \ldots \ldots \ldots \ldots \ldots \text{(Eq. 7.11)}$$

For several indicators, instead of the maximum value, a suitable target value is used. The targets have been set by the UN at the global level for 74 indicators, for instance, the target of reducing Maternal Mortality Ratio (MMR) to 70 per 1,00,000 live births by 2030. For 28 indicators, targets set by the Government of India are used. Benchmark values set by international development organisations or international standards are used with respect to nine indicators, for instance, the World Health Organization (WHO) target of 50 per cent reduction of anaemia in women of reproductive age by 2025. For indicators where no specified quantitative target is available, the target value is set by deriving an average of top three states.

For indicators where a higher value implies lower performance, the following formula was used:

$$\text{Normalised Value} = 1 - \frac{\text{Actual value} - \text{Minimum Value}}{\text{Target value} - \text{Minimum Value}} \quad \text{...........................(Eq. 7.12)}$$

After normalisation, the SDG value is estimated as the arithmetic mean of the normalised values of all indicators under the Goal, for each State/UT. Equal weight is assigned to each indicator in the index. The justification for assigning equal weight to all SDGs and also to indicators within every SDG is the normative assumption that all goals and indicators are equally significant. Once the normalised value of each indicator within a goal is obtained, then the arithmetic mean of these indicators is calculated to obtain the normalised value for the goal. Similarly, the arithmetic mean of all the normalised goal values is calculated to get the SDG score of a state or union territory.

Based on the SDG score obtained by a state or UT, they are grouped into the following categories: (a) Achiever: when the Index score equals 100; (b) Front Runner: when the Index score is between 65 and 99, including both; (c) Performer: when the Index score is between 50 and 64, including both and (d) Aspirant: when the Index score is less than 50. The data for the indicators in the index are obtained from national survey reports of Union ministries, national data portals of Union ministries, government schemes, etc. Nearly 80 per cent of the indicators have data obtained from the last three years. Only about 20 per cent indicators have data from 2015 to 2018, whereas just two indicators have been from prior to 2015.

SDG India Report 2020–2021: The composite SDG score for India in 2020–2021 was 66. The performance of India has been consistently improving since the index was first launched. The range of SDG values was between 52 and 75 for states and between 62 and 79 for union territories. Overall, the best performance was of Chandigarh that scored 79 while the best-performing state was Kerala which ranked first among the states scoring 75. The second-ranked states were Tamil Nadu and Himachal Pradesh, both scoring 72. Goa, Uttarakhand, Karnataka and Andhra Pradesh shared the fourth spot. Fifteen states/UTs were in the performer category while there were 22 states/UTs in the front-runner category. There was no states/UT in the aspirant category. Bihar, Jharkhand and Assam were the worst-performing states. Each goal in turn is also scored between 0 and 100 (Figure 7.3). Overall, the

216 Measuring Social Well-Being

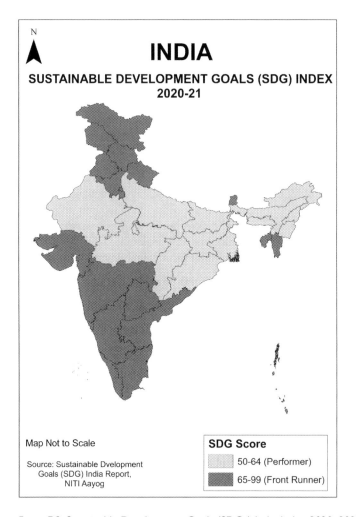

Figure 7.3 Sustainable Development Goals (SDGs) India Index 2020–2021

best score was in SDG 7 (affordable and clean energy) and SDG 6 (clean water and sanitation) in which the scores were 92 and 83, respectively. SDG 14 (life below water) in the report is assessed with respect to only nine coastal states and, hence, is qualitatively analysed. Goal 6 has the highest number of Front Runners with 25 States in this category while SDG 5 and SDG 9 have the highest number of aspirants with 14 States each in the category. Among the goals in which considerable efforts are required are SDG 10 (reduced inequalities), SDG 13 (climate action) and SDG 4 (quality education).

There are various issues related to the SDG Index, such as the quantum of data required to be collected and operated upon. Another issue is that each goal and indicator is weighted equally, which is based on a normative assumption that all goals are equally significant. Some goals like SDG (life under water) and SDG 17 (partnership for action) are difficult to quantify and assess (Scown, 2020). It is difficult to understand the progress of each goal based on a single SDG Index score.

SDG Targets: The 17 SDGs and the targets as adopted by India are listed below (NITI-Aayog, 2021):

1. **No Poverty**: Goal 1 encompasses the aim of eradicating poverty – not only in monetary terms but in all forms and dimensions by 2030
   1.1. By 2030, eradicate extreme poverty for all people everywhere, currently measured as people living on less than USD 1.25 a day
   1.2. By 2030, reduce at least by half the proportion of men, women and children of all ages living in poverty in all its dimensions according to national definitions
   1.3. Implement nationally appropriate social protection systems and measures for all, including floors, and by 2030 achieve substantial coverage of the poor and the vulnerable
   1.4. By 2030, ensure that all men and women, in particular the poor and the vulnerable, have equal rights to economic resources, as well as access to basic services, ownership and control over land and other forms of property, inheritance, natural resources, appropriate new technology and financial services, including microfinance
   1.5. By 2030, build the resilience of the poor and those in vulnerable situations and reduce their exposure and vulnerability to climate-related extreme events and other economic, social and environmental shocks and disasters
   1.6. Ensure significant mobilisation of resources from a variety of sources, including through enhanced development cooperation, in order to provide adequate and predictable means for developing countries, in particular least developed countries, to implement programmes and policies to end poverty in all its dimensions
   1.7. Create sound policy frameworks at the national, regional and international levels, based on pro-poor and gender-sensitive development strategies, to support accelerated investment in poverty eradication actions
2. **Zero Hunger**: End hunger, achieve food security, improve nutrition and promote sustainable agriculture
   2.1. By 2030, end hunger and ensure access by all people, in particular the poor and people in vulnerable situations, including infants, to safe, nutritious and sufficient food all year round
   2.2. By 2030, end all forms of malnutrition, including achieving, by 2025, the internationally agreed targets on stunting and wasting in children under five years of age, and address the nutritional needs of adolescent girls, pregnant and lactating women and older persons
   2.3. By 2030, double the agricultural productivity and incomes of small-scale food producers, in particular women, indigenous peoples, family farmers, pastoralists and fishers, including through secure and equal access to land, other productive resources and inputs, knowledge, financial services, markets and opportunities for value addition and non-farm employment

2.4. By 2030, ensure sustainable food production systems and implement resilient agricultural practices that increase productivity and production, that help maintain ecosystems, that strengthen capacity for adaptation to climate change, extreme weather, drought, flooding and other disasters, and that progressively improve land and soil quality

2.5. By 2020, maintain the genetic diversity of seeds, cultivated plants and farmed and domesticated animals and their related wild species, including through soundly managed and diversified seed and plant banks at the national, regional and international levels, and promote access to and fair and equitable sharing of benefits arising from the utilisation of genetic resources and associated traditional knowledge, as internationally agreed

2.6. (2.a) Increase investment, including through enhanced international cooperation, in rural infrastructure, agricultural research and extension services, technology development and plant and livestock gene banks in order to enhance agricultural productive capacity in developing countries, in particular, least developed countries

2.7. (2.b) Correct and prevent trade restrictions and distortions in world agricultural markets, including through the parallel elimination of all forms of agricultural export subsidies and all export measures with equivalent effect, in accordance with the mandate of the Doha Development Round

2.8. (2.c) Adopt measures to ensure the proper functioning of food commodity markets and their derivatives and facilitate timely access to market information, including on food reserves, in order to help limit extreme food price volatility

3. **Good Health and Well-Being**: Ensure healthy lives and promote well-being for all at all ages

   3.1. By 2030, reduce the global Maternal Mortality Ratio to less than 70 per 1,00,000 live births

   3.2. By 2030, end preventable deaths of newborns and children under 5 years of age, with all countries aiming to reduce neonatal mortality to at least as low as 12 per 1,000 live births and under-5 mortality to at least as low as 25 per 1,000 live births

   3.3. By 2030, end the epidemics of AIDS, tuberculosis, malaria and neglected tropical diseases and combat hepatitis, water-borne diseases and other communicable diseases

   3.4. By 2030, reduce by one-third premature mortality from non-communicable diseases through prevention and treatment and promote mental health and well-being

   3.5. Strengthen the prevention and treatment of substance abuse, including narcotic drug abuse and harmful use of alcohol

   3.6. By 2020, halve the number of global deaths and injuries from road traffic accidents

   3.7. By 2030, ensure universal access to sexual and reproductive healthcare services, including family planning, information and education, and the integration of reproductive health into national strategies and programmes

3.8. Achieve universal health coverage, including financial risk protection, access to quality essential healthcare services and access to safe, effective, quality and affordable essential medicines and vaccines for all

3.9. By 2030, substantially reduce the number of deaths and illnesses from hazardous chemicals and air, water and soil pollution and contamination

3.10. (3.a) Strengthen the implementation of the World Health Organization Framework Convention on Tobacco Control in all countries, as appropriate

3.11. (3.b) Support the research and development of vaccines and medicines for the communicable and non-communicable diseases that primarily affect developing countries, provide access to affordable essential medicines and vaccines, in accordance with the Doha Declaration on the TRIPS Agreement and Public Health, which affirms the right of developing countries to use to the full the provisions in the Agreement on Trade-Related Aspects of Intellectual Property Rights regarding flexibilities to protect public health, and, in particular, provide access to medicines for all

3.12. (3.c) Substantially increase health financing and the recruitment, development, training and retention of the health workforce in developing countries, especially in least developed countries and small island developing States

3.13. (3.d) Strengthen the capacity of all countries, in particular developing countries, for early warning, risk reduction and management of national and global health risks

4. **Quality Education**: Ensure inclusive and equitable quality education and promote lifelong learning opportunities for all

    4.1. By 2030, ensure that all girls and boys complete free, equitable and quality primary and secondary education leading to relevant and effective learning outcomes

    4.2. By 2030, ensure that all girls and boys have access to quality early childhood development, care and pre-primary education so that they are ready for primary education

    4.3. By 2030, ensure equal access for all women and men to affordable and quality technical, vocational and tertiary education, including university

    4.4. By 2030, substantially increase the number of youth and adults who have relevant skills, including technical and vocational skills, for employment, decent jobs and entrepreneurship

    4.5. By 2030, eliminate gender disparities in education and ensure equal access to all levels of education and vocational training for the vulnerable, including persons with disabilities, indigenous peoples and children in vulnerable situations

    4.6. By 2030, ensure that all youth and a substantial proportion of adults, both men and women, achieve literacy and numeracy

    4.7. By 2030, ensure that all learners acquire the knowledge and skills needed to promote sustainable development, including, among others, through education for sustainable development and sustainable lifestyles, human rights, gender equality, promotion of a culture of peace and non-violence,

global citizenship and appreciation of cultural diversity and of culture's contribution to sustainable development
- 4.8. (4.a) Build and upgrade education facilities that are child, disability and gender sensitive and provide safe, non-violent, inclusive and effective learning environments for all
- 4.9. (4.b) By 2020, substantially expand globally the number of scholarships available to developing countries, in particular least developed countries, small island developing States and African countries, for enrolment in higher education, including vocational training and information and communications technology, technical, engineering and scientific programmes, in developed countries and other developing countries
- 4.10. (4.c) By 2030, substantially increase the supply of qualified teachers, including through international cooperation for teacher training in developing countries, especially least developed countries and small island developing States

5. **Gender Equality**: Achieve gender equality and empower all women and girls
   - 5.1. End all forms of discrimination against all women and girls everywhere
   - 5.2. Eliminate all forms of violence against all women and girls in public and private spheres, including trafficking and sexual and other types of exploitation
   - 5.3. Eliminate all harmful practices, such as child, early and forced marriage and female genital mutilation
   - 5.4. Recognise and value unpaid care and domestic work through the provision of public services, infrastructure and social protection policies and the promotion of shared responsibility within the household and the family as nationally appropriate
   - 5.5. Ensure women's full and effective participation and equal opportunities for leadership at all levels of decision-making in political, economic and public life
   - 5.6. Ensure universal access to sexual and reproductive health and reproductive rights as agreed in accordance with the Programme of Action of the International Conference on Population and Development and the Beijing Platform for Action and the outcome documents of their review conferences
   - 5.7. (5.a) Undertake reforms to give women equal rights to economic resources, as well as access to ownership and control over land and other forms of property, financial services, inheritance and natural resources, in accordance with national laws
   - 5.8. (5.b) Enhance the use of enabling technology, in particular information and communications technology, to promote the empowerment of women
   - 5.9. (5.c) Adopt and strengthen sound policies and enforceable legislation for the promotion of gender equality and the empowerment of all women and girls at all levels

6. **Clean Water and Sanitation**: Ensure availability and sustainable management of water and sanitation for all

6.1. By 2030, achieve universal and equitable access to safe and affordable drinking water for all
6.2. By 2030, achieve access to adequate and equitable sanitation and hygiene for all and end open defecation, paying special attention to the needs of women and girls and those in vulnerable situations
6.3. By 2030, improve water quality by reducing pollution, eliminating dumping and minimising the release of hazardous chemicals and materials, halving the proportion of untreated wastewater and substantially increasing recycling and safe reuse globally
6.4. By 2030, substantially increase water-use efficiency across all sectors and ensure sustainable withdrawals and supply of freshwater to address water scarcity and substantially reduce the number of people suffering from water scarcity
6.5. By 2030, implement integrated water resources management at all levels, including through transboundary cooperation as appropriate
6.6. By 2020, protect and restore water-related ecosystems, including mountains, forests, wetlands, rivers, aquifers and lakes
6.7. (6.a) By 2030, expand international cooperation and capacity-building support to developing countries in water- and sanitation-related activities and programmes, including water harvesting, desalination, water efficiency, wastewater treatment, recycling and reuse technologies
6.8. (6.b) Support and strengthen the participation of local communities in improving water and sanitation management

7. **Affordable and Clean Energy**: Ensure access to affordable, reliable, sustainable and modern energy for all
    7.1. By 2030, ensure universal access to affordable, reliable and modern energy services
    7.2. By 2030, increase substantially the share of renewable energy in the global energy mix
    7.3. By 2030, double the global rate of improvement in energy efficiency
    7.4. (7.a) By 2030, enhance international cooperation to facilitate access to clean energy research and technology, including renewable energy, energy efficiency and advanced and cleaner fossil-fuel technology, and promote investment in energy infrastructure and clean energy technology
    7.5. (7.b) By 2030, expand infrastructure and upgrade technology for supplying modern and sustainable energy services for all in developing countries, in particular least developed countries, small island developing States and landlocked developing countries, in accordance with their respective programmes of support

8. **Decent Work and Economic Growth**: Promote sustained, inclusive and sustainable economic growth, full and productive employment and decent work for all
    8.1. Sustain per capita economic growth in accordance with national circumstances and, in particular, at least 7 per cent gross domestic product growth per annum in the least developed countries
    8.2. Achieve higher levels of economic productivity through diversification, technological upgrading and innovation, including through a focus on high-value added and labour-intensive sectors

8.3. Promote development-oriented policies that support productive activities, decent job creation, entrepreneurship, creativity and innovation, and encourage the formalisation and growth of micro-, small- and medium-sized enterprises, including through access to financial services

8.4. Improve progressively, through 2030, global resource efficiency in consumption and production and endeavour to decouple economic growth from environmental degradation, in accordance with the 10-Year Framework of Programmes on Sustainable Consumption and Production, with developed countries taking the lead

8.5. By 2030, achieve full and productive employment and decent work for all women and men, including for young people and persons with disabilities, and equal pay for work of equal value

8.6. By 2020, substantially reduce the proportion of youth not in employment, education or training

8.7. Take immediate and effective measures to eradicate forced labour, end modern slavery and human trafficking and secure the prohibition and elimination of the worst forms of child labour, including recruitment and use of child soldiers, and by 2025 end child labour in all its forms

8.8. Protect labour rights and promote safe and secure working environments for all workers, including migrant workers, in particular women migrants, and those in precarious employment

8.9. By 2030, devise and implement policies to promote sustainable tourism that creates jobs and promotes local culture and products

8.10. Strengthen the capacity of domestic financial institutions to encourage and expand access to banking, insurance and financial services for all

8.11. (8.a) Increase Aid for Trade support for developing countries, in particular least developed countries, including through the Enhanced Integrated Framework for Trade-related Technical Assistance to Least Developed Countries

8.12. (8.b) By 2020, develop and operationalise a global strategy for youth employment and implement the Global Jobs Pact of the International Labour Organisation

9. **Industry, Innovation and Infrastructure**: Build resilient infrastructure, promote inclusive and sustainable industrialisation and foster innovation

9.1. Develop quality, reliable, sustainable and resilient infrastructure, including regional and transborder infrastructure, to support economic development and human well-being, with a focus on affordable and equitable access for all

9.2. Promote inclusive and sustainable industrialisation and, by 2030, significantly raise industry's share of employment and gross domestic product, in line with national circumstances, and double its share in the least developed countries

9.3. Increase the access of small-scale industrial and other enterprises, in particular in developing countries, to financial services, including affordable credit, and their integration into value chains and markets

9.4. By 2030, upgrade infrastructure and retrofit industries to make them sustainable, with increased resource-use efficiency and greater adoption of

clean and environmentally sound technologies and industrial processes, with all countries taking action in accordance with their respective capabilities
- 9.5. Enhance scientific research, upgrade the technological capabilities of industrial sectors in all countries, in particular developing countries, including, by 2030, encouraging innovation and substantially increasing the number of research and development workers per 1 million people and public and private research and development spending
- 9.6. (9.a) Facilitate sustainable and resilient infrastructure development in developing countries through enhanced financial, technological and technical support to African countries, least developed countries, landlocked developing countries and small island developing States
- 9.7. (9.b) Support domestic technology development, research and innovation in developing countries, including by ensuring a conducive policy environment for, *inter alia*, industrial diversification and value addition to commodities
- 9.8. (9.c) Significantly increase access to information and communications technology and strive to provide universal and affordable access to the internet in the least developed countries by 2020
10. **Reduced Inequality**: Reduce inequality within and among countries
    - 10.1. By 2030, progressively achieve and sustain income growth of the bottom 40 per cent of the population at a rate higher than the national average
    - 10.2. By 2030, empower and promote the social, economic and political inclusion of all, irrespective of age, sex, disability, race, ethnicity, origin, religion or economic or other status
    - 10.3. Ensure equal opportunity and reduce inequalities of outcome, including by eliminating discriminatory laws, policies and practices and promoting appropriate legislation, policies and action in this regard
    - 10.4. Adopt policies, especially fiscal, wage and social protection policies, and progressively achieve greater equality
    - 10.5. Improve the regulation and monitoring of global financial markets and institutions and strengthen the implementation of such regulations
    - 10.6. Ensure enhanced representation and voice for developing countries in decision making in global international economic and financial institutions in order to deliver more effective, credible, accountable and legitimate institutions
    - 10.7. Facilitate orderly, safe, regular and responsible migration and mobility of people, including through the implementation of planned and well-managed migration policies
    - 10.8. (10.a) Implement the principle of special and differential treatment for developing countries, in particular least developed countries, in accordance with World Trade Organisation agreements
    - 10.9. (10.b) Encourage official development assistance and financial flows, including foreign direct investment, to States where the need is greatest, in particular least developed countries, African countries, small island developing States and landlocked developing countries, in accordance with their national plans and programmes

10.10. (10.c) By 2030, reduce to less than 3 per cent the transaction costs of migrant remittances and eliminate remittance corridors with costs higher than 5 per cent
11. **Sustainable Cities and Communities**: Make cities and human settlements inclusive, safe, resilient and sustainable
    11.1. By 2030, ensure access for all to adequate, safe and affordable housing and basic services and upgrade slums
    11.2. By 2030, provide access to safe, affordable, accessible and sustainable transport systems for all, improving road safety, notably by expanding public transport, with special attention to the needs of those in vulnerable situations, women, children, persons with disabilities and older persons
    11.3. By 2030, enhance inclusive and sustainable urbanisation and capacity for participatory, integrated and sustainable human settlement planning and management in all countries
    11.4. Strengthen efforts to protect and safeguard the world's cultural and natural heritage
    11.5. By 2030, significantly reduce the number of deaths and the number of people affected and substantially decrease the direct economic losses relative to the global gross domestic product caused by disasters, including water-related disasters, with a focus on protecting the poor and people in vulnerable situations
    11.6. By 2030, reduce the adverse per capita environmental impact of cities, including by paying special attention to air quality and municipal and other waste management
    11.7. By 2030, provide universal access to safe, inclusive and accessible, green and public spaces, in particular for women and children, older persons and persons with disabilities
    11.8. (11.a) Support positive economic, social and environmental links between urban, peri-urban and rural areas by strengthening national and regional development planning
    11.9. (11.b) By 2020, substantially increase the number of cities and human settlements adopting and implementing integrated policies and plans towards inclusion, resource efficiency, mitigation and adaptation to climate change, resilience to disasters, and develop and implement, in line with the Sendai Framework for Disaster Risk Reduction 2015–2030, holistic disaster risk management at all levels
    11.10. (11.c) Support least developed countries, including through financial and technical assistance, in building sustainable and resilient buildings utilising local materials
12. **Responsible Consumption and Production**: Ensure sustainable consumption and production patterns
    12.1. Implement the 10-Year Framework of Programmes on Sustainable Consumption and Production Patterns, all countries taking action, with developed countries taking the lead, taking into account the development and capabilities of developing countries
    12.2. By 2030, achieve the sustainable management and efficient use of natural resources

12.3. By 2030, halve per capita global food waste at the retail and consumer levels and reduce food losses along production and supply chains, including post-harvest losses

12.4. By 2020, achieve the environmentally sound management of chemicals and all wastes throughout their life cycle, in accordance with agreed international frameworks, and significantly reduce their release to air, water and soil in order to minimise their adverse impacts on human health and the environment

12.5. By 2030, substantially reduce waste generation through prevention, reduction, recycling and reuse

12.6. Encourage companies, especially large and transnational companies, to adopt sustainable practices and to integrate sustainability information into their reporting cycle

12.7. Promote public procurement practices that are sustainable, in accordance with national policies and priorities

12.8. By 2030, ensure that people everywhere have the relevant information and awareness for sustainable development and lifestyles in harmony with nature

12.9. (12.a) Support developing countries to strengthen their scientific and technological capacity to move towards more sustainable patterns of consumption and production

12.10. (12.b) Develop and implement tools to monitor sustainable development impacts for sustainable tourism that creates jobs and promotes local culture and products

12.11. (12.c) Rationalise inefficient fossil-fuel subsidies that encourage wasteful consumption by removing market distortions, in accordance with national circumstances, including by restructuring taxation and phasing out those harmful subsidies, where they exist, to reflect their environmental impacts, taking fully into account the specific needs and conditions of developing countries and minimising the possible adverse impacts on their development in a manner that protects the poor and the affected communities

13. **Climate Action**: Take urgent action to combat climate change and its impacts

    13.1. Strengthen resilience and adaptive capacity to climate-related hazards and natural disasters in all countries

    13.2. Integrate climate change measures into national policies, strategies and planning

    13.3. Improve education, awareness-raising and human and institutional capacity on climate change mitigation, adaptation, impact reduction and early warning

    13.4. (13.a) Implement the commitment undertaken by developed-country parties to the United Nations Framework Convention on Climate Change (UNFCC) to a goal of mobilising jointly USD 100 billion annually by 2020 from all sources to address the needs of developing countries in the context of meaningful mitigation actions and transparency on implementation and fully operationalise the Green Climate Fund through its capitalisation as soon as possible

13.5. (13.b) Promote mechanisms for raising capacity for effective climate change-related planning and management in least developed countries and small island developing States, including focusing on women, youth and local and marginalised communities
14. **Life Below Water**: Conserve and sustainably use the oceans, seas and marine resources for sustainable development
    14.1. By 2025, prevent and significantly reduce marine pollution of all kinds, in particular from land-based activities, including marine debris and nutrient pollution
    14.2. By 2020, sustainably manage and protect marine and coastal ecosystems to avoid significant adverse impacts, including by strengthening their resilience, and take action for their restoration in order to achieve healthy and productive oceans
    14.3. Minimise and address the impacts of ocean acidification, including through enhanced scientific cooperation at all levels
    14.4. By 2020, effectively regulate harvesting and end overfishing, illegal, unreported and unregulated fishing and destructive fishing practices and implement science-based management plans, in order to restore fish stocks in the shortest time feasible, at least to levels that can produce maximum sustainable yield as determined by their biological characteristics
    14.5. By 2020, conserve at least 10 per cent of coastal and marine areas, consistent with national and international law and based on the best available scientific information
    14.6. By 2020, prohibit certain forms of fisheries subsidies which contribute to overcapacity and overfishing, eliminate subsidies that contribute to illegal, unreported and unregulated fishing and refrain from introducing new such subsidies, recognising that appropriate and effective special and differential treatment for developing and least developed countries should be an integral part of the World Trade Organisation fisheries subsidies negotiation
    14.7. By 2030, increase the economic benefits to small island developing States and least developed countries from the sustainable use of marine resources, including through sustainable management of fisheries, aquaculture and tourism
    14.8. 14.a Increase scientific knowledge, develop research capacity and transfer marine technology, taking into account the Intergovernmental Oceanographic Commission Criteria and Guidelines on the Transfer of Marine Technology, in order to improve ocean health and to enhance the contribution of marine biodiversity to the development of developing countries, in particular small island developing States and least developed countries
    14.9. 14.b Provide access for small-scale artisanal fishers to marine resources and markets
    14.10. 14.c Enhance the conservation and sustainable use of oceans and their resources by implementing international law as reflected in the United Nations Convention on the Law of the Sea, which provides the legal

framework for the conservation and sustainable use of oceans and their resources
15. **Life On Land**: Protect, restore and promote sustainable use of terrestrial ecosystems, sustainably manage forests, combat desertification, and halt and reverse land degradation and halt biodiversity loss
    15.1. By 2020, ensure the conservation, restoration and sustainable use of terrestrial and inland freshwater ecosystems and their services, in particular forests, wetlands, mountains and drylands, in line with obligations under international agreements
    15.2. By 2020, promote the implementation of sustainable management of all types of forests, halt deforestation, restore degraded forests and substantially increase afforestation and reforestation globally
    15.3. By 2030, combat desertification, restore degraded land and soil, including land affected by desertification, drought and floods, and strive to achieve a land degradation- neutral world
    15.4. By 2030, ensure the conservation of mountain ecosystems, including their biodiversity, in order to enhance their capacity to provide benefits that are essential for sustainable development
    15.5. Take urgent and significant action to reduce the degradation of natural habitats, halt the loss of biodiversity and, by 2020, protect and prevent the extinction of threatened species
    15.6. Promote fair and equitable sharing of the benefits arising from the utilisation of genetic resources and promote appropriate access to such resources, as internationally agreed
    15.7. Take urgent action to end poaching and trafficking of protected species of flora and fauna and address both demand and supply of illegal wildlife products
    15.8. By 2020, introduce measures to prevent the introduction and significantly reduce the impact of invasive alien species on land and water ecosystems and control or eradicate the priority species
    15.9. By 2020, integrate ecosystem and biodiversity values into national and local planning, development processes, poverty reduction strategies and accounts
    15.10. (15.a) Mobilise and significantly increase financial resources from all sources to conserve and sustainably use biodiversity and ecosystems
    15.11 (15.b) Mobilise significant resources from all sources and at all levels to finance sustainable forest management and provide adequate incentives to developing countries to advance such management, including for conservation and reforestation
    15.12. (15.c) Enhance global support for efforts to combat poaching and trafficking of protected species, including by increasing the capacity of local communities to pursue sustainable livelihood opportunities
16. **Peace, Justice and Strong Institutions**: Promote peaceful and inclusive societies for sustainable development, provide access to justice for all and build effective, accountable and inclusive institutions at all levels
    16.1. Significantly reduce all forms of violence and related death rates everywhere

16.2. End abuse, exploitation, trafficking and all forms of violence against and torture of children
16.3. Promote the rule of law at the national and international levels and ensure equal access to justice for all
16.4. By 2030, significantly reduce illicit financial and arms flows, strengthen the recovery and return of stolen assets and combat all forms of organised crime
16.5. Substantially reduce corruption and bribery in all their forms
16.6. Develop effective, accountable and transparent institutions at all levels
16.7. Ensure responsive, inclusive, participatory and representative decision-making at all levels
16.8. Broaden and strengthen the participation of developing countries in the institutions of global governance
16.9. By 2030, provide legal identity for all, including birth registration
16.10. Ensure public access to information and protect fundamental freedoms, in accordance with national legislation and international agreements
16.11. (16.a) Strengthen relevant national institutions, including through international cooperation, for building capacity at all levels, in particular in developing countries, to prevent violence and combat terrorism and crime
16.12. (16.b) Promote and enforce non-discriminatory laws and policies for sustainable development
17. **Partnerships for the Goals**: Strengthen the means of implementation and revitalise the Global Partnership for Sustainable Development

Gender Development Index (GDI)

The Gender Development Index (GDI) is a composite index that measures the level of human development among women. It is published by the UN Development Programme (UNDP) and is among the four composite indices that are released along with the Human Development Report, the others being Inequality-Adjusted Human Development Index (HDI), Multidimensional Poverty Index (MPI) and the Gender Inequality Index (GII).

The GDI was introduced in 1995 as part of the Human Development Report with the objective to make the HDI gender sensitive. It expresses the gaps in gender development across regions. GDI measures the gender gaps in human development by using a methodology that accounts for the disparities between women and men in the three basic dimensions of human development as used in the Human Development Index (HDI). These three dimensions are: (a) health, measured by female and male life expectancy at birth; (b) education, measured by female and male Expected Years of Schooling for children and female and male Mean Years of Schooling for adults aged 25 years or more and (c) income, measured by female and male estimated earned income.

The GDI is the ratio of HDIs calculated separately for females and males that use the same methodology as in the HDI. It is a direct measure of gender gap. A GDI value equal to 1 means that there is human development parity between the genders. A smaller value of GDI indicates less development equality between genders.

Table 7.6 Dimensions and Indicators of Gender Development Index (GDI)

Dimensions	Indicator	Weight	Maximum	Minimum
Health	Female Life Expectancy (years)	1/6	87.5	22.5
	Male Life Expectancy (years)	1/6	82.5	17.5
Education	Expected Years of Schooling	1/6	18	0
	Mean Years of Schooling	1/6	15	0
Income	Estimated Earned Income (Rupees)	1/3	400,000	2000

In India, the estimation of GDI for different states and union territories is done by the National Statistics Office (NSO) of the Ministry of Statistics and Programme Implementation. This estimation is not done regularly. The indicators used by NSO in estimating the GDI are similar to those used by the UNDP. These indicators are as follows (Table 7.6).

These indicators have different units which need to be normalised by using the following general formula:

$$\text{Normalised Index} = \frac{\text{Actual value} - \text{Minimum Value}}{\text{Maximum value} - \text{Minimum Value}} \quad \text{...............(from Eq. 7.1)}$$

Like the HDI, three normalised sub-indices are calculated, namely the Life Expectancy Index, Education Index and Income Index, separately for males and females. The justification for the selection of maximum and minimum values has been discussed earlier in the section on Human Development Index.

Life Expectancy Index (LEI): Life Expectancy Index for a state is calculated by the following formula, for females by,

$$LEI_f = (LE_f - 22.5) / (87.5 - 22.5) \quad \text{.................................... (from Eq. 7.2)}$$

and for males by,

$$LEI_m = (LE_m - 17.5) / (82.5 - 17.5) \quad \text{.................................... (from Eq. 7.2)}$$

where

LEI_f and LEI_{fm} are the Life Expectancy Index for females and males, respectively, and

LE_f and LE_m are the Life Expectancy for females and males, respectively.

Education Index (EI): Education Index for a state is calculated by the following formula for females and males, respectively:

$$EI_f = (MYSI_f + EYSI_f) / 2 \quad \text{.. (from Eq. 7.3)}$$

$$EI_m = (MYSI_m + EYSI_m) / 2 \quad \text{.. (from Eq. 7.3)}$$

where,

EI_f and EI_{fm} are the Education Index for females and males, respectively,

$MYSI_f$ and $MYSI_m$ are the Mean Years of Schooling Index for females and males, respectively, and

$EYSI_f$ and $EYSI_m$ are the Exoected Years of Schooling Index for females and males, respectively.

Mean Years of Schooling Index (MYSI) is calculated by using the following formula for females and males, respectively:

$$MYSI_f = (MYS_f - 0) / (15 - 0) \quad \text{... (from Eq. 7.4)}$$

$$MYSI_m = (MYS_m - 0) / (15 - 0) \quad \text{...(from Eq. 7.4)}$$

where,

MYS_f and MYS_m are the Mean Years of Schooling for females and males, respectively.

The minimum means years of schooling is zero years because people can live without any formal education, i.e. with zero years of schooling. The maximum Mean Years of Schooling is set at 15 years till the period of 2025 based on previously recorded data.

Expected Years of Schooling Index (EYSI) is calculated by the following formula:

$$EYSI_f = (EYS_f - 0) / (18 - 0) \quad \text{...(from Eq. 7.5)}$$

$$EYSI_m = (EYS_m - 0) / (18 - 0) \quad \text{...(from Eq. 7.5)}$$

where,

EYS_f and EYS_m are the Expected Years of Schooling for females and males, respectively.

The minimum Expected Years of Schooling (EYS) is set at zero years. The maximum value for the Expected Years of Schooling is set at 18 which is equivalent to achieving a postgraduate degree in most of the countries. The MYSI and EYSI are calculated separately for males and females. Hence, two indices of education EI_f and EI_m are obtained.

Income Index (II): Income Index for a state is calculated by the following formula:

$$II = [\ln(GSDP_{pc}) - \ln(2{,}000)] / [(\ln(400{,}000) - \ln(2{,}000))] \quad \text{.............. (from Eq. 7.6)}$$

When GSDP per capita ($GSDP_{pc}$) is equal to Rs 4,00,000, Income Index is equal to 1 and it is 0 when GNI per capita is $100. The natural logarithm of GSDP per capita is used because each additional rupee of income has a smaller effect on human development. The GSDP per capita for a state both for males and females is calculated separately. The data for GSDP is provided by the National Statistics Office (NSO) under Ministry of Statistics and Programme Implementation. GSDP per capita ($GSDP_{pc}$) is obtained by dividing the GSDP of a state by its total population, data for which is provided by the Census of India. However, the GSDP per capita for a state both for males ($GSDP_{pcm}$)

and females (GSDP$_{pcf}$) is calculated by using a complex formula using estimated earned income as an indicator based on the data for wage per day, both for casual and regular labour wage, provided by the Periodic Labour Force Survey (PLFS). For calculating estimated earned incomes, the share of the wage bill is calculated separately for both males and females. The female share of the wage bill (S$_f$) is calculated as:

$$S_f = (W_f / W_m * EA_f) / \{ (W_f / W_m) * (EA_f + EA_m) \} \quad \text{(Eq. 7.13)}$$

where S$_f$ is the female share of the wage bill, W$_f$/W$_m$ is the ratio of female to male wage per day, EA$_f$ is the share of economically active female population and EA$_m$ is the share of economically active male population.

The male share of the wage bill is calculated as:

$$S_m = 1 - S_f \quad \text{(Eq. 7.14)}$$

Estimated female earned income per capita is obtained in the form of GSDP per capita for females (GSDP$_{pcf}$) from GSDP per capita (GSDP$_{pc}$), by multiplying it by the female share of the wage bill, S$_f$, and then rescaling it with the share of females in the population.

$$GSDP_{pcf} = GSDP_{pc} * S_f / P_f \quad \text{(Eq. 7.15)}$$

where,

$$P_f = N_f / N \quad \text{(Eq. 7.16)}$$

where P$_f$ is the share of females in the population, N$_f$ is the number of females and N is the total population of the state.

Similarly GSDP per capita for males (GSDP$_{pcm}$) for a state is estimated using the following formula:

$$GSDP_{pcm} = GSDP_{pc} * S_m / P_m \quad \text{(Eq. 7.17)}$$

where

$$P_m = N_m / N \quad \text{(Eq. 7.18)}$$

where P$_m$ is the share of males in the population, N$_m$ is the number of males and N is the total population of the state. The GSDP$_{pcf}$ and GSDP$_{pcm}$ is used to calculate the income index (II) separately for males and females.

The three indices are calculated separately for males and females, Life Expectancy Index (LEI$_f$ and LEI$_m$), Education Index (EI$_f$ and EI$_m$) and Income Index (II$_f$ and II$_m$). The HDI for males and females is calculated using the following formula:

$$HDI_f = (LEI_f * EI_f * II_f)^{1/3} \quad \text{(from Eq. 7.7)}$$

$$HDI_m = (LEI_m * EI_m * II_m)^{1/3} \quad \text{(from Eq. 7.7)}$$

Table 7.7 Categories of the Gender Development Index (GDI)

GDI Category	GDI Score
Low Gender Equality	<0.901
Medium Low Gender Equality	0.901 to 0.925
Medium Gender Equality	0.926 to 0.950
Medium High Gender Equality	0.951 to 0.975
High Gender Equality	>0.975

The HDI_f and HDI_m values obtained range between 0 and 1. The GDI is finally calculated as the ratio of female HDI to male HDI as follows:

$$GDI = HDI_f / HDI_m \quad\quad\quad\quad\quad\quad\quad\quad\quad\quad\quad\quad\quad\quad\quad\quad (Eq.\ 7.19)$$

The smaller the GDI values, the greater the gender disparity, and the larger the value of GDI, the greater the level of gender development. The value of GDI is not limited between 0 and 1. It can exceed 1. For instance, if the GDI value is 1.5, it means that the level of development in females is 1.5 times greater than for males.

The GDI groups are based on the absolute deviation of GDI from gender parity, $|GDI - 1|$ and grouped in the following categories (Table 7.7):

According to the National Statistical Office (NSO), in 2017–2018, the GDI score of India was 0.876, indicating low gender equality. The states that reported the highest level of gender development were Goa (0.994), Himachal Pradesh (0.990) and Chandigarh (0.984), having a high equality of gender development. The lowest level of gender development was in Bihar (0.550), Jharkhand (0.747) and Assam (0.765) (Figure 7.4). 15 states had low gender equality while only five states and union territories had high gender equality, all of which have small population.

The indicator of estimated earned income in the form of gender-wise GSDP per capita is estimated indirectly using data related to wages and economically active population, which does not really depict the value added by females in the economy. The GDI is a composite index which measures development within a country then negatively corrects for gender inequality (Beneria & Permanyer, 2010). Hence, GDI is considered to be an index that is only a modified version of the HDI and does not represent true inequalities between the genders (Hirway & Mahadevia, 1996). However, the GDI is relevant and is a progress upon the HDI as it helps to better understand the gender gap in human development achievements across nations and sub-national units. It provides insights into gender disparities in achievements in three basic capabilities: health, education and command over economic resources, and is useful for designing and monitoring policies to close the gaps.

Gender Inequality Index (GII)

Gender Inequality Index (GII) is a composite index that measures gender disparity. It was introduced in the 2010 as a part of the 20th edition of the Human Development Report by the United Nations Development Programme (UNDP). It was introduced as an experimental measure to remedy the shortcomings of the previous indicators, the

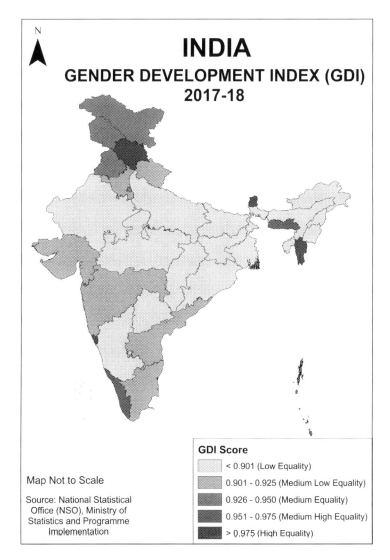

Figure 7.4 Gender Development Index (GDI) of India (2017–2018). Figures for Jammu and Kashmir and Ladakh have not been disaggregated

Gender Development Index (GDI). The Gender Inequality Index (GII) represents gender-based disparities in three dimensions of reproductive health, empowerment and the labour market. The GII as a composite index shows the loss in potential human development as a result of the inequality between the two genders across these dimensions. The value of GII, like the HDI ranges between 0 and 1. A GII value of 0 represents equality between males and females while a GII value of 1 represents complete inequality between the two genders.

Table 7.8 Gender Inequality Index

Dimensions	Indicator
Health	Maternal Mortality Ratio (Maternal Death per 100,000 live births within 42 days (MMR)
	Adolescent Birth Rate (Birth per 1000 women ages 15-19 years) (ABR)
Empowerment	Women's share of seats in Parliament in Per cent (PR)
	Per cent of female Population of age 25+ years with at least secondary education (SE)
Labour Market	Female Labour Force Participation Rate in Per cent (LFPR)

The GII is computed using the association-sensitive inequality measure suggested by Suman Seth in 2009. The index is based on the general mean of general means of different orders—the first aggregation is by a geometric mean across dimensions; these means, calculated separately for women and men, are then aggregated using a harmonic mean across genders (Ferrant, 2010). The dimensions used in the GII are listed as follows (Table 7.8):

Calculation of the Gender Inequality Index: First, the indicators are aggregated across the three dimensions for each gender group by the geometric mean to make the GII association sensitive.

$$G_f = \left[\left(\frac{10}{MMR} \times \frac{1}{ABR} \right)^{1/2} \times (PR_f \times SE_f)^{1/2} \times LFPR_f \right]^{1/3} \quad \text{(Eq. 7.20)}$$

$$G_m = \left[1 \times (PR_m \times SE_m)^{1/2} \times LFPR_m \right]^{1/3} \quad \text{(Eq. 7.21)}$$

The female and male indices are aggregated using the harmonic mean for the creation of equally distributed gender index G_f, G_m.

$$HM(G_f, G_m) = \left(\frac{\frac{1}{G_f} + \frac{1}{G_m}}{2} \right)^{-1} \quad \text{(Eq. 7.22)}$$

Using the harmonic mean of within-group geometric mean helps to capture the inequality between women and men and adjust for association between dimensions, that is, by accounting for the overlapping inequalities in dimensions.

The geometric mean of the arithmetic means for each indicator is calculated. The reference standard for computing inequality is obtained by aggregating female and male indices by using equal weights and then aggregating the indices across dimensions.

Table 7.9 Categories of the Gender Inequality Index (GII)

GII Category	GII Score
Category I	<0.400
Category II	0.400–0.499
Category III	0.500–0.599
Category IV	0.600–0.699
Category V	>0.700

$$G_{f,m} = \left(\overline{\text{Health}} \times \overline{\text{Empowerment}} \times \overline{\text{LFPR}}\right)^{\frac{1}{3}} \quad \text{.................................(Eq. 7.23)}$$

where,

$$\overline{\text{Health}} = \frac{\left[\left(\frac{10}{\text{MMR}} \times \frac{1}{\text{ABR}}\right)^{\frac{1}{2}} + 1\right]}{2} \quad \text{...............................(Eq. 7.24)}$$

$$\overline{\text{Empowerment}} = \frac{(PR_m \times SE_m)^{\frac{1}{2}} + (PR_f \times SE_f)^{\frac{1}{2}}}{2} \quad \text{.......................(Eq. 7.25)}$$

$$\overline{\text{LFPR}} = \frac{LFPR_f + LFPR_m}{2} \quad \text{.....................................(Eq. 7.26)}$$

Finally, the GII value is calculated by the following formula:

$$GII = 1 - \frac{HM(G_f, G_m)}{G_{f,m}} \quad \text{......................................(Eq. 7.27)}$$

Categories: Based on the GII values, five categories of nations or sub-national units are identified (Table 7.9):

The GII score of India in 2017–2018, according to the National Statistical Office (NSO) was 0.462. Andhra Pradesh (0.361), Himachal Pradesh (0.373), Jammu and Kashmir (0.374) and Punjab (0.398) had the least level of gender inequality. The states and union territories which recorded the highest inequalities between the genders were Arunachal Pradesh (0.789), Lakshadweep (0.785), Manipur (0.777) and Nagaland (0.765). (Figure 7.5)

There are several criticisms of the GII as a measurement of gender inequality. It is a complex indicator and its components are both difficult to interpret and calculate. The non-linear nature of the index makes its interpretation complex. The indicators like Maternal Mortality Rate (MMR) and Adolescent Birth Rate (ABR) may or may not be truly representative of the health of women (Malik, 2018). Similarly parliamentary

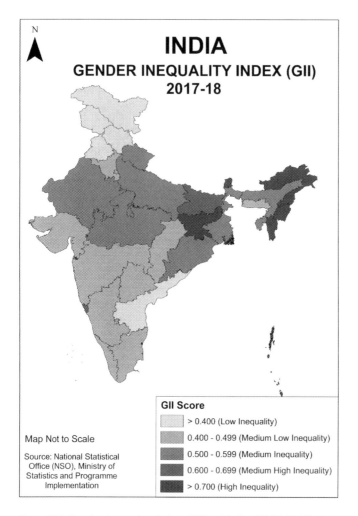

Figure 7.5 Gender Inequality Index (GII) of India (2017–2018). Figures for Jammu and Kashmir and Ladakh have not been disaggregated

representation (PR) of women is very less in most of the developing countries and may not be represent the empowerment of a large number of women. However, GII presents a diverse and novel approach to measuring inequality between males and females.

Notes

1 Children under five years (60 months or less) are considered undernourished if their z-score of either height-for-age (stunting) or weight-for-age (underweight) is below minus two standard deviations from the median of the reference population. Children 5–19 years (61–228 months) are identified as deprived if their age-specific BMI cut-off is below minus two standard deviations. Adults older than 19–70 years (229–840 months) are considered undernourished if their Body Mass Index (BMI) is below 18.5 kg/m^2.

2   A household is considered to have access to improved sanitation if it has some type of flush toilet or latrine, or ventilated improved pit or composting toilet, provided that they are not shared.
3   A household has access to clean drinking water if the water source is any of the following types: piped water, public tap, borehole or pump, protected well, protected spring or rainwater, and it is within 30-minute walk, round trip.
4   Deprived if floor is made of natural materials or if dwelling has no roof or walls or if either the roof or walls are constructed using natural or rudimentary materials.

References

Bandura, R. (2008). *A Survey of Composite Indices Measuring Country Performance*. New York: UNDP Working Papers.

Beneria, L., & Permanyer, I. (2010). Revisited: The Measurement of Socio-Economic Gender Inequality. *Development and Change*, 41(3), 375–399.

Booysen, F. (2022, August). An Overview and Evaluation of Composite Indices of Development. *Social Indicators Research*, 59(2), 115–151.

Bourguignon, F., Bussolo, M., & Silva, L. A. (2008). *The Impact of Macroeconomic Policies on Poverty and Income Distribution: Macro-Micro Evaluation Techniques and Tools*. Washington DC: World Bank and Palgrave Macmillan.

Cavapozzi, D., Han, W., & Miniaci, R. (2015). Alternative Weighting Structures For Multidimensional Poverty Assessment. *Journal of Economic Inequality*, 13(3), 425–447.

Ferrant, G. (2010). The Gender Inequalities Index (GII) as a New Way to Measure Gender Inequalities in Developing Countries, *Proceedings of the German Development Economics Conference*, Hannover 2010, No. 20.

Foster, J., & Alkire, S. (2011). Counting and Multidimensional Poverty Measurement. *Journal of Public Economics*, 95(7–8), 476–487.

Foster, J., Alkire, S., & Seth, S. (2013). *The Global Multidimensional Poverty Index*. Oxford: Oxford Poverty & Human Development Initiative.

Greeve, B. (2020). *Poverty: The Basics*. Oxon: Routledge.

Haq, M. u. (1999). *Reflections on Human Development*. Delhi: Oxford University Press.

Hirway, I., & Mahadevia, D. (1996). Critique of Gender Development Index: Towards an Alternative. *Economic and Political Weekly*, 31(43), 87–96.

Kahneman, D., & Deaton, A. (2010, September 21). High Income Improves Evaluation of Life But Not Emotional Well-Being. *Proceedings of the National Academy of Sciences of the United States of America*, 107(38), 16489–16493. doi:10.1073/pnas.1011492107.

Lugo, A., & Decancq, K. (2013) Weights in Multidimensional Indices of Wellbeing: An Overview. *Econometric Reviews*, 32, 7–34.

Malik, R. (2018). HDI and Gender Development Index: Current Status of Women Development in India. *PRAGATI Journal of Indian Economy*, 5, 30–43.

Mazziotta, M., & Pareto, A. (2016). Methods for Constructing Non-Compensatory Composite Indices: A Comparative Study. *Forum for Social Economics*, 45(2/3), 213–229.

McGillivray, M. (1991). The Human Development Index: Yet Another Redundant Composite Development Indicator? *World Development*, 19(10), 1461–1468.

McGranahan, D. (1972). Development Indicators and Development Models. *The Journal of Development Studies*, 8(3), 91–102.

Nagar, A. L., & Basu, S. R. (2004). Statistical Properties of a Composite Index as Estimate of Single Latent Variable. *Journal of Quantitative Economics*, 2(2), 19–27.

NITI-Aayog. (2021). SDG India Index & Dashboard 2020–21: Partnerships in the Decade of Action. New Delhi: NITI Aayog. Retrieved August 9, 2022, from https://www.niti.gov.in/writereaddata/files/SDG_3.0_Final_04.03.2021_Web_Spreads.pdf.

Noorbaksh. (1998). The Human Development Index: Some Technical Issues and Alternative Indices. *Journal of International Development*, 10, 589–605.

Saltelli, A. (2006). Composite Indicators Between Analysis and Advocacy. *Social Indicators Research*, 81, 65–77.

Scown, M. W. (2020). The Sustainable Development Goals Need Geoscience. *Nature Geoscience*, 13, 714–715.

Sen, A. (1987). *The Standard of Living*. Cambridge: Cambridge University Press.

Sen, A., & Anand, S. (2000). Human Development and Economic Sustainability. *World Development*, 28, 2029–2049.

Stanton, E. A. (2007). *The Human Development Index: A History*. Massachusetts: Political Economy Research Institute.

Walker, R., & Godinot, X. (2020). Poverty in All Its Forms: Determining the Dimensions of Poverty Through Merging Knowledge. In Dimensions of Poverty (pp. 263–279). Cham: Springer.

Index

Academic Bank of Credit 125
Accredited Social Health Activist 147
adolescent birth rate 73, 234-5
age-sex pyramid 70-1
Age Structure 70-1, 74
age-specific fertility rate 72-3, 138
Alkire-Foster method 207
All India Council for Technical Education 113, 117, 129
anaemia 134, 142, 153, 161
areal differentiation 11, 13
Astana Declaration 131
Austro-Asiatic language family 85
Autonomous Institutes 114-5
AYUSH 157, 161

Basic Minimum Needs 28-30
behaviouralism 16
Bhore Committee 136, 147
Bismarckian-Corporatist Welfare State 39, 42
brain drain 128

cancer 78, 134, 153-5, 159
capabilities approach 29, 200
cardiovascular disease 134, 153-5
Census of India 50, 79, 81, 91, 187, 189-90, 230
Central Board of Secondary Education 99
Central Business District 10
central university 114-5
chatuspadis 95
child sex ratio 64
Chipko Movement 13
chronic respiratory disease 153-5, 159
climate change 218, 224-6
communicable disease 152
Community Health Centres 77, 147
composite indicator 198-204
Confucian Welfare State 41
Conservative Welfare State 41
constant price 172-84
Council for the Indian School Certificate Examinations 100
Covid-19 125, 152, 162-4, 175, 179, 181

critical geography 17, 34
cultural geography 9, 11
cultural landscape 7, 9
current price 170-2, 176-85
curriculum framework 99, 124

Dardic Aryan languages 83
De facto method 49-51
De jure method 49
deemed university 114
deficiency disease 142, 153
degenerative disease 153
delimitation 50
demographic transition 43, 59-60, 72, 74
demographic window 70
deprivation score 207, 211-2
diabetes 134, 153-4
Directive Principles of State Policy 44, 137
directly transmitted disease 152
disguised unemployment 195
disposable income 173-4
Distance Education Bureau 113
Dravidian languages 85
dropout rate 108-10

economic activity 128, 167, 176, 178, 182-4
economically weaker section 97
economics 8-9, 20, 34, 36, 166
Education Index 202, 229-31
elementary education 45, 92-97, 106
emotional health 133
emotional well-being 26
employability 129
empowerment 161, 220, 233-5
environmental stress surface 17
environmental well-being 27
esteem needs 28-9
ethnographic approach 15
Expected Years of Schooling Index 202, 230
expenditure approach 169-70

factor cost 170-1
factorial ecology 14

Index

feminism 18-9
financial well-being 27
formal education 64, 92, 202, 230
formal worker 190
free market 12, 38
frictional unemployment 195

GDP deflator 172, 179
GDP growth 126, 175, 181-3
Gender Development Index 228-32
gender gap 67, 228, 232
Gender Inequality Index 232-6
genre de vie 7
Germanic language 85
Ghetto 4, 12
Gross Domestic Product 43, 45, 122, 155, 168, 172-9, 222
Gross Enrolment Ratio 105-6, 119, 124
Gross National Product 172
Gross State Domestic Product 173, 183-5
Gross Value Added 170, 175-6

headcount ratio 192, 207, 211
health insurance 40, 45, 144-5
healthcare infrastructure 76, 147
heredity 134-5
home area studies 9
homo economicus 16
Human Development Index 30, 41, 198, 200-6, 228
Human Development Report 200-6, 228
Humanism 17
hybrid geography 20

immunization 77-8, 145, 157-8, 162
income approach 169-70
Income Index 203, 229-30
indeterminism 10
indirectly transmitted disease 152
Indo-Aryan languages 83
Inequality-Adjusted Human Development Index 228
infant mortality rate 77, 140, 156-9
informal education 92
informal worker 190
Institute of National Importance 114
institutional delivery 142
intellectual well-being 26
intensity of poverty 206-7, 211
International Baccalaureate 100
International Covenant on Economic, Social and Cultural Rights 131
Iranian languages 83

Kindergarten 93-4
Kothari Commission 94, 121

labour force participation rate 185, 234
laissez faire 38
Liberal Welfare State 40
life expectancy at birth 138, 159, 202, 228
Life Expectancy Index 202, 229
literacy rate 13, 43, 64-5

main worker 187-9
maktabas 95
marginal social space 33
marginal worker 187-9
market price 170, 174
Marxism 18
Maslow's Hierarchy of Needs 27-8
maternal mortality rate 140, 157-8
Mean Years of Schooling Index 202-3
medical colleges 136, 149-50
mental health 131-4, 153, 161
Millennium Development Goals 207, 213
Mission Indradhanush 145
mixed reference period 193
morbidity 34, 142, 153-4
Mudaliar Committee 136
Multidimensional Poverty Index 206, 211-2
multiple entry exit system 124

National Council for Teacher Education 113, 117, 124
National Education Mission 120
National Education Policy 1968 121, 126
National Education Policy 1986 121-2
National Education Policy 2020 122-6
National Health Policy 1983 156
National Health Policy 2002 157
National Health Policy 2017 158-62
national income 168-73, 200
National Institute of Open Schooling 100
National Medical Commission 113
National Research Foundation 125
Naturalism 15
neo-liberalism 40
Net National Product 173-4
New Deal 39
nominal GDP 171-2, 175
non-communicable disease 152-3
non-worker 187
normalisation 199

objective social indicators 31
occupational well-being 27
open university 114
out-of-pocket expenditure (OOPE) on health 143
overpopulation 52

Pay 7
Periodic Labour Force Survey 183, 190, 196, 231

physical health 133
physical well-being 26
place-work-folk 7, 32
Poor Law 41
population density 52, 53-7
population growth rate 57, 58, 60-2
population projection 86-7
positivism 6, 9, 16-7
possibilism 7
Post-colonialism 19
Posthumanism 19
Postmodernism 19
pre-primary education 93, 119
Primary Health Centres 136-7, 147
primary sector 167-8, 176-7
production approach 169-70
pupil teacher ratio 97, 102-3, 118
purchasing power parity 172, 175, 200

quality of life 3, 27, 30-1
quantitative method 14, 16, 34
quantitative revolution 13-6, 34
quaternary sector 167-8
quinary sector 168

rate maps 10
Residual Welfare State 41
Right to Education 45, 90, 96, 98, 106
right to health 131, 137-8, 143
rurality index 15

Sample Registration System 72, 138, 140, 142
sample survey 49
scarcity 167
Scheduled Castes 43, 67, 109, 121
school board 100
School Management Committees 97
secondary education 121
secondary sector 167, 183
sense of place 17
sex ratio 52, 62
social area analysis 14
social change 3, 5, 11
Social Democratic Welfare State 41
social group 20, 21
social health 133
social identity 3
social indicators 30-4
social institution 3
social interaction 3-4
social justice 3, 20, 36
social phenomena 6, 11, 13, 17
social process 3, 5, 9, 13, 14

social regions 13
social relationship 3
social space 4, 5, 8, 12-5
social structure 3, 5, 10, 11, 14, 15, 17-8
social system 3, 8
social theory 4-5, 9
social values 3, 15
social welfare 3, 21, 34, 39-43
social well-being 27, 30
societal scale 14
sociography 8-9
socio-spatial dialectic 21
sozialstaat 38
spatial method 15
spatial organization 16, 18, 21
spatiality 21
spiritual health 133
spiritual well-being 26
spot maps 10
state university 114
structural unemployment 128, 195
structuralism 17
Sub-health Centres 147, 155
subjective social indicators 31
subsidiary status 196
Sustainable Development Goals 207, 213-4
Sustainable Development Solutions Network 214
syn-ecological complex 9

Targeted Welfare State 42
tertiary sector 167, 176, 183
Tibeto-burmese language family 85
Topography 9 17, 54
total fertility rate 72, 74-6

under five mortality rate 140, 157, 159
underemployment 195
unemployment rate 196-7
United Nations Development Programme 30, 129, 200, 211, 232
Universal Declaration of Human Rights 131
Universal Immunisation Programme 145, 158
University Grants Commission 112-4
usual principal status 196
utilities 35

value freedom 168
Voluntary Welfare State 42

WASH 104, 134
welfare geography 12, 34-6

zone maps 10

Printed in the United States
by Baker & Taylor Publisher Services